Town Life in the Fif

Volume

Alice Stopford Green

Alpha Editions

This edition published in 2024

ISBN : 9789357961721

Design and Setting By
Alpha Editions
www.alphaedis.com
Email - info@alphaedis.com

As per information held with us this book is in Public Domain.
This book is a reproduction of an important historical work. Alpha Editions uses the best technology to reproduce historical work in the same manner it was first published to preserve its original nature. Any marks or number seen are left intentionally to preserve its true form.

Contents

VOLUME 2 .... - 1 -
CHAPTER I .... - 3 -
CHAPTER II .... - 13 -
CHAPTER III .... - 27 -
CHAPTER IV .... - 40 -
CHAPTER V .... - 50 -
CHAPTER VI .... - 61 -
CHAPTER VII .... - 77 -
CHAPTER VIII .... - 88 -
CHAPTER IX .... - 100 -
CHAPTER X .... - 109 -
CHAPTER XI .... - 122 -
CHAPTER XII .... - 132 -
CHAPTER XIII .... - 147 -
CHAPTER XIV .... - 164 -
CHAPTER XV .... - 183 -
CHAPTER XVI .... - 194 -
CHAPTER XVII .... - 199 -
FOOTNOTES: .... - 205 -

VOLUME 2

CHAPTER I

THE TOWN MANNERS

THE controversy concerning the bounds and limits of their freedom, which the English boroughs were forced to maintain with powerful organizations already settled in the land—with the monarchy, the baronage, or the Church—represented in the history of each municipality that which in the case of States of greater magnitude we call the foreign policy of the commonwealth. But whatever may be the compass of a dominion, whether it be a borough or an empire, no influence is more potent in shaping the character and destiny of the community than the nature of its external relations. It was in the single-handed conflict with foreign powers, whether superior lord or insidious rival, that the drapers and mercers, the smiths and butchers and weavers of every country town were forced, with a patriotism quickened by necessity, to meddle in matters of State and to concern themselves about the public weal; their ardours were stirred by legends of an ancient freedom, while their political instinct was trained by incessant discussion of legal precedent and right; and in the strain of perpetual taxation, in heavy burdens imposed upon a people whose prosperity was new, uncertain, or shifting; above all in the strengthening of certain forms of narrow municipal despotism born of the struggle against external danger, they paid the price of a bracing public discipline.

But there is another side of the town history which is not less important, and which is far more complicated than the question of its foreign relations and policy—that is, the problem of its own nature, of the spirit by which it was animated and the inherent resources of its corporate life. In the town a new world had grown up with an organization and a polity of its own wholly different from that of the country. Members who joined its community were compelled to renounce all other allegiance and forego any protection from other patrons. The chief magistrate set over its inhabitants must be one of their own fellow-citizens—"not a far dweller" unless in time of special need, such as war, and then only "by the pleasure of the commonalty."[1] Adventurers from the manor-houses of the neighbourhood and strangers in search of fortune were equally shut out; and it was only when a county squire was willing to throw in his lot with the burghers, to turn into a good citizen and honest tradesman, and to prove his credit and capacity by serving in a subordinate post,[2] that he could hope to rise to the highest office. It is true that country folk were welcome to pay a double price for having a stall in the market, or a store-room in the Common House for their wool; while the impoverished knight might come in search of a renewal of his wasted fortunes through the dowry of some rich mercer's daughter. But otherwise the town carried on its existence apart, in a watchful and jealous independence. Its way of life, its code of manners, its habits, aims, and interests, the condition of the people, the local theories of trade by which its conduct of business was guided, the popular views of citizenship and government under the influence of which the burghers regulated their civic policy—all these things must be kept in view if we would gain a clear idea of the growth of the borough from within.

The way of thinking and acting of the new world of traders and shopkeepers and artizans lives again for us in a wholly new literature which first sprang up in England about the middle of the fifteenth century—in Books of Courtesy and popular rhymes as to the conduct of daily life. The first English manual of etiquette appeared about 1430. Germany had had its book of courtesy more than two hundred years before, a set of rules composed for a distinguished society by equally fastidious writers, one of whom laments that his pen had been made "common" by writing about masters and servants, and explains that it was never happy save in describing knights and ladies. In northern Italy a similar book drawn up in the thirteenth century had taken a very different character. There the merchants and shopkeepers of the towns, impatient of "new ceremonies" brought in from over the mountains which they deemed contrary to all the traditions of the traders of Lucca and Florence and only fit for the degenerate Neapolitans, framed rules to suit their own needs and aspirations. The French followed rather later, at the end of the fourteenth century; and then last of all came the English experiment.[3]

The very appearance of such a book at this time is most significant. The nobles had already their own literary traditions handed down from an older world; and in the ideal of chivalrous conduct which was enshrined for them in the "Morte d'Arthur," the Knights of the Round Table still served as a standard of social virtue and good bearing for the upper classes—a standard with which the burghers had nothing whatever to do. But the new literature was for the townsfolk themselves, and it bore on every line the impress of its origin. A growing sense of dignity and self-respect in the middle class of traders and artizans wakened aspirations for polite manners, and intercourse with strangers abroad gave fresh stimulus to social ambition. Englishmen who visited Flanders towards the end of the century were as much impressed by the Flemish manners as by the Flemish wealth: "they can best behave them and most like gentlemen," was their comment.[4] In England the new society, with no heritage of tradition and no recognized array of models in the past, had to create its own standard of behaviour, to shape its own social code, to realize for itself the art of life. Compilers worked busily in the service of the middle-class aspirants. One book of courtesy after another was adapted for the vulgar use. The "Rules of S. Robert," the good Bishop of Lincoln, whereby "whosoever will keep these rules well will be able to live on his means and keep himself and those belonging to him," were put into

English in a brief form, after wearing a more courtly garb of French or Latin for three centuries.[5] A Latin treatise on manners was translated for the unlearned by a writer who prayed for help in his work from Him who formed man after His own image, from Mary the gracious Mother, and from Lady Facetia the Mother of all virtue.[6] Sound codes of morals were put in the form of an A B C.[7] The right conduct of life, especially as it concerned polite behaviour, was set out in little songs "made for children young, at the school that bide not long."[8] Plain directions in verse pointed out the duties of girls, of young men, of housewives, of wandering youths looking for service. The rhymes are of the homeliest kind, with trite and prosaic illustrations taken from the common sights of the market-place, the tavern, the workshop, or the street with its wandering pigs and its swinging signs; it is in their very rudeness and simpleness that their interest lies. Meanwhile political and satirical songs which had been so common in the foregoing centuries mostly died out of fashion and were heard no more, as the burghers, quickened into a new self-consciousness, began to be concerned for a time with matters nearer home.

These fragments of old speech and song lead us into the very midst of the lanes and workshops of a mediæval town. They recall for us the countless political and social troubles amid which the trader was slowly fighting his way upward, and which left their deep impress on his character and view of life. A pervading suspicion, a distrustful caution, are the ground-note of many a song. Rude proverbs of daily speech, jingling rhymes of wise counsel, all are profoundly marked by the narrow prudence of people set in the midst of pitfalls, to whom danger was ever present, whether at the council chamber or at the tavern or at a friend's dinner table, and among whom talk and clatter with the tongue were looked on as an unspeakable indiscretion.[9] They picture a life anxious and difficult, whose recognized condition is one of toil that knows no relaxation and no end, of hardship borne with unquestioning endurance—a life amid whose humble prosperity family affection and the family welfare are best assured by having one roof, one entrance door, one fire, and one dining table, and a "back door" is looked on as an extravagance which would bring any household to ruin. After a man had lived hard and worked strenuously he still stood in need of the constantly recurring warning against any bitterness of envy at the prosperity of a lucky dealer next door. The limits of his ambition and his duty are bounded by rigid lines; and the standard of conduct is one framed for a laborious middle class, with its plain-spoken seriousness, its sturdy morality, its activity and rectitude and independence, its dulness and vigilance and thrift. It is the duty of good men to set their people well to work, to keep house carefully, to get through any heavy job steadily and swiftly, to pay wages regularly, to give true weight, to remember ever that "Borrowed thing must needs go home." They are not to ape their betters in dress, only

"Be as pure as flour taken from the bran
In all thy clothing and all thine array."

With one whom "thou knowest of greater state" there should be no easy fellowship, no dining or betting or playing at dice; above all there must be no show of overmuch "meekness" or servility, "for else a fool thou wilt be told."[10] A practical religion adds its simple obligations.[11] Men ought to pay their tithes, to give to the poor, to be strong and stiff against the devil. The prayer on awaking, the daily mass before working hours, the duties of self-control and submission, must ever be kept in mind. For the trader indeed the way of virtue was a narrow one and straight. Three deaths ever stand menacingly before him. First comes the common lot, the mere severing of soul and body.

"The tother death is death of Shame,
If he die in debt or wicked fame;
The third death, so saith the clerks,
If he hath no good works."[12]

But side by side with directions about mercy, truth, and fulfilling the law, come other warnings—warnings about carving meat and cutting bread and dividing cheese, about a formal and dignified bearing, how to walk and stand and kneel, how to enter a house or greet a friend in the street—all carefully and laboriously shaped into rhyme. In the new sense of changing customs, of fashions that came and went with the revolutions of society,[13] training and thought and conscious endeavour were called in to replace the simplicity of the old unvarying forms. Manners became a subject of serious anxiety. Throwing aside the mass of tradition handed down from century to century, when every usage was consecrated by custom, and determined by immemorial laws as to the relations of class to class, the burghers, side by side with the professional and middle classes all over the kingdom, were tending towards the realization of a new social order, in which men were no longer obliged as formerly to pass through the door of the Church to find the way of social advancement, but might attain to it along the common high road of secular enterprise. The notion of the worth of the individual man was none the less important for the homely and practical form given to it in their rude and untrained expression. No one, they declared simply, need be shamefaced, of whatever lowly position he might come, for

"In hall or chamber, or where thou gon,
Nurture and good manners maketh man."

In whatever society he might find himself, the humblest citizen should therefore so order his behaviour that when he left the table men would say "A gentleman was here."[14] The practical divinity of plain people easily drew the graciousness of outward demeanour within the sphere of religion, and "clerks that knew the seven arts" explained

"That courtesy from heaven came
When Gabriel our Lady grette
And Elizabeth with Mary mette."[15]

Since "all virtues are closed in courtesy and all vices in villany" or rudeness, the best prayer one could make was to be well-mannered, for the virtues of a fine behaviour reached as far as thought could go.

"In courtesy He make you so expert,
That through your nurture and your governance,
In lasting bliss He may yourself advance."

These books of courtesy show us one side of the great change that passed over society[16] when the mediæval theory of *status* was broken down by the increase of riches which trade brought with it, and the new chances of rising in the world through wealth. The yeoman might become a gentleman by getting into a lord's household, and "spending large and plenty." The squire who would be a knight without the danger of bearing arms need only go to the king's court with his purse full of money. The man of letters, the merchant, the seeker after pleasure, whoever and whatever a man might be, he could win neither degree nor worship "but he have the penny ready to take to."[17] When the acquisition of wealth or the passage from one class to another was practically impossible, poverty and a low estate might still be dignified. But as soon as fortune and position had been brought within the reach of all, the man who remained poor might be looked on as idle or incapable. A new test of superiority was applied, a test of material prosperity, and by this measure the townsman was judged by his neighbours and naturally judged himself. On all sides we find indications of the excited ambition which had begun to stir in every class,

"Now every boy will counterfeit a knight,
Report himself as good as he."[18]

New distinctions of rank and caste began to appear, and an aristocracy of energy and skill constantly recruited and invigorated made its influence felt in every borough, as public honour was attached to trade in proportion to the wealth which its followers could win. The wool trade especially held a place of distinction in common esteem; and people who took to the selling of cloth were supposed to "live like gentlemen" and rejoice in a really superior station.[19] More and more the enriched burgher hastened to give proof that he had risen into the leisured class by donning the fine dress whose cumbrous folds bespoke a sedate idleness and luxury, so that whereas "sometime afar men might lords know by their array from other folk, now a man shall stand or muse a long throw which is which."[20]

As the chance of rising in the world stirred in the trader a new ambition, so it stirred too the sense of the power of knowledge. When the writer of Piers Ploughman counts up the gifts of the Spirit that were distributed among the commons at the descent of the Holy Ghost as "treasure to live by to their lives' end," and "weapon to fight with when Anti-Christ assaileth," he carefully reckons in with the rest the wit to use words skilfully as preachers and prentices of law who live leally by labour of tongue, the crafts and "connynge" of sight by which men win their livelihood with selling and buying, the wisdom to till and thatch and cook as their wit would when the time came; the art of divining and dividing numbers, and all such learning of the schools.[21] Already the workers of the town were reaching forward, as some of their rough rhymes show, to a true love of learning.[22] Their zeal took very practical form. Side by side with the great movement for education which was going on under the patronage of kings and queens, of archbishops and bishops, and great lords and ladies, humbler work was taken in hand by burghers and tradesmen for the teaching of their own people.[23] The founding of free grammar schools all over England was the work of the trading classes themselves. Sometimes the schools were founded by Guilds.[24] Sometimes townsmen who had thriven in the world remembered gratefully the place of their birth or their education. "By some divine chance" a "teacher of grammar learning" came to live in Rotherham about the beginning of the fifteenth century, and one of the town boys, Thomas Scott, who had been taught by him about 1430, became in 1474 Lord Chancellor, and in 1480 Archbishop of York. In 1483 he founded a college in his old home with a Provost and three Fellows who were to teach freely any one who came to them. One was to give lessons in grammar, poetry, and rhetoric; the second in music, especially singing, playing, and broken song; and if possible these two were to be priests, or at least one of them. The third Fellow was to teach writing and arithmetic to youths who were not intended for the priesthood, but for trades and other employments; for among the children of Rotherham, said the archbishop, there were many who were "valde acuti in ingenio."[25] In the same way bishop Alcock of Rochester, the son of a Hull merchant, established a free grammar school at Hull, where the master was to "teach all scholars thither resorting without taking any stipend or wages for the same, and should have for his own wages £10."[26]

So in one way or another the work of education went on throughout the fifteenth century—a work whose magnitude and importance have been too long obscured by the busy organizers of the Reformation days, who, for the giving of a new charter or adapting the school to the new system established by law, clothed themselves with the glory of founders and bore away from their silent predecessors the honour of inaugurating a new world. Not only in the busy centres of commerce, but in the obscure villages that lay hidden in forest or waste or clung to the slopes of the northern moors, the children of the later middle ages were gathered into schools. Apparently, reading and writing were everywhere common among the people,[27] and as early as the reign of Richard the Second the word "townsmen" had come to mean people instructed and trained, and no longer ignorant rustics.[28] But the most remarkable thing about the growth of the new grammar schools was the part taken in their foundation by laymen—by the traders and merchants of the towns. The great benefactor of Sandwich, Thomas Elys, left provision in 1392 for one of the chaplains of his chantry to serve as schoolmaster for the town boys; and the son of a draper who had had his education in this school afterwards founded a grammar school. Sir Edmund Shaa, goldsmith and once Lord Mayor of London, established a school at Stockport by will in 1457, and appointed a chantry priest of the parish church, who, being "cunning in grammar," should "freely without any wages or salary asking or taking of any person, except only any salary hereunder specified, shall teach all manner persons, children and other, that will come to him to learn as well of the said town of Stopford as of other towns thereabouts, the science of grammar as far as lieth in him for to do." And another London mayor, Sir John Percyvale, who had been born close to Macclesfield, left money in 1502 to endow a free grammar school there, because there were few schoolmasters in that country and the children for lack of teaching "fall to idleness and so consequently live dissolutely all their days."[29] It seems also that the Manchester Grammar School was first planned by a Manchester clothier, who at his death left money for its foundation; and was completed in 1524 by Hugh Oldham, Bishop of Exeter, a native of Oldham;[30] the children were to be taught "after the manner of the school of Banbury," and inhabitants of the town were compelled to contribute to its support by being forced to grind their corn at the school mills—a custom which was kept up till 1759.

The new movement marked the beginning of that revolution which was ultimately to take education out of the exclusive control of the Church and hand it over to the people themselves. Up to this time the privileges and profits of teaching had been practically a monopoly of the clergy, and there was no possible competition save that which might spring up between licensed and unlicensed teachers within the ecclesiastical order.[31] A document drawn up by order of the abbot of Walden tells how the clergy of the parish church there had taught some children of the village the alphabet, and even more advanced lessons, without leave from the abbot, who claimed by the statutes and customs of the monastery a perpetual monopoly of teaching or licensing schoolmasters. A petition was made by the inhabitants in favour of the priests, and in consequence of this petition the abbot, to the great satisfaction of the townsfolk, graciously allowed that every priest of the Church might (during the goodwill of the abbot and convent) receive one "very little child" of each inhabitant, and might teach the child in "alphabete et graciis"[32] but not in any higher learning; a legal instrument embodying this concession was drawn up by a clerk of the York diocese, and signed with a beautiful notarial monogram which must have cost him the greater part of a day to draw.[33]

But under the new state of things another element was brought into the controversy. The town itself occasionally became the aggressive party, and took the teaching straight out of the hands of the priest. An order was made at Bridgenorth in 1503 "that there shall no priest keep no school, save only one child to help him to say mass, after that a schoolmaster cometh to town, but that every child to resort to the common school in pain of forfeiting to the chamber of the town twenty shillings of every priest that doeth the contrary."[34] Burghers accustomed to manage their own affairs easily assumed the direction of education, and the control of schools gradually passed from clerical to lay hands and became the charge of the whole community. In Nottingham, where there had been a grammar school before 1382 at which it would seem that a boy's education cost eightpence a term,[35] a new free school was founded in 1512, probably by the widow of a former mayor, and was put directly under the management of the mayor and town council,[36] and as these apparently proved somewhat negligent in the business the Leet jury constantly interfered in the most officious way in the government of the school and the choice and supervision of its teachers. "It will be a credit," they said, "to have a good master and a good ussher in one school."[37]

Of the intellectual life of the towns we know scarcely anything, and there is perhaps not much to be known. Scholars naturally drifted away to the Universities or London, and the society of the borough was occupied with other matters than learning. In Nottingham, in spite of the educational zeal of the jury, the first evidence we have of a town clerk who knew enough of the classics to quote a line of Vergil and a line of Horace is in 1534-1545; while it is not till 1587 that we find a clerk who had learned Greek.[38] On the other hand Bristol was evidently a centre of radiant light. An excellent education was given in its school, if we judge from the famous Grocyn, who was brought up there and left the school in 1463;[39] and its society was adorned by men of culture and wide intellectual curiosity. William of Worcester, the enquirer after universal knowledge, a man of science who practised medicine and cultivated his garden of herbs, as well as a man of letters, who at forty-three "hath gone to school to a Lombard called Karoll Giles to learn and to be read in poetry or else in French," and to whom "a good book of French or of poetry" seemed as fine a purchase as "a fair manor," might be seen in his later days at Bristol, practising the art of annalist, in which character he surveyed the whole town and carefully measured it by paces from end to end.[40] His friend Ricart, town clerk and historian, spent the twenty-seven years of his clerkship in writing his Calendar or Chronicle of 332 leaves in six carefully arranged parts, the first three being devoted to history and the last three to local customs and laws, in which he carried the story of Bristol through 3,000 years from the days of Brut to the reign of Edward the Fourth.[41]

It was inevitable that the purpose and theory of education should ultimately be modified by the change of masters, as well as by the change of manners, and already fervent reformers like Caxton began to look beyond "the alphabet and humanities" and discuss training in the mysteries of the English tongue itself. Among the "fathers ancient" who should command the reverence of scholars they counted the famous men of their own race and speech—men removed from them by but a generation or two—Chaucer "the father and founder of ornate eloquence," Lydgate, the maker of "volumes that be large and wide," and Occleve; and it is touching to see men, on the very eve of the heroic age of English literature, wistfully looking back to the vanished glories of their grandfather days, when, as it seemed to them, all the "fresh flowers" of style had been reaped by this handful of ancient worthies, and "of silver language the great riches" stored away in their treasury, so that the painful toiler who came after in search of "the embalmed tongue and aureate sentence," could now get it only by piece-meal, or at the most might glean here and there by busy diligence something to show that he had reverently visited the fields of the blest.[42] The enlightened zeal of the learned indeed had still to wage a long warfare with the pedants of the schools and the barbaric notions of education that governed men's minds; and the training vouchsafed to the poor boys of the fifteenth century was then and for many a century afterwards a rude and brutal one.[43] No doubt, too, the trader's view of education, practical as it was, had a touch of unashamed vulgarity. "To my mind," says the Capper in the Commonweal, "it made no matter if there were no learned men at all," for "the devil a whit good do ye with your studies but set men together by the ears;" what men wanted was "to write and read, and learn the languages used in countries about us, that we might write our minds to them and they to us." Scholars, on the other hand, trembled at the results to civilization and knowledge of the crude ideals of the mere man of business, who if he had his way would "in a short space make this realm empty of wise and politic men, and consequently barbarous, and at the last thrall and subject to other nations; for empire is not so much won and kept by the manhood or force of men as by wisdom and policy,[44] which is gotten chiefly by learning." But whatever were their faults it was in the schools as much as in the council-chamber or shop that the revolution of the next century was being prepared; and the wide-reaching results of the spread of education in town and village were potent factors in the developement of a later England. "The fault is in yourselves, ye noblemen's sons," wrote Ascham, "and therefore ye deserve the greater blame, that commonly the meaner men's children come to be the wisest counsellors and greatest doers in the weighty affairs of this realm."[45]

CHAPTER II

THE TOWN MARKET

CLOSE under the sheltering walls of the parish church we may look for the market of a mediæval town, with stalls leaning against the building where possibly the first beginnings of trade had found shelter, where before any market was held the people of the neighbourhood assembled on feast days and sold meat and bread at the church without fear of being called on for any payment for toll and stallage;[46] and in which, after the community had been endowed with market rights, the rulers and governors of the market met, the guardians of its weights and measures, the makers of its laws, the assessors of its tolls, the supervisors of its wares. There, while the national government was drifting in perplexity at the mercy of court factions, agitated by problems of the King's civil list, pensions to nobles, and the conquest of France, the towns were rapidly sketching out their commercial system and tentatively laying down the main lines into which the national policy was ultimately to be driven.

The market had long been kept out of view by its more showy predecessor the fair—the offspring of an immemorial antiquity, whose very name[47] betrays its origin in the ancient gatherings at feasts heathen or Christian, and reveals it as an institution derived from old tribal and national usages. Gradually expanding in later times with the growth of the royal prerogative and necessities of commerce, and drawing to its miscellaneous gatherings strange merchants fetched from far and near, the fair had a brilliant history of its own; it had given birth to universal commerce and watched over its growth; it became the foster-mother of the Merchant Law; even now it still appears with the lavish airs of an antique benefactor casting on the green its faded gifts of holyday and merry-go-round and quack delights. But as long ago as the fifteenth century the superannuated fair was already falling into a slow decrepitude, and giving place to its successor, the product of a later order of things.[48] For the market had another origin and might trace back its descent to the traditions of the Roman *municipia*, and claim the Roman Pandects for its sponsors, and show itself fortified by customs and modes of administration handed down to England with many another legacy from the laws of the Frankish kings.[49] With all its air of being the very work and possession of the people, the market was by descent no popular or tribal right; it was the king's prerogative; its tolls and customs were regulated by the authority of the Justices of the King's Bench, and its prices were proclaimed by the king's Clerk of the Market.[50]

What kings could not themselves profitably enjoy, however, was generally to be bought at some reasonable price. The privilege of holding a market could be transferred as a franchise to a subject, and the whole market system in England grew up by means of royal grants of monopolies to individuals or to corporations. Between the years 1200 and 1482, almost 5000 local centres of organized trade were established by grants of markets and fairs,[51] and the towns were naturally well to the fore in securing whatever bargains were being distributed. But the origin of the privilege was always independent in theory of the ordinary municipal franchises;[52] and in many important boroughs freedom from the Steward and Marshal of the Household and the royal Clerk of the Market was one of the last rights given to the people.[53]

Closely connected with the right to hold a market was the right to keep a Beam or Steelyard with its weights, a yard measure, and a bushel.[54] On the day that each new mayor entered on his office, he received from his predecessor the common chest, the town treasure, and the standard measures; and was required forthwith to send out his councillors to the house of every shopkeeper, baker, brewer, or innkeeper, that they might carry all bushels, gallons, quarts, yards, or weights back to the Mayor's house to be compared with the standard models and duly sealed.[55] Thenceforth it was his business to make war on spicers and grocers who sold by horn or aim of hand or by subtlety deceived the poor commons, on brewers who used cups and dishes instead of lawful measures,[56] on drapers who measured after their own devices, on weavers who used stones and not sealed weights to buy their wool; even merchants of the Staple and country squires and foreign dealers brought their wool to the "Trove" or Balance, with a fee for the "Fermour of the Beme,"[57] as soon as general trade proved the inconvenience of a variety of local weights, or of the primitive method of using stones which still survived in the fifteenth century, when a Yorkshire steward writes to his master, "I have a counterpoise weight of the weight stone that the wool was weighed with, and that ye see that the stone be kept that the shipman brings."[58]

Thus the market with its Beam and measures became the source and centre of an activity absolutely new—an activity which crowded the roads not only with merchants and chapmen, but with the new race of carriers that was created at the end of the fourteenth century to transport the dealer's wares throughout the length and breadth of the country.[59] Dealers and manufacturers gathered in groups round the central Cheap and its Balance with authentic sealed weights, and gave the names of their several trades to the alleys in which butchers or milksellers clustered together, or where spurriers and goldsmiths had their shops, and grocers, mercers, wool-dealers, and cloth merchants were ranged in ordered ranks round the Guildhall for the greater convenience of the municipal officers. What the new movement meant we can see in the change that passed over the face of English boroughs. The first sight of a mediæval town must have carried little promise to the visitor. We have a lively picture of the state of Hythe given by the presentments of its reforming jury in the beginning of the fifteenth century, from which it is not easy to understand how the inhabitants ever made their way about the town at all. Streets were choked with the refuse of the stable, made impassable by the "skaldynge de hogges," flooded by the overflow of a house, drowned by the turning of a watercourse out of its way or the putting up of a dam by some private citizen heedless of all consequences to the public road. Timber dealers cast trunks of trees right across the street, dyers poured their waste waters over it till it became a mere swamp, builders blocked it up utterly with the framework of their new houses, and traders made their wharves upon it. Not only the most thriving and respectable merchants, such as the Honywodes, but the butcher and swine-keeper as well, threw the waste of house and shambles and swine-cote into the open street till there was scarcely any passage left for the wayfarer; or established a "hoggestok," "which smells very badly and is abominable to all men coming to market, as well as to all dwelling in the town," say the jury. There was hardly a street or lane which was not described as "almost stinking and a nuisance." The "Cherche Weye" was occupied by the pits of a skinner. "There was no carrying through Brokhellislane." The street by which the procession went on Holy Thursday, the day of perambulation of the town, could scarcely be traversed. Everywhere gates and bridges were falling to decay, ditches unrepaired, and hedges overgrown; and one offender who had obstructed a road by neglecting to repair the ditches found an easy way of escape from his obligations by a courtesy to the Bailiff—"the dyeing of two cloths that the said ditches may not have to be repaired." Worse still the Holy Well was choked with refuse, and so was the well in West Hythe, and "the water in the cart of Geoffrey Waterleader by which the whole community is refreshed" was equally obstructed and spoiled by the refuse of the butchers' shambles. It is no wonder that pestilence devastated Hythe in 1412, as throughout the century it swept over one town after another. But it has been calculated that even without the aid of pestilence the ordinary mortality of a borough in the Middle Ages was almost equal to that of a town during a visitation of cholera to-day. Even the first well-meant efforts of Corporations to shut pigs out of their streets and banish wandering dogs, by levying fines from any inhabitant who had an "irrational animal going about" in the churchyard[60] or the market, doubtless added to the dangers of pestilence by removing the only scavengers known to the early borough.

Nor was this the condition of the smaller towns only. In Nottingham, a thriving and prosperous borough, we read in the same way of streets blocked with piles of cinders cast out smoking hot from the bell-foundry or the iron workshops, or with heaps of corn which the householders winnowed, or as they said "windowed," by the simple method of throwing it from an upper window or door into the street that the wind might carry away the chaff.[61]

In the yet wealthier manufacturing city of Norwich the market place was not yet paved in 1507, but a judicious order was issued that no one should dig holes in it to get sand without the mayor's licence.[62] The very attempt to get access to a town was often not wholly free from peril. In 1499 a glover from Leighton Buzzard travelled with his wares to Aylesbury for the market before Christmas Day. It happened that an Aylesbury miller, Richard Boose, finding that his mill needed repairs, sent a couple of servants to dig clay "called Ramming clay" for him on the highway, and was in no way dismayed because the digging of this clay made a great pit in the middle of the road ten feet wide, eight feet broad, and eight feet deep, which was quickly filled with water by the winter rains. But the unhappy glover, making his way from the town in the dusk, with his horse laden with paniers full of gloves, straightway fell into the pit, and man and horse were drowned. The miller was charged with his death, but was acquitted by the court on the ground that he had had no malicious intent, and had only dug the pit to repair his mill, and because he really did not know of any other place to get the kind of clay he wanted save the highroad.[63]

All this heritage of squalor and rough disorder however was no longer accepted without protest. Old abuses were brought to light and denounced.[64] Towns were swept and garnished, stately market crosses set up, and new Guild-halls everywhere built with shops and stalls and storage rooms for the traders. A new interest was awakened in the state of streets[65] and lanes and central squares when waggons and pack horses began to struggle through the mire with their loads on market day. And as travellers multiplied—busy men intent on bargains, traders flocking to buy and sell, mayors and clerks of distant boroughs come to negotiate a commercial treaty, men of law having the conduct of a new charter, common earners—all travellers who no longer cared (and some of them for very obvious reasons) to depend on the hospitality of monasteries, the towns with one accord began to provide inns where, to the greater profit of the community, such men might turn for shelter; and the more luxurious among them might discover good cheer which demanded a grateful entry—"paid for our bed there, and it was well worth it, witness, a feather bed 1*d.*"[66] Everywhere a new order reigned under the busy rule of the municipal officers, as they leased out the market stalls and sheds,[67] appointed the corresponding pews in the church, allotted storage rooms in the Guildhall, issued licenses to alien traders, and controlled the wayward will of the sellers by regulating their prices and their profits. Goods landed at the wharves of a seaport were delivered up to the public porters and measurers of the Strand[68] employed by the town to unload vessels with pulleys and ropes supplied at the common expense, and to carry them to the appointed place for toll or for inspection; and the town brokers—public officers sworn to make no private profit while they held their posts—conducted bargains in the name of the whole community,[69] freighted vessels, and measured cargoes of corn or canvas or cloth. Before the mayor the endless officials of the market were sworn—the clerk of the market who had to search and survey all victuals, the sergeant who carried the toll-box on market days after the bailiffs,[70] the "leave-lookers," the "decennaries," the "prud'hommes,"[71] the butchers chosen to oversee the meat market, the men appointed to control the sale of fish and poultry, the common weigher, and so on through the long and various list of officials.

A vast system of ingenious and elaborate regulations[72] marked the long effort of the townspeople to carry out in their new markets the apparently simple end which lay at the heart of the democracy, that food and necessaries of life both good and cheap should be within the reach of every man. According to the theory which still held its ground in the sixteenth century that "victual being a necessary sustenance for the body should not be esteemed at the seller's liberty,"[73] a fixed price was set on all provisions. Hence the Assize of Bread[74] (apparently quite neglected by the feudal lords[75]) and the Assizes of Beer and of Wine were secured by the towns, whether as a part of their market rights or as an independent privilege.[76] Victuallers were closely watched lest in selling meat, eggs, butter, or oatmeal they should take "excess lucre upon them, selling that is to say more than 1*d.* in the shilling;"[77] innholders were allowed a penny of gain on every bushel of corn and a half-penny on every seven pounds of hay, so that if a man could buy a bushel of corn[78] for 2*s.* 8*d.* he was not allowed to sell it for 3*s.*; tavern-keepers might have twopence profit on a gallon of white or red wine, and on sweet wines brought by Italian merchants, fourpence;[79] cooks must make their meat "well seasoned and wholesome, and sell it for reasonable winning, and that they reboil nor rebake no meat in hurt of the King's people;" while fishmongers—a class most important in the mediæval world, and among whom it was impossible to prevent the growth of the middleman, were subjected to endless regulations.[80] In the unceasing effort to save themselves from dearth or from fraud the poor commons had their authorized protector in the Mayor—a protector who on entering office took oath before the community not only to obey the King but also to serve the people, and to "keep truly correction on all bakers and brewers and taverners and cooks and such like people." No sooner was the Mayor of Bristol installed than he was bound to call all the bakers of the town to the Guild Hall, to understand from them what stuff they had of wheat, to counsel them in their buying and bargaining with the "Bagers" who brought corn to the town, and to decide on the size of the loaves. Then all the Bristol brewers were summoned before him, that he might commune with them about the cost of malt, and decree a fixed price which no brewer might evade or alter.

In like manner he proceeded to set a price on wood "by his wise discretion," and to order the hours of its sale; and he had to examine the colliers' sacks, and to assure himself that standard measures for coal were set in the proper places of the town. Further, throughout the year it was his duty constantly to watch that his ordinances were duly observed. Occasionally his walk was extended along the river side, that he might keep an eye on the timber trade and observe whether the great wood called Berkeley wood was discharged at one quay, and the smaller faggots at another landing-place; and that he might from spring to spring watch prices, and see that there was small wood enough to supply the poor people with bundles at 1/2*d.* or 1*d.* kept at the "Back," a waterside street where the merchants' stores were piled. At divers times he went to oversee the quality of the bread and try its weight (for which perhaps, as at Sandwich, he engaged a goldsmith who was liberally paid for his experience at the scales); while at Christmas, or whenever there was holiday or a pilgrimage in the town, it was his business to make sure that there was bread enough in the shops to supply all needs. And in order to know certainly that the brewers not only made good ale for the rich but also a cheap small drink for the poor, on Wednesdays and Saturdays he was "used to walk in the mornings to the brewers' houses, to oversee them in serving of their ale to the poor commons of the town, and that they have their true measures; and his ale-konner with him to taste and understand that the ale be good"[81]—a very necessary task if we accept the picture given us in Piers Ploughman of the typical beer-seller of his day—

"Yea, bawe," quoth a brewer, "I will not be ruled,
By Jesus, for all your jangling after *spiritus justicie*;
Nor after conscience, by Christ, for I could sell
Both dregs and draff, and draw at one hole
Thick ale and thin ale, and that is my kind,
And not to hack after holiness; hold thy tongue, Conscience!
Of *spiritus justicie* thou speakest much and idle."[82]

The Nottingham jury a century or two later would have drawn the same picture. "Master Mayor," they cry, "we beseech you to be good master to us, and see a remedy for our brewers, for we find us grieved with them all."[83]

Nor did legislation stop here. The moment a trader came within reach of a town he became the object of universal suspicion lest he should be a dealer travelling with an alert intention to outwit the public and force an artificial value in the market by some contrivance of forestalling or regrating or engrossing—that is of intercepting goods on the way to market in order to buy them more cheaply; of thus buying at advantage to sell at increased prices; or of keeping back goods bought at wholesale prices in order to sell them later at a better value. A jealous watch was kept on him. He was not allowed to do any business secretly or outside the proper limits, but "openly in the market thereto assigned," and even there he was ordered to stand aside till the townsmen had come back from early mass and had first been served with such stores of corn and malt, of butter and poultry and meat as their households needed, and the bell struck the hour when he might take his turn for what was left.[84] And as he bought so must he sell only in the established and customary place; and food once displayed on his shelf or stall could not be taken out of the town unsold without leave of the bailiffs.[85] Any citizen who helped a "foreign" merchant by buying or selling goods for him under his own name lost his freedom.[86] Men who lived "upland"[87] were rejected from the society of privileged traders of the towns, and sharp distinctions such as we find at Worcester between the "citizens denizen" and the "citizens foreign"[88] separated the folk within and without the walls.[89] In one borough strangers' stalls in the market were separated from those of the burghers[90] so that they might not hinder the townsfolk in their business; in another they were forbidden to carry their wares from house to house;[91] here they might not sell their goods with their own hands, there they must dispose of them wholesale, or forfeit their entire stock to the town if they attempted to sell by retail; elsewhere they had to wait for a given number of weeks after their arrival before they could offer their merchandise to the buyer; if for public convenience aliens were allowed to bring into the market victuals[92] and a few other articles, the monopoly of all valuable trade was kept in the hands of the burgesses or of their Merchant Guild.[93]

It is however needless to multiply instances of monopoly. The system was universal, and a curious attempt which was once made to establish free trade at Liverpool died almost as soon as it was born. The charter of Henry the Third contained the usual provision that members of the Guild alone might trade in the borough, unless by consent of the burgesses, but in a new charter of Richard the Second for which he was paid £5 this clause was left out and free trade practically established. No sooner however did Henry the Fourth appear in 1399 than the burgesses bought from him for £4 a fresh grant of privileges with the former clause restored, and the old monopoly was consequently reasserted, till oddly enough an outburst of religious bigotry abolished trade restrictions; for seeing that the Liverpool Protestants were shutting out Roman Catholics from their market, Queen Mary in 1555 proclaimed anew the charter of Richard the Second and the right of free commerce.[94] Sometimes a lively smuggling trade betrays the weak side of the monopolists' position; as when Bristol claimed entire control of all ports and creeks as high as Worcester, and the only lawful trade left to Gloucester was the shipping of supplies, mostly of corn, to Bristol. The shippers of Gloucester saw their chance of a rich lawless traffic; small boats quickly and easily laden and drawing little water, shot out of the channel by shallow passages where the bigger Bristol ships could not follow them, and Irish vessels made their way direct to Gloucester and escaped the heavy dues at the Bristol port; and while Gloucester traders grew rich fast, the Bristol folk made complaint that they were threatened with ruin.[95]

This elaborate system of trade regulation was no doubt mainly due to the effort which men were forced to make, as centres of thicker population grew up in a country where the carriage of goods[96] was a slow and difficult matter, to protect themselves from violent changes in the price of food;[97] while it is also possible that a society which dictated wages and profits was naturally drawn on to undertake the corresponding duty of fixing the value in food and clothing of these wages and profits. It would seem that for some centuries the cost of mere subsistence remained almost stationary; and even in exceptional cases, like the Jubilee of 1420 which brought a hundred thousand pilgrims to Canterbury, the corporation which had charge of the preparations was able to ensure that there should be no increase in the ordinary price of provisions.

It has been commonly held, however, that the old trade laws were not only invented to protect the people's food, but to protect wages and profits as well; and they have been denounced as the outcome of an ignorant selfishness; and as proving the belief of the mediæval burghers that the industrial prosperity of the whole community could only be assured by their securing so complete a monopoly of the entire trade of the borough that they might themselves reap all the fruit of their enterprise and gather wealth undisturbed—a belief to which modern democracies (with one great exception) still cling, though they throw a grander air over their creed now-a-days by discussing protection in continents instead of protection in a little market town. But it seems likely that protection in the modern sense had scarcely anything to say to the great mass of mediæval legislation about trade. No doubt it was the natural ideal of every craft to have the State for its nursing-mother; but the voice of the crafts was lost in the monotonous reiteration by the general public of their dominant principle, that manufactures and commerce only existed for the benefit of the whole community—the "poor commons of the realm," to use the phrase of that day. It was for *their* protection that no unlicensed or unregulated trade should be allowed to exist, that there should be no fraudulent manufactures, no secret breaking down of barriers set up by Parliament for the orderly division and control of crafts, no buying and selling by forestallers, public enemies to the community and to the country, hastening by land and by water to oppress the poor;[98] and rules devised to check a public mischief or secure a public good are no more to be classed as protective than regulations for the sale of drugs or the licensing of public houses in our own day. Such rules indeed were often as unsolicited by the trader as they were agreeable to the public, and all his cunning was exerted to elude them. Some little margin of profit was to be won beyond the city boundaries where there was freedom from the city law and from the city tolls. Therefore the London corporation complained that the butchers of London "who have bought their freedom and are sworn of the franchise, do rent their houses at Stratford and round Stratford, and never come at any summons nor bear their part in the franchise of the city; but shut out the citizens (resident butchers) in divers markets where they ought to buy their wares, so that through them no wares they can get to the great undoing of the citizens."[99] Bakers withdrew themselves "into the foreign" to avoid punishment for frauds.[100] Candlemakers established themselves in the suburbs, and butchers were presented "for selling of his tallow into the country and will not sell it to a man within the town,"[101] or for carrying tallow in sacks at night out of the city for the making up of candles; and being punished were ordered to leave candle-making to the chandlers, who on their part were commanded to keep within the boundaries. In Canterbury, where owing to the great number of ecclesiastical tenants the main burden of taxation was thrown on a part only of the population, and where doubtless taxes were correspondingly high, there came a time at last when traders of every kind, cloth-makers and brewers and bakers, carried their business outside the "liberties," so that according to the story of the mayor and council "formerly there were divers and many habitations in which of time past were kept good and notable households, by the which many men and women were relieved and had their living and increase, being now uninhabited and greatly decayed, and some of them fall to ruin and utter destitution ... and it is well understood and known that the principal cause thereof" was this wicked device of the independent dealers, by which the tradesmen in the city who had to pay "tax, tallage, and other impositions," could not compete with those outside and "have not the sale and utterance of their bread and ale, as they in times past have had, to their great impoverishing, and manifold hurt and prejudice to the commonweal of the said city." The suburban bakers sold their goods to "divers and many simple and evil disposed persons of the city as well to Scots, Irish, and other, which in no wise will apply themselves to any labour or other lawful occupations, but only they live upon sale and huckstry of the said bread, beer, and ale, and for that they have resorting unto them many vagabonds ... whereby many well disposed persons be greatly annoyed and grieved."[102] To restore trade to its primitive simplicity a law was passed with clauses against the mercenary Scotch and Irish, the troublers of the city's peace, and dealers were forbidden to sell their provisions "to no inhabitant within the said city, but only to such persons as shall be thought by the mayor and aldermen of good disposition and conversation."[103]

The prejudice against unregulated trade was no doubt reinforced by the hostility of the town dealer to competitors who throve at his expense on illegal profits; but it was probably the governing body of the town which maintained the most serious opposition to all traffic that depended on the cheating of the common treasury of the borough.[104] For no trifling part of the town revenue came, as we see from the Nottingham records, from fines paid yearly by non-freemen for the privilege of holding a stall in street or market. In Canterbury "Tollerati" paid for the right of buying and selling during a limited period, and at the end of the time renewed the right by a fresh payment of what was called "Tolleration money";[105] alien traders living without the liberties, there known as "intrantes," took in Romney the name of "extravagantes." Some towns shewed a jealousy of strangers, dictated no doubt by special circumstances; as in Preston, where the "Foreign Burgesses," as distinguished from the "Inn Burgesses," were drawn from the country gentry and squires and some inhabitants of the town,[106] and were merely freed from toll[107] for any goods bought for the use of their families, but were allowed no other profits of trade, and even though they were inhabitants had no right of common on marsh or moor, nor could they join in the election of any town officer nor be themselves elected;[108] while even with these restrictions no trader who lived outside the walls was admitted among them,[109] and it was only in course of time that alien dealers were gradually allowed on payment of a fine to set up stalls in the market-place and carry on their business under the name of "stallingers." In general, however, an open purse was all that was needed to commend a stranger; and if the charge on it was sometimes excessive it seems to have been enforced mainly as a means of persuasion to enter the Merchant Guild.

But for whatever reason the regulation of trade was thought desirable, whether to protect the consumer's pocket or to fill the town treasury, it certainly was not intended to keep buyers and sellers at home, to hamper their enterprise, or to abolish competition. If protection and monopoly were allowed to look big, they were never allowed to get seriously in the way of business. In theory and sometimes in fact iron chains might be flung across the King's highway, bars thrown athwart the river, and custom house officers set at the gate to levy toll and stallage.[110] But gates and bars and chains swung open everywhere before the trader "if he have the penny ready to take to;" the guilds enlarged their rolls for foreigners,[111] the towns granted them their privileges liberally. Since a man could hold citizenship in more than one borough a speculator or merchant doing business in a large way might always circumvent the rules against foreign dealers by being made citizen in some convenient trading centre as well as in his own town,[112] and so obtain power to carry on the business proper to an alien speculator with all the privileges of a resident burgher. Every pedantic hindrance, indeed, was removed out of the way of his enterprise, for a very slight study of town records disposes of the idea that mediæval trade was ultimately governed by the formal laws of statute books. Monopoly was broken through whenever it was advisable or convenient for special occasions. Bakers and victuallers who rose to municipal offices turned the assize of bread and the inspection of cooking houses and fish stalls into an idle tale. In the hands of merchants the laws of buying and selling were manipulated so as to interfere neither with the free circulation of goods nor with the instinct of the dealer to buy in the cheapest market and sell in the dearest; and it was still left possible to carry food where it was most needed, whether to supply a manufacturing centre such as Norwich or a city which was rapidly doubling its population like London.[113] If the law ordained that the forestaller was to be heavily fined for the first offence; for the second to lose his merchandise and be put in the pillory; and for the third to be deprived of the freedom of the city, the law was simply ignored, or some trifling fine was inflicted—a paltry sum which a prosperous trader might easily disregard.[114] In fact it would almost seem that the actual result of the trade laws was mainly to give the rich wholesale merchant an additional advantage over the poor trader. Forestalling and regrating became the fashionable privilege of town councillors and magnates who through their position and their wealth found it doubly easy to evade local ordinances, of London merchants who were buying all over the country to supply the needs of the growing city, and of dealers on a large scale interested in the export trade; while the terrors of the law served as an effective deterrent to struggling hawkers and chapmen against meddling with the profits won by more exalted speculators from a customary if illegal traffic.

The real foundation of free trade throughout the country, however, and that which alone gave any value to local arrangements and individual privileges, is to be found in the early town charters, where this great gift had a leading place. Almost the first boon asked for by a borough was a grant which should make its burghers or its merchant guild quit of tolls and pontage, and stallage and lastage, throughout the whole kingdom, in fairs and throughout sea-ports, in lands on this and on the other side of the sea; and give them power to buy and sell throughout all England, within cities and without, all kinds of merchandise; with the right to have stalls in other markets than their own without paying stallage, and to buy in such markets at all hours and not only those allowed to strangers. Each charter moreover had wrapped up in it a kind of "favoured nation" clause which gave to boroughs "such liberties as the city of London hath"—a clause which seems to have been interpreted (at least as to one of its meanings) as implying the right for burghers to buy and sell in gross in another town than their own on other than market days, and that "they may have in this respect as much liberty as the citizens of London."[115]

In its wide and unstinted privileges a charter such as this—the grant of a king who was lord of all fairs and markets—expressed the whole spirit of free trade; at a word local monopoly and protection in its true sense were swept away, and every market in the country opened to any trader duly enrolled as a burgher or a member of the Merchant Guild. The question indeed still bristled with difficulties. As the king was constantly giving away or selling his rights, or part of his rights, over markets, there were innumerable cases when the special grant to one town to hold a market without disturbance, and the more general license to its neighbour to consider itself free of all market dues, were wholly irreconcilable; and the law held that no charter of freedom could interfere with any earlier rights granted to any other person or corporation to levy tolls on transport, on crossing a bridge, on entering a gate, on taking up a standing in the market, or the like. In cases where two charters were found to bestow conflicting rights, therefore, the towns set their best lawyers to search out old evidences and records, and to claim the protection of judges of the King's Bench or of Parliament for the grant that boasted of the greater age.[116] The preliminary question of priority of rights having been thus decided, the next step was to remedy the dead-lock of business to which the two communities had been brought by means of formal treaties such as nations make to-day, in which the right to levy toll and custom was probably used as systems of tariffs have been used in modern states—as a means of bribing or threatening refractory neighbours into some concession of free trade.[117] Southampton made its separate treaties with at least seventy-three towns or trading corporations besides all the "honours" of the kingdom, releasing them from payment of its tolls and customs; its burghers had their own compact with Marlborough[118] in which they waived such privileges as they possessed by their own earlier charter; with Bristol they settled the amount of the tax to be levied on Bristol men who brought merchandise to their market; they agreed with the men of Winchester that no tolls should be asked on either side;[119] and in 1501 their treaty with the Cinque Ports was ratified by "your lovers the bailiff and jurats of Hastings."[120] Undermined as they were on all sides, and with gaping breaches everywhere, the walls of protection which the boroughs had thrown up round their markets certainly formed no impediment to the movement of local trade. Before the impatience of traders greedy for gain, artificial frontiers and barriers and tariffs were swept away, and from little self-contained communities where the cottagers grew their own food and spun their own wool and asked scarcely anything from outside save fish and salt and a little iron, the boroughs grew rapidly into centres of expanding commerce. To supply their needs or their luxuries they despatched their traders far and wide. When Ely sent for John of Gloucester, the famous bell-founder, to make the four great bells for the cathedral, messengers had to go to Erith for clay, and to Lynn and Northampton for copper and tin.[121] The Nottingham goldsmith was employed to repair the cross in Clifton Church, and its "alablaster man" supplied the faithful in London with little statues of the Baptist in appropriate shrines.[122] Buyers of wool and sellers of cloth, saddlers, butchers, fishmongers, hawkers of all sorts, obtained from the mayor and commonalty of their borough letters of free passage throughout the kingdom for the carrying on of their business[123] and kept up incessant intercourse between town and town. Everywhere busy forestallers were on the look out for eggs and meat and corn, and bought up supplies all over the country for London or some big town or for the export trade, or turned their privileges under the clause of London liberties into a means of buying wholesale all the week long as regrators in order to sell at a profit on market day, while on that day itself they were out at cock-crow to buy privately when the citizens were at mass, so that by six o'clock there was nothing left in the market for the good folk of the town.[124]

As we look at this mighty volume of commerce pouring from town to town with a steady force that swept all obstacles out of its channel, we may well begin to doubt whether the burghers of the middle ages were indeed stupidly putting their necks under a hard yoke of arbitrary law, and wilfully destroying their own prospects by preferring bondage to freedom, or sacrificing general prosperity to local greeds. The mediæval system, until it began to fall into the decay that precedes death, was in fact the minister to fine and worthy ends. In a society where few rights existed save by way of privilege, the trading "communitas," whether the borough or the guild, did actually serve as the great engine for the abolition of restrictions, for extending privilege, and throwing open a national commerce. There was a time when every new chartered association was an actual widening of free trade; and a man entered the community of a town for the same reasons that he might to-day take out letters of naturalization in a country where his business lay—not to be ensured against competition, but to share in all commercial privileges which it had won by treaty, and in case of peril to own the protection of its flag. Each town had its own privileged "community" and recognized the "community" of the neighbouring borough; and it was by this mutual recognition only that intermunicipal treaties became possible, or that any borough could ascertain the limits of its responsibility for members in foreign fair or market, could pledge itself to the fulfilment of its treaties, or have any guarantee for redress in case of wrong.[125] In the detailed municipal legislation about debt and surety and mutual responsibility, about punishment of violence, the suppression of an individual traitor to the common weal, the protection of a community from false dealing of any of its confederate states, we may plainly see how local monopolies had come to be far more significant from the point of view of public order and general intercourse than of private wealth. Monopoly and protection in fact had put on the garb of a necessary office and service. Instead of gaolers who kept the trader fast bound at home, they were the strong guardians who attended him as he went abroad, the fore-runners who cut down before him the chains that barred the highway, the ministers of justice that tracked out in his service the fraudulent debtor, the pledges to him in every danger of the vigilance and power of his native town. To each community they were the bonds of a civil order and the tokens of a corporate fidelity.

CHAPTER III

THE TOWN TRADER

WITH the appearance of the new commercial society in the boroughs we feel that the history of modern England has begun. By the formation of a prosperous middle class, a new type of character was introduced into English life—a type which lay altogether outside old traditions, and was as far from imitating the confident superiority of classes that held the mastery by traditional right, as it was from preserving the simplicity and resignation of the masses of those who confessed a hereditary duty of subjection. The mediæval burgher was trained in a rough school. Owing nothing to class or family or patron, roughly judged and consigned to his own place in the ranks by the test of competition in its simplest form, the industrial rivalry between man and man, the trader had no helper if he did not help himself. Merchants burdened with little capital, like the trader pictured by Holbein in his Dance of Death carrying all their store of wealth bound up on their persons, and free to change their residence as often as commerce offered brighter prospects elsewhere, wandered from town to town, leaving no trade unlearned, no fair unvisited at home, and no market forgotten abroad. Craftmasters equally destitute of money had to trust to their own wit in the struggle for life, and became practised in vigilance and patience, thrift and caution, in the contempt of hardship, in strenuous and ceaseless activity. The discipline of trade was severe, and the conditions of prosperity hard. If a gentleman intruder appeared among these men hoping to find an easy way to wealth in the more respectable forms of business to which the county families alone condescended, his experiences were watched with contemptuous good humour by the burghers, who knew the hardships of the road.

"I have made many a knight both mercer and draper,"

says the merchant in a mediæval poem,

"Paid never for their prenticehood not a pair of gloves;
But chaffered with my chevesance, [bargains] cheved [prospered] seldom after."[126]

The feeble and incompetent fell away before the severity of the tests applied, and the trading class was constantly undergoing change. Perhaps some sturdy Jewish stock, like the Phillips of Birmingham, held their own for three or four centuries;[127] but more commonly families spring up into importance and for one or two generations hold the first place in the payment of taxes, and have control of the chief offices of government, till after the third generation the name disappears from the account books.[128] The family has died out, or broken down under the stress of competition, or it has settled upon an estate bought in the country and become merged among the county squires; and some new stock comes in to fight its way with fresh energy and enterprise.

In picturing to ourselves the life of a mediæval borough it sometimes happens that, with our constant tendency to exaggerate the strangeness of the past, we perceive only an existence so straitened and humble in condition that all sense of distinctions is lost, and we create a false monotony, supposing that because in that remote world business was carried on in a narrow sphere men's fortunes were therefore more equal, or that the general level of commercial prosperity was necessarily more uniform than it is now. But everything we know of town life, from the moment when the boroughs come into view, forces home the conviction of an inequality of circumstance and wealth as sensible as any that we recognize in the later Middle Ages; of a society which was at no time either simple or homogeneous, and where the plutocrat and capitalist held as imposing a place and bore himself in as lordly a fashion, considering the limits of his stage, as his descendants of modern times. The secret of wealth was first found, as it was long kept, by the butchers, brewers, and victuallers of one kind or another. There were in every borough men like Andrew Bate, the butcher of Lydd, who became "farmer of Dengemarsh," and kept the town in a ferment for years, whether with his herds of cattle which overran the marsh pastures and trespassed on his neighbours' fields or commons so that they could not "occupy in peace," and would rather sell their land than be so "grievously hurted by the cattle of Andrew Bate;" or with his heavy tolls for the "Western men" who came to dry their whiting on the nesse, and found him a hard "extortioner" who "had driven away half Dengemarsh"; above all with his ceaseless activity in extending his borders over the doubtful limits that parted the lands of the town from the lands of the Abbot; so that though the corporation in 1462 insisted on a careful marking out of their frontiers, and years later were labouring to have him supplanted in Dengemarsh by another burgher, Bate was evidently victorious, and ended by seeing his brother, who had been trained in the law probably with this object, appointed Town Clerk and practical controller of the affairs of Lydd.[129] In like manner the rich fishmonger, Daniel Rowe of Romney, who sent his oysters, crabs, lampreys, and trout to London, the eastern counties, Cambridge, and along the valley of the Thames as far as Wallingford, and fetched back in their stead boars, calves, porkers, and bacon, ended by being made Town Clerk of Romney[130]—as indeed became an educated man, who kept his daybooks, where all the travelling expenses of men and horses were carefully set down, in Latin. So also the Romney vintner, James Tyece, who began life in a very small way in 1387, was important enough in 1394 to be sent on a deputation to the archbishop; in 1398 he was Jurat, and in 1414 held so much land that his property was made into a separate ward named after him in 1432.[131]

In short in every town the bakers, brewers, vintners, cooks, hostellers, and publicans "built their nests high" buying burgages out of the pence of the poor,[132] and in spite of law and ordinance walked the streets in the furred mantles of aldermen, entered the council chamber, kept the treasure chest as chamberlains—issuing prudent versions of the town accounts calculated for the public eye, and themselves regulating the assessments for taxes in the interests of their wealthy fellowship—and presided over the courts of justice, where they administered the assizes of bread and beer for the benefit of the fraternity; while for their services they required a part of the common land to be enclosed for their use, or pastured their flocks at the public expense, and in a thousand ways gathered in for generations the harvest that then ripened for men in authority.[133] No law could shut them out from the mayor's seat; and carrying away from office the robe of "clean scarlet" which gave them the chief places among the powerful members of "the Clothing,"[134] they still dominated over a helpless people, with scarcely any check save from the jealousy of their fellow traders. Thus all Canterbury was disturbed in 1507 by the brewer Crompe who, having been mayor for a year, returned to his former business on leaving office, and went about busily canvassing the small retailers, promising that if they would sell Crompe's beer he would be their "very good master whatsoever they had to do in the Court Hall," and that he would see to it that their pots should not be carried off on charges of short measure to the Hall. In cases of this kind remonstrance from the people seems invariably to have been perfectly useless, and the only complaint recorded in Canterbury was that of the rival brewers, who met Crompe's competition by an appeal to a custom of the town that the mayor should altogether forsake the victualling trades; in the course of the half century there had been, it was said, at least six mayors who had "lived like gentlemen" for the rest of their lives after leaving office, and though this polite profession allowed them to carry on the business of drapers or cloth manufacturers, it was proved that one ex-mayor who had been a brewer as well as draper left off his brewery and never returned to it; while another who was a baker sold his business, hired his house to another man, and "lived after as a gentleman." Crompe however remained obstinate, contemptuously protesting that the alleged "custom" was but fifty years old (a bit of special pleading on his part since this was just the age of the mayoralty itself in Canterbury) and, that the mayors had ceased to be victuallers out of self-indulgence, and because they preferred to live at their ease.[135]

At the first victuallers and publicans owed their supremacy in the town society to the fact that among a people needy and thrifty the trader's only way to fortune lay in selling the common necessaries of life. The great bulk of the people lived poorly. In general perhaps the master craftsman scarcely earned a higher wage than his journeymen,[136] and may have often eked out his livelihood by ploughing and reaping his lot of the common land at one time, while at another he worked at his occupation with two or three helpers—servants and apprentices "which be of no great having," and who were by law compelled to cut, gather, and bring in the corn[137] if they were employed in a trade "of which craft or mystery a man hath no great need in harvest time." The first speculators who were tempted by visions of a great public with its exhaustless needs and unfathomable purse pursued their dreams with the guile of petty schemers. If a dealer proposed to make his fortune in malt he opened proceedings with the strictest economies. A penny or a half-penny served as earnest money to the peasants from whom he bought his corn, and who were told to come to the house for payment. "And when they come there and think to have their payment directly, the buyer says that his wife at his house has gone out, and has taken the key of the room, so that he cannot get at his money; but that the other must go away and come again soon and receive his pay. And when he comes back a second time, then the buyer is not to be found; or else, if he is found, he feigns something else, by reason whereof the poor men cannot have their pay. And sometimes while the poor men are waiting for their pay the buyer causes the corn to be wetted," and then tells the peasant he may take it away with him if he does not like the price offered.[138] In the same way the cloth contractor started with a modest business that needed no outlay of money, taking the raw material which his customers brought to him and handing it over to weavers, who on their side provided their own tools and did the work in their own homes. As he prospered in the world he may have become the owner of a few looms which he let out to the weavers he employed; or he perhaps added to his trade the keeping of a little shop or some small pedlar's business for the sake of such petty gains as the law, looking in those days with scant favour on dealers, might allow. Often hard set to carry on his business, he sought to help out his poverty by cunning, and the expedients to which he was driven—the giving out of bad material or short weight to his workmen, the devices to save a few pence here and there by deducting it on one pretext or another from payments due, the giving wages in victuals or needles or mercery or the waste trifles of his little shop—must often indicate the distracting pressure of immediate need under which he anticipated the devices of the small working employer of to-day.[139]

But from the earliest times it is evident that there were many of the more successful traders who rose to a position which, in a humbler degree, closely resembles that of our modern capitalists and employers, and that this class constantly tended to increase in wealth and in numbers. They evidently rivalled in astuteness their brethren of lowlier fortunes.

"Ne had the grace of guile gone among my ware
It had been unsold this seven year, so me God help,"[140]

the merchant in Piers Ploughman admits frankly. His wife who made the cloth for sale was diligent in her sphere of economies, ordering her spinning women to spin the yarn out to great length, and paying for it by a pound measure that weighed a quarter more than her husband's weighing machine—when he weighed true. At the draper's he was taught how to stretch out the list of the cloth, or to fasten rich pieces together with a pack needle, and lengthen them out with pressers till ten or twelve yards reached to thirteen; and to get rid of his goods at Winchester and Wayhill fairs he carefully learned to lie and use false weights. To add to these resources he would go to the Lombards for lessons in clipping coin and in lending money out at usury.[141] Weaknesses of remorse troubled him little.

"'Repentedst thou never?' quoth Repentance, 'nor restitution madest?'
'Yea, once,' quoth he, 'I was y harboured with a heap of chapmen,
I arose and rifled their mails when they a'rest were.'
'That was a rueful restitution,' quoth Repentance, 'forsooth!'"

No age, indeed, has a monopoly of clever dealers, and every artifice practised in earlier days was familiar to the fifteenth century, and so loudly resented by the consumers, that many people, mistaking the signs of a public zeal to check abuses for the evidences of a growing audacity in evil, have discovered in the later middle ages an accumulating mass of corruption which gradually covered with its blackness the felicity of a purer age.[142] But whether from "the grace of guile," or from sheer ability, the traders prospered on every side. Langland looking out over all classes of men sees how with them above all lay the secret of fatness and good cheer:

"And some chose chaffer, they cheved [prospered] the better,
As it seemeth to our sight that such man thriveth."[143]

The large sums that passed from hand to hand—the imposing debts registered in the town accounts—the complaints of a master being in arrears to his apprentice for a sum of £100, or an apprentice to his master for £138—the leasing out of the customs of a great port like Southampton to a single merchant—all these things indicate the new plutocracy that was beginning to appear.[144] Drapers and clothiers were admitted into the select circles of privilege; in the towns the rank of "gentleman" became the appropriate reward of a successful cloth merchant,[145] and even in the county society the clothier was beginning to oust the old proprietors. The Tames of Gloucestershire were ordinary dealers who made cloth and traded at Cirencester till about 1480 when John Tame rented great tracts of land at

Fairford for his flocks of sheep, and in the new industrial centre which he developed there, wool was collected to feed the Cirencester manufactory. All over the country he bought at a cheap rate lands which the ruined nobles could no longer hold; and his enormous wealth increased yet further under his son Edmund, who took his place among the "gentry" by becoming High Sheriff of Gloucestershire in 1505, receiving the reward of knighthood in 1516, and entertaining Henry the Eighth at his house at Fairford in 1520.[146]

The most wealthy folk in the towns, however, were probably the class that had grown up with the developement of foreign commerce and the export trade[147]—the merchants who forsook handicrafts and lived wholly by "grete aventour."[148] Their lot was not altogether an easy one in a society perplexed by the mighty rush of the new commerce, where men trained in an earlier system looked with a mixture of fear and dislike on the intrusion of a dubious profession not vouched for by familiar custom—"covetous people who seek their own advantage," and who not only lay under suspicion as men who refused to work, but were reproached with the destruction of trade by underselling the goods of English artizans with cheaper foreign wares. The government was concerned lest by their dealings the merchants should diminish the stock of gold to be kept in the country;[149] while, on the other hand, Church and people unanimously saw in bargains with bills and pledges and sums bearing interest, which were then known as "dry exchange," something not to be distinguished from the sin of usury, and called on the government to declare void all such "damnable bargains grounded in usury, coloured by the name of new chevesaunce contrary to the law of natural justice"—"corrupt bargains which be most usually had within cities and boroughs."[150] To the delicate conscience of theologian or social preacher trade could only be defended on the ground that honestly conducted it made no profit.[151] As for the "poor commons," they held that while a man might live by trading, and perhaps make a modest competence, he had no right to grow rich;[152] his gains represented to the people the wages of iniquity, and the hungry toiler sitting over his mess of beans and bacon-rind comforted himself as best he could with thoughts of the weary ages merchants must at last count in purgatory, watching kings and knights and bishops pass out of its gates, while they themselves still lingered to pay the penalty of great oaths and innumerable taken

"Against clean conscience, for covetyse of winning."[153]

Meanwhile their way was made difficult on earth, and along the road to fair or market the wandering merchant or chapman was held to ransom by the rustics, while the harmless messenger who travelled by his side was sent merrily on his road.[154]

To the mediæval mind indeed the merchant burdened with his goods was the very type of the soul laden with sins, and painfully battling its doubtful way to heaven. He passed from peril to peril in the transport of the packages on which he had set the sign that distinguished his wares, the tall cross with shrouds[155] or the flag. No navy protected his vessels on seas that swarmed with pirates, and companies of ships as ready for battle as for commerce, set out together, under command of one of the captains chosen as admiral,[156] to fight their way as best they could, while at home fear beset the owner on every side. If a merchant sent his servant over sea to Bruges, or despatched an apprentice to one of the Baltic ports to gather in the profits due to him or to carry merchandise, no man might comfort him, and no religious thought distract his spirit till his messengers returned;[157] and even when his goods reached port all his experience and cunning were needed to deal with the exactions of the king, who demanded the first choice of his wine or precious cargo, or to baffle the rapacity of the officers of the sheriff, the officers of the staple, the collectors of customs, the treasurers of the town, the searchers, or the clerk of the market.[158]

If, however, the risks of the merchant who dared the "great adventure" increased a hundredfold, so the chances open to courage and skill became more brilliant,[159] and the triumphant trader became the object of national pride. London had its hero—

"The son

Of Merchandy, Richard of Whittingdon
That loadstar and chief chosen flower
What hath by him our England of honour?

That pen and paper may not me suffice
Him to describe so high he was of prise."[160]

A brass in the church of Chipping Camden, dated 1401, commemorates the "flower of the wool merchants of all England." In Dartmouth the long prosperity of the Hawleys[161] was recalled in the local proverb—

"Blow the wind high, blow the wind low:
It bloweth good to Hauley's hoe."

There were none who surpassed the merchants of Bristol—men who had made of their town the chief depot for the wine trade of southern France, a staple for leather, lead, and tin, the great mart for the fish of the Channel and for the salt trade of Brittany, whose cloth and leather were carried to Denmark to be exchanged for stock-fish, and to France and Spain for wine; who as early as 1420 made their way by compass to Iceland; whose vessels were the first from England to enter the Levant; and who when calamity fell on their business by the loss of Bordeaux, and by the competition of London merchants and the concentration of commerce in the hands of its Adventurers, turned their faces to the New World; sending out in 1480, and year after year from that time, two, three, or four light ships to sail "west of Ireland" in search of the "Island of Brasylle and the seven Cities," till in 1496 Cabot started with five vessels on his voyage of discovery, whence he came back to live in great honour among his fellow-townsmen, dressing in silk, and known as the "Great Admiral."[162] The Bristol merchants of those days lived splendidly in fine houses three stories high, the grander ones having each its own tower. Underground stretched vast cellars with groined stone roofs: the ground floor was a warehouse or shop opening to the street; above this were the parlour and bedroom, with attics in the gables; while the great hall was built out behind with a lofty roof of carved timber.[163] In the towers treasures of plate were stored which rivalled those of the nobles, and the walls were hung with the richest tapestries, or with at least "counterfeit Arras." Perhaps it was some such house which suggested to the poet, born perhaps in a village "cote," and who knew Bristol well, the idea of an abode which might be offered to the Lord of heaven—

"Neither in cot neither in caitiff house was Christ y bore,
But in a burgess house, the best of all the town."[164]

But the growing luxury of private life is a far less striking feature of the mediæval borough than the splendid tradition of civic patriotism and generosity which seems to have prevailed. Burghers who prospered in the world left their noblest records in the memories of their public munificence; and there were hundreds of benefactors like Thomas Elys, the Sandwich draper, who in 1392 founded the hospital of S. Thomas-the-Martyr, and endowed it with a messuage and 132 acres of land; and within five months after founded the chantry of S. Thomas-the-Martyr;[165] or like Simon Grendon, three times mayor of Exeter, who left money to found a hospital for the poor. Gifts to churches of plate and vestments and books, legacies for chantries or for priests are too numerous to mention;[166] but there was a steady tendency among the townspeople to turn their benefactions into very different channels, and bequeathing their money to the town corporation instead of a religious body, to devote it directly to secular purposes and charities of the new fashion—founding free schools, building walls, repairing bridges, maintaining harbours for their borough, or leaving a fund for the payment of the ferm rent or certain fixed taxes. An Abingdon merchant gave a thousand marks towards the bridges over the two dangerous fords, Borough Ford and Culham Ford, which had to be built by the Abingdon men "at their own cost and charges, the alms of the town, and the benevolence of well-disposed persons," and which were to make Abingdon the high road from Gloucester to London.[167] In 1421, when the Friars who owned the sources from which Southampton had its supply of water could no longer afford to replace the decayed pipes, a burgher "for the good of his soul" left money for new leaden pipes sufficient for the whole town as well as for the friars.[168] An Ipswich burgess gave the very considerable sum of £140 to relieve his fellow-townsmen of certain yearly tolls;[169] and money was always forthcoming for gates and walls and market crosses, for the buying of new charters, the adorning of the Town Hall, or gifts of plate to the corporation;[170] while as we have seen, a new system of education was practically founded by the free schools which were so largely endowed by their liberality.

For the first time in fact since the expulsion of the Jews from England we find a class of men with money to dispose of; for whatever gold and silver was available for practical purposes was gathered into the coffers of the burghers. The noble "wasters" who with gluttony destroyed what plougher and sower won[171] carried a light purse; while timid country-folk, terrified by the disorder and insecurity of the times, unused to commerce and speculation, buried their treasures in the earth, or laid away bags of "old nobles" with their plate in safe hiding places,[172] industriously hoarding against the evil day that haunted their imagination. But among spendthrifts and faint-hearted economists the burghers came with habits of large winnings and generous outgoings. They became the usurers and moneylenders of the age. When the county families had exhausted all possibilities of borrowing from their cousins and neighbours[173] they had to turn to the shopkeepers of the nearest town, who seem to have been willing to make special and private arrangements on better terms than those of the common usurer.[174] John Paston borrowed from the sheriff of London; Sir William Parr pawned his plate to a London fishmonger for £120, which he was to pay over to him in the church of S. Mary-on-the-Hill beside Billingsgate.[175] From Richard the Second onwards kings borrowed as readily as their subjects from the drapers and mercers of the towns. The prosperous merchant in his prouder moments matched his substantial merits against the haughty pretensions of lords who could go about begging of burgesses in towns and be "not the better of a bean though they borrow ever,"[176] and was not without an occasional touch of disdain for aristocratic poverty. Sir William Plumpton married the daughter of a citizen and merchant of York, who out of her rich dowry of houses in Ripon and York was able to leave large fortunes to her children. One of these wrote a description of a visit she paid to the house of some aristocratic cousins, Sir John Scrope and his daughter Mistress Darcy, and of their supercilious bearing. "By my troth I stood there a large hour, and yet I might neither see Lord nor Lady ... and yet I had five men in a suit (of livery). There is no such five men in *his* house, I dare say."[177]

But the constant fusion of classes which went on steadily throughout the century showed how solid were the reasons which drew together the rich traders of the towns and the half bankrupt families of the county. Impoverished country gentry were tempted by the money made in business, just as the "merchants and new gentlemen" hoped to reach distinction by marriage into landed families. Squires built for themselves houses in the neighbouring boroughs, turned into traders on their own account, and commonly took office at last in the municipal government;[178] while on the other hand successful city merchants were becoming landed proprietors all over the country, were decorated with the ornaments of the Bath, and distinguished by fashionable marriages,[179] in spite of the fretful sarcasms of a "gentle" class consoled in the hard necessities of poverty by a faint pride. "Merchants or new gentlemen I deem will proffer large," Edmund Paston wrote when a marriage of one of his family was in question; "well I wot if ye depart to London ye shall have proffers large."[180] He seems to have preferred that the Pastons should look out for good connections; and possibly this anxiety was especially present in the case of the women, for the family seem to have been rather excited when Margery Paston in 1449 married one Richard Calle, and went, as John said, "to sell candles and mustard in Framlingham."[181] But John Paston felt no hesitation about marrying the daughter of a London draper. One brother considered the solid merits of a London mercer's daughter, and another was very anxious to secure as his wife the widow of a worsted merchant at Worstead, who had been left a hundred marks in money, a hundred marks in plate and furniture, and £10 a year in land.[182] The money side of marriage with a substantial burgher must have had its attractive side also to the county ladies. In Nottingham, according to the "custom of the English borough," half of the property of the husband passed at his death to his widow;[183] and a London mercer setting up in business promises in his contract of marriage "to find surety that if he die she to have £100 besides her part of his goods after the custom of the city."[184]

All interests in fact conspired in effacing class distinctions to an extent unknown in European countries; and in a land where "new men" had long been recognized among the king's greatest officials, and where law created no barriers in social life, all roads to eminence lay open before the adventurer. Notwithstanding this freedom, however, the English merchant never rose to the same height of wealth and power as the great traders of the Continent. We have no such figures as that of Jacques Cœur,[185] burgher of Bourges, whose ships were to be seen in England carrying martens and sables and cloth of gold; or trading up the Rhone; or competing with rivals from Genoa, Venice, and Catalonia for the coasting trade of the Mediterranean; or sailing to the Levant, each vessel laden with sixteen or twenty thousand ducats for trade adventures. Three hundred agents in various towns acted as his factors in business; and his ambassadors were to be found at the court of the Egyptian Sultan, or sitting as arbitrators in the quarrels of political parties in Genoa. "I know," he writes with frank consciousness of power, "that the winning of the San Grail cannot be done without me."[186] He had bought more than twenty estates or lordships, had two houses at Paris, two at Tours, four houses and two hotels at Lyons, houses at Beaucaire, Béziers, Narbonne, S. Pourçain, Marseilles, Montpellier, Perpignan, and Bourges. In 1450 he had spent 100,000 crowns of gold on the new house he was building out of Roman remains at Bourges, and it was still unfinished. As Master of the Mint at Bourges and at Paris, and as the greatest capitalist of his nation, he practically controlled the whole finances of France; and, indeed, held in his hands the fortunes of French commerce, and even of the French nation, for it was his loans to the King that alone enabled Charles to drive the English out of Normandy. At a time when all trade was strictly forbidden to the noble class, a grateful monarch, mindful of timely loans and of jewels redeemed from pawn by his useful money-lender, ennobled Jacques Cœur, with his wife and children. His eldest son was Archbishop of Bourges; his brother was Bishop of Luçon; his nephew and chief factor was Councillor of King Réné, and Chamberlain of the Duke of Calabria. But just as far as he went beyond the English trader in his glory and success, so far he exceeded him in the greatness of his ruin. The same arbitrary power which had set him above his fellows could as easily be used to cast him down; and after twenty years of prosperity Jacques Cœur was a State prisoner, robbed of all his goods, and condemned to perpetual exile. Transforming banishment into opportunity for new ventures, he set off eastward at the head of a crusade in 1456 to die on the journey, and find a grave in Chios.[187]

Beside such a career as this, and measured by the prizes that hung before the adventurers of the Continent, the life of the English trader was indeed homely and monotonous. Triumph and ruin alike were on a modest scale. No great figure stands out from the rest as the associate of princes or the political agent of kings. No name has come down to us glorified by a vast ambition, or dignified by an intellectual inspiration, or made famous for turning the balance of a political situation. And it is just in this fact that we discover the essential character of the new commercial society in England. Instead of colossal fortunes we find a large middle class enjoying everywhere without fear a solid and substantial comfort. And, perhaps as a consequence of the widespread diffusion of material prosperity, the republic of traders had succeeded in developing a marvellous art of organization, with all its necessary discipline. The triumphs of the English merchants were won by a solid phalanx of men alike endowed with good average capacity, possessing extraordinary gifts of endurance and genius for combination, and moving all together with irresistible determination to their ends. The uniformity and regularity of their ranks was never broken by the intrusion of a leader of genius pre-eminent among his fellows; and whether in towns or in commercial fraternities, the little despotisms that were set up were despotisms, not of a single master, but of groups of men who had devised a common policy and by whose voluntary and united efforts it was sustained. In fact the very spirit of the people seemed to have entered into the great industrial system which had sprung up in their midst—a growth free and independent, nourished out of the common soil from which it came, obedient to its own laws, expanding by the force of its own nature.

No doubt there was loss as well as gain for a society so constituted. The special genius of the people, their remoteness from outer influences, the concentration of the national forces on the pressing industrial and commercial problems of the moment; all these things evidently affected the developement of the national life, and tended in many ways to leave civilization still rude and imperfect. But in addition to this we are also conscious of the influence of a certain prevailing mediocrity of station. The horizon of the trading and industrial classes was bounded by a practical materialism where intellect had as little play as imagination. Neither the glamour of ancient Rome nor the romance of a crusade ever touched the fancy of an English merchant, busy with the problems of the hour. There is no stately dwelling of those days to show the magnificent conceptions which might occupy a merchant builder, and a "palace of King John" at Nottingham,[188] or a turreted house at Bristol, "the best of all the town," telling their tale of a comfortable domesticity, contrast strangely with the famous building of Bourges. So far as we know no trader or burgher possessed a library; out of the lost past not so much as a line of Horace found an echo among even the more lettered men of business till over a hundred years later; not a picture was carried home from the schools of Italy or the Netherlands; of the mighty commerce of the world beyond the sea the trader knew everything, of its culture nothing; and England remained without any distinguished patrons of the arts or fosterers of learning save those found in bishops' palaces. And not only was the trader limited on the side of art and letters; in the hurry of business he had no time and less attention to give to political problems that lay beyond his own parish or his industrial domain. Fortunately for his country he reaped an exact reward. His business prospered, but the work of statesmanship in its finer sense was given to others; and in the political and commercial crises through which England had to pass she for a time chose her leaders from men trained in another and more comprehensive school. It was only in the next century that the merchant by degrees began to enter on a new dominion in the world of politics. Under the early Tudors it became the custom to appoint as representatives of England in foreign countries traders resident in the place, and though the system is commonly put down to the niggardliness of the Court, it was more probably due to the ruler's sagacity. In England itself it was with Thomas Cromwell, the clerk of Antwerp, the wool merchant of Middelburg, scrivener, banker, and attorney, that for the first time the man of business made his vigorous entry into the Court, struck aside at a blow the venerable traditions that had gathered there round Church and State, and from the wreck and ruin of the past proclaimed the triumph of a new age.[189]

CHAPTER IV

THE LABOUR QUESTION

Perhaps no complaint is at first sight so startling amid the vigorous growth of manufacture and commerce which marked the fifteenth century, and in a society where pestilence and plague apparently kept population stationary, as the complaint of surplus labour; and the elusive way in which the problem appears and vanishes again makes it yet more bewildering. People complained at one moment of labourers unemployed, and at the next they modified old laws because they could not get workmen enough. Masters on all sides were evading the regulations which limited the number of their apprentices and journeymen, and still cried to the State for protection for their craft because the artizan could find no work to do. Men talked of foreign competition and too many workers in every trade, and took forcible measures to keep down prices and wages. The lawmakers were forbidding the import of foreign goods so as to give employment to destitute artizans at home, and the artizans were conspiring to limit their output and raise their prices. That there was some real trouble whose indeterminate presence can be felt behind all these conflicting appearances we cannot doubt; but it may be questioned whether the trouble was that of labour for which there was no demand.

Many of the complaints no doubt arose in some period of peculiar suffering, when an outbreak of war or the rivalry between England and the Netherlands shut the great markets across the sea, and left weavers with idle looms and bales of cloth unsold; and we must occasionally take the phrases of statutes passed under the stress of some temporary calamity as merely describing a distress too unaccustomed to be borne in silence. For instance the statute of 1488 which was passed during the depression of trade that marked the first years of the reign of Henry the Seventh proposed to restore prosperity to the drapers' craftsmen, for "they that should obtain their needy sustentation and living by means of the same drapery, for lack of such occupation daily fall in great number to idleness and poverty;"[190] but the commercial treaties which distinguished the next three or four years of Henry's reign were probably more effectual than any statute of this kind, and they sufficiently prove that the trade was not in a dying or decrepit state.

Occasionally too the murmurings of the people only tell of troubles that follow every industrial change. To an employer the new industry came to search out the extent of his resources and his activity. What with the haste to make wealth, and the hurry of keeping pace with the demands of foreign traders and of big markets, he was hard pressed by the necessity of cheap and swift production, and his attempts to improve his industrial methods brought him into collision with workers to whom ruder and more wasteful ways of doing business were often more immediately profitable. Labour disputes arose over questions of wages and piece-work, of holidays, of the employment of women[191] and cheap workers. Occasionally the master carried on an illicit industry—keeping workmen privately engaged in his own house or on board a ship in the port,[192] so as to withdraw his servants from the supervision of the town council, and his goods from charges for the town dues. If he had accumulated a little capital he perhaps moved out to the valleys of Yorkshire or Gloucestershire in search of water-power for his fulling-mills, or of finer wool for his weavers; or forsook the manufacturing town for some rural district where labour was plentiful, and where he could escape the heavy municipal dues which his business could ill afford to pay. While the valley of the Stroud was welcoming Flemish settlers and seeing mills spring up along every stream, London and Canterbury found their manufacturing trade slipping away from them;[193] and the glory of Norwich departed as cloth-makers pushed along the moorland streams of Yorkshire to Wakefield and Huddersfield and Halifax, and set up fulling-mills among the few peasant huts of remote hamlets.

Difficulties also arose when the manufacturer began to contrive the first rude form of a factory system, and so disturbed the occasional labour of his neighbourhood; after the manner of the brewers of Kent, who besides having to supply London and the big trading ports of the coast were also beginning to send out beer to Flanders, and who no longer as of old bought their malt from the people, making only some trifling hundred quarters or so in their own houses, but began to make at home as much as a thousand or even eighteen hundred quarters, to the hurt of those farmers and youths who had once gained a livelihood by preparing malt for sale.[194] Or perhaps enterprising masters began to introduce new machinery to keep pace with the increasing demand for their wares. Such an innovation was resisted as hotly as in our own century. The shearers of cloth raised a cry against a new iron instrument invented for raising the nap of cloth so that it could be quickly burned off without the old labour, while shearers were left idly loitering.[195] Among the cap-makers "some of the trade provided a water-mill for fulling their caps" in 1376, by which apprentices and freemen of the trade found themselves deprived of work and "at the point of perishing." Their appeal to the town was of course on the ground that caps so fulled were bad wear for the community, and the mills were in consequence forbidden;[196] but a century of disobedience and evasions and wranglings followed until the working fullers appealed to Parliament itself, and in 1482 it was decreed that hats, bonnets, and caps, which "were wont to be faithfully ... thicked by men's strength, that is to say with hands and feet," should never again be fulled in fulling-mills invented "by subtle imagination to the destruction of the labours and sustenance of many men," and to the "final undoing" of the cap-makers.[197]

Even the question of foreign immigration stirred up contention between clothiers and weavers. Manufacturers trading in marts where the fine work of Flemish experts—the most skilful weavers in Europe—had been displayed, required for the success of their trade the services of the finely trained artizans who took refuge in England from the ruin that awaited them in Flanders, and in many a town skilled immigrants found themselves welcome guests.[198] Under the protection of the classes to whom the foreign artizan can never have been unwelcome—the consumer, the merchant, and the master—he fared well enough; for so long as he was subjected to the local control of the guild or the municipality, forced to dwell in the house of an Englishman, forbidden to sell in retail, kept under a supervision so strict as practically to shut him out from the market, the employers of labour saw no reason for anxiety.[199] On the other hand the complacent view of the manufacturer was not shared by the English artizan; and in places where trade was shrinking or where there was financial trouble the foreigner might chance to be made into the luckless scape-goat of the community, and have heaped on his head all the calamities that burdened the guild or the municipality. For example, in the middle of the fifteenth century when the Bristol wool trade was half ruined by the loss of Bordeaux which destroyed its great market and brought about lasting changes in the French manufacturing centres; and by the determination of the Merchant Adventurers to establish in London and in favour of London merchants a practical monopoly of the cloth trade with the Northern Seas, a complaint was made by the journeymen against the master-weavers who had "brought in and put in occupation of the craft strangers, persons of divers countries, not born under the King's obeisance but rebellious," urged the desperate working man in search of an unassailable argument which should finally decide the matter, "which been sold to them as it were heathen people"; and the Mayor granted the desired order that no foreign weaver should be brought into Bristol[200]—a law which did not however restore the cloth trade to their city.

In this case we seem really to hear the complaint of the poor journeyman; and elsewhere, in appeals for compassion and protection, in statutes of Parliament and royal charters,[201] or in ordinances of Town Councils for his relief, we seem from time to time to find ourselves on the brink of a labour problem present to the modern as to the ancient world. But generally the story of foreign immigration as it has been handed down to us is in no sense the story of the labour question. An association of masters seeking to secure a strict monopoly for their own advantage could not bring a more powerful argument than the desperate situation of their workmen—an argument which might be used by a powerful corporation confident of official support, or by a dying trade which had been utterly beaten in the competitive struggle—and which taken alone throws little light on the subject. When the dispute with the foreigner emerges it generally seems to bear the character of a quarrel among dealers rather than a grudge of artizans. The working man had no doubt his grievance, but it is not his voice which we hear—it is the voice of his more noisy neighbour the shopkeeper or the trader, who knowing that he himself had little to expect from the sympathy of the English consumer, passed briefly over the subject of his own immediate interests, and used with artistic skill the sufferings of the wage-earner to kindle a general compassion and heighten the effect of an appeal to an anxious government or an alarmed public. For as we read the Town Ordinances and Acts of Parliament[202] these strange "artificers" who were setting the world on fire put on the guise of pedlars or small dealers who "bring much foreign wares with them to sell," and were thus especially obnoxious to the native traders; such foreign pests, it appears, were going "to men's doors" "taking up standings" and there "showing" their wares to the undoing of the natives, and hiring servants of their own people to retail their goods about the country—an unpardonable offence in the eyes of London merchants, who were moving heaven and earth to become the only middlemen of the foreign trade. With varying success the native dealers clamoured for protective legislation, praying that the strangers might be forbidden to engage freely in trade, and forced as journeymen to serve only an English master, or as masters to employ only English servants. A usurper like Richard the Third, anxious to conciliate the leading burghers of the towns, was ready among other things to forbid any alien whatever to become a handicraftsman, or any foreigner to take an apprentice of his own people save his own son or daughter;[203] while on the other hand, Henry the Seventh carried out his own views of industrial policy by bringing weavers over to develop the trade of Yorkshire and Devonshire.

But under whatever restrictions the foreigners still came, and the same cry against them went up loudly from time to time. Manufacturers and middlemen who would have gladly welcomed immigrants so long as they gave themselves out as men working for hire, resented the invasion of strangers coming from over sea "with their wives, children, and household, and will not take upon them any laborious occupation as carting and ploughing but use making of cloths and other handicrafts and easy occupations;" and this apparently as masters, for the complaint was that they employed only foreign apprentices, so that English people were falling into idleness and becoming thieves, beggars, and vagabonds.[204] "The land is so inhabited with a great multitude of needy people, strangers of divers nations ... that your liege people, Englishmen, cannot imagine or tell whereto or to what occupation that they shall use or put their children to learn or occupy within your said cities or boroughs"—so the Londoners complain in 1514: and add that if this went on Englishmen would no longer be able to pay their rents, maintain their households, and subdue and vanquish their ancient enemies the French.[205] Hopeless, in fact, of combating the theory of his time that trade legislation was meant in the first instance to serve the interests of the buyer rather than the dealer, and fearing lest an argument for monopoly of sale might hardly withstand the criticism of a hostile public, the trader was tempted to discover some circuitous course, and catch at the cause of the poor workman, the terror of the French, and the patriotic vision of a nation of warrior weavers,[206] as infallible appeals to the sentiment of his time.

We find animosities and complaints of the same kind directed against the struggling suburban manufacturers, who competed with the townsfolk by dint of braving every hardship, and accustoming their hands to every form of labour. To the town manufacturer they were an abomination; and he sought to enlist the sympathy of the public by loud complaints that it was only workmen who had scarcely learned their trade who thus left their masters to set up for themselves and make an independent living. It is probable indeed that their numbers were often recruited by small masters who had fallen through poverty out of the regular ranks of industry; as for example when an apprentice or a stranger set up in business to try his luck, and having been given perhaps three or four years in which to pay by instalments the sum charged by the guild for opening shop, made his escape out of the borough just before his last fine became due,[207] being by that time possibly ready to start as a free trader in an "upland" hovel, and to eke out a scanty living by working at his hand loom or his rope-making in the intervals of cultivating field or garden. But such home industries, however they originated, were inevitably disallowed by the municipal organizers of labour. They diverted trade, established a formidable competition of unregulated labour, reduced tolls, and emptied the tax-gatherer's collecting box. Town councillors and shopkeepers and journeymen with one accord declared war on those who for their own "singular advantages and commodities, nothing regarding the upholding of the said towns, nor the common wealth of the handicrafts ... nor the poor people which had living by the same," hired farms and became graziers and husbandmen, and yet took to weaving, fulling, and shearing cloths in their own houses;[208] or who, like the grasping people that withdrew from Bridport, took farms "for their private lucre" and not only "used husbandry" but made cables, ropes, ships' tackling, and halters in their idle hours.[209]

Disputes of the kind which have been mentioned, however, were of trifling importance in the secular controversy between the leaders of industry and the general body of workers, as it presented itself in the Middle Ages; and the great problem of all—that which concerned no separate groups or industries, but the whole mass of labour that was to be let out for hire—was one inarticulate through its very magnitude. While workers were being set free from the land wherever arable farms were turned into enclosed pastures for sheep farming, they were called for by the manufacturer whose new business of making cloth needed more hands than the old business of selling wool. But the labour released from the field was perhaps not always easily transferred to the shop; and when the countryman who with his fellows had toiled on the land

"All for dread of their death such dints gave hunger,"[210]

and, save when harvest time gave a brief plenty, ate in suffering his cake of oats with a few curds, his "bread of beans and peases," his onions and half-ripe cherries, and little baked apples,[211]—when he forsook his "cote" and carried to the town nothing but his hunger, his ignorance, his want of skill, he did not necessarily mend his fortune by turning from the serf of the landlord into the wretched dependent of the employer. Moreover, as though the obstacles in the way of his helplessness were not already sufficiently overwhelming, by the ingenious device of man the difficulty was made yet more acute. Artificial barriers to keep in check the labour that clamoured at their gates were thrown up with all the united strength of State and Town and Guild. The State in order to protect the agricultural interest strictly forbade the poor countryman to leave husbandry for trade, or to apprentice his child to any craft.[212] The towns for reasons of their own hastened to intensify the effect of these laws by local regulations, or by the strictness with which they carried out old enactments.[213] Finally the guilds fenced themselves about with rules to protect their monopoly by limiting their numbers and shutting out intruders. As the fifteenth century went on all these bodies alike enforced their provisions with increasing severity, and the danger that threatened the working-class through the industrial revolution was hardened into a present calamity.

It is impossible to conceive that regulations of this kind were self-denying ordinances on the part of employers to limit the supply of labour; they rather come to us as echoes of the first great controversy concerning the position and privileges of the hired worker. The "protection" of industry from all competition was the first and the last creed of the crafts (as distinguished from the general public)—a protection by which every conceivable danger that might threaten the interests of the monopolists was struck down, whether it was the competition of other allied trades, or that introduced by machinery and new methods of organizing labour, or rivalry between members in the same craft, or the intrusion of dealers from the provinces, or the immigration of alien manufacturers from abroad. As to the main principle there was no dispute; and there were some of its less important developements where the interests of the masters and the journeymen coincided. But to employers and dealers the monopoly of trade chiefly meant their own monopoly of production and sale; while the wage-earner's dominant anxiety was to keep surplus labour out of the craft, lest the regular workman might be deprived of his comfortable certainty of subsistence. Labour however was too sorely needed in the enormously increasing trade of the country for masters to deny themselves its services; nor did any of their ordinances necessarily tend in the least to produce a result so disastrous to themselves. In their eyes the important matter was that workers should be kept docile and obedient, retained in country districts where they were most advantageous to the contractor, and prevented from making claims on the control or the profits of industry which must have hampered the great business of the moment—the expansion of English trade; and the ability of the craft-leaders was shown in the masterly tactics which they adopted, the success which they achieved, and the political sagacity by which they accomplished their purpose without open strife or public agitation.

For it seems probable that the labour question had its origin with the very beginning of manufacturing industries, and that long before the fifteenth century a large class of hired workers already existed. We know that in the fourteenth century the wage-earners in the crafts already constituted a force which the State and the municipality had come to fear, and that not only in London but in other towns journeymen had learned discontent, and had begun to combine for self-protection.[214] We know also that before 1340 one manufacturing town at least (and no doubt the records will ultimately tell of more) owned its miserable race of labourers who worked by the day at a bare subsistence wage of a penny, an outcast people whose abject poverty was their only protection; men possessing absolutely nothing by which they could be attached for crimes or offences, and who could laugh at any attempt of the court to summon or to fine them; while their employers, not being held legally responsible save under some special ordinance for such day labourers as these, took no care for the debt or crime of a class without privilege or standing in the eye of the law.[215] And obscure as the subject still is, we seem at a very early time to detect behind the guild system a growing class of "uncovenanted" labour, which the policy of the employers constantly tended to foster, their aim being on the one hand to limit the number of privileged serving-men, and on the other to increase the supply of unprotected workers.

It was for this reason that while the demand for manufactures was increasing beyond all experience, the number of men who sought through apprenticeship to enter the trade was most strictly limited by law;[216] and when a man had finished his apprenticeship cunning devices were found for casting him back among the rank and file of hired labourers;[217] so that the skilled workman who had passed through his time of service but had not been admitted to the freedom of his trade[218]—whether because he failed to secure the recommendation of the heads of the guild, or because he was unable to pay the double fees demanded for the franchise of the city and the franchise of the craft[219]—was condemned henceforth to remain a mere journeyman without apparently much hope of promotion. For the enrolled journeyman there was some protection, though of a very limited kind, in the guild; but a lower and more helpless class of serving-men was recruited from the apprentices who had not worked out their full time—poor children whose service had begun at seven or twelve, and who while yet mere lads were induced to cut short the seven or ten years fixed in their trade for apprenticeship, and entering hastily on work for a daily wage found themselves from that time forward counted as unskilled labourers;[220] apparently deprived of the protection of the law in the matter of wages, without any standing in the guild, and lying in the power of the craft-masters for their hire, they were for the rest of their lives admitted to work on sufferance as bringing cheap labour into the market. Finally even the statutes which forbade poor country people to apprentice their children in the towns,[221] far from proving any intention of withdrawing the villagers from the service of the manufacturer, may have been the result of an alliance between landowner and employer to serve their several ends, and have been designed by the town magnate merely to prevent the dependent country workers from flocking into the boroughs in search of apprenticeship and subsequent freedom of the trade.[222] For it seems probable that the town dealers had very early been accustomed to contract with the country folk for the lower and rougher kinds of work. In Norwich, for example, all the tanners' business was at first done in the country, and the skins sent into Norwich to be worked and finished by the parmenters; and it was perhaps but a generation before the passing of the Act of Henry the Fourth that the tanners came into Norwich and settled down by its river side. And in like manner all cloth brought to the Norwich market was country-made, and originally no wool was sold in the Norwich streets and no cloth manufactured in its workshops.[223] The same system of contracting for work in surrounding villages[224] was known far beyond Norwich, but its local history varied greatly with local circumstances. In that city, where trade was manifestly too vigorous to be shut up into a few square miles, and where the surrounding population had turned into a people of journeymen and artizans, the municipality seems to have inaugurated the policy of governing an industry it had no desire to suppress, by seizing the organization of the country districts into the same hands as that of the town, and bringing the workers under the same municipal control[225]—a policy, it would seem, of merchants and employers mainly occupied with the expansion of commerce, and blind to the danger which their experiment implied of the breaking up of municipal life. But in other towns we seem to detect a vain attempt of the working population to clutch at a trade which had grown into a free maturity, and force it back into the old municipal nursery under the tutors and governors of its infancy; as in Worcester, where the ordinances contain many proofs of having been drawn up under strong popular influences, and where the masters were forbidden to give out wool to weavers so long as there were people enough in the city to do the work, "in the hindering of the poor commonalty of the same."[226] It is evident that the manufacturer might, from his own point of view, feel the strongest objection to flooding the towns with an unmanageable number of workers attached to the guild who could, by virtue of their numbers and their covenanted position, call on the municipal government to interfere for their special benefit in the management of the trade.[227]

If we consider therefore the case of the working population in town or country—whether we remember the poor folk of the hamlets, known to Langland, that "have no chattel but their crafts and few pence taketh;"[228] or consider in the towns the lowest class of casual labourers working at a wage of a penny a day, or the little more fortunate groups of unskilled serving-men, or the depressed company of the skilled journeymen; whether we trace in villages or boroughs the astonishing multitude of religious fraternities which sometimes at least concealed an illicit attempt at self-protection by the wage-earners; or examine the rigour with which towns and guilds repressed every attempt of the working men to combine in any association for their common benefit—we find ourselves again and again confronted with the problem of labour. In the thick darkness which still envelopes the subject dogmatism itself is swallowed up. But as we look into the obscurity, the borderland of the covenanted trades and the dim regions that lie beyond their recognized limits become crowded with the masses of the common workers—dreary groups of labourers seething with inarticulate discontent, themselves suffering the terrors and bondage of a harsh law, and from time to time, as they emerge into a brief light of riot and disorder,[229] kindling the alarms of the settled and protected classes above them. Associations of the richer merchants inspired by a common interest drew together for mutual support; and friendly Town Councils whose policy was to keep down the number of voters—especially of poor craftsmen who might be troublesome—and all whose members were indeed themselves employers and craft masters, made alliance with the guilds, and passed laws which, by shutting out apprentices from the freedom of the craft, debarred them from the franchise of the town. It was in vain that from time to time as the evil increased the central government sought to interfere with craft-masters and wardens who "for their own singular profit" made ingenious bye-laws or ordinances for the exclusion of new comers;[230] local alliances were too strong for it, and local wits too cunning, and one of the main results of the triumphant guild system was to develope throughout the country a formless and incoherent multitude of hired labourers, who could by no possibility rise to positions of independence, and had no means of association in self-defence. As the weaker members of the crowd from time to time sank back into utter penury, the outcasts of the industrial system slowly gathered into a new brotherhood of the destitute; and even in the fifteenth century, long before they had been reinforced by the waifs and strays of town and country that flocked into their sad fellowship on the dissolution of the monasteries, the advanced guard of the army of paupers appears in the streets of the boroughs to trouble the counsels of municipal rulers.

CHAPTER V

THE CRAFTS

THE early history of the craft guilds, like that of the municipalities, is the story of communities in the first strength of youth, growing by the force of their own vitality into forms which can be reduced to no mechanical regularity or order, and ever plastic to take on new shapes according to the shifting exigencies of an age when industry, commerce, local government, were all in a state of revolution. In the pride of their first creation, in the humiliation of their later apparent subjection, in the victorious results at last of their long discipline, the guilds reflected successive movements in the great change that transformed English society; and it would be hard to find a single formula in which to express a life so free and various. Like the boroughs their systems of government ranged from constitutions which, if not democratic, were at least republican, to constitutions which placed in command an oligarchy, whether limited or despotic; so that we can scarcely say that the towns borrowed their methods from the guilds, or the guilds from the towns, at a time when both alike were perhaps tentatively feeling their way towards the only solutions of the problem of government which the time and occasion admitted. They had the same period of intense activity, from the awakening of the new life of England under the Norman kings, till under Henry the Seventh its industrial and commercial position was definitely established. The very difficulties by which they were hemmed in were the true conditions of any lively growth; and it was not till the sixteenth century, when the militant life of the crafts came to an end, that a fatal monotony settled down on their associations—a dreary uniformity[231] both of constitution and of policy, which makes their period of triumphant prosperity and imminent decay a record at once tedious and disheartening.

In dealing with the history of commerce the craft guilds necessarily take a foremost place in their character of trading or manufacturing associations; but we are here mainly concerned with what we may call their political relations to the borough, and their influence on the growth of municipal life. The constitution of the craft becomes therefore important, not from its economic results, but as indicating the character and complexion of the guild, the policy which it might be expected to pursue if it attained to authority, and the extent to which it could be supposed to favour popular or democratic theories of government. How far the crafts were actually able to make their influence felt depends on a second question as to the connexion that existed—of what kind and closeness it may have been—between the guilds and the governing body of the borough.

We must remember that the various craft guilds represented all ranks and classes in the industrial world—the capitalist, the middleman, and the working man. There were aristocratic fraternities of the Merchant Adventurers, and of dealers living by the profits of commerce alone, who were grouped in the great mercantile companies such as the vintners and spicers and grocers and mercers. In a lower scale were the middlemen and traders who produced little or nothing themselves, but made their living mainly by selling the produce of the labour of others—such as the saddlers, the drapers, the leather-sellers, the hatters—and whose unions were in fact formidable combinations of employers. Below these again came guilds of artizans employed in preparing work for the dealers, to be by them sold to the general public, as the smiths who worked for the tailors or linen-armourers,[232] the weavers who supplied the clothiers; the joiners, painters, ironsmiths, and coppersmiths who made the saddles and harness for the saddlers; the tawyers who prepared skins for the leather-sellers; the cap-makers who fulled the caps which the hatters sold.[233] Finally there remained the crafts which both manufactured and sold their own wares, like the bakers, tailors, or shoemakers, and who dealt directly with the consumer without the intervention of any other guild. It is evident that these various associations had all their own business to do,[234] and that their policy differed as widely as did the interests of the several classes. We do not find a guild of merchants or dealers trying to raise wages or shorten hours; or a guild of artizans seeking to depress labour and assert the supremacy of the middleman; or a mixed guild of masters and men intent upon lowering prices for the public. But we may still ask whether behind all obvious divergences of interest and of power, there was any ruling instinct common to all these brotherhoods of trade.

The original motives which drew men together into craft guilds were no doubt everywhere the same—the desire to obtain the monopoly of their trade and complete control over it;[235] and also to find the security which in those days organized associations alone could give to the poor and helpless against tyrannical and corrupt administration of the law, just as in the country men enrolled themselves under the livery of a lord or knight who was their adequate protector against the iniquities of the courts[236] and by whose arbitration their quarrels were adjusted.[237] For these purposes associations were formed of the entire trades of various districts. All the members of the craft, great and small, were enrolled in the fraternity; and thus every guild, to whatever order in the hierarchy of industry it belonged, contained within itself the various ranks of workers who belonged to that particular occupation. It is in this organization of the whole craft into a compact body arrayed in self-defence against the world outside, and in the means that were used to maintain it, that we trace the peculiar characteristics of the mediæval guild as opposed to those of modern associations. From the very outset its society was based on compulsion. Dealer or artizan had no choice as to whether he would join the association of his trade or no, that question being settled by the charter which gave the craft power to compel every workman to enter into its circle. A constitution such as this left a profound mark on the conduct and ultimate policy of every guild, for where there was no real freedom of association there proved at last to be no real freedom of government. Societies such as the modern trade union, created and maintained by the good will of men naturally bound to one another by common occupation and interests, and who expect from their association a common benefit, may long persist as voluntary institutions with a democratic government. But the ancient guild—a fraternity of the whole trade with all its ranks and classes, employers and wage-earners alike, compulsorily bound together into one fellowship as against the world without, and whose common interest in association tended to become more and more visionary—was inevitably driven to preserve by force an artificial and ill-compacted union; and instead of a free self-governing community, there grew up a society ruled by its leading members in a more or less despotic fashion, according to the character of the trade itself and to the support given to its governors by the authorities at Westminster or in the municipality.[238]

(1) For it is plain that no intimate union can ever have existed between the three orders that practically made up the guild.[239] At the head of the society stood the master and the aldermen or wardens, drawn from among the wealthiest men of the trade; and grouped immediately round them were all those who, after having passed through these offices, retained for life a position of dignity among the members, and from whom the court of assistants or governing council was wholly or partly formed.

(2) Then came the commonalty, the craft-holders or shopkeepers or "masters" of the trade—a term which by no means necessarily implies *employers* of labour, but rather artificers admitted into the "mestier"[240] or mistery—who were alone responsible before the law for offences[241] committed in their shops or work-rooms, and were therefore alone authorized by the guild to take work from a customer.[242]

(3) Last came the hired workers—that is the trained journeymen or serving-men; for the unskilled labourers working for a daily hire and apprentices can scarcely be reckoned as in any sense members of the guild.

In a society thus constituted the notion of self-government never for a moment implied the modern notion of democracy, or even the idea that authority should be exercised only by the will of the majority. In some fraternities indeed the whole community of craft-masters took part directly in the yearly election of officers, though probably this was the extreme bound and limit of their influence;[243] but in general there was the same tendency in the guilds as in the boroughs to choose their governors by some indirect and complicated system through which the commonalty was kept well in restraint. Either the alderman himself nominated candidates for the various offices, from among whom the select council or fellowship made their choice, or he appointed a few picked men, five or seven or eight as the case might be, to choose the rulers for the next year.[244] In the same way the two or four "sufficient and discreet men" who were to assist the alderman, "the helpmen and overseers," or the council of eight or twelve or twenty-four, were chosen either by a similar committee, or by the direct choice of the alderman himself "with the aid of his fraternity."[245] Nor is there any evidence that this method of government by the select few was a growth of later corruption; it is more probable that in societies which could only be founded at the wish of the more prosperous men in the trade, since they alone could undertake to raise the money for its charter or guarantee the payment of its yearly rent, these men were accustomed, in return for their money or as a security for it, to hold the management of the community in their own hands; and this seems confirmed by traces of the system which we find in very early times, as well as by what we know of the origins of later fraternities.

If the power of the masters was thus limited, the mere journeymen were practically of no account at all in such great matters as election and legislation. Perhaps in some trades they occasionally exercized a slight influence, as in the case of the London bowyers, whose ordinances were agreed to "as well by serving-men as by masters."[246] But in general it is doubtful whether the voice of the hired worker was ever heard or his will consulted, however much his obedience to the ordinances was required and enforced. It was supposed that his interests were sufficiently protected by the town authorities, to whom an alien who was cheated by his master, a journeyman who found his wages paid on the truck system, or a weaver who saw his labour supplanted by that of a woman or a foreigner, could make his complaint; and who were bound to see that no freeman of the borough took more apprentices into his household than he could promise to support comfortably; that the apprentice was not chastised beyond measure, nor turned out penniless at the end of his service;[247] and that no fraudulent action of his master should rob him of the benefit of the exact tale of the years of service he had fulfilled.[248]

In all that concerned the hired worker, indeed, law had become so rigid and so detailed by the time that Parliament, the Town Council, and the Craft wardens, had taken their turn at legislation, that it might be plausibly assumed that nothing remained for the discussion of the working man. By a series of statutes Parliament endeavoured to keep the hire of the workers and the length of the working day fixed in spite of the increase of trade;[249] and mayors and bailiffs in all boroughs[250] were ordered to compel labour to keep its allotted times, and to proclaim the wages of craftsmen twice a year, "and that a pair of stocks be in every town to justify the same servants and labourers."[251] Whatever was left undefined by Parliament was put under rule by the subordinate authorities. Town Councils made provision for the punishment of "rebel and contrarious" men in the mayor's court, examined and corrected the customs of the crafts, forbade workmen to make their bargains anywhere save openly at the market cross, and fined them if they stood there beyond one day in the week,[252] probably on the supposition that they were holding out for a higher wage or shorter hours. The guild-masters regulated the prices to be paid for piece-work,[253] issued orders allowing work to be done by night, and made rules as to apprenticeship and service.[254] For greater security moreover the masters were accustomed to enter into covenants for mutual protection against their servants—"And if any serving-man shall conduct himself in any other manner than properly towards his master, and act rebelliously towards him," said the Whittawyers, "no one of the trade shall set him to work until he shall have made amends before the mayor and aldermen."[255] On the other hand journeymen were invariably bound by oath not to make any sort of confederation among themselves,[256]—a precaution which State and town and guild were equally vigilant in enforcing. Under such a system as this, if at any time the workers proposed to disturb the statute wage or the statute day, they had to contend not only against the upper class of their own craft, the masters and wardens and shopkeepers, but against the governing body of the town, and the opposition of the whole community.

Neither oaths nor laws nor public opinion however could permanently prevent men from combining to better their position, and from time to time we can follow the fortunes of a struggle which, when the town records are published, will probably be shown to have been very general. In London alone we have during a single century records of strikes among the workmen of four trades—the shearmen, the saddlers, the shoemakers, and the tailors.

The journeymen of the cloth shearers took a lesson in combination from the employers. "If there was any dispute between a master in the said trade and his man," ran the complaint of the masters about 1350, "such man has been wont to go to all the men within the city of the same trade, and then by covin and conspiracy between them made, they would order that no one among them should work or serve his own master, until the said master and his servant or man had come to an agreement; by reason whereof the masters in the said trade have been in great trouble and the people left unserved." These men were also making a covert attempt to raise their payment by refusing to work at day wages, and insisting on piece-work through which they could gain more money; while the masters, so long as they were forced by law to sell at a fixed price, had a valid reason for protesting before the mayor that there must be some relation between lowering the price of their wares and raising the wages of their workmen, or they themselves would be set between the upper and nether mill-stone; and for making a petition that the men might be chastised and commanded to work according to the ancient usage "as matter of charity and for the profit of the people." The city magistrates granted ordinances which forbade any attempt to settle trade disputes by strikes, and ordered all complaints to be brought before the warden of the craft (himself of course a master), and failing him before the mayor. Though the court did not forbid piece-work, it fixed its price at the low rate that prevailed before the Plague.[257] On the whole the victory therefore lay with the masters.

The shoemakers' servants were early in the field. They made their first rebellion before 1306, the main results of which seem to have been a decree added to their old ordinances that the journeymen of the trade should make no provisions to the prejudice of the public;[258] and perhaps the imposition of an oath that they would not make among themselves any union or confederation.[259] For eighty years they waited before making a new attempt. At last in 1387 a "great congregation" of them met at the Black Friars "and there did conspire and confederate to hold together ... and because that Richard Bonet of the trade aforesaid would not agree with them made assault upon him so that he hardly escaped with his life ... to the alarm of the neighbours." The meeting was illegal, not only because of their oath, but because of a law passed four years before to forbid any confederation among workers; so to make their position more regular the poor shoemakers hit upon the plan of calling in the help of a friendly friar preacher, "Brother William Bartone by name, who had made an agreement with their companions that he would make suit in the Court of Rome for confirmation of that fraternity by the Pope; so that on pain of excommunication and of still more grievous sentence (!) afterwards to be fulminated, no man should dare to interfere with the well-being of the fraternity. For doing the which he had received a certain sum of money which had been collected among their said companions." This form of Papal interference, however, was not to the mind of Londoners—"a deed," they said, "which notoriously redounds to the weakening of the liberties of the said city and of the powers of the officers of the same." The mayor accordingly threw the leaders into prison,[260] and the attempt of the luckless journeymen came to an end.

The serving men of the saddlers tried another plan, and formed in 1383 a religious fraternity whose ostensible duties were perfectly harmless. Its members were wont once a year to array themselves in a like suit and go out beyond the city bounds to Stratford (in other words, out of reach for the moment of the city authorities) where they held a meeting, and returned to hear mass in honour of the Virgin in the church next to the Saddlers' Hall;

also from time to time their beadle would summon journeymen to attend at vigils of the dead and pray for the souls of their old comrades. According to the masters, however, this was but "a certain feigned colour of sanctity" under which the men merely wasted their masters' time and conspired to "raise wages greatly in excess"—in fact in the space of thirteen years, from 1373 to 1396, they had increased their hire to twice or three times the old customary rate. The mayor and aldermen agreed with the masters as to the dangerous character of these proceedings, forbade any such meetings or any fraternities for the future, and ordered that the serving-men should be under the masters, and that the "masters must properly treat and govern" them as in all other trades.[261]

The journeymen tailors took a bolder line, for they not only held illegal meetings both within and without the city bounds, at which they assembled wearing a common livery, but also hired houses in the city where they lived in companies, and defied both their own masters and the officers of the city. Whereupon the masters and wardens of the trade notified to the mayor and aldermen "that they were exceedingly sorrowful at there being such offenders and such misdeeds"; and the mayor and aldermen "after holding careful council and conference thereon" decided that it was manifestly to the public peril to allow journeymen and serving-men—a race at once youthful and unstable—to have a common livery at their assemblies, or common dwelling-houses by themselves. The settlement was broken up, and livery and meetings forbidden. Then the tailors also put on the colour of sanctity, and a couple of years later (in 1417) we find them petitioning to be allowed to meet for prayers and offerings for the souls of deceased tailors.[262]

That similar attempts, with the same impotent conclusions, took place in other manufacturing towns is certain; though we have not yet the means of measuring the extent of the movement. The uniform failure of every effort at revolt, even the acquiescence of the workmen when revolt was impossible, declare the helplessness of the mediæval labourer, entangled as he was in a vast net-work of commercial theories, administrative maxims, and arguments of vested interests public and private. For in a society where law ruled all industry, the whole community was on the alert to resist any defiance of ordinances avowedly made for their own protection.[263] The right to strike was denied by law and vehemently resisted by public opinion as contrary to the common good; and disputes were settled, not as now by an agreement voluntarily made within the trade, but by the formal decision of the municipality, against which there was no appeal.

At the same time it is evident that in their dealings with journeymen and hired servants, if in no other respect, the municipalities did no more than carry out exactly the intentions of the guilds themselves. From the moment that they come into view the crafts—that is, all the more important ones, for from the nature of the case we know very little about the poorer sort of associations or the humbler trades concealed under the form of religious societies—are distinguished by the same creed and policy. Their essential character was laid down in the oligarchic schemes of administration to which they inclined; and, as we have seen, the purity of the guild government was further maintained by the pains which was taken to prevent the journeymen from pressing on into the upper ranks and weakening the established system by multiplying the number of small masters; and to select with adequate care the people admitted to be subjects with constitutional rights—a people chosen as far as possible from an upper class and even from the hereditary stock of the guild.[264] By an original stringent constitution therefore, and by their own later discipline, the governing oligarchy was protected as by a double course of entrenchments; and a third line of defence was formed by keeping guard over every entrance through which the common workman might make his way into the superior class of artizans who, in however inferior a degree, might still be recognized as more or less officially attached to the craft. In its very nature, therefore, the guild organization was adverse to the claims of the men who worked for hire, and under its government the journeyman was practically condemned without a hearing. What with the influence exercised by the masters in the Town Council and government, and what with the credulous fears of the public of consumers when they were told what "contrarious" workmen might do in raising prices and limiting supply, and "the many losses which might happen in future times" through combinations of hired labour, the victory of the employers was never for a moment doubtful,[265] and unions of journeymen such as those which sprang up in the fourteenth and first half of the fifteenth centuries, broken and disabled almost at the outset, seem, so far as we can see, to have been again and again crushed out of existence by the overwhelming forces of guild and town and state brought to bear on them, and to have found no permanent life till the eighteenth century.

There was no doubt a sense in which the strong rule of a governing oligarchy fully justified itself throughout the course of the struggle for autonomy between the rising crafts and the rising municipalities. Shaking itself free from discussions and divisions within its own body by asserting the triumph of the stronger party, the guild was able to maintain in practice the consistent theory of its constitution—the undisputed supremacy of the masters in the regulation of the trade policy, and through centuries of varying and doubtful fortunes the crafts still contrived to present to the world outside an unbroken front and a certain air of independence; holding together in companies under leaders of their own choosing, and, save in rare instances, scorning to stoop to the custom common in France or Germany of having their chief officer appointed by some external authority.[266] But this bold militant attitude was only maintained through a rigid discipline, and by a ruthless suppression of every attempt to break the ranks. A body to all appearance uniform, but in fact split up into two or three hostile groups, the craft only preserved its air of harmony by abandoning all pretence at democratic government, and avowedly subduing the weaker classes to the stronger. The policy which had been its safety in the time of conflict remained its settled creed in the time of power. It is clear, therefore, that if ever the members of the guild forced their way into the council chamber of the town, their appearance can scarcely be taken as marking a popular or democratic movement. That it enlarged the governing class by bringing in a new group of men to take part in the active political life of the country is evident; but on the other hand these men do not seem to have contributed a single idea to political experience, or carried political experiment a single step further. Saturated with the customary views of administration which were the fashion in the upper class of town society, and by which their own interests had been so well served, the craft-masters sent their representatives to the council only to give new strength to the coercive policy of the governing oligarchy. The character of the trade fraternity was fully shown when, victorious over the foes of its own household, strong in its complete organization, the craft guild rose out of its long subjection to public control, and seizing into its own hands municipal authority, destroyed its terrors for the trader. When this last step was taken the crafts stood forth in full realization of their ideal—close corporations fully equipped against the whole body of consumers, and masters of the labour of the country. What has been called the decline of the guild system may more truly be called its triumph—the revelation of its constant aim and true significance.

NOTE A

STATUTE WAGES IN 1388.

	s.	d.	
Bailiff for husbandry	13	4	a year with clothing.
Master-hind, carter, shepherd	10	0	
Ox-herd and cow-herd	6	8	
Cowdriver	7	0	
Swine-herd and woman labourer	6	0	

No servant of artificer or victualler in a town was to take more than those in the country (12 Richard II. cap. 4.).

IN 1444.

	s.	d.		s.	d.	
Bailiff of husbandry	23	4	With clothing	5	0	and food
Hind, carter, shepherd	20	0	,,	4	0	,,
Labourer	15	0	,,	3	4	,,
Woman servant	10	0	,,	4	0	,,
Child under 14	6	0	,,	3	0	,,

Summer wages of mason or carpenter 4*d.* a day with food, without 5*d.*; tiler, slater, rough mason, and builders 3*d.* with food; other labourers 2*d.* Without food 1*d.* more in all cases. Winter wages 1*d.* less all round. In harvest a mower 4*d.*, reaper 3*d.*; labourers 2*d.*; 2*d.* more for meat and drink. (23 Henry VI. cap. 12.)

IN 1495.

	s.	d.		s.	d.	
Bailiffs had risen to	26	8	With clothing	5	0	
Carters, shepherd, &c., remained at	20	0	,,——,,	5	0	
Labourers had risen to	16	8	,,——,,	4	0	and food

The hire of women, children, and artificers remained the same. (11 Henry VII. cap. 22.)

By 12 Henry VII. cap. 3, all statutes fixing the wages of artificers and labourers were made void for masons and all concerned in building, and servants in husbandry. Rogers (Work and Wages, ii. 327) fixes the wages of the ordinary artizan in the fifteenth century at 6*d* a day and agricultural wages at 4*d.*, carpenters a little under 6*d.*, plumbers 6-1/2*d.*, masons 6*d.* The board of a skilled artizan might cost in 1438 about 2*s.*, of a common labourer about 1*s.*, very commonly from 8*d.* to 10*d.*, most generally 8*d.* (Agriculture and Prices, iv. 505, 751-2.) In 1395 a Nottingham "layer" was charged for working two days as stone-cutter for 12*d.* against the law, and the jury stated that "all the carpenters, all the plasterers, all the stone-cutters, all the labourers, take too much for their craft by the day, against the statute of our lord the King." (Nott. Rec. i. 275.) For a list of wages paid in 1464 see ibid. ii. 370-373; in 1511 iii. 328-337. In 1495 a man was employed to dig stones at 3*d.* a day without food.

That there was difficulty in enforcing the legal wage and that there was often a difference between the prices actually paid and those which the law books spoke of as still valid is evident from the ingenious methods in use of evading the law. Sometimes the workman was paid his board wages and given his food besides; or false entries were made in the account books; or a yearly fee was given in addition to wages; or he was paid a sum of so much a mile for coming to and going from his work; or his wages were calculated at 6*d.* or 5*d.* according to ability for 365 days in the year, against the statute which forbade the workman to receive hire for holidays or for the eves of feasts. (Rogers' Agric. and Prices, i. 255; Work and Wages, ii. 328-330; Stat. 4 Henry IV. cap. 14.)

The legal hours of work for country labourers from March to September were from 5 A.M. till between 7 and 8 P.M., with half an hour for breakfast, an hour and a half for dinner; from September to March, from the springing of the day till the night of the same day. They were not to sleep in day-time save after dinner from May to August. (Stat. 11 Henry VII. cap. 22.) The Saturday half-holiday from noon seems to have been universal. In shops trading on Sundays, holidays and vigils was very generally forbidden in the middle of the fifteenth century, save in harvest time, and unless "great high need may excuse." (Kingdon's Grocers' Company, ii. 190; Hist. MSS. Com. xi. 3, 169.) Rogers (Work and Wages, i. 180-2) calculates that an artizan working three hundred days a year could earn from £3 15*s.* 0*d.* to £4 7*s.* 6*d.*, and in London might get from £6 5*s.* 0*d.* to £6 17*s.* 6 *d.* a year. Walter of Henley (ed. by Miss Lamond, p. 9) gives forty-four weeks, leaving eight weeks "for holidays and other hindrances." But in his translation of Walter's Husbandry, Bishop Grosseteste adds a phrase (ibid. 45) which throws a new light on the matter. "In these forty-four weeks be 264 days besides Sundays"—an explanation which certainly expands the amount of leisure allowed to country labourers, whether it applied to town artizans or no.

CHAPTER VI

THE CRAFTS AND THE TOWN

FROM the mediæval Craft Association to the modern Trade Union the distance, as we have seen, is great. In the guild or "mistery" of the older world, instead of associations of working men we have to deal mainly with associations of producers or middlemen, whose battle is not the organized attack of wage-earners on the profits of their masters, but an attempt of dealers and manufacturers to stand out for their interests against the whole body of consumers or against the aggressions of competing trades; while far from being a voluntary association, or a self-governed institution of spontaneous growth, its individual members were if necessary enrolled by compulsion, and governed with little regard to their own consent. But the relations between the trades and the municipalities show a yet more striking contrast. According to a modern English theory the common good is best served when we allow every artizan and trader perfect liberty to develope his own industry in his own way.[267] But the mediæval world was fully convinced that since all trade and manufacture was carried on for the benefit of the public, all trade and manufacture should be subject to public control; and no one then questioned that it was the duty and the right of the State or the municipality to fix hours of labour, rates of wages, prices of goods, times and places of sale, the quality of the wares to be sold, and so on. In the interest, not of the trader or manufacturer, but of the whole community, the central government made general laws for regulating industry, and the towns carried out these laws by their officers and filled up the blanks of legislation after their own will; while in the exercise of the enormous power which law and public opinion gave to the authorities, the power of the people was supposed to be used with impartial justice alike against the dealer or the employer and the artizan or serving man, whenever individual claims clashed with what seemed to be the public advantage. Hence to the governing body of the borough the trade association was a mere matter of public convenience; and was so little regarded as depending on the free will of the craft itself that it was frequently founded by order of the town, and was invariably compelled to make submission to superior force and receive orders from its master the municipality. Unable to secure the passing of any new rule save by convincing the authorities on some pretext or other that it was devised in the interest of the whole commonwealth, the craft came at last to be considered as a society which existed mainly for the advantage of "the common people of the realm," and indeed, bowing to a hard necessity, itself contracted the habit of solemnly disavowing any special regard for "its own singular profit," and apologetically described itself as the humble servant of the municipality and the obedient minister of the public, in phrases which the modern trade union would scarcely accept as an adequate description of its uses.

This service of the public, however, was in no sense a voluntary tribute of the guilds, nor did it enter in the slightest degree into their original scheme; and if through long and severe compulsion the crafts learned to wear with decorum their odd cloke of apparent devotion to the common weal, behind this ostensible policy and feigned colour of self-abnegation they had still their own purposes to serve, which were by no means the purposes of the rest of the community. Occasions of discord were probably far more frequent than provocations to unity and concord in the society of a mediæval town, with its hierarchy of struggling workers—the rising dealers, the small masters who employed two or three servants, the artizans who let down the ledge from their window to display the goods which they had themselves made, journeymen working for a statute wage, and unskilled labourers for whatever they could get—men for the most part living meagrely by incessant toil, and to whom the public, thrifty and inclined to bargains, was "the enemy"; and with its population of consumers, poor and ignorant, without the means of travelling, forced to buy what they wanted on the spot and thus deprived of such protection as may be given by a larger competition, able to afford little beyond the mere necessaries of life so that every fraud brought to them real suffering, and to whom the trader represented the ancient adversary lying in wait among the gins which he had privily set for the innocent. The thin veil of civility thrown over the situation by the polite phrases of contemporary convention which have come down to us in ordinance and compact deceived nobody concerned; and between the "poor commons" and the whole army of crafts reconciliation never went farther than an armed truce. To the consumer the dealers seemed all alike steeped in iniquity. Shopkeepers measured out their wares "by horn or by aim of hand," or in chance cups and dishes; and sold in dark corners where a man could not see what scamped work and deceitful goods were being handed over to him. Clothiers gave out bad yarn in scanty measure, and stretched out the list of their cloth with cunning presses "in deceit of the poor commons." Hatters because they knew that everyone must needs wear hats charged exorbitantly for their wares, and shoemakers were no better, so that statute after statute vainly sought to mend them. Chandlers asked scandalous prices for wax candles, images, and figures, "by which means divers of the people be defrauded of their good intent and devotion."[268] "All the bakers, butchers, fishers, taverners, poulterers, chandlers, tanners, shoemakers, cooks, hostelers, weavers, and fullers," according to the comprehensive statement of the Nottingham Mickletorn jury in 1395, were asking too high prices and selling bad goods; and they go on the next year to repeat the same complaints.[269] Above all the anger of the common folk burned hot against the traders they knew best, the powerful licensed victuallers who heaped up to themselves riches with the food that should have fed the starving workers: "for took they on truly, they timbered not so high." The "sundry sorrows in cities," fevers and murrains and floods, or fires which burned down half the town and seemed ever to begin by the falling of a candle at a brewer's or some "cursed place," were the vivid testimony of the anathema of the poor and the righteous vengeance of heaven falling on the sinful traders;[270] and the common rumour of the market is still heard behind the poet's parable of the day when Guile was at the point of death, and when it was only the shopkeepers who recovered him to life:

"But merchants met with him and made him abide,
And shutten him in their shops to showen their ware,
And parrelled him like their prentice the people to serve."[271]

As for the crafts, on the other hand, whether they were combinations of employers, or associations of middlemen or dealers, or unions of wage-earners, or societies of masters and men, in one respect their unanimity was unbroken; for inspired by a reasonable hostility to the consumer who wanted to cheapen their wares, they were all ranged on the same side in the common controversy as to who was ultimately to fix prices, the seller or the buyer. Then obvious policy was declared in a number of conspiracies which were constantly made in the various trades to raise prices by combination among the dealers; but unfortunately for the traders, always on the watch as they were for opportunities, they still found the public as alert as themselves, and more powerful to accomplish their will. When Edward the Third in 1331 fixed the price of wine of Gascony at 4$d.$ a gallon the retail dealers, who had apparently found their profit best secured by the absence of any statutory prices for their goods, broke into open rebellion, and "all the taverners of the city making a confederacy and alliance among them" closed the doors of their taverns and would not allow their wines to be sold; till to "put a check upon this malignancy" the mayor and sheriffs proceeded through the city, and had the names of the taverners so closing their taverns written down, twenty-nine in number, and twelve men from each ward of the city were summoned by the authorities to decide in the name of the injured wine-drinkers upon the punishment to be awarded to the taverners for their contumacy.[272] In 1363 and again in 1411 the consumer was protected by law against the rich Pepperers who had formed a company in 1345, and were accused of raising prices.[273] The whole body of chandlers in Norwich were presented at the Court Leet in 1300 for a certain agreement made among themselves that "no one of them shall sell a pound of candles for less than another."[274] And in 1329 when a lime-burner of London bound all the members of his trade by oath not to sell lime below a fixed price, and "by reason of his great conspiracy" almost doubled the price of lime, the city rulers imprisoned him and the "conspiracy" was cut short.[275]

Alliances of this kind to increase profits or raise prices were universally met by a determined resistance on the part of the public.[276] But the "poor commons" went far beyond a policy of mere self-defence. They aimed in fact at nothing less than putting the crafts altogether under the yoke of the community, at seizing the whole organization of trade which had been built up and binding it over to perpetual service. Nothing could have been more distasteful to the guilds. In the twelfth century, while municipal government was in its very infancy, they had already aimed at complete independence and a real autonomy; and certain crafts did in fact succeed in making a special bargain with the King over the heads of the local magistrates. By charters bought at Westminster fraternities were made dependent for their existence on the royal will alone; and were granted rights of supervision and jurisdiction over their workmen without any reference to the borough;[277] and since in these early charters the only definite provision was that all the men of the trade in that particular district should be enrolled in the guild, the freedom of the craft as a whole remained for the moment unquestioned even if the freedom of the individual was limited. An independence so complete however was bitterly resented by town governments. In London for example the weavers lived in a quarter by themselves into which the city officers never entered. They had their own courts and special privileges, and raised their taxes through their own officers. Under the protection of the King's writ they successfully defied the town authorities, and when in the time of Henry the Third the citizens seemed likely to overpower them by force they laid up their charter of rights in the Exchequer as a perpetual record of their privileges. The jealousy excited in municipal bodies by an alien society settled in their midst, where the town writs did not run, is not surprising. Every interest of the city was threatened—the monopoly of the sale of cloth claimed by the burgesses, the authority of the town magistrates, the orderly system of administration which the kings were building up, and the interests of the whole body of consumers. A natural apprehension of any danger to the unity of the borough was shown not only in London, but in Winchester, Oxford, Marlborough, Beverley,[278] and possibly in other towns; the weavers were shut out of the franchise and all its privileges, hampered in their trade by all sorts of oppressive regulations, forbidden to buy their tools, or possess any wealth, or sell their goods save to freemen of the city, while the status of villeins and aliens in the city courts was allotted to them. But mere repression left the real evil untouched; and by 1300 the city authorities in London had found a more radical cure. The Mayor had gained the right to preside in the weavers' court if he chose, and to nominate the wardens of the guild;[279] and no sooner was all danger from an independent rule thus averted than the weavers were granted power to buy and sell "like other free citizens."[280]

From this time all independent trade jurisdictions in the towns came to an end.[281] No more charters such as that of the weavers were sold by the crown;[282] and the crafts were presently forced to conciliate the local powers according to their measure of art or cunning—to beg from the municipal government a formal recognition for their association with such limited liberties as the town officers could be induced to give; to secure a more or less precarious existence by the payment of fines to the town treasury;[283] or to wrap round them a solemn conventional disguise, and conceal wholly or in part the fact of their union for trade purposes by sheltering themselves under the form of a religious association, and seeking independence "under a feigned colour of sanctity"[284] as men wholly moved by a zealous care for the souls of their dead comrades but taking no thought for the bodily welfare of living brethren.

But by whatever means the fraternities hoped to compass liberty, it was in vain that they sought to elude the heavy hand of the municipal government. Trade associations were laid hold of by the boroughs, brought under the discipline and authority of the public magistrates, and forced to take their due part in the developement of the municipal organisation.[285] Towns which obtained a grant to have "all reasonable guilds" took care to maintain a reasonable authority, and craft fraternities were only given leave to exist on the express plea that they were "consonant with reason and redounding to the public honour and to the advantage of the common weal";[286] while privileges were meted out to them on the distinct understanding of the gain which was to spring from these to the whole commonalty. By a dexterous move on the part of the town governors the officers of the guild were transformed into the officers of the community, and the machinery of the guild became the means by which the public sought to provide for a full and cheap supply of the necessaries of life, and protected itself from overcharges and false measures and bad wares, from uproar and disorder, from drunken workmen, from the flying sparks of the smith's forge, or the noise of his hammer at night. In London for example there was a constant succession of customers complaining at the Mayor's Court of the bad bargains they had made in buying cloth, so that the fullers found themselves excessively "hard worked" in appearing at the Guildhall to examine the cloths of discontented buyers, and begged that every one might buy at his own risk.[287]

The masterly manœuvre executed by the town magistrates is revealed in the self-denying ordinances passed by the later guilds. Crafts "petition," as we are gravely told, to have masters and ordinances, and these being granted the new rules turn out to be simply regulations to supply wares to the people of a fixed quality and price.[288] We can scarcely believe that the farriers should of their own free will have devised the rule that if any one of them, through negligence or any excess of pride which hindered his asking advice of the craft, failed in curing a horse of sickness, "then he shall be accused thereof before the Mayor and Aldermen and be punished at their discretion, in the way of making restitution for such horse to the person to whom the same belongs."[289] Nor is it likely that masons and carpenters should have volunteered to take oath before Mayor and Aldermen that they would do their duty in their trade;[290] or that the masons should themselves propose that if a mason failed to fulfil his contract certain men of the trade who acted as his securities should be bound to finish his task.[291] Even the universal rule against night work was never among the London guilds (save in the single instance of the hat-makers)[292] made in the interest of the working-man; but on the contrary was dictated by the sagacious observation of the buyers that "sight is not so profitable by night, or so certain, as by day—*to the profit, that is, of the community*;"[293] and if spurriers "who compass how to practise deception in their work desire to work by night rather than by day"[294] the reason given for interfering with them was that they wandered about all day idle, and "then when they have become drunk and frantic they take to their work to the annoyance of the sick and all their neighbourhood ... and then they blow up their fires so vigorously that their forges begin all at once to blaze ... and all the neighbours are much in dread of the sparks which so vigorously issue forth in all directions from the mouths of the chimneys in their forges."[295] Sunday closing itself was ordered as a matter of public convenience, because apprentices "could not be trusted to carry on work in the absence of their masters at church."[296]

In thus bringing the crafts into subjection the towns were greatly strengthened by the sympathy of the State, which was the more inclined to make common cause with them from a growing apprehension of guilds of artificers and other labourers which in troubled times might prove centres of disturbance throughout the country. By a series of statutes the ancient powers of crafts were carefully pruned, and new authority grafted on to the town governments. "Congregations and confederacies" were jealously watched and forbidden.[297] The guilds were ordered to have their charters registered, and their rules and bye-laws approved by the chief magistrates of the town. They were forbidden to make ordinances to the damage of the King or the people. Sometimes jurisdiction over their own members was taken from them; and the right of search for any articles that "be not pure lawful and able chaffers," or even the duty of seeing that the workers were duly paid their wages in ready money, was handed over to the town officers.[298]

Thus it came about that by the triple alliance of the officials at Westminster with the governing class of the town and the general body of consumers, all alike bent on organizing industry in their several interests, the primitive free associations of workers were gradually forced into the singular position of deferential servants of the community. Within its own little realm each guild might use a narrow independence or a petty tyranny, but in its public aspect it could assert few pretensions.[299] No craft fraternity could be formed without the leave of the municipality, and every Warden took his oath of office before the Mayor, at whose bidding and subject to whose approval he had been elected.[300] The rules made by any trade for its government had no force till they had been approved by the Mayor and Corporation, enrolled by them on the city records, and sealed with the common seal.[301] And since they reserved the right of making any addition to these ordinances which they might deem necessary,[302] the town magistrates could interfere whenever they chose in the interests of order. Not only did they bear rule over the seller in the market, but they followed the craftsman to his little workroom and ordered every smallest detail of his trade, material, wages, apprentices, cost, the fit of a coat and the quality of a shoe, according to the laws that "reserved all time to the Mayor and to the Council of the town power to correct, to punish, amerce, and redress, as well the masters and all other persons of the said crafts, each after their deserving and trespass, as the case asketh."[303] Men who offended against the rules of the trade were brought before the town officers for punishment, and half their fines went into the town treasury.[304] Even the wandering artizans who moved from place to place, who had no fixed shops and no complete guild organization, found themselves subjected to the town authorities as soon as they had crossed the borders of the borough. Carpenters, masons, plasterers, daubers, tilers, and paviours had to take whatever wages the law decreed and to accept the supervision of the municipal rulers,[305] and their regulations were framed according to the convenience of the borough. Thus after the big storm of 1362 in London they were forbidden to raise their prices for repairing the citizens' roofs;[306] and the same ordinances of Worcester which direct that chimneys of timber and thatched houses should be done away with, and stone or brick chimneys and tiled roofs everywhere made by midsummer day, contain regulations for the tilers who must have flocked to the city on such an occasion. They must set up no parliament to make any one of them "as a master and all other tilers to be as his servant and at his commandment, but that every tiler be free to come and go to work with every man and citizen freely as they may accord." No stranger tiler coming to the city was to be forced to work for any city tiler, but might take whatever work he liked by the day.[307]

The rapidity with which the whole movement was conceived and carried out is one of the most surprising things about it; and nothing was wanting to the thoroughness with which mediæval society carried out its theory of the use which the craft guilds might be made to serve, whether willingly or no, in protecting the interests of the public. One discovery followed on another. As the King for convenience of administration constantly delegated new powers to the Mayor, and successive Acts and Charters added to his load of responsibilities for supervising work and wages and wares, so the Mayor in his turn passed on these charges to the craft—apparently exalting its power, in reality undermining its independence. Town governors embarrassed by the difficulty of overawing a turbulent community and keeping the peace with the aid of a couple of constables, found in the guild organization an admirable machinery all ready to their hands, and turned its officers, responsible as they were for the good behaviour and order of the whole trade, into an effective city police; so that when Bristol was in danger of a general riot in consequence of the imprisonment of its Mayor, the sheriff and recorder simply summoned the masters of the various crafts, and ordered them to keep the peace in their several trades. In the same way the crafts might be charged with the duty of "setting the watch" at night.[308] Difficulties of taxation were lightened by shifting responsibility from the municipal officers to the guilds—by charging for example the bakers or blanket-makers or fullers with a certain proportion of the ferm, to be collected among their members and paid in by their officers.[309] If walls were to be repaired and gates and towers and piers maintained, or if the expenses of a public festival were to be met,[310] the craft might again be brought into use, and for the due performance of the allotted task their common funds or individual profits might be reckoned as security.

When the town had thus laid firm hold on the guilds and discovered the various uses to which these bodies might be put in the municipal scheme, it began to look on them with as much favour as it had formerly shown distrust,[311] and proceeded industriously to multiply their numbers both by creating new fraternities and reorganizing the old ones.[312] The public opinion of the day showed itself strongly in favour of guilds, and indeed often outran the desires of the workin-gmen, so that the drawing together of artizans into the later craft fraternities was not always a matter of free will. If trades did not associate at their own wish they were presently forced to do so, and at the end of the fifteenth century we find the towns everywhere issuing orders that crafts which had hitherto escaped should be compelled to group themselves into companies. In Sandwich, for example, barbers, surgeons, and wax-chandlers were incorporated in 1482; and in 1494 wardens were appointed of the companies of tailors, shoemakers, weavers, and shearmen.[313] In Canterbury, where a spirit of revolt against the rules of the corporation seems to have gone abroad, where strangers were setting up trades within the liberties and laws had to be made to insure their paying "reasonable fine" for so doing, where masters neglected to enroll their apprentices in the books of the Common Chamber, and where the servants in husbandry riotously resisted the Statute of Labourers, the outraged city authorities declared that the crafts needed new regulations "to maintain due order for the weal and increase of the same," and set to work to tighten the hold of the government on manufacturer and artizan, by forcing the trades to form themselves into companies, and setting at the head of every craft or mystery two of the city aldermen.[314] In very many cases the later incorporation of trades was connected with a pledge to undertake certain town works such as the building or repairing of gates;[315] and here we probably find the clue to the growing custom of combining several poor societies into one substantial association. When the crafts of Canterbury began to grudge spending their money on the Corpus Christi Play and on the Pageant of St. Thomas (which had to be revived in 1504 and paid for by the corporation), and also neglected "setting the watch," the Town Council would have none of the excuse of poverty, only made "for lack of good ordering of certain crafts within the same city not corporate"; and it was settled that every trade "being not corporate for the nonsufficiency of their craft be associate, incorporate, and adjoining to some other craft most needing support, if they will not labour to be corporate within themselves"; any obstinate craft that did not make suit to the Burghmote by next Michaelmas to be incorporate was to pay 20s. and give up their bodies for punishment. The shoemakers were accordingly joined in one guild with the leather-sellers and pouchmakers, the apothecaries with the grocers and chandlers.[316]

But if the town carried on business in this high-handed and imperious fashion, still in the double bargain made between the municipalities and the crafts it is not to be supposed that the advantage was all on one side. If the guild had services to sell to the community, it in its turn demanded a fair price. The trading society received all the benefits which fall upon communities by law established; and municipalities fostered with tender care the fraternities whose discipline they had first seized into their hands.[317] If trade was reaching out its branches to markets beyond the sea or if it was withering away, if the serving-men were growing poor or if they were waxing prosperous and threatening to dictate wages and prices, if new machinery was introduced to replace human labour, if foreign craftsmen came in to supplant the home-bred artizan—whatever the trouble might be the government of the people bravely stepped in to set the matter right. Craft rules once entered on the city records became an admitted part of the city statutes, to be enforced by the authority of the whole community, and the master found his jurisdiction recognized and enforced, and might call on the mayor, "if the men are rebels or contrarious and will not work," to deal with them "according to law and reason."[318] The whole strength of the town government could be invoked to suppress "foreign" labour or alien dealers and manufacturers, or combinations of men against their employers. No remedy was too heroic for patriotic burghers if they thought the prosperity of the local manufacturers was in danger. When the cloth trade of Canterbury had fallen into an evil plight the Town Council passed a law ordaining that in the next year the mayor and each of the twelve aldermen should buy a certain amount of cloth, the forty-eight councillors one-half that amount, and certain well-to-do inhabitants a like measure according to their degree.[319]

The system in fact was a curious balance of compromise among three distinct parties to a triangular strife—the whole body of traders and manufacturers organized in craft guilds, whose primary object was naturally to secure "their own singular profit," as the phrase went, and to take on themselves as few of the common burdens as possible—the body of householders organized for civic purposes as the mayor, council, and commonalty, whose business was to keep order and carry on government—and the entire population of the town considered as consumers, who were thinking only of the supply of their own wants and whose chief aim was to buy the trader's goods at the lowest possible price. For a time the borough corporations and the big public had the triumph on their side, and the traders were held in a position which was judged to be "consonant to reason." But if the crafts passed through a period of subjection while their organization and discipline were being perfected, this by no means implied the practice of a like humility when they had learned how to manipulate the narrow oligarchy that formed the corporation, and to despise the incoherent masses that made up the body of consumers. For all this time the guilds were steadily, by the help of the town customs and administration, fortifying themselves in their position, strengthening their monopoly, closing their ranks, shutting out competitors from their gains. There came at last a moment when the crafts matched their strength with that of their masters, and the municipalities surrendered to the forces which they themselves had drilled. How completely the mediæval theory of the consumer's interest in legislation about industry was swept away by the final success of the crafts in enforcing by their compact majority the original purpose of their own members, we may see from the chasm that separates in principle the ancient trade guild from the modern trade union. To-day we also are constantly making attempts to regulate industry through combinations whether of capitalists or of wage-earners. We have our associations of employers which have grown up to resist their workmen, and our unions of working-men formed to fight the employers; but neither is in the least concerned with the interests of the public, and not even in a phrase of courtesy are any of our modern associations supposed to "redound to the common profit" of the buyers. In this profound difference between the old and the new organizations of industry we may find a measure of the tremendous importance of the victory achieved by the crafts, when they had learned to use the disciplined forces of the guild for the capture of the municipal government. In later times, when public opinion almost ceased to work through the machinery of local government and only found occasional or incoherent expression, teaching societies under their more modern name of companies employed the same compact organization of monopolists to press their claims with redoubled success on the attention of the all-powerful central authorities, and the protection of the consumer was more and more forgotten in the protection of the privileged trader.

NOTE A.

Besides the instances which have been given of the interference of the town with the crafts in questions that concerned the public, or that concerned the journeymen, there were other interesting cases in which it took part in struggles between the guilds of artizan producers and the guilds of dealers or middlemen for whom they worked. For the difference between the greater and the lesser crafts must always be borne in mind, and the fact that some of them were mere associations of working-men whose ordinances prove their subordinate position; though except possibly in rare instances the association was not originally formed, or at any time mainly used, for the purpose of resisting the middlemen.

The weavers in London for example who lived by themselves in a special quarter of the city formed a union of independent artizans, each of whom possessed his own loom; if by chance he became rich enough to own a second, he set his son or his wife to work at it, being forbidden by the craft-guild to hire it out of his own house and so increase the number of workers. They worked for the guild of "burellers" or cloth-makers, who gave out the yarn which they wove into a coarse cloth, and paid them a fixed wage or price by the piece. In very early times the weavers complained of the bad quality and short quantity of yarn supplied to them by the burellers, and of the prices paid for weaving; and about 1290 they planned a whole scheme of organized resistance. They reduced the hours of labour by stopping night-work, and appointing seasons when no work at all might be done; they limited the number of workers by excluding new comers and forbidding looms to be let out on hire; and as their work was necessarily done by the piece, they ruled that a given length of cloth which could easily be made in two or three days should always count as four days' work and no less; and apparently further devised means for making plausible overcharges for work done. To compel the obedience of members of the guild they ordered that any weaver who offended against these regulations should be called up for judgement before their governing council of twenty-four, and punished by it in formal fashion in the same way as for offences against legal ordinances. And to force the submission of the burellers, they commanded a general strike among the weavers in case of complaint, and that all work should be stopped until amends were made for the wrong done. In the face of a public which had already fixed prices and wages by law and considered that question finally closed, the weavers who found themselves shut out from direct methods of gaining their ends had thus taken the crooked way, at least so their enemies said, of raising prices by limiting production, and thus forcing up the price of cloth.

For ten years middlemen and workmen seem to have fought out their quarrel together; but in 1300 the burellers brought their grievances to the mayor's court, and charged the weavers with making new ordinances contrary to all law. There was little sympathy in the city courts for craftsmen whose rules were framed "for their singular profit and to the common injury of the people," and the jury decided that the weavers had no right to limit the production of cheap cloth for the public by any device whatever. They were forbidden to shorten hours of labour by stopping work at any time save at night, or to check manufacture by preventing weavers from hiring out their looms to men of the craft; piece-work might be done as fast as any weaver chose to do it; all overcharges for work were forbidden. And lastly strikes were absolutely prohibited. In a second trial in 1321, when the obstinate weavers were called up before the king's judges at the Tower, charged with making a "conspiracy and confederation" in the Church of St. Margaret de Patyns to raise the price of weaving each cloth by 6*d.*, the king's serjeant, who prosecuted, explained with precision that an unlimited number of workers working at full speed meant low wages and an abundance of cheap cloth, and that any attempt to reduce the number of labourers, to bring in short hours, or slow work—every device in fact by which the output of cloth was limited, was a device to empty the burgher's purse into the workman's pocket. In the common interest such "malicious machinations" must needs be put down; and indeed it would seem that some doubts were entertained about the wisdom of interfering even with night-work if the public was to have cheap cloth. (Riley's Liber Custumarum, 123, 416-425.)

The guild, which by this time had declined from three hundred and eighty to eighty looms, was probably never strong enough in London to renew the strife. Perhaps the Flemish weavers supplanted them and took up the battle, for we find that in 1362 and 1366 they in their turn were making congregations and collecting money among the people of the trade through their bailiffs. By the ordinances which were drawn up to meet this emergency it was settled that in future congregations of the workers and collections of money among them might only be made with the consent of the twenty-four best men of the trade, and that these twenty-four should be chosen at the discretion of the mayor and aldermen. (Mem. Lond. 306-7, 332.)

A yet more complicated controversy divided the various crafts concerned in the making of saddles, where we have the reverse case of a union of middlemen conspiring to put under their feet the crafts of artizans with which they were connected. The London Saddlers who sold to the public formed as early as the twelfth century a guild of employers and middlemen. (Madox, 26.) Of the different crafts that worked for them were the Joiners who made the wooden framework, the fore and hind saddle-bows cut out of a quarter of a horizontal section of a tree and hollowed to fit the horse's back; the Painters who painted these frames; and the Lorimers (that is the coppersmiths and ironsmiths) who made the metal work for the trapping and the harness of the horses. As for the saddlers themselves they seem only to have put the finishing touches to the saddles, or put on the leather covering for the great lords who were not contented with painted wood; but as all orders and all sales were carried out by them they had the ultimate control of the whole trade.

The first dispute arose out of the complaints of the public of the badness of saddles supplied to them; the saddlers threw the blame on the joiners; and the joiners seem to have in their turn pushed it back on an illegal or "blackleg" labour encouraged by the saddlers for their own advantage. "Bad apprentices who fly from their masters, and other false men, betake themselves to the woods, and there make up their work of saddle-bows glued together and send them by night to painters and to saddlers within the franchise" who profited largely by the cheap labour of the "bad apprentices" working under the cover of the woods. The authorities forbade these practices, and in 1308 granted to the joiners' guild ordinances to protect their monopoly of the trade and check irregular labour. (Lib. Cus. 80.)

A few years later the joiners made common cause with the painters and lorimers—a formidable conspiracy, for the lorimers had already been organized as a craft for half a century, and ordinances which strictly protected their monopoly lay for safe keeping in the city treasury. (Lib. Cus. 78-9. The lorimers included two ranks—the master who kept house and forge and paid fine to the commune of London; and the journeymen who paid to the mistery but not to the city.) In 1320, however, the saddlers contrived to have the lorimers' ordinances annulled and publicly burnt in Cheapside. (Lib. Cus. lix.) In 1327 the combined trades broke out into open war one day in Cheapside and Cripplegate, and "strongly provided with an armed force exchanged blows and manfully began to fight." (Riley's Mem. 156-162.) Mayor and sheriffs came to stop the riot; the trades were summoned to appear at the Guildhall, and complaints were presented on both sides. The story of the saddlers was (1) that the three trades had organized a union for strike purposes, in case any one of them should have a quarrel with any saddler.

(2) That the coppersmiths were "out of their own heads" refusing to receive any strange workman of the same trade into their craft until he shall have made oath to conceal their misdeeds, the implication being of course an attempt to raise prices by limiting numbers.

(3) And further the joiners and painters "do set every point of their trade at a fixed price ... by reason whereof they are making themselves kings of the

land, to the destruction of all the people of the land and to the annihilation of the saddlers."

The trades emphatically denied both the strike conspiracy and the fixing of prices, which at all events indicates that they knew such claims would never be conceded by the public, and formulated their counter-charges.

(1) That the saddlers had formed a "conspiracy and collusion among themselves" and bound themselves to it by oath that they would compel the joiners, painters, and lorimers not to sell to any one but themselves any work they did pertaining to saddlery. The workman was thus to be bound to them hand and foot.

(2) That when the workmen come to ask for payment due to them they are so bandied about among the said saddlers with offensive words, beaten, and otherwise maltreated, that they have no longer the daring to demand their just debts.

(3) That the saddlers make old saddles into new, thus cheating the workmen of trade that ought to come to them.

The first charge was denied by the saddlers, but as they promised henceforth never to make any confederacy again their denial was scarcely conclusive. They pleaded that the sheriff's court was the place for questions of debt. And they promised never again to sell old saddles for new.

Evidently the excitement in London over this trade dispute was extreme, for when arbitration by the city officers was proposed, and the crafts summoned to meet in the church of St. Martin's le Grand before six chosen aldermen, they arrived there in so great multitudes and with such a concourse of people eager to hear the solution of the great trade problem, that no business could be done. The aldermen ordered another meeting at which elected representatives from each craft only should attend. Six saddlers therefore were confronted with two ironsmiths, two coppersmiths, two painters, and two joiners; and after a day's discussion a new group of thirteen was chosen by the trades and a concord was made "by the ordinance of these common friends and presented to the mayor and aldermen." The result was a decided victory of the working crafts over the dealers. The nine chief offenders among the saddlers were driven out of the trade, and the saddlers bound in a heavy penalty never again to take them back, to sustain them, or to help them, till they had made peace with the crafts. (Mem. Lond. 156-162.) As to the introduction of "blackleg" labour by the masters, it was decreed that no stranger was to be brought into the trades till he had been received at the husting by the assent of eight respectable men of the craft. The regulation that no repaired work was to be sold for new prevented another form of irregular labour, since trades might not legally repair for any but private customers.

In this instance it was the employers' union that was beaten; but it is evident that the question mainly turned on the convenience of the public, and their dislike to have bad saddles supplied to them. It is also evident that save in the case of some unusually powerful combination of working crafts there was but little hope for the humbler trades in a conflict with dealers or employers backed by the public in keeping down prices. The Tawyers or dressers of skins made ordinances in 1365 "as to how they shall serve the pelterers and how much they shall take for their labour." (Riley's Mem. Lond. 330.) The records may state that the ordinances were "provided and made by the serving-men called tawyers," but it is hard to believe that these "serving-men" acted of their own free will in framing rules which put their necks mercilessly and irrevocably under the yoke of the pelterers, binding themselves to serve them only, to work for the old fixed prices, and to bow to their jurisdiction in trade offences "according to the award and discretion of the rulers of the trade of pelterers."

There were other grounds of dispute between craft and craft, and battles raged at times between guilds as to the boundaries of the trades, and the relations between them—disputes which sprang from the "overlapping" of different crafts engaged upon one and the same product; or from the "apportionment" of work between closely related trades. Shoemakers were forbidden to be tanners (Stat. 13 Rich. II. i. cap. 12); then allowed to tan leather till the next Parliament (Stat. 4 Henry IV. cap. 35); and in 1423 again forbidden to be tanners (2 Henry VI. cap. 7). And as the tanners were protected against the shoemakers, so shoemakers were protected against cobblers. There was many a quarrel between the cordwainers who made new boots and the cobblers who mended old ones, the cobblers complaining that the cordwainers were preventing them from gaining their living as they had done of old. In 1395 at the king's order the mayor summoned twelve of each craft to state their grievances. The question of how much mending might be supposed to make a new boot required the most detailed inquiry: and the apportionment of labour was exact. No person who meddled with old shoes was to make new ones; all work with new leather was declared to be within the sphere of the cordwainers, and the cobblers were restricted to mending, and that with very small pieces of leather. Fourteen years later the lines were drawn still more precisely; the re-soling of old boots was reserved to the cordwainers, but the cobblers were allowed to mend with pieces of new leather boots that were burnt or broken. (Mem. Lond. 539-40, 572-3.) Ordinances of this kind were not necessarily designed for the protection of the workers, though no doubt that may often have been partly intended; but in the first instance were probably meant to make the supervision of trades and inspection of wares more efficient in the public interest.

CHAPTER VII

THE TAILORS OF EXETER

It was in the fifteenth century, at the very time when the towns seem to have been most energetic in tightening the bonds that held the crafts fast to their service, that we find the crafts on their side most impatient of subjection, and eager to test their strength in a direct conflict with the civic rulers. Their restless energy broke down all barriers between trade and politics, and forced each into the service of the other; for by whatever stratagem the crafts proposed to compel the constituted authorities to recognize them in a partnership of power—whether a wealthy guild planned the winning of a charter which should make it a free and independent corporation in the town; or whether a combination of less powerful trades demanded to be officially included in the municipal government which regulated their business, or in any other way to control its action—in any and every conflict with the ruling oligarchy the guilds were forced to enlist the sympathy of the burghers and to become leaders of popular discontent. On the other hand the commons, with no resource against the official class save an occasional mass meeting, eagerly welcomed the aid of the disciplined army enrolled in the guild, and under the politic guidance of expert leaders, to give weight to their claims for more power. Thus under the stress of the growing passion for political emancipation, trading interests constantly seem to merge altogether into the ambitions and animosities of parties wholly occupied in a conflict about civic rights. No doubt a prevailing suspicion of some such intimate connection between the desire of the crafts to escape from municipal control and a democratic movement in city politics, gave fire to the discussions which from the first origin of the question disturbed market-place and council-chamber, law-court and Parliament, and proclaimed the vehemence of feeling with which so great a matter was debated.

In the Tailors' Fraternity of Exeter we have a very curious example of the part which the Guild organization played in municipal politics. We have already seen the optimistic view taken by the Mayor and his Fellowship of "the great commonalty of the city," united and harmonious, and worthily represented by the patriotic officers into whose hands an absolute and unquestioned power had been committed; so that when John Shillingford sends to the Recorder and the Fellowship an account of his doings in London in the matter of the Dean and Chapter, he simply begs them first to make such corrections as they saw fit, and adds, "This done I pray you to call before you at the Hall the substance of the commonalty praying every one of them in my name and charging them in the most straightest wise in the King's behalf to come before you in haste for the tidings that I have sent home to you; and that ye wisely declare before them these answers; so that they say manly yea and nay *in such points as you think to be done.*"[320] Throughout the whole of the Mayor's letters there is not the slightest indication that he had ever heard of any "impetuous clamours" of a revolutionary Exeter mob, little mindful of the honour of the city; nor that after a hundred years or more of gathering discontent a crisis was close at hand when the commonalty was to measure its strength against the corporation. Nevertheless the union of the moment was but the union that comes of confronting a common enemy; and the townsmen seemed to be only waiting till that strife was temporarily hushed to fling themselves again into the discussion of their own domestic differences.

It is probable that from the time when the people of Exeter began to elect their own mayor, bailiff, and eight aldermen of the wards, they were also accustomed to appoint a body of twelve men to aid the mayor in all difficult business.[321] As at Colchester, Norwich, and many other towns, the elections were made by a double jury of Twenty-four; but how the Twenty-four were themselves elected we do not know. In the fourteenth century they seem already established, like the Twenty-four of Norwich, as a permanent council to advise and assist the Mayor; but the Twelve apparently survived alongside of them, for freemen were forbidden to assemble for the election of a mayor "in the absence of the Thirty-six"; and the Twenty-four were unable to perform any act save in the presence of Twelve men.[322] Until the records of Exeter are published, however, it is impossible to define the relations of the two bodies; and the manner in which the Twenty-four took possession of the Council Chamber is unknown.[323]

In Exeter, as elsewhere, trouble broke out in the middle of the fourteenth century between the two factions of the community—between the commons, discontented and rebellious; and the governing class, who appear, not as innovators or usurpers, but as the conservative guardians of "the ancient orders and customs of the city." The quarrel began in 1339 with "impetuous clamours" of the people against the constant re-election of one or two men as mayors; and for one year at least they carried their point, perhaps by some breach of former customs of election, for a decree was immediately issued that the people were not to gather together on the day of the mayor's election "in the absence of the Thirty-six"; perhaps by some help from the Church and from country patrons, for it was further ordered that no clerk of the Consistory Court, nor any man who did not live in the city should be elected mayor or allowed in any way to meddle with the election. The decree that no burgher might be excluded from the office who was resident, had been seneschal and had the hundred shillings of property which was generally required in all boroughs was, if we may judge from other boroughs, simply a recapitulation of the common custom.

That the quarrel was still agitating the people's minds some years later is shown by the ordinances of 1346 and 1347. The first forbade that a mayor should be immediately re-elected—an order evidently made to quiet public opinion but which the Twenty-four had no intention of observing. The second ordinance of 1347 decreed that the election should be made "by Twenty-four persons who upon their several and respective oaths shall make the election"—in fact it declared anew the custom which had been already recognized for fifty years, and probably from the first institution of the office, though of late years it had been called in question.

The victory of the governing body was apparently complete,[324] and it was indeed inevitable that so long as the city had to keep up its struggle with Earl and Bishop the needs and discipline of war should strengthen the position of the leaders and tighten their hold on their fellow-citizens. In 1427 the Twenty-four appear with the name of "the Common Council," ordinances are issued in the name of "the Mayor and the Common Council," and "in open court the Mayor and Bailiffs by the assent of the Twenty-four" transact all manner of town business, whether it concerned the city franchise, the hearing and carrying out of the King's orders, or the voting of money for public purposes.[325] To them also undoubtedly Shillingford wrote his long letters from London, respectfully addressing them as the "Fellowship" or "his Fellows," with whom he was accustomed to take counsel.

The ordinary burgesses of Exeter therefore, so far back as we can trace its history, played a modest part in city politics, nor had their attempt to assert themselves in 1339 won for them any advantage whatever. In 1460 the townsfolk made a new effort of a different and singularly interesting kind.

There was in Exeter a certain Tailors' Guild. Its rules, written or copied in 1460, ordained that every full tailor worth £20 "shall be of the Master's Fellowship and Clothing" and pay as his entrance "a spoon of silver weighing one ounce and the fashion," besides buying a livery once a year and giving twelve pence to the yearly feast. Other shop-holders were entered as of the Fellowship of the Bachelors, each paying 8d. to the feast and his offering.[326] There were special charges for the "free sewers"; and every servant who took wages was also brought into the organization and had to pay his sixpence yearly to the Guild.[327] The master and wardens sat every Thursday at nine o'clock to do business, and general meetings of the wardens and shop-holders were held four times a year, where after they had dined the free sewers were given the remains of the feast. There was a council of Eight;[328] and the usual rules for protecting the trade monopoly, for maintaining discipline, and for collecting funds were made.

So far the Guild was as other Guilds. But rich, powerful, and well drilled, it cherished ambitions beyond the perfecting of the tailors' art.[329] In the struggle between York and Lancaster, the sympathies of official Exeter were apparently Lancastrian, and when Edward the Fourth came to the throne[330] he probably found it politic or necessary, by a generous grant to the Tailors' Company, to make friends of the trading classes that had been left outside the governing caste. By the charter of incorporation which he allowed them they were granted singular privileges, of a kind which the municipal government bitterly resented. The charter placed the guild in direct dependence on the King, not on the mayor. They were given a rare liberty—the right "to make ordinances among themselves, as to them might beseem most necessary and behovefull for the said fraternity," and to "make search" and correct faults, apparently without need of the mayor's sanction.[331] Not only so, but they obtained authority to "augment and enlarge" their Guild as they chose; and did forthwith begin daily to take into their company "divers crafts other than of themselves, and divers others not inhabitants within the same city"—men in fact of every conceivable trade and occupation, free brethren who swore to be true and loving brothers of the guild, never to go to law with any of the fraternity, to pay their fines duly during life to the treasure box, and leave a legacy to it at their death. The usual rule that no man of the craft could be admitted to the freedom of the city save by the consent of the master and wardens gained a new political significance when the bulk of the inhabitants were thus enrolled under the Tailors' Guild, and when consequently it was the master of the Tailors who decided what men should or should not be made free of the borough.

From this moment the Tailors' Guild was really a great political association. The Master and Fellowship of the company were scarcely less powerful than the Mayor and Fellowship of the Corporation. By their right of search the guild officers could enter by day or night almost any house in the city or suburbs. By their authority to amend defaults they were able to leave the city courts deserted and the city treasury empty of its accustomed fines. The granting of citizenship was practically in their hands. Their funds and organization afforded the means for a steady and ordered attack on the governing oligarchy. Taking into their ranks all crafts and all classes, they gathered into one body the overtaxed and discontented populace whose anger at the authorities had grown big with long suppression; while they also enlisted members that lay beyond the authority of the corporation—country people as well as church tenants who, as we know, were already murmuring at the assessing of their taxes, and prepared to make common cause with the burghers.

Up to this time the authority of the Mayor over the trades of Exeter had been unquestioned. Merchants, grocers, drapers, mercers, the tailors themselves had been subject to his rule as in other towns; till by this alarming conspiracy the Mayor and Fellowship found themselves confronted with what naturally seemed to them a "great disorderly body" of revolutionists, who held conventicles and stirred up commotions in the town, who even overawed the Mayor and threatened to destroy his authority—men of "such evil disposition and unpeaceable that the Mayor of the said city may not guide and rule the people ... nor correct such defaults as ought by him to be correct," so that "evil example" was "likely to grow to subversion and destruction of the same city."[332] The royal charter obtained by the Guild was looked upon by the Corporation as a breach of municipal privilege; and the Guild members were required to renounce it by oath or to lose the city franchise; while the Mayor made an example of some of the burgesses who belonged to the fraternity by striking them off the roll of citizens. The shop windows of the refractory were fastened down, and inhabitants were forbidden to have garments made by certain tailors whose names were set down in a black list, "nor with no other of their opinion." Members of the craft who were on the city council were refused the Christmas gifts of wine and canon bread given to the councillors, and if they held to the craft were indeed excluded from the Chamber.[333] On the other hand if a luckless inhabitant sought to make his peace with the Corporation by withdrawing from the Tailors, and swearing upon the Crucifix and the Holy Evangelists to renounce their charter as contrary to the liberties of the city, the armed brethren of the Guild visited his house and levied his contributions by force of arms, that is to say by jacks, doublets of defence, swords, bucklers, glaives, and stones.[334] Then the town officers retorted by "presenting" the guilty tailors at the next court for the crime of riotously collecting fees, and throwing them into prison; and so the war went on, evidently at the expense of the weakest members of the community.

Presently however the quarrel was carried beyond the city courts. The Corporation appealed to Westminster and was once more plunged into legal expenses. In 1477 both parties appeared by attorneys before Edward the Fourth, who used the opportunity of the strife to tighten the hold of the central authority both on the town and on the craft. He set aside the contention of Exeter that the Corporation had any exclusive right of granting charters: the Guild had received its incorporation from the King and this remained valid; and in future all disputes between city and guild were to be laid before the King and his Council. But the royal rights being thus secured, the sympathy of the central government veered round to the side of the town as against the craft; and the conditions imposed on the Guild if it would preserve its charter were such as must necessarily break up the organization in its actual form. The fraternity was cut down again to the limits of the tailors' trade, and might enlist no members and make no search among those of other occupations, nor beyond the city boundaries; and even within these limits "saving always the franchises of the Mayor and Commonalty." It might issue no order against the rights of Bishop or Mayor: nor might it admit any man to the freedom of the city by enrolling him in the craft unless he were first presented to the Mayor. They suffered indeed a yet further humiliation, for while the Mayor was given the right of refusing to accept a candidate if he were suspected of not being of good disposition or conversation; yet if the master and wardens attempted to prevent a man from gaining the freedom of the city by refusing to testify in his favour and to make him free of the craft, the Mayor, bailiffs, and common council might insist on his being accepted by the Guild.[335]

Provisions such as these, involving the dissolution of the actual fraternity as it then existed, the ruin of its political position, and the end of its control over the roll of burgesses, proclaimed the triumph of the municipal authorities; and "the malice and grief which was conceived thereof could not in long time be satisfied or appeased." The Guild indeed apparently refused to accept defeat; for ordinances were made in 1479 requiring fresh contributions fixed for seven years from masters, shop-holders, and free sewers "to the finding of a priest"[336]—contributions which were assessed so high as to suggest some "feigned colour of sanctity" in the desire to provide for a chaplain so unwonted an opulence, in addition to his board at the Mayor's cost; and which evidently lasted beyond the seven years, since in 1500 an order was again made that all serving-men, whether working by the year, by the week, or by the piece, should pay a penny a quarter to maintain the priest, and at Michaelmas for the wax. The Guild indeed was still in good repute and able to hold its own. One of the Tailors was Mayor before 1482;[337] and in 1481 the Company arrogantly defied the authority of the Corporation. A tailor summoned to choose between keeping his place as member of the Guild and retaining the freedom of the city solemnly renounced his oath to the Guild before the Mayor, whereupon the master and wardens sued him for perjury; so "by the mean of gentlemen and money" he made peace with them and was again sworn to the Guild. But absenting himself from the duties it required of him "without cause reasonable" he was fetched out of his house, brought to Tailors' Hall and set in the stocks, and finally compelled to find sureties for good conduct in the future.[338] The town councillors of Exeter learned caution from such incidents; and when in this same year they granted to the Cordwainers a confirmation of their charter, it was on condition that the master and wardens of the guild should yearly come before the Mayor and surrender all their powers, after which on payment of a fine they should receive them back again by grant of the Mayor.[339] The next year, 1482, when the Bakers desired to have new ordinances,[340] the Corporation stipulated that all corn must be ground in the city mills; that the wardens in making search in bakers' shops or in hucksters' houses should always be accompanied by a city officer or serjeant; and that if any guild rules were made which were against the city liberties, the Mayor and council might change them at their will.

The rebellious Tailors, however, had fought their last battle. In 1482 a new petition was laid by the city authorities before Edward the Fourth praying, in spite of the King's award, for the total abolition of the Tailors' charter; and the Twenty-four voted in this and the following years over £50 for business in Parliament and legal expenses "touching the annulling of the charter."[341] From the history of other towns about this time, it would seem that considerable anxiety was beginning to grow up at Court as to the commotions of the populace and the growth of democracy in the boroughs; the petition was granted as a matter of course, and the Tailors' Fraternity sank back into the subject position of an ordinary craft guild. Discontent and murmurings were still heard in the city streets, but the corporation had no reason for fear. In 1496 when one John Atwill was about to be chosen for the fifth time, "a great division happened amongst the citizens about the election of the mayor, and for avoiding the like for the future, was ordered by the mayor and common council hereof, that no man should be mayor or bear any office here, nor any election hold good, unless the same were held according to the ancient orders and customs of the said city, and withal that the Mayor and four and twenty of the said Common Council should elect the Mayor and all other officers of the said city." To make matters quite safe the city got a charter the next year from Henry the Seventh. The new charter did indeed slightly limit the claims which the Council had freely set forth in 1496: they were no longer allowed to elect the Mayor, but were to choose two candidates for the office, one of whom was to be appointed by the freemen; but on the other hand they still retained absolute power to fill up their own vacancies, and to choose the bailiffs. Their name too was for the first time recognized, and instead of using any longer the old style of the city, "the Mayor, Bailiffs, and Commonalty of the city," the king legislated "by the assent and consent of the Common Council."[342]

The Tailors, thus beaten in open fight, could only fall back on the indirect influence of their wealth and compact majority, and make alliance with the power which they could not destroy. In 1516 the Master of the craft was also Steward of the city, another member was Receiver or Treasurer, and others were of the Council of Twenty-four; while others again had been Mayors or Treasurers of past years. By the will and consent of these officers of City and Guild, the constitution of the Tailors' Company was amended, so as to blot out the last trace of government by the will of the fraternity; and the Eight men, "the sent of the occupation," by whose authority laws had once been made for the trade, were replaced by a council of those who had once been masters of the craft, to be summoned by the Master.[343] The full significance of this step can only be understood by taking it in connexion with the position which was at this time being given to "the Clothing" in municipal government.[344] But it is plain that the ancient strife was now closed by a division of the spoils of power; and the sorrows of defeat were left to the populace at large. These lay more hopelessly than before at the mercy of their rulers, for masters of crafts when they controlled town government had a double reason for maintaining the authority of the corporation—the instinct of the master tradesman and the instinct of the town councillor.

The story of Exeter is invaluable from the light it throws on the mutual attitude of town and craft in the struggle for autonomy. Nothing is more intelligible than the passionate resistance of a corporation to royal charters given over the heads of the town officers,[345] if we realize the quick alarms to which a municipality which had had experience of the long fight for supremacy with king and church and baron, was liable when it saw a new enemy, an enemy which it had long supposed vanquished, springing up in its very midst to threaten with a fresh danger the unity of the borough. It was speedily discovered how great an internal weakness must follow from this cleavage in the political society of the towns; and how the very appeals for arbitration to the State, and the interference of King and Parliament, must constantly tend yet further to limit municipal independence; while there were other hints of danger in the new chances offered for the country gentry to interfere with the independence of the town life, when they could make the guild, detached from the town, an engine for their own political projects.[346] Even for the guilds themselves, there were to be set against the advantages, whatever these amounted to, which they actually won by emancipation, grave dangers for the future—dangers from the difficulty of enforcing discipline without government support; from the hostility of the corporation and the annoyances it could inflict by rendering honour to their most unruly members; and from the encouragement given to a more aggressive animosity on the part of other companies, rivals in independence and determined foes in monopoly.[347] The emancipation of the greater trading companies from local control may have been a necessary step in setting free a growing national commerce; but it was the evident sign that the age of municipal freedom and local self-government had entered on its decline.

Usually, however, it seems that the big trading companies had their own methods of making terms with authority, or of leading the corporation captive and peacefully installing themselves in the place of power; as we may see in the case of the great merchant fraternities and wholesale dealers who, like the Drapers and Mercers of Coventry, the Drapers of Shrewsbury, and possibly guilds of the same kind at Walsall,[348] had made of their combinations the dictators of the civic administration. But commercial unions such as these, standing in a group by themselves, somewhat apart from the Exeter Tailors, must be separately considered. The Tailors' fraternity may perhaps be taken as holding a sort of intermediate position—on one side figuring almost as a merchant company, and on the other as an ordinary manufacturing craft; and it is in this second aspect that its history indicates to us the very important part which the trades played in rallying the elements of revolt, drilling their forces, and lending the guild organization for the strife. No single instance can ever be taken as in any way typical or representative, for everywhere the position of the crafts resolves itself into questions of local circumstances, and of delicate changes from place to place in the balance of conflicting forces. Whether there was any town under normal conditions in which successful resistance was made to a governing oligarchy save with the help of a good craft organization we cannot as yet say. In every borough there seem to have been disputes, more or less acute, between the governing and the governed, whether the conflict took the form of the attack and defence of a close corporation as at Exeter; or of a powerful guild merchant controlling the corporation as at Lynn; or of the great mercantile fraternities as at Coventry. And in some boroughs in which the commons succeeded in modifying the old oligarchic system, we can certainly trace the direct action of the manufacturing crafts. Occasionally the working trades rose against the merchant societies, and forced their way into the Council Chamber. In Carlisle the Merchant Guild, while remaining distinct from the municipal body, gave to the town more mayors and aldermen than any other guild; and as it admitted no strangers to membership of its society "for no money whatsoever"[349] its posts and honours became practically hereditary, until eight crafts or occupations of the town (seven of them being unions of artificers, and the eighth a union of shopkeepers, seedsmen, apothecaries, haberdashers, and so on) put an end to this despotism in the sixteenth century by creating a council of thirty-two, four from each trade, who joined the council of the mayor and aldermen, and claiming to act in the name of the whole community took part in making bye-laws; in choosing the "out-men" who were to be made burgesses; in auditing accounts; in removing the town officers if necessary; and in keeping the keys of the common chest.[350] That such powers as these were voluntarily or even quite peaceably handed over by the ruling guild is conceivable, though its improbability is shewn by all analogy. In Newcastle it was after "great commotions, unlawful assemblies, confederacies," and general riots that the mercers, drapers, and corn-dealers were forced in 1516 to admit nine other crafts to share with them the government.[351] In Norwich, where it was found possible even for guilds proscribed and forbidden to force an honourable compromise with their opponents, the settlement was only brought about after discords by which the city was "divided and dissolved and in point to have been destroyed."[352] When Edward the Fourth, in 1464, sent a royal patent to York ordering that for the future the craftsmen of the trades should nominate two aldermen, one of whom was to be chosen mayor, the action must imply that there had been dissension in the city society, out of which the king perhaps hoped to make his profit[353] by attaching to himself an important faction in the community. No doubt there were many cases where the trades had to confess the entire failure of their attempts, or where their success was but partial, as in London where the crafts would willingly have increased their influence if popular opinion could have been taken out of the way.[354] In a great number of boroughs we know that the crafts insisted that the only way to the municipal franchise should lie through their societies;[355] but to what extent this condition prevailed, to what political uses it was put, and how far it served as a trial of strength between parties in power and revolutionary factions, are as yet only matters of guess-work.

The scanty state of our knowledge indeed makes it impossible to sum up in a phrase the character of a strife which was universal, which involved every class in a most complicated and highly organized industrial society, and of which the history has not yet been fully made out for a single borough. But so far as our evidence yet goes, the developement of municipal government involved everywhere a struggle between the classes triumphant and the classes put under subjection. To discuss whether the subject class who attempted to create new associations or use old ones to fight their battles, were mere common burgesses contending with a municipal corporation, or bodies of artificers resisting a guild of merchants, or an indiscriminate mob opposed to a religious fraternity of the Holy Trinity or the Holy Cross, is often a mere juggling with words. For as we shall see, it was possible for one group of men to bear the three names, and in their character of "magnates" or "potentiores" to act not only as the Town Council but also as the Guild Merchant; and to shelter both functions under a specious colour of sanctity. Under such circumstances it is of no great consequence under which name they fought, nor by what name they called the mob, whether commonalty or another; since no change in their nominal relations materially affected the attitude of men in power towards those outside, or the policy of merchant and master tradesmen towards the working people. We must always remember, too, in discussing the social changes that took place in England, that the absence of violent dramatic effects, the limited and provincial character of the contests of classes, were but necessary consequences of the conditions of English life, at a time when industrial and political disputes were carried on by the local forces of every little town independently, in a series of particular conflicts fought out with varying success by groups of combatants trained in small detachments for separate service. It would be too much to imagine, because we read of no open war of classes, no burning of towns or insurrections quenched in blood, that the whole industrial society of mediæval England moved together in a harmonious and orderly progression, each new group as it arrived being peacefully lifted to its destined place in wealth and council, without the jealousy of predecessors, or the bitter grudge of after-comers. On the contrary all evidence goes to show that the tenacity of Englishmen in holding to power, and their stubbornness in insisting on freedom, were as characteristic of the race in the fifteenth as in the nineteenth century; that antagonism between the man who asks and the man who pays a wage, were very much the same as now; and that class interests were if anything far more powerful. If therefore we suppose the social and political developement of the later middle-ages in this country was naturally brought about by the logical sequence of economic developement, we must allow that stern sequence to include then, as it would include now, the passionate efforts of a strong people to turn aside by their might the impending calamities of fate, and to lay a violent grasp on her uncertain benefactions.

CHAPTER VIII

THE GUILD MERCHANT

IN the conflicts of the fourteenth and fifteenth centuries we see the town society rent into two factions; and whether the contending groups call themselves the Burghers and Commonalty, or "the rich" and "the poor people of the city," or the Merchant Guild and the Crafts, or by any other names, they seem practically to represent the same broad sections of the community. In town quarrels it is hard for us to draw any valid distinction between groups of citizens and companies of craftsmen, as though they were led by different passions; for however numerous were the mere inhabitants who must have lain outside the organization of the crafts, usually every freeman was a member of some company, and the whole voting population was thus enrolled under the banners of the various trades. The real line of cleavage on which we have to concentrate attention is not the thin line which may be drawn between the Town Council and the Merchant Guild, the Commonalty and the Crafts, but rather the broad chasm which breaks the whole industrial society itself into two factions—on the one side the merchant traders, on the other the artificers and small retail dealers. Wherever the lesser crafts who represented the middle classes of the borough, and whose interests were more or less identified with the cause of the commons and "poor people of the city," were forcing their claim to a share in the counsels of the town; to which their way was barred by a solid phalanx of hereditary "magnates" and wealthy merchants who had abandoned the meaner employments of trade and thrown in their lot with the governing oligarchy of "the rich," and who fought in alliance with or under cover of the burghers; there the revolt of the commons against the Town Council becomes practically a battle of the working crafts against the rule of the mercantile fraternities—a battle which may be fought at one time for the winning of civic privileges, at another for industrial freedom.

If we ask how old this conflict was, and at what time the peace of the town was first disturbed by the antagonism of the greater commerce and the lesser crafts, of the trader and the artificer, we must go back for an answer to the very much earlier period when commercial societies first became organized, or at least to the twelfth century when the Merchant Guild and the Crafts come prominently to the front.[356] Unfortunately the history of the Guild Merchant,[357] from its obscure beginnings in the days of the Confessor, or of the Norman kings, down to the time when its organization had spread all over England, and its fraternities were to be found in most of the trading boroughs, is still enveloped in the darkness which covers the early records of our towns, and problems await solution which involve the whole developement of the Guild. We know that from a remote period men had banded themselves together in associations to secure protection and monopoly of trade, and before the close of the twelfth century the majority of trading towns had each its "Merchant Guild" with rights guaranteed by royal charter. First born into life in a society where a merchant class such as we understand it was unknown, we are told that the Guild may have first consisted mainly of agriculturists busied in tilling their common lands, and increasing their herds of cows and sheep and pigs; and whose chief anxiety was to sell the butter and honey and salt meat and wool that remained over when they had supplied their own wants, and to buy fish for the fasting seasons, ploughs and spades for their fields and the simplest furniture for their humble households. But, in the opinion of its latest historian, from the twelfth century artizans were freely admitted to its society, and presently formed the majority of the Guild[358]—each craftsman being a small trader on his own account, buying his raw material, and selling his manufactured goods at the stall he rented in the market or on the folding shelf that he let down to the street from the window of his little workroom. With these were clergy and women who busied themselves in trade;[359] travelling dealers among the townsfolk to whom exemptions from jurisdictions outside the town and freedom from toll were important (things which mattered little to the homekeeping citizens); and strangers who brought their wares to the town market,[360] paid their entrance fee and pledged themselves to bear henceforth their share of the town taxes, though they were considered free from all other charges that lay on the "downlying and uprising and pot-boiling" householders. It is therefore supposed that when the time came for the Guild to emerge from its humble state of private association, and rise into the dignity of an official civic body, charged with the protection of the trading interests of the borough,[361] it formed a really popular institution, which from its very nature could never become entangled in a conflict with the crafts—an organization of the whole community for the control of trade by the common consent of the people, which was in many respects peculiarly characteristic of English life,[362] and which was the natural product of an age of freedom before the people had been trodden under foot of a despotic oligarchy. Theoretically subject to the authority of the town as part of its regular administrative machinery,[363] but ruled over by its own officers, and exercising independent jurisdiction through its voluntary tribunals of arbitration, the Guild by virtue of its trade monopoly,[364] its powerful organization and discipline, and the fact that the men who formed its governing body were generally the same as those who sat on the governing body of the borough, maintained a far more independent position than any department of town government to-day.[365]

But according to Dr. Gross the Gilda Mercatoria was doomed to vanish away before the growth of new industrial conditions. The first blow was struck at its supremacy by the appearance early in the twelfth century of crafts, which bought from the king the right to exist as independent fraternities during his pleasure.[366] From this time the decline of the Merchant Guild from its old estate kept pace with the commercial revolution that caused its ruin. It began to undergo its great change at the close of the thirteenth century, and in the two following centuries it may be said to have practically ceased to exist. Broken up into a multitude of independent associations, each of which carried on business for itself,[367] deprived of all its old functions, it died because it had no longer any adequate reason to live. Perhaps it lingered on here and there in agricultural towns where few or no craft guilds had been formed;[368] or in ecclesiastical boroughs where its organization provided the only rallying point for the community in any struggle for freedom; but everywhere else its machinery fell to pieces;[369] and so completely did it vanish away as a distinct body that the very name only survived by taking to itself new meanings. Sometimes the old Merchant Guild became indistinguishably blended with the town and gave its name to the whole community;[370] though in another place it perhaps handed over name and functions to the narrow select governing body of the borough as distinguished from the general community of citizens.[371] Elsewhere its title was in some vague way transferred to the aggregate of the craft guilds.[372] As a mere shadow of its former self, with nothing but the word to mark its identity, the Merchant Guild might survive as a simple social-religious fraternity;[373] or perhaps without conflict or bitterness it merely faded away before the crafts, leaving not so much as a name behind it.[374] But however the implicit, unspoken compact was carried out, by whatever means the Gilda Mercatoria, obedient to a final destiny, effected its renunciation of an inconvenient supremacy, there was no possible occasion left for strife between Guild and crafts,[375] and the suggestion of any such quarrel, or of revolt on the part of the crafts against the superior fraternity from the twelfth to the fifteenth centuries, must be looked on as a wanton "myth".[376] Having fulfilled its course the Merchant Guild took its doom without noise or struggle, and entered decently into the shades with a grave decorum before which jarring sounds of contention were put to silence. It was at a later time, when the old popular organization had died, that the harmony of the commons was destroyed by the coming in of a tyranny unknown till then—the tyranny of a select and irresponsible governing body which by its corrupt administration stirred up a new spirit of dissension in the boroughs.

Unfortunately this picture of the successive stages of the guild history, from the free republican period through which they are all apparently supposed to have passed, down to their extinction or absorption into a governing oligarchy, a whole borough community, or a group of trades, has not been verified by following out the continuous story of any single guild. Moreover it would seem that the difficulty of making any general statement about the groups of traders who made the fortunes of the English boroughs, is as great as the difficulty of making a general statement as to the position and grouping of a host of irregular troops in rapid march over a tangled country. Amid the intense activity and the transformation scenes of mediæval life there is no exact definition which does not prove false with a little lapse of time, a little change of place; and theories of "natural tendency" are but as traps set for the unwary. So far as the Guild Merchant is concerned, there were probably as many various exceptions to any general rule as there were towns which contained a Guild. Let but a generation pass away and the institution is perhaps wholly changed; here it existed in some special form; a few miles off it never existed at all; in some boroughs it dominated the history of the town, while in others it left but the bare echo of its name behind.[377] There may possibly have been towns where at one time the Guild included within its ranks the majority of the burghers, and perhaps mainly consisted of craftsmen;[378] but there were evidently others where from the first it formed a society far narrower and more restricted,[379] or where it rapidly tended to become a limited body of wealthy citizens out of whose midst the craft guilds cannot possibly have been developed; while occasionally it may have happened that the craft guilds preceded the Merchant Guild.[380] Even if the theory was ostensibly maintained that craftsmen "were freely enrolled among the members of the Guild Merchant"[381]—in practice "gifts and entrance fees of a collation, a bull, beer, and wine" could effectually keep out the poorer sort, and allow the association[382] to develop rapidly into an exclusive and comparatively aristocratic society, which demanded from all save owners of a house or burgage, or men entitled by direct descent to belong to the fraternity, admission fees big enough to guarantee the new comer's fitness to be of their fine company. The two ranks established in the Andover Guild[383] as early as the thirteenth century suggest how privilege might creep in even among Guild members themselves; as the merchants of Bristol teach us how it could be fought for;[384] and there is no doubt that the policy of each separate fraternity must have largely depended on whether it adopted the custom of having its officers chosen by consent of the whole community of Guildsmen,[385] or by a handful of electors of the superior class.[386] Even if a considerable number of burghers was admitted to trading privileges, it by no means follows that they were allowed any voice in the control of business.

Nor are we less in the dark as to that "natural process" by which the Guild is believed to have passed to its resigned and painless end. The "transference of authority from the ancient general Guild Merchant to a number of distinct bodies and the consequent disintegration and decay of the former,"[387] the weakening of its strength by the creation of new crafts, the splitting up of its monopoly into fragments, the annihilation of its original being to make place for "the aggregate of the crafts," the turning of the Guild into a "simple social-religious fraternity"—a kind of quiet haven of rest for wealthy merchants who had given up the sweets of power and the real government of trade in which their fortunes were concerned, to busy themselves with dirges and masses and chaplains, or even with a Corpus Christi procession—in fact the whole "gradual and spontaneous" movement in which lay the death of the primitive fraternity is still enveloped in mystery. If craftsmen, associated in their own peculiar guilds, yet remained in the common Guild Merchant[388] which had once made regulations for their trade, and in many cases still did so,[389] the instances (apart from cases where the Guild Merchant either was the municipal body, or had simply handed over to it its name) are rare or perhaps unknown in the fourteenth and fifteenth centuries; nor can we easily follow the far more complicated transformation said to have taken place when the burgesses became the heirs of the general body of guildsmen, by a double process which changed the idea of citizenship from the conception of the freeman holding a burgage tenure into the later idea of a man holding the right to exercise a trade, and which turned the governors of the guild into the rulers of the town;[390] so that by natural growth the fraternity of the Guild Merchant, once wholly distinct from the borough, became identical with it.[391]

It is very possible—indeed it is very probable if we remember the thrift of the English people in politics, their habit of fetching out the old machinery whenever there seems a chance of making it useful; their aversion to repairs or patches beyond what imperative necessity demands; their indifference to new inventions if the old wheels and cranks can still be induced to turn—that we may learn something of the working of the original Guild Merchant by watching the doings of its successors in the fourteenth and fifteenth centuries. For whether the primitive Guild had ceased to exist or no, something going by its name and clothed in its form confronts us constantly in the later times, soberly masquerading in an ancient habit which seems scarcely the worse for wear or out of fashion for all the lapse of centuries; and figuring before us as a robust survival, as an old organization fitted out afresh for a pressing emergency, or even as a new creation. We may watch in Coventry such a Guild, which bears none of the signs of decrepitude or symptoms of decay—a guild which was in no sense a simple social-religious fraternity, nor yet an ordinary craft guild; which was far from being an aggregate of the trades; which refused to the lesser crafts the right to combine, and despotically governed their business in its own interests; which was the municipal body of the city and carried on its entire administration, but never gave its name either to the community or to the governing body; anti-democratic in its origin, in its maturity, and in its old age; jealous of dominion; incapable of making terms from behind its barricaded doors with dissolution. Late as was its date, it has features in its origin, its constitution, and its policy far too like those of much earlier guilds, not to claim our interest.[392]

Born two or three hundred years out of due time (for it was not till Queen Isabella became owner of part of Coventry and interested in defending her tenants' rights against the Prior, that the city was able to obtain the grant of a Gilda Mercatoria), it was only in 1340 that the Merchant Guild of S. Mary's was founded[393]—an association apparently of dealers in cloth, wool, and general merchandise.[394] Even then it failed to secure license to mortmain, perhaps through the resistance of the Prior, the lord of the soil; but it is possible that the charter of incorporation for the town, granted in 1344, was bought by the Guild, and at least as early as 1347 and 1350 two of its masters were mayors; while the Town Hall, where the mayor and council met and where the chest containing the town treasure and the charter were kept, always bore the name of S. Mary's Guild.

In the meantime two other societies had sprung up—the guild of S. John Baptist[395] in 1342, and the guild of S. Catherine in 1343—and the three companies of S. Mary, S. John, and S. Catherine united into one body between 1364 and 1369; and finally joined themselves to the Trinity Guild, which had received license to mortmain in 1364, and gave its name to the whole association.[396] Considerable property was handed over in trust for the combined societies to six of the chief citizens of the town, most of whom had been mayors several times, and one of whom had been founder of S. John's Guild. From this time the history of the municipality is the history of its leading guilds; and the further step taken in 1392, when the four guilds were more formally united by a patent of incorporation, and when fresh donations of land were given to the whole body, was only a fortifying of the position which it already held.

Though the name of the Merchant Guild was sacrificed, doubtless for some sufficient reason, the Trinity Guild was nothing more than an extension of the primitive association under a new title. The founders and donors and the early mayors are usually classed together as "mercatores" in the deeds, and the union seems to have represented the wealthy upper class (drapers and mercers for the most part, with a few leading members of other trades),[397] living in S. Michael's parish, of which Queen Isabella and her successors were the owners. Only one other society was allowed to exist alongside of it,—the fraternity of rich traders in Trinity parish (the Prior's half of the town), who were in 1348 licensed to form the Corpus Christi Guild. Drawn from the same rank, sharing the same interests, they cast in their lot with the merchants of the neighbouring parish, contributed to the general town expenses, and were admitted to a corresponding degree of influence in the municipal government.[398]

For the Trinity and Corpus Christi Guilds were in fact the governing body of the town. According to the general custom the Master of the Corpus Christi Guild was made Mayor in the second year after his laying down that post, and two years after his mayoralty he was set at the head of the Trinity Guild.[399] All important town officials were sworn members of both the great companies; so were the Leet Jury and the Twenty-four who elected the mayor (these two bodies consisting of almost the same individuals); and so were all the men who might be summoned on the Mayor's Council to aid the Twenty-four. By this simple device, the fear of an alien party being formed in the Council was once for all banished; for if the Corpus Christi Guild held its elections in the Bishop's palace[400] and had its centre in Trinity Church on the Prior's land,—if its members included the Prior and his bailiff, the vicar, and strangers, some of them of great estate, from near and far[401]—all dangerous elements were made harmless by the order that none of its members should meddle with town affairs unless he had been first approved and accepted by the Trinity Guild. The Corpus Christi fraternity in fact was admitted to its position by a sort of cautious sufferance, and all real power lay with the Guild of the Trinity. Its master was a Justice of the Peace, and therefore took a leading part in all the most important business of the courts; he was first on the list of the Twenty-four who elected the mayor and who also sat at the Leet Court. Invariably he was one of the five men chosen by the mayor to keep the keys of the common chest—being, in fact, in matters of finance supreme; for at the end of the mayor's year of office it was to the master that he delivered up his accounts and his balance "and is quit"; and the Guild was not only charged with the payment of salaries to public officials—the recorder, the grammar-school master, the priests in the Lady Chapel of S. Michael's, and the warden and priests at Bablake—but as early as 1384 it was ordered by the Leet to pay yearly the ferm to the Prior, in return for which a certain part of the common lands was made over into its possession. The keeping of Bablake Gate was committed to it; and it was given possession of the Drapery Hall, which was used as the cloth mart under the control of the municipality.[402]

But this great society, known on the one side as the Trinity Guild, on the other as the Town Corporation, owed in neither aspect anything whatever to popular election,[403] and made no pretence at government according to the will of the people.[404] From the very moment of the first union of the fraternities the story of revolt among the 7,000 workers who thronged the streets of Coventry begins, and is repeated from generation to generation for the next hundred and fifty years. Incessant riots declared the discontent of the commons at the light loaves sold under mayors who neglected to keep the assize of bread, at false measures allowed for selling corn, at the encroachments on common lands by chamberlains and councillors, at the government of trade by the drapers and mercers enrolled in the two great guilds of the city, while weavers, shearmen, fullers, and tailors, lying for the most part outside these guilds, had little hope of ever rising to municipal power.[405] The crafts, in fact, were kept in uncompromising subjection. When the fullers and tailors tried to set up a fraternity,[406] the ruling guilds obtained a charter in 1407 which forbade the creation of any other society than their own. They had this grant confirmed in 1414; and the next year they appealed to Parliament against the dyers[407] who endeavoured to form a confederation of cloth-makers and wool-sellers. S. George's Guild—a union of the "young men, serving men of the tailors and other artificers, and labourers working by the day called journeymen," who defiantly gathered in S. George's Chapel and elected "masters and clerks and other officials to fulfil their youthful and insolent desires," and "abet each other in their quarrels"—was put down because it was "to the ruin and destruction of the Guilds of Holy Trinity and Corpus Christi and disturbance of all the community."[408] Though the fullers and tailors once more obtained license in 1438 to hold property, their union was broken up in the next ten years;[409] and the persistence of the dyers in clinging to their illegal combinations was opposed in 1475 by an ordinance that unlawful writings and oaths made by dyers and other crafts were to be "void, quashed, and annulled," and members of the craft should not be sued for not observing these illegal ordinances.[410] Circuitous attempts to win independence by informally setting up voluntary tribunals where the members of the trade assembled to settle disputes, were met by the order that no masters of crafts should sue any of their craft in any kind of suit in special courts until the mayor have heard the matter and licensed the suit; on the plea that "discord falls out continually because masters of crafts sue in special courts divers people of their crafts, affirming they have broken their oaths made in breaking divers rules, which rules are ofttimes unreasonable, and the punishment of the said masters excessive, which, if it continue, by likelihood will cause much people to void out of this city."[411] With regard to customs on wool, or the conditions of sale for the coarse cloth of the people, or the regulations for apprentices, the merchants passed laws which drove the commons to impotent fury;[412] and the wild dreams of revolution that passed from street to street for the century after John Ball found his hiding-place in the lanes of Coventry, are told in the rhymes nailed by the people on the church door side by side with the official announcements, where we hear their passionate outcry for the freedom of the good old days of Godiva, and threats of a time when the "littel small been" and "wappys" should "also sting";[413] or in the teaching of the leader of the populace that the city would have no peace till three or four of the churls that ruled them had their heads stricken off.

But if the Trinity Guild was in this complete sense the governing body of the town—if its legislation was at once so characteristic and so irresistible—by what strange access of modesty was it restrained from taking to itself the glory, and letting its name blot out all others on the city roll?[414] Such renunciation, we can scarcely doubt, whether in Coventry or in other places where the problem presents itself, was more likely to spring from the "grace of guile" than from modesty. From the point of view of worldly wisdom, indeed, the arguments for a diplomatic self-effacement were overwhelming; for it was easy to discern the dangers to its hoarded treasure which a guild must incur from the moment when in the eyes of the law or of its officers it became confounded with the municipality. Safety lay in silence, and if the name of the guild lingered in the Guildhall, it did not pass the precincts; while by a wise precaution the actual mayor of the borough was never allowed to be the same person as the actual master of the guild,[415] lest the higher authorities should in some emergency make an easy confusion between the keys with which he opened the treasure-box of the community, and those which unlocked the coffers of the guild.[416] If there were any doubt before 1392[417] about the meaning of thus carefully preserving the double aspect of the fraternity, there seems but little after it. For in that year when the Coventry Guild got its new formal patent and its increased income, it was only following a somewhat common fashion of the day.[418] In 1392 the bailiffs and commonalty of Birmingham obtained leave to have their Guild of the Holy Cross—"a guild and brotherhood of brethren and sisteren among themselves in that town ... and men and women well disposed in other towns and in the neighbourhood"—which might hold lands in mortmain, and which was intimately connected with the governing body of the town. The Town Hall or Guild Hall was built by it, and charities were distributed "according to the ordering and will of the bailiffs and commonalty"; and it "kept in good reparacioune two great stone bridges and divers foul and dangerous highways, the charge whereof the town of itself is not able to maintain."[419] In the same year, 1392, "the seneschalls of the Guild Merchant of Bridgewater and of the community of the same town" obtained a grant to assign certain lands in mortmain,[420] and an indenture which probably belongs to the beginning of the reign of Edward the First[421] proves that there was a close relation of this guild on one side to the fraternity of S. Mary or of the Holy Cross, and on the other to the corporation of the town. The brotherhood of the Holy Cross at Abingdon, which was established under Richard the Second, seems to have been practically the governing body of the borough, owned most of the landed property in the town in the fifteenth century, and spent money liberally in the building of churches and the market cross.[422]

Such guilds as these seem to have been the quick retort of the towns to the Act of 1391, which for the first time extended to cities and boroughs the Statute of Mortmain passed in 1279, and placed them in a position where they could thenceforth boast of no advantage over religious corporations, and like them had to buy leave to hold property. But it seemed beyond the wit of man to put English traders into a difficulty which was not by their very touch turned into a new opportunity for gain. If right to hold corporate property must now be bought, whatever claimant appeared, then why should it not be bought by a private society of merchants, sheltered under the Holy Cross or the Trinity, rather than by the town community or the burgesses? On the one hand the leading citizens, the intelligent and prosperous men of the town, thus secured an indestructible claim to guide its fortunes aright; on the other hand the town funds were by the same measure garnered once for all in a safe hiding-place—in other words, if troublesome officers from the exchequer should come with demands for inconvenient rent or forfeitures, they were met by the fact that the men of the town *had* nothing, while the men of the guild *owed* nothing. The system seems to have worked as effectively as the British constitution itself. We know that the Coventry Guild, besides the property it already held, had taken over yet more at its incorporation in 1392. But in 1468, Coventry being then the fourth city in the kingdom, it was £800 in arrears for its ferm; and since the goods of "the mayor and men of Coventry" only amounted to 106*s.*, and since the said "mayor and men" had no other goods or lands within the bailiwick that could be taken into the king's hands, no further payment was then made.[423] If we remember the wealth of the Trinity and Corpus Christi Guilds, the fact that they probably held the main portion of the common property,[424] and their close connexion with the city government,[425] it is plain that the town was doing very good business in withdrawing its funds from the reach of the king's officers; and that the traders had adequately realized their purpose in setting up in their Townhall one of those familiar companies which was admitted at home to be in effect the corporation, but which was officially known at Westminster only as a "simple" social-religious fraternity that yearly carried S. George and his Dragon or some other poetic emblem through the streets with solemn festival, or kept great tendrilles of wax burning before the Holy Cross in the parish church.

That the Trinity society of Coventry was not the last of these astute fraternities of traders we know;[426] that it was not the first we may safely believe. Indeed, it might well have been modelled on the fraternity of the Trinity at Lynn[427]—an older company by a hundred and fifty years, whose members would at no time have found any trouble in discussing the secrets of their policy with the merchants of Coventry. It may be that the texture of society was never so simple or so uniform as historians have believed, that the humble mediæval merchant loomed big in the eyes of his yet humbler fellow-citizens, and that in many a trading town the Guild Merchant was the monument of the successful capitalists of the village, and of a triumph so complete that the petty details of its progress fell out of memory. How many typical forms the early guild may have taken from town to town, as it squeezed its way with or without a welcome into communities of every shape and consistence, we have not yet materials to say; nor do we yet know by what varieties of compact it may have become the indispensable minister or the master of the municipal authority; or what was its common relation to the lesser forms of trade. It is indeed conceivable that later research may show us that in many cases the subjection of the crafts to the town—a subjection so astonishing in the silence, the calm, the rapidity with which it is affected—was carried out by the indissoluble union of guild and corporation. Organized in days when the way to wealth lay in the buying and selling of raw material, and in consequence by its constitution destitute of powers to follow the artizan into his workroom and meddle with his tools and the stuff of his trade, the Guild Merchant must very early have seen its officers falling behind the officers of the town before whom all bars and doors were thrown open; but if, suiting their policy to the necessities of the situation, seneschals and scavins of the Guild preserved their power by becoming bailiffs and councillors of the borough, not by laying down their authority before the wardens of the cobblers or the tailors, or even by taking them into its councils; such a guild might make its end neither by resigning to the crafts its cherished prerogatives nor by a spontaneous death, but by a consecrated alliance, in which it only seemed to merge its identity in the borough corporation, while in reality it secured the preservation of its ancient name and guaranteed the traditions and authority of its order. As in Coventry, the force which had first served to overthrow the mastery of the lord of the soil might be employed later to enforce its own despotism over a subject people; and the question whether it used an old or a new name was a matter of little consequence to the inferior and dependent class. In either case the control of the town rested in the hands of an oligarchy of the richer sort of traders, who by combination were able to exact from the mass of the working people an unlimited submission, and practically held at their mercy the fortunes of the free commons of the city.

NOTE A.

The satisfactory working of the system may be inferred from its continued use in the next century. Plymouth may serve as an illustration. Among the three little fishing hamlets, the Augustinian Priors' Sutton or South Town at the mouth of the Plym, and two King's Suttons which had been granted out to noble families, the first stirrings of independent life seem to have begun about 1282, when the Sutton people, wanting to be free burgesses and to have their fair and market, begged for a piece of waste ground near the port, five perches long and one broad, and a piece of land "in the withdrawal of the sea" six acres big, where the King's bailiff held his court in a certain house, and where every fishing boat coming to dry nets or sails paid toll to the King. They set up a stone cross and a stall for their market; in 1311 they made a final agreement with the Prior, and then or very soon after began yearly to elect a "Præpositus, or Custos Ville de Sutton Priors, which did then rule and govern under the King." (In the time of Edward the Third he was called mayor; Hist. MSS. Com. ix. 274-5, 279, see also 297.) In 1411 the townsmen petition that they may yearly elect a mayor and be incorporated so as to be able to buy tenements without royal license (Gross, i. 94); but apparently it was not till 1440 that they really gained their wish by the efforts of a rich merchant of Bristol, Richard Trenode, who traded with Plymouth, and of his sister Thomasine, widow of a Plymouth citizen; who at great cost and labour won for the group of hamlets their final union into the free borough of Plymouth "with one Mayor and one perpetual Commonalty"; for which the town in gratitude bound itself in a sum of £200 to maintain a chaplain in the parish church of S. Andrew to pray daily for their souls.

The important point is, however, that it was in this year, 1440, that the Plymouth Guild Merchant was either first established, or formally confirmed and given a definite position. (Gross, i. 15.) On one side a religious guild, on the other it was the governing body of the town, very jealous of its monopoly of power, as we see from the order of 1472, that every man made a freeman should be either a whole or a half-brother in Our Lady and S. George's Guild, a whole brother paying 12$d.$ yearly, and a half-brother 6$d.$; and that if any of the commons was made one of the Twenty-four he must pay 8$d.$ yearly to the Guild, while if one of the Twenty-four was made one of the Twelve he must pay 1$s.$ (Hist. MSS. Com. ix. 272.) Like the Guild at Coventry of a century earlier the fraternity seems to have been at first an organization of the more enterprising inhabitants to secure the liberties promised by charter, to make a stand against any aggressions of the Earl of Devon, and to rid themselves of some of their obligations to the Prior, on the plea of a convenient poverty, and a subtle appeal to the new King Edward the Fourth to revise arrangements made by Henry the Sixth "late in deed and not of right King of England." (Hist. MSS. Com. ix. 272.) The ancient Guild of Totnes, known as the "Guild of the Commonalty" as late as 1333, survived in full power in 1449, when it was ordered that no one shall carry the mace before the mayor save a member of the Merchant Guild (Hist. MSS. Com. iii. 344-5).

CHAPTER IX

THE TOWN DEMOCRACY

ACCORDING to a theory which is commonly accepted the English borough in its first condition, and probably during a considerable part of the twelfth and thirteenth centuries, did actually realize the ideal of a true democratic society; the spirit of popular liberty penetrated the whole community, pervading the council and assembly of the town, the leet court, the guild merchant, the companies of artizans; and under the favouring influences of equality and fraternity government was guided by common consent of the burgesses, by whom elections were conducted and administration controlled. Elsewhere it is known that the early communes, however strong their protest against the tyranny of alien despots, were within their own circle far from democratic in temper or practice; but it has been believed that in England, possibly by virtue of her people's passionate instinct for liberty, town societies wore a more popular character and expressed a loftier freedom. If this theory be exact, however, the reign of the democracy was brief, and the later history of the towns from the fourteenth century onwards is the tale of a swift decline from the enjoyment of primitive liberty into impotent subjection to the rule of a narrow and selfish oligarchy, the usurpers of the people's rights.[428] The hypothesis of a constant degradation of municipal liberty from the thirteenth to the sixteenth centuries becomes invested with extraordinary interest, since all our judgments of the part that England has played in the history of free government must be coloured and determined by the ideas we accept as to the kind of civil freedom in which her people have really believed, the classes who have held to that faith, and the means by which they have pursued it. In the absence of some strong compulsion, forcing men to yield obedience to a "select" body, we question what outward influences or what inward apathy could have led the boroughs, at the moment when wealth and prosperity crowned their vast activity, thus unanimously to betray the privileges of their constitution and to deny their early faith; for in view of the whole drift of English history, and remembering how great a part the men of the towns played at this time in English life, it may well seem inconceivable that the mental and political emancipation of the sixteenth century should have been attained by a people who in the conduct of their own local affairs had already universally abandoned a noble tradition of ancient rights and idly consented to the tyranny of a mere plutocracy.

To find an example of the primitive form of municipal institutions, and how they were at the outset understood by the people, we naturally turn to the well-known story of Ipswich. On June 29, 1200, "the whole community of the borough" elected the two bailiffs by whom it was to be governed, and four coroners, whose business it was to keep the pleas of the crown and see that the bailiffs treat rich and poor justly; and on the same day by common counsel of the town it was ordered that there should be "twelve sworn capital portmen, just as there are in other boroughs in England, who are to have full power to govern and uphold the said borough with all its liberties, to render the judgments of the town, and to ordain and do all things necessary for the maintenance of its honour." From this moment "the community" as it were unclothed itself of power to lay it on the shoulders of the bailiffs and coroners, who thereupon proceeded to act with all the authority with which they had been endued. They first appointed four approved and lawful men of each parish, who in their turn elected the twelve portmen. This being done, bailiffs, coroners, and portmen met—a little company of twelve, since bailiffs and coroners had all been appointed capital portmen too—to make ordinances about the collection of customs and the police officers by whom their decrees were to be carried out. In due time the whole community was called together to give their assent and consent to these ordinances; and they once more assembled to bestow a portion of their common land on the portmen in return for their labour in the common service, and to agree that all the laws and free customs of the town should be entered in a doomsday roll to be kept by the bailiffs.[429]

Here then we have the simplest form of early government—a council of twelve "worthy and sufficient men" to assist the mayor or bailiffs in the administration of the town, controlled by a *referendum* to the general body of burghers. The doors of the common house or the church where the councillors met stood open to all the freemen of the borough who might attend to hear discussions, even in cases where they were not allowed to join in them.[430] And in the original idea of the free borough every public act was legally supposed to require the whole consent of the community from which theoretically at least all power was ultimately derived; so that whether a new distribution of the common fields was made, or soldiers were called out and a settlement agreed upon as to their payment, or guns bought or hired for the common house or the church tower; whether an inquiry was ordained about the "livelihood" of the inhabitants and the taxes to be imposed on them, or a new law proposed, or new freemen admitted to the city liberties, or municipal officers elected, it was officially assumed that the unanimous assent of the whole people had been given in their common assembly.

The privileges of the common assembly are perhaps best defined in the customs of Hereford, drawn up in 1383, but which doubtless embody customs of older times. There we learn that at the great meetings held at Michaelmas and Easter, to which the whole people were gathered for view of frankpledge (in other words at the court leet), "the pleas of the court being finished, the bailiff and steward, on the behalf of our lord the king and the commonalty, may command that all those which are not of the liberty should go out of the house and depart from the court; and then the bailiff and steward may take notice if there are any secrets or business which may concern the state of the city or the citizens thereof, and let them proceed therein as they ought to do."[431] To these assemblies, according to the custom of Hereford, the people ought to come, and if there was anyone "which will complain of any trespasses committed, or any other thing touching the state of the city or themselves, they ought to speak the truth upon their own peril, not bringing with them any stranger ... because we do not use that strangers shall come and implead amongst us and know the secrets of the court for divers dangers that thereby may ensue."[432] In case of necessity the bailiff "by all kinds of rigour" might compel the discreeter citizens to come to the court and take their due part in its labours; and in Sandwich we know that if the burgesses summoned by bell or horn failed to appear, the "rigour" of the mayor might go as far as the sending of a serjeant to shut up all shops and work-rooms in the town, and thus compel the burghers' attention to public instead of private business.

In the general assembly there was always present the most conspicuous, if the most unwieldy, symbol of the authority of the people, and of the supreme power which was theirs, not only by law, but by an ancient customary right which to the last remained independent of statute or charter. It is true that the common gathering of the people—without executive authority, without power to initiate laws, called together merely to give or refuse assent to the deeds of the government—would in itself have given the democracy very little hold on the town magistrats in the exercise of their office. The theory of the constitution, however, was that those who were mainly charged with making and administering the laws should be yearly chosen for their work by the people whom they were called to govern. The mayor who stood at the head of the administration was, according to the common formula which pointed back to the fundamental right and first intention of the institution, elected "by assent and consent of the whole community of the town," and "in the place from of old accustomed;"[433] and as each community was allowed to decide for itself how this "assent and consent" should be ascertained, there were perhaps towns where the practice followed the theory. Thus in Sandwich the unanimous consent of the whole town was given by public vote in a general assembly. On the first Monday in December at one o'clock of the day, the town serjeant sounded the common horn, and made his cry at the fourteen accustomed places, "Every man of twelve years or more go to St. Clement's Church; there our commonalty hath need. Haste, haste!"; and when the people had gathered in the church, having first ordered the mayor to withdraw, they named him and three other natives of the town to be "put in election," one of whom was then appointed by the whole assembly voting after their degree, jurats first and freemen afterwards.[434]

This practice was no doubt rare, but the theory that the mayor was the elected servant of the whole people, enshrined in the town book of customs, in ordinance and statute, never died out of the common speech and belief of the people. "We must obey our chief bailiff as one presenting the person of the king," the burghers of Hereford say deferentially, and proceed to make him swear on assuming office "that he shall do all things belonging to his office by the counsel of his faithful citizens"; and to order that if he refused to answer complaints he should be proceeded against as for perjury; that if his accounts were not faithfully rendered all his goods should be seized; and that if "he shall be dishonest or proclaimed or suspected or convicted of any crime, he shall forthwith be put out of his place."[435] And as the mayor was the people's servant, so in theory at least his election was supposed to be of their pure free-will. "From this time forth," say the inhabitants of Wycombe in 1505, "no burgess nor foreigner make no labour, nor desire no man to speak before the day of election of the mayor for no singular desire, but every man to show their voices at their own mind, without trouble or unreasonable doing there in the time of their election."[436]

The chosen head of the people was thus to the popular sentiment the type and symbol of their freedom, and a Bristol chronicler tells us how, the mayor being accused by an enemy of the king's household, the townspeople followed after him as he was led to prison, lamenting and weeping "as sons for their natural father."[437] He was assisted by councillors also chosen to uphold the liberties of the borough; and the frequent use of elected juries in public business served still further to maintain the ancient tradition of rights vested in the people. In the manor courts of the country the jury made its way slowly and with difficulty, but in the town courts it seems to have taken complete hold very early, and to have been worked constantly and elaborately.[438] The system was applied to all manner of local business. Not only did the Leet jury in some towns, as in Nottingham and Andover, occupy itself with a vast range of affairs connected with government and legislation; but it was a universal custom to appoint representatives of the community for any special purpose. Everywhere we have glimpses of bodies of jurors chosen to elect officers, to assess taxes, to make statements as to a broken bridge, to hold discussions about tallages or about disputed boundaries[439]— transient apparitions supposed, when their work is done, to dissolve into their constituent householders, and which appear and vanish again as the centuries pass, till the burghers, recognizing in them an admirable machinery for larger uses, fix or seek to fix them into permanent existence as town councils. To a people inheriting the high and inalienable prerogatives of a chartered borough, with the right of free meeting and free speech in their general assembly, presided over by a "natural father" of their own choosing, the jury system might seem to afford the final safeguard of liberty.

Such was the ideal of a self-governing community in early times—an ideal to which in later ages men looked back wistfully, as summing up the faith and practice of a golden age. Whenever the mayor was summoned to take his oath to the people on "the Black Book" of the city, instead of the Gospels;[440] whenever according to custom the ancient ordinances of the town were yearly read before the people gathered together, the ideal of a noble liberty was proclaimed anew. The boast that the borough's rights were founded and grounded upon franchises, liberties, and free ancient customs, and not upon common law,[441] remained a living faith; and a tradition of independence sanctioned and enjoined by authority was handed down from generation to generation, by men who believed themselves born into a birthright of freedom for which they need plead neither the law of nature nor the law of Rome,[442] since it was the honest handicraft of English kings and English lawyers, and paid for in hard cash out of their own grandfathers' pockets.

But behind law and charter there lay always the great appeal to immemorial custom. In that dim time of which no memory is, a power yet more venerable and imposing than law itself had been the keeper of popular liberties; and to the last we may perhaps trace the obscure record of a double origin of rights in the two words by which the borough expressed its corporate existence— the "Citizens" or "Burgesses," and the "Commonalty" or "Community." By the common explanation of these terms they are supposed originally to have borne exactly the same meaning, and alike served to express the general body of freemen in the borough; but presently to have diverged in sense as the more important "citizens" gradually absorbed the management of public business, and appropriated to themselves the name of honour, while the lower classes were massed together as "the communitas," so that this word at last came to be little more than a contemptuous nick-name given to the mob in the later days of oligarchic rule. In the town records, however, we find these two words used from first to last in a precise and formal manner which is most characteristic of the Middle Ages; each one having its own character and meaning, and neither of them invading the place of the other. As far back as the thirteenth century "the Burgesses" already appear as distinct from the commons at large, and use their title with an official and technical significance attached to the phrase which gives it a special value.[443] The use of the word in charters and deeds seems then to denote the corporate body of citizens who had been legally endowed with certain privileges, whose association had been created by charter and was dissolved if the borough lost its franchise; and who in a vast mass of business, and especially in relations of the borough to the crown, were represented by the official body of the town which acted in their name, and especially assumed the title of "the Burgesses."

But behind this corporate body lies the "communitas"—a term which has a far earlier origin and a far deeper meaning. Whatever may be the base use of the word which has crept into chronicles and common talk, in municipal deeds and ordinances it is a name of dignity and honour—an ancient title of nobility. It carries the mind far back to the primitive society of householders in the ville, bound by mutual ties and protected by customary rights, which had preceded the free borough, and by its discipline had created the advanced type of commonwealth which is discovered to us in Ipswich at the inauguration of its new career as a chartered town. We feel the story of new beginnings such as this to be the consummation of a long history; and even under the corporate life of the citizens recognized by law we may sometimes detect the persistent survival of the ancient community, which still emerges in the half light with its consecrated title, and the remnants of its old functions ever clinging to its shadowy form. For it seems that in municipal records the "community" or "commune" possibly appears as something which existed before the corporation in time,[444] which might have its common seal separate from the mayor's seal,[445] which held property and exercised certain powers, and independent as it was of all charters, survived all loss of franchises conferred by royal grant alone. We seem to find it asserting its existence when the borough had been dismembered, and there was no longer any place for "the citizens." It sends its appeals to the King over the heads of the official caste; when an intermunicipal treaty has to be drawn up the "communitas" usually appears as the contracting body, whose members are bound together in mutual responsibility; it claimed to hold common property of the borough under its own name and apparently by some other title than the burgesses; and by its very existence it maintained to the last the tradition of an ancient free community reaching back to a time of which no memory was, and endowed with prerogatives on which neither mayor nor council dared to lay their hands.

The privileges of the early community were no doubt quickly merged in the more liberal rights which were made sure to the borough by its charter; but there was one department, the management of their common lands, in which the existence of a separate power seems to exhibit itself beyond all doubt.[446] Never did the commonalty abandon their right of control over the public estate. The division of strips of arable ground, the apportionment of pastures and closes, the letting of stalls or fields, the gathering in of rents for burgages or common property let on lease, these were things done by the act and in the name of the whole community, without any mention of "council" or "citizens"; and in one borough after another any tampering with the public estate by the governing class drove the whole body of inhabitants into the streets threatening revolution. In their claim to "have knowledge from year to year how the common ground is occupied and by whom, and if that it be not rented the commons to seize it into their hands, to that end that they may be remembered of their right, and to have profit and avail thereof" ... and "to know verily what their rent cometh to,"[447] the freemen of the fifteenth century carried on a tradition known in the boroughs two hundred years before, and in many instances their tenacious grip on the town lands was evidently one of the most important factors in the shaping of town politics.[448]

From the very beginning of municipal records, therefore, we find the town living as it were a double life—the one buttressed on either side by law and charter—the other sending roots deep down into the past, and drawing from primitive custom and tradition a sustenance which "Westminster law"[449] could neither give nor take away; the one regularly expressed in the stately proceedings of "the Citizens"—the other finding a fitful and incoherent, but no less distinctive utterance in the doings of "the commonalty;" and the two, intimately allied and constantly hostile, persisting side by side through centuries of strained but honourable union. With these immemorial traditions of franchises, liberties, and free ancient customs, it followed that when burghers set up any plea for liberties old or new they imported no revolutionary note into their demands. It is hard to tell from what source they drew their faith in a freedom which they confessed to have been lost, which indeed neither they nor their fathers had known; but it seems that the conviction never failed of an ancient type and pattern of liberty which had been proved once for all by remote ancestors of the heroic age. Townsmen professed to claim nothing more than such privileges as were "according to our Red Book as we do think"; or that had been bestowed by a charter of the House of Alfred which had once compassed them about with liberty, though it was now, alas, *casualiter amissa*; or that dated back to the time when the grace of the Lady Godiva had broken the bonds of slavery. Just as Englishmen under the rule of the foreign kings looked back with desire to the good laws of the Confessor, so the burghers had their fiction, too, of the joy of their first estate as by law established, and turned over the rolls of their treasure chest and bought copies of Magna Charta, to discover anew the light of privilege that had once irradiated the whole commonalty. We have seen in the case of Exeter how this essential faith of the people survived, as it had preceded, their study of historical documents. As the spirit of independence and discussion awoke, the conflict that was presently to be waged in the domain of religion was oddly foreshadowed in the realm of municipal politics; when the common folk demanded that they should be allowed to return to the written law in its primitive and unadulterated purity; while the guardians of established order, aldermen and councillors and great people of "the clothing,"—resting on the theory of a living tradition and its secular "developement,"—appealed with no less confidence and insistence to the majesty of law as it appeared when interpreted by the custom of generations and expounded by the scarlet-robed officials who surrounded the mayor.

NOTE A.

Mr. Maitland (Law Quarterly, January, 1893) gives a most interesting account of the customs of holding and dividing lands in various boroughs. On the whole he doubts whether the holding of land by burgesses subject to communal regulations is generally a very ancient arrangement. There seems, however, to be evidence for the antiquity of the holding of common property by the community; and it may be possible further to discover the existence of a permanent distinction between the property thus held by the community for the common use, and that held by the corporation for certain special purposes, such as payment of ferm, taxes, public servants, and the like—a distinction which rests on the different function which I have suggested in the case of those bodies.

The community of Ipswich apparently possessed land before 1200. (Gross, ii. 122, cap. xviii. 115.) For its common lands see also Hist. MSS. Com. ix. 234-7, 246. Lands were held by Wycombe (Ibid. v. 556-7). In Morpeth the "burgesses and community" make grants of land in the thirteenth century. (Ibid. vi. 527.) Andover in 1314 owned land managed by the community. (Gross, ii. 307, 326, 330.) Oxford (Boase, 47) and Chester might also be cited. Also Hythe (Hist. MSS. Com. iv. i. 432, 433), and Worcester (English Guilds, 386) and Preston (Preston Guild Records, xxiv.). The Nottingham Records mention the "land of the community" (ii. 269. See also 304-6). A grant of six acres of mosses was given to Liverpool in 1309 (Picton's Municipal Records, i. 8, 12. For the results of holding this property see 11). Birmingham held land and rights of common (Survey of the Borough and Manor, xiv. 74, 102).

Romney held the Salt Marsh, the Gorse, the Horseho, and the Harpe pastures, the old bed of the Rother, the forelands and saltpits and warrens and gardens and marshlands, "the land of the commonalty" (Hist. MSS. Com. v. 536, 537, 539, 540 3).

Lydd (Ibid. v. 525, 531-2) seems to have held marshland common on the Ripe for at least four hundred sheep, and the boroughs of Dengemarsh and Orwellstow. Its ownership of the shore as against the claims of the crown was proved in the time of Elizabeth by evidence from "the face and vieu of the antienty of the town and church, and buryall of men cross-legged and such like monuments." A seal given to the community by the archbishop at the beginning of their incorporation "long before the Conquest," as rumour said, was used (as distinguished from the bailiff's seal) as late as Elizabeth's time for the selling or letting of lands by the town. (Ibid. v. 530-2.) The cases of Lydd and Morpeth illustrate the way in which the lord of a borough granted it the possession of land along with grants of local government and independence.

Colchester had 500 acres of Lammas lands besides Mile End Heath, etc. (Cutts' Colchester, 142-4); and meadow still divided by boundary stones into strips. (Ibid. 67-8. See also for 1322 p. 142.)

Coventry owned common lands in the fourteenth century, of which there is no suggestion that they were newly acquired, and which belonged to the community and not to the corporation, and were distinct from lands or property acquired under the statute of mortmain and used for the payment of town officers, etc.

There were boroughs whose disputes about their property dated from the very beginning of their corporate existence. Southampton was already quarrelling about its common in the thirteenth century; and the Norwich citizens were engaged in a lawsuit in 1205 as to their rights of pasture on land for which rent was due to the Prior, but which the Prior could not legally either enclose or cultivate without a grant from the city. (Norwich Town Close Evidences, 4, 5. For the common lands see ibid. pp. 52-64.)

In some instances the burghers apparently did not profess to own the soil but only to hold an exclusive right to its use; and the furious excitement of the Norwich citizens (see p. 392) about a tribute of 4*s.* yearly to the Prior for a certain meadow proves how very thin the boundary line between possession and use might become.

The main evidence as to the possession of lands lies in the town archives and not in public records. It is a question for lawyers why disputes concerning them apparently were not brought before the judges of the King's Bench, but seem to have been settled at home by fighting or by arbitration. Possibly because the "communitas" had no power to sue in the law courts as a legal person. In any case it must have had all kinds of dangers to fear—the danger of having local customary law overridden by Westminster law, the danger of advertising the amount of their possessions, and a danger which is constantly present in town records, of encroachments under one pretence or another by the corporation or members of it, and the fear of which, in days when "the law is ended as a man is friended," would give reason enough for keeping out of the courts.

CHAPTER X

THE TOWN OLIGARCHY

IT is evident that if the towns had been called on for a confession of faith, the declaration of a pure and unadulterated freedom would have been in every mouth. There remains the question of how far it was found possible to carry that faith into the common practice of daily life.

We have seen how freedom was enthroned at Ipswich before the whole community of townsmen, who with outstretched hands and loud unanimous voice swore before heaven to maintain the liberties of the new republic. If, however, we glance again at Ipswich when it next comes clearly into view, a century after it had obtained its grant of privileges, there is very little trace of a golden age save for publicans and portmen. For in 1321 we find a narrow official class in the noontide of their power. Since there was no fixed day for elections they had been used by "lordly usurpation and private covin" to make bailiffs at their own pleasure secretly without consent of the people; they grievously taxed and amerced the commons for their own private purposes; they used the common seal without the common consent to the great burden and damage of the commonalty; and made new burgesses at their own pleasure without the public knowledge, so as to divide the entrance money among themselves; and by a regular system of forestalling and secret sale, merchants and inn-keepers had combined to rob the commons of their right to free and equal trade.[450] Against these abuses the burgesses sought to repeat and reinforce the ordinances of the town, but it may well be doubted whether the customary defiance of the laws of 1200 was likely to be corrected by the mere re-enactment or amendment of rules in the book of ordinances.

For it was not in Ipswich alone that the commonalty were held at the mercy of a handful of men in power, without hope of redress through their assemblies or constitutional methods at home. In 1304 justices were sent down from Westminster to inquire into a complaint of "the poor men of our city of Norwich," where, according to the petition of the commons, the rich, in defiance of all laws against forestalling, bought up victuals and goods before they came into the market, and daily inflicted other grievances on the said poor men "to the manifest deterioration of the city."[451] And again in 1307, "les menes gentz de la communaute de la ville de Norweiz" appeal to the king on the ground that an inquiry by justices had been promised them concerning the fines and tallages which weighed them down; the poor people, they said, had been unjustly taxed by the bailiffs and the rich ("les riches"), "but on the hearing, the bailiffs and the rich spoke so fair to the said poor people, promising them redress and that they should have no cause to complain in future, and that no tallage should be levied from them without their common assent, that the poor men ceased from their suit. But now the said bailiffs and rich have levied two hundred marks without warrant and threaten to levy a still higher tallage."[452] The law of the matter was clear enough, for only a year or two before the principle that the bailiffs could only assess taxes "by the assent of the whole of the commonalty or of the greater part of the same" had been re-affirmed;[453] and the king accordingly sent answer, "If tallage have been made without assent of the commonalty, let them have a writ against those who have imposed such tallage to answer before the king, and that henceforth it be not done."

It is, however, hard to say what amount of relief to the mean folk was actually given by such an order from high quarters. At the very same time, in 1304, the people of the neighbouring borough of Lynn were seeking protection against the ruling burgesses, and charged them with the usual trespasses—with assessing tallages without the unanimous consent of the community; levying these tallages and other great sums of money from the poor and but moderately endowed men of the community; employing the sums thus raised for their own use and not for the advantage of the community or the reparation of the town; forestalling goods on the way to market; and establishing and using corruptions contrary both to common and to merchant law. The great people of Lynn, however, easily put themselves beyond all fear of justice by simply buying from the king in 1305[454] letters of pardon and release for the crimes of which they were accused—letters which evidently left them free to go on in the same course. Upon which the people instinctively turned to their natural ally, the lord of the manor himself, and through the powerful aid of the Bishop, and his aid only, were able to win from the mayor in 1309 the composition which became the charter of their liberties, according to which all the "unreasonable grievous" tasks and tallages laid by "the great men of the town upon the mean people and the poor"—or as the Latin version has it by the potentiores on the mediocres and inferiores—and their "grievous distressing so violently of them," were to come to an end, and taxes were henceforth to be assessed in due measure according to the three degrees of prosperity.[455]

It is evident that we need not wait for the fifteenth century to discover an oligarchical system of administration which was in its full strength in the English boroughs as early as 1300, and can even be traced back at least fifty years earlier. In the middle of the thirteenth century the commons of Lincoln, having a dispute with the lord of S. Botolph's fair about tolls, formally withdrew altogether from the fair till they should obtain a remedy from the king; but two sons of the mayor and two other burghers, rich traders who did not want their business interrupted, and who were evidently town officials with command of the common seal, gave the lord a charter promising a yearly rent of £10 from the Lincoln citizens, and this "without any assent or consent of the commonalty." It was in vain that the people made remonstrance; the charter was still binding in 1276,[456] and in 1325 the inhabitants of Lincoln were still without defence against the "great lords of the said city" who formed the corporation. While "les grauntz Seigneurs" themselves paid nothing, the "mean people" were arbitrarily taxed without their own consent; they alone were forced to keep the nightly watch; they paid their murage tax for the building of the wall, and the rulers used the money for their own purposes and rendered no accounts to the people;[457] and the pitiful appeal of the commonalty to the king praying him to provide some remedy for their grievances only proved how helpless they were to influence the governing body which was supposed to rule solely by their consent. In like manner the mayor and other officers of Oxford were charged in 1294 with exacting tallages without the king's order or the town's consent, applying the town revenues to their own uses, raising loans without proper receipts, and collecting money for expenses of the rich on juries and assizes while the poor were left to pay their own costs.[458] Probably the richer party secured the jury, for the verdict was given against the burgher who had instituted the suit; but his complaint is so absolutely similar to those raised in other towns at the same time that we can scarcely doubt its truth.[459]

The inner contentions of Bristol[460] and of Andover[461] in the early years of the fourteenth century repeat in varying forms the same story of a few rich burghers managing the whole machinery of administration, and of a commonalty whose voice was often scarcely heard in elections, who were unable to secure the just assessment of taxes, or to prevent the money from being devoted to improper uses, and who daily saw the laws of trade—the assize of bread or beer, the injunctions against forestalling and regrating and a thousand tricks of commerce—diverted to the convenience of the rich officials, while the common folk patiently expiated their sins before the judgment seat of the great offenders who sat in careless immunity on their high places.

It is manifestly hard to find in the thirteenth and fourteenth centuries the happy age of the historian's dream, when "there was a warmer relation between high and low, when each class thought more of its duties than its interests, and religion, which was the same to all, was really believed in. Under such conditions," we are told, "inequality was natural and wholesome;" and apparently an age of innocence and peace attested the fostering care of a universal faith; for according to this theory, so highly commended and so widely believed, it was only "when religion became opinion, dubious more or less and divorced from conduct, while pleasures became more various and more attainable, the favoured classes fell away from the intention of their institution, monopolized the sweets of life and left the bitter to the poor."[462]

Whatever "the intention of their institution" may have been, however, there is not a particle of proof that the intention of the favoured classes themselves did at this time differ sensibly from that which prevailed at the Reformation; nor were the dominant folk of town or country disposed voluntarily to nail their interests on the cross of duty—whether we consider the knight "hunting hardily" hares and foxes,[463] and wholly regardless of his oath to the labourer "to keep him and his chattel as covenant was between them;"[464] or the lord with his loud laugh calling for his rent;[465] or the trader filling his pockets in "deceit of the poor commons," the alderman adding field to field, the cook and brewer building their burgages out of the pence of the poor. The relations of inequality, in the exceedingly bitter form in which they were then known, may have seemed natural, or perhaps supernatural, to an age when all life, social, economic, and political, was brought under the universal sway of dogma and superstition; but it is certain that they were not held to be wholesome by those who suffered, and whose struggles to win the freedom so long promised to them in ordinance and charter fill the town records of succeeding centuries.

For in these young republics formidable difficulties lay in the way of securing any popular control whatever over administration. In the first place the general assembly, which was to be the pledge of the people's liberties, and to assure to them the final word about the taxes they had to pay and the manner in which they were to be governed, proved in its actual working but a poor security for freedom. It would seem sometimes that in the hurry and excitement of expanding trade, men busy in their shops had as little time or attention to bestow on serious politics as American citizens of a later date; or perhaps the very opposite accident might befall the borough, and a heterogeneous and unmanageable mob gathered at the place of assembly, where strangers and unenfranchised journeymen pushed their way in among the lawful citizens. But a tumultuous gathering of ignorant and over-tasked artizans and poor householders crowding from the narrow lanes of the borough must manifestly have been a very rare and occasional expedient, and at the best meant an assembly incapable of real business. In general it would seem that any small number of burgesses who happened to be present at a meeting in the common hall or at the court leet, or a select group of the better class specially summoned by the mayor,[466] were taken to represent the general body of inhabitants, and their consent was legally counted as conveying the assent of the burghers at large. From the very first, and under the most favourable circumstances, it is evident that the assembly gave no real security to the commonalty, that through its gatherings they could never hope to bring sustained or efficient pressure to bear on the governing class, and that "the entire assent and consent of the whole community" was for the most part simply taken for granted. If the theory of government by the people for the people already existed in law books and ordinances the means of realizing such an ideal had yet to be found.

Nor must it be forgotten that from the very first no man of the people could hope to aspire to any post in the administration of the town. All important public offices were confined to persons of a certain station, and "the rank of a mayor" or "the rank of a sheriff" were well-known mediæval phrases which expressed a comfortable social position maintained by an adequate income. Councillors and chief officers were chosen from the class of "magnates"[467]—men not bound by the law of frankpledge and possibly holding a position of some authority—of whom there are traces in Norwich and possibly in other cities; or from the "good and sufficient" men of the borough; or from the class who were technically known as the "probi homines," the "good" or "credible" or "lawful men" privileged to serve as legal assessors in the civic courts and "credible witnesses" to bargains, and who had probably come to be regarded as an official class and gradually organized into a separate caste.[468] This choice of wealthy officials ultimately depended of course on the custom of those days by which the chief officers and the townsfolk were held mutually responsible for defaults; so that in the interests of the people themselves, as well as of the king, it was important to secure men of substance whose possessions formed a guarantee to both parties—a guarantee which was by no means originally a figure of speech, as we see from the case of the Lincoln bailiffs in 1276, when the receipts for paying the ferm were diminished, "wherefore they who have once been bailiffs of Lincoln can scarcely rise from poverty and misery."[469] The opulent class who bore the chief burden of responsibility shared the compensating pleasures of power. We have seen the primitive simplicity with which at Ipswich twelve portmen divided among themselves all the posts of bailiffs, coroners, and councillors; and in fact among the handful of "worthy" men which could be produced in modest little market-towns,[470] whose clustered dwellings of wood and plaster, bordering narrow alleys that ran to the central market-place, lay almost hidden in fields and gardens, the burghers had actually no great choice of rulers. From generation to generation the chief municipal offices were handed down in the few leading families of the place. A great merchant would take the command again and again while the whole town lay at his discretion, for though a universal law forbade the continuous holding of office and usually fixed an interval of two or more years before re-election, either the law was persistently ignored, or as soon as the period of retirement had elapsed, power inevitably fell back to its former possessor.[471] How greatly this state of things was determined by economic conditions we may see from the fact that in a place like Nottingham, where wealth was widely distributed, it does not seem that any single family rose to very marked supremacy;[472] and in general a comparison of lists of town officers indicates that as the growth of trade in the fifteenth century increased the numbers of well-to-do burghers and merchants, there was a corresponding variety in the names of men entrusted with office. At the best however the upper class was but a little one, and usually the corporation with its one or two councils composed of twelve and twenty-four members, or even of twenty-four and forty-eight, as well as the retired magnates who constituted "the clothing," and a whole army of officials of various kinds, recorder, town clerk, chamberlains or treasurers, aldermen, decennaries of the market, bailiffs, coroners, arbitrators, jurors, and the like, must have absorbed a very considerable proportion of the well-to-do inhabitants. A close caste was easily developed out of the compact body of merchants and thriving traders who formed the undisputed aristocracy of the town, and whose social pre-eminence doubtless went far to establish their political dominion.

And if very little space was practically found in mediæval times for democratic theories of government, whether in the conception of a governing class, or in the working of the general assembly, still less are they to be found in the prevailing views as to representation. In the case of Ipswich we have seen how rapidly the great body of the townspeople retire from the scene when they have fulfilled their first simple function of electing bailiffs and coroners. It is the bailiffs and coroners who nominate the committee to elect the portmen,[473] and then the twelve between them take charge in a general way of the borough and its affairs, while the commons go back to attend to their own business and are henceforth only from time to time summoned for a general assembly, where they gather like a Greek chorus to view with official eyes the progress of the drama, and to applaud in due form the action of the ultimate executive or express an expected and resigned acquiescence with all their will. People talked, it is true, of election by the whole community, and this was the theory of ordinance and charter, but the universal fashion of the day in all ranks and classes was to adopt some more or less complicated system of indirect election which, whether intentionally or not, was admirably suited to the use and convenience of the minority. The nobles who under the provisions of Oxford formed the council of Fifteen to assist Henry the Third used exactly the same devices as were of common experience among merchants and artizans and burghers; for not only in trading or in social-religious guilds were the members accustomed to choose their governor through a select committee of four, five, seven, eight, or twelve men; but in the boroughs themselves the plans by which the sovereign people delegated their power to a few "worthy and sufficient" citizens were so ingenious and elaborate that we may well doubt whether the majority had ever any chance at all of making their will prevail. In some cases indeed the leading people of the town were altogether independent of popular election, and hereditary owners of the wards sat in the high places of the hall in virtue of their landed property,[474] not of the people's will; while in others a guild merchant apparently imposed its own council on the community at large.[475]

Nor can we wonder at anxiety to secure an efficient governing class if we consider for a moment the work that lay before the council. From the affairs of a pig-market and the letting of butchers' stalls they were required to pass to business of the most complicated kind—to constitute a Board of Trade concerned with inland and foreign commerce; a Foreign Office constantly busied with the external relations of the town, whether to overlord, or king, or rival boroughs; a legal committee responsible for all the complicated law business that might arise out of any one of these relations, or out of the defence of the chartered privileges of the borough; a Treasury Board whose incomings were drawn in infinitesimal proportions from the most varied and precarious sources, and whose outgoings included every possible payment with which any public body has ever had to deal. The king might call on them for the supervision of the staple trade, the management of river basins, the draining of marshes, the collection of taxes, the administration of justice, the local carrying out of laws framed by Parliament, the guarding of the coast, the provisioning and training of detachments of the national army. The responsibility thrown on them by the central government was constantly increased as time went on; and there was probably nothing which proved so important in tightening the hold of the oligarchy on government as the appointment of a certain number of the upper council to be justices of the peace, having a formidable authority over the working classes, besides the power to draw into their own hands a mass of business which had once gone to the court leet of the burghers.

No doubt the official caste from the beginning sufficiently appreciated the pleasures of power not to deprecate their increase; but apart from any question of greedy usurpation, it was inevitable under such conditions that a strong government should have been formed of experts who need not necessarily be changed every year or elected by a popular vote. The date at which some custom of this kind became established is probably much earlier than is commonly supposed; and there is evidence to shew that it often preceded by a long time the charters which make it legally binding. Possibly indeed the administrative despotism of a narrow oligarchy was often as old as the independence of the borough itself. The need for capable rulers may have been even greater at the perilous outset of its life than in its later times of confident strength; and when we remember the imperfection of the primitive machinery for ascertaining the popular will, the weakness of the general assembly, and the limitations put on public election, it is evident that the theory of a free and equal people electing their own government by the unanimous consent of the whole community, and controlling administration by a constant criticism, was a theory which could never have been practically carried into effect; which as a matter of fact the governing class had no wish to encourage, and which the mass of the governed had neither the cohesion nor the intelligence to enforce.

Once in authority it must be admitted that the ruling class carried themselves bravely, shirking neither responsibility nor power. In their splendid robes of office, with furs and stripes and rich colours changed at every great occasion to make a more imposing show, the municipal officers were the dazzling centre of every procession and public function in the town—at Advent services, at the bull-baiting and public games,[476] at the pageant of Corpus Christi, or the yearly solemnity of recounting to the people the ordinances and liberties of the borough. Strict discipline, unquestioned authority, a belief in firm government, were prominent in their administration. Of the general body of burgesses and craft guilds implicit obedience was required, and the corporation allowed neither discussion nor interference with its decrees. Windows through which inquisitive townsmen peeped into the chamber where they consulted were blocked up; listeners under the eaves "to hear the words of the council" were violently discouraged; severe rules forbade the meddling of too active citizens, and fines and imprisonment fell on those who "in an abusive manner" called a councillor a "Fliperarde,"[477] or who wickedly "wished that all the jurats had been burnt in the common ship," or with "opprobrious and crooked words" declared that they were "false thieves," or that they "were looked upon at Dover as so many grooms."[478] Administrative capacity went hand in hand with the self-assertion and exclusive temper of a successful class. To the townspeople, amid the confusion of national revolutions and civil war, the mayor remained a standing witness to the enduring forces of an order triumphant over discord and confusion; as in Exeter, where between 1477 and 1497 the citizens had seen a skilfully organized revolt shattered before the municipal power, and a victorious mayor holding office undisturbed under four successive kings, three of whom had come to the crown by the violent death or deposition of their predecessors.[479]

There is perhaps no better type of the superior town official than the Common Clerk, in his dress of sanguine cloth striped with violet rays, or of more sober green bordered with fur.[480] The business of his office came into great consideration with the growth of local liberties. In the fifteenth century there was scarcely a single town which did not require to have its "Custumal" written out afresh from the faded and worn-out copies made in earlier centuries,[481] while in a vast number of cases, where the old French or Latin was no longer understood by the townsfolk, the writer had not only to decipher and copy the old tattered roll, but to translate it.[482] Perhaps portions of the gospels were needed—"enough to swear by."[483] Every town also instituted the making of its own "Domesday Book," its black book or white book or red book as the case might be, with copies of all deeds, wills, and charters relating to municipal affairs;[484] and whenever a legal question arose or local liberties were imperilled new search was made in the chest containing the town "evidences" on which the municipal privileges depended, and copies were written out of Acts of Parliament,[485] extracts from Domesday, Magna Charta,[486] or legal documents such as the New Tenures by Lyttleton.[487] The clerk must be able to translate and to read in the mother tongue to the community any letters or orders sent from Westminster. He had to expound legal technicalities to the council, and to use them effectively in the town's interest, not only at Westminster, but in the innumerable disputes that arose between borough and borough as to the interpretation of conflicting charters.[488] Elaborate accounts of municipal expenditure were made yet more arduous by the system of Roman numerals which constantly baffled his best efforts at exact addition. The keeping of the town rolls in general was a very serious occupation; in the time of Edward the Fourth the yearly rolls of Ipswich (called Dogget Rolls from the clerk's docquet or table of contents) form bundles as big as a garden roller;[489] and in Nottingham twenty rolls were covered within and without in a single year with the list of pleas against foreigners alone. In fact, the supply of parchment began to fall short of the prodigious demands of the town clerks, who were driven to take to paper, either to economize the trifling sum allowed them for the expense of parchment, or in obedience to a direct order from the corporation.[490] As they added roll to roll and book to book, they from time to time relieved the tedious labour by adorning the town accounts with sketches and ornaments, with a snatch of French song or a few quibbles or catches of very moderate wit,[491] with a rugged ballad on the evils of over-eating,[492] or a final sigh of satisfaction from a German copyist, "Explicit hic totum; pro Christo da mihi potum!"[493]

The town clerk, in fact, was to the local government what two centuries earlier the trained lay-lawyers had been to the central administration. From mere superiority of education, as a scholar and linguist, an accomplished lawyer, something of a historian and an antiquary, a skilled accountant, a scribe trained to finer penmanship and more exact views of spelling than the ordinary councillor, or even than the mayor himself, the clerk must have exercised an easy intellectual supremacy.[494] Responsible only to the mayor, holding his post year after year in perfect security, he remained among the changing officers about him a permanent force, a municipal chancellor in whom was embodied a continuous tradition of administration and a fixed jurisprudence.[495] Thriving towns of the fifteenth century vied with one another in seeking out able professionals for the post. Bridgewater engaged a man who seems to have been in practice as attorney or notary public in Oxford; and as early as the fourteenth century a chamberlain of London wrote letters under the common seal at Romney. Winchester looked yet farther afield, and seems to have employed a German.[496] An able lawyer in those days could command the market, as we see by the story of Thomas Caxton (probably a brother of William Caxton the printer), who spent a busy professional career of forty years going from town to town wherever he could best sell his services. A native of Tenterden, he was brought up to the law, and in 1436 was engaged in a plea of debt in Romney against one William-at-the-Mill. In 1454 he was practising as an attorney at Tenterden, and was the leading man of law in its negotiations with Rye to resist the union of the two towns into a single corporation. In 1458 he entered the service of Lydd, which was then in the thick of its troubles about boundaries and franchises, and was paid £2 13s. 4d. a year, or double the salary of his predecessor, and in addition was soon after promised a gown every year, while ultimately his pay was raised to £4—a sum which at that time was only given by great commercial towns such as Bristol or Southampton.[497] On his resignation Lydd returned to its old custom and once more paid to his successor the original salary of 6s. 8d. a quarter, but the corporation still continued to employ Caxton constantly on very profitable terms for himself, often sending him to London on business, or to carry on negotiations with the king. In 1470, when Lydd had been running into danger on every side, first sending men to fight under Warwick, and then paying £9 for another body of troops to go to the help of King Edward, the burghers made Caxton their treasurer, and two years later he was elected bailiff, and a town clerk put under him of his own training. We next find him in 1474 as clerk in Romney; but he was called back again to Lydd in 1476, and employed to write out its "customall" in his fine bold hand. A yet more important town however now cast longing eyes on the successful lawyer, and he was drawn away from Lydd to Sandwich, where he finally settled down as common clerk.

In fact for professional men of talent in the middle class a new and comparatively brilliant career was now opened in the towns.[498] Nicholas Lancaster, town clerk of York from 1477 to 1480, was a bachelor of laws, who in 1483 became one of the king's council, was in 1484 alderman of York, and in 1485 mayor.[499] Easingwold, who kept the rolls of Nottingham for nearly thirty years (from 1478 to 1506), wrote himself down as "gentleman" among the yeomen, braziers, and smiths, who paid their 6s. 8d. along with him to gain the freedom of the borough,[500] and in his later signatures still kept up the solitary distinction of this title, which scarcely occurs in the records save after his name. An educated man with a very tolerable knowledge of Latin, though he preferred English, he served his adopted town well, and in his time the old court rolls, which had been carelessly kept in paper books for thirty years before his coming, were replaced by parchment rolls with very full and elaborate accounts in a singularly beautiful and exact writing.[501]

It is obvious that in governing bodies whose members were thus distinguished from the common mass of burghers by wealth, social position, culture, who were independent of the people they ruled, very watchful in the matter of their legal or customary rights, and abundantly supplied in case of difficulty with advice in the law by the recorder or the town clerk or the special counsel retained in their service, no influence was wanting which could foster the official spirit in its most extreme form, with its pride of position, its administrative pretensions, its love of legal definition, and its anxiety for "good order." "The worshipful men of the great clothing" or "the imperial co-citizens" of some very minor borough ruled for their own ends with frankness and capacity; while their natural rallying cry of "good rule and substantial order"[502] was so well understood at court that they could always confidently count on support from that quarter. The alarm of the mob, which since the Peasant Revolt had troubled statesmen at Westminster as well as aldermen in the boroughs, drew the ruling classes generally into close alliance; and towards the end of the fifteenth century, we constantly find the town officers turning with apprehension to the court for aid, and kings anxiously lending succour to the corporations. The Wars of the Roses and dynastic quarrels which once appeared to pass so lightly over the boroughs, scarcely touching them with a passing alarm of material calamity, were not brought to a close before they had left a terrible and abiding impress on the civil life of the people. The shaking of the national security, the wild hopes and the panic-stricken fears of rebellion, had their inevitable conclusion in tightening the hold of authority. In the boroughs the governing bodies, terrified at the signs of bitter discontent in the subject populace, and justly trembling lest under some feint of political obedience, the mass of the people might be arrayed against their rulers and clamour against wrong and injustice might fill the streets, raised a cry for protection against social anarchy; and the cry was eagerly responded to by kings whose title to the crown was their strong will and heavy hand. The progress of liberty was violently arrested by the fears that shook the settled classes before threatenings of revolt. "It seemeth that the world is all quavering; it will reboil somewhere," onlookers said; men walked with redoubled wariness in an "unstable" and "right queasy" world,[503] and while anxious kings urged the mayor and his council to make good and fearful example of indisposed commons, aldermen gladly locked the doors of the town-hall, and cast into the freeman's dungeon the burgher who still prated of a free community.

NOTE A.

We do not know when or how the leading men of Bristol assumed a position of special privilege. All we know is that troubles grew out of a quarrel about customs in the port and market, &c., in which fourteen of the citizens "were seen to have the prerogative," while the community asserted that the burgesses were all of one condition and were equals in liberties and privileges. After many disputes the case was brought before the judges of the king's court, but the Fourteen so arranged matters that foreigners or aliens were associated with them in the inquisition, which the community alleged to be against the liberties of the town. Seeing that their arguments were rejected and that their cause was going to be lost, not by reason but by favour, the leaders of the people angrily went out of the judgment hall and proclaimed to the mob that the judges were favouring their enemies. The whole people, called out by the ringing of the common bell, flocked into the hall; and there was terrible clamour and a free fight with fists and clubs; twenty men were killed; and terror seized alike on the noble and ignoble, who tried to escape by windows and roofs at the risk of their lives; while even the judges prayed to be allowed to fly by the help of the mayor, who himself could scarcely soothe the "vast crowd of malefactors." About eighty men were summoned for the riot, and not appearing before the judges were banished, but stayed on nevertheless comfortably in the town and were well cared for by their fellow rebels. It was in fact the Fourteen who judged it wise to leave Bristol, thinking it useless to remain in such a storm. (See the extract from the life of Edward the Second by a monk of Malmesbury given in Seyer's Bristol, ii. 94.)

To quell this tumult the king in 1312 took the government into his own hand and appointed Bartholomew of Baddlesmere, constable of the castle, as custos; but the mayor and bailiffs, asserting that the letter had not been addressed to the *community*, and further that the custody of the town had been previously given to them, refused to obey orders, and kept the gates of the castle and town for thirty-five weeks, building a wall against the castle and refusing to let the king's men go out to fetch victuals save at the will of the community. Of their own authority they made John the Taverner mayor, John of Horncastle and Richard Legate bailiffs, and John Hazard coroner, without making them take their oath of king or constable; and by force of arms seized the custody of the prison, levied for their own purposes the revenues from the town and port which ought to have been collected for the king, and administered justice. The king's judges and servants were imprisoned or driven from the town; the Fourteen and half a dozen partizans, who had mostly been in office, were not allowed to return to the town in spite of the king's injunction, and the community seized their goods to the value of £2,000, and drove out their wives, freemen, and tenants.

The rebellion lasted for two years. In 1316 six citizens representing the community of Bristol were summoned before the king's council to answer for these offences. They denied the charges, and refused to submit unless life and limb, rents and land, were secured to them. The king, looking on the case as one of evil example, ordered Bristol to be besieged by sea and land, and after attempting to hold out for some days in the hope that the troops might be called away to the Scotch war, the town surrendered half in ruins. The leaders were put in prison and the multitude terrified by a series of heavy punishments. The banished party returned in triumph to power, and appeared, twelve of them, before the king's council, with the allotted fine of four thousand marks to have pardon for all the city's offences, and to have back the franchise of the town. The rebel mayor and his immediate friends, excluded from mercy, went in their turn into exile. (See the account extracted from Rolls of Parliament 9 Edward II. by Seyer. Memoirs of Bristol, ii. 89 to 105.)

After this matters seem to have gone on as before, a few influential families still taking the leading place. One, Turtle, was mayor ten times, and another, Tilly, held office for four years. But in 1344, the popular party insisted on the appointment of Forty-eight "of the chiefest and discreetest" burgesses, to be the mayor's councillors and assistants. When Bristol was made into a county in 1373 the new charter recognized the system established in 1344, and provided that the mayor and sheriff with the assent of the commonalty should choose a Council of Forty, whose consent was required for all ordinances, and who took part in municipal elections; while the five aldermen of the wards were chosen by the people from among the ex-mayors or members of the common council. By a later charter of 1499 it was settled that six aldermen were to be elected for life by the mayor and common council, and were to have the authority of London aldermen (Charter Henry VII., 1499. Seyer's Charters and Letters Patent of Bristol, 123), while the common council itself was to be elected by the mayor and two aldermen chosen by him, with the assent of the commonalty.

CHAPTER XI

THE TOWN COUNCIL

THE fifteenth century has been popularly taken as the time when victory crowned the local oligarchies and liberty fled from the English boroughs, and the restriction of popular rights has sometimes been attributed to the charters of incorporation given under Henry the Sixth. In this, as in many other respects, the luckless age has long lain under a heavy weight of accusations which might more fairly be distributed among other centuries; for in most towns the work of adapting the primitive town constitutions to oligarchic government had practically been accomplished long before the days of Henry.[504] Indeed it seems as though the characteristic movement of this time, a movement which naturally sprang out of the industrial developement of the Middle Ages, was the effort to enlarge the sphere of political activity. Far from being a time of apathy in local politics, it was a time of acute excitement. Townspeople on all sides were awakening to the sense that the free community of which their fathers had talked had still to be created; and were making perhaps the first organized attack on the monopoly of "the magnates," and the first practical attempt to deal with the problem which confronts Englishmen to-day—the problem of how to combine popular control with good administration. Traditions of ancient rights which the commonalty theoretically held by law and charter mingled with the ambitions of a new world of enterprise, and, as we have seen, the manufacturing classes by asserting their right to have some share in the work of government, did here and there for the first time bring the commonalty into the council chamber.

The problem of government was indeed no longer so simple as it had been when "the magnates" first easily assumed the control of the town destinies. As the centuries went on, bringing their commercial and industrial revolutions, the growth of capital and the organization of labour, new standards of administration and a more anxious vigilance on the part of the central authority, the balance of power in local governments began to sway to one side or the other under the pressure of contending forces. Every political tendency of the time went to strengthen the administrative body, and maintain the authority of the select council. But, on the other hand, the mass of the commons were neither so poor nor so helpless as they had once been. The manufacturing classes waxed fat and kicked. Enriched by trade and disciplined by industrial training, organized in guilds, and practised in such self-government as this implied, restless under growing taxation, clamorous for advancement in well-being, tormented by petty tyranny, they were growing into a real power; and amid all the ugliness and violence and suffering of the troubled crowd which Langland brings before us at the close of the fourteenth century, we cannot but feel the stir of the coming revolution, and of a world transforming itself under the power of some new force. To the eye of the contemporary observer the merchants have become too clever at their business, the lawyers too shrewd, the common people everywhere too independent; the poor are less content to starve, and are looking for the easiest ways of getting hot meat and ale and comfortable chimney corners; the ploughman will not work till hunger has buffeted him so "that he looked like a lantern all his life after";[505] if the peasant was for a moment safe from actual starvation, he was ready to defy the very Statute of Labourers itself.[506] On all sides there is the movement of a growing discontent[507]—the criticism and impatience that are born of a new hope. We have a sense of the vague trouble of a people grown too rich and too busy and too energetic for the old restraints—a people that had outgrown its "childish things." Nature itself seemed to have been dragged within the circle of some mysterious change, and its old stately courses turned into confusion—

"Neither the sea nor the sand nor the seed yieldeth
As they wont were....
.   .   .   .   .   .

Weatherwise shipmen now and other witty people
Have no belief to the lyft nor to the lode star.
Astronomers all day in their art failen
That whilom warned men before what should befall after."[508]

In presence of such a world—a world in restless and perpetual movement—it is difficult to make general statements of what was likely or "natural" to happen. In some cases the governing class, terrified by the new force which was stirring the masses of the people, eluded any serious conflict by making terms with the upper groups of the middle class, thus detaching to their own side the leaders of revolt; and a new oligarchy was formed out of the upper and middle sections of the community—an oligarchy stronger and wider than the old, and with promise of more permanent existence. In other cases the people had the advantage, and a more liberal settlement was for a time brought about in the interests of the commonalty; so that while the Town Council of one borough appears as a chosen band ostentatiously arrayed for the protection of a successful oligarchy, we may see it figuring in another as the advanced guard of the commons entrenched in the enemy's country. Never, in fact, did any people endeavour to solve the difficulty of creating an efficient government with such endless resource and ingenuity as the mediæval burghers, who as need arose, flung themselves into the art of constitution making with all the persistence, temperance, energy, and economy in patching up ancient models and finding new use for old materials in which Englishmen for centuries have found their pride.[509] The charters granted to them allowed wide limits within which they might try their experiments and plan their own mode of government at their will. A local scheme of administration was devised; and when they had framed their system it might depend on the sanction of local custom, or for greater security and authority it might be defined and ordained by a new charter; and if again the chartered constitution proved unsatisfactory, the townsfolk had only to agree among themselves on new methods, and have them once more embodied in a fresh grant from the Crown.

The whole character of municipal government was thus indefinitely modified by local circumstances—by the position or the special industry of the borough, the nature of its tenure and its compact with the lord of the manor, the power of the merchants or the owners of property within its walls; and nothing is more surprising than the variety and intricacy of political systems with which the mediæval burghers were familiar. As free in theory as they were free in practice, under bondage to no fixed democratic creed, they adopted indiscriminately any method that commended itself—whether of election direct or indirect, election tempered by nomination, minority representation, public voting, or arrangements by which voters recorded their will secretly one by one.[510] Every borough, for example, had its own fashion of choosing its mayor. We have seen that in Sandwich the whole people made the election; but in Winchester the council of twenty-four chose two men and the outgoing mayor nominated one of them as his successor;[511] while in Southampton the plan was reversed and the outgoing mayor in the presence of bailiffs and council nominated two burgesses from whom the assembly was bound to elect one,[512] nor could an occasional outbreak of popular discontent do more than convince the commons afresh of their true impotence. Midway between these extremes came an endless variety of customs, often of elaborate complexity.[513] When the selection of the mayor was nominally left to the whole "people in the hall," their choice was often limited and checked in one way or another. They must take him from among the upper council; or from among men who had already served as mayors or sheriffs; or they must send two names to the first chamber for approval, of whom this discreet company might choose one; or perhaps the council itself nominated two or three candidates for the freemen's choice, as a curb to the license of popular judgment; or the matter was yet more effectually settled by a decision that the council alone should elect the mayor.[514] In some boroughs a special jury was chosen by the citizens for the purpose of electing the chief officers—either a single jury of twelve as at Bridgnorth,[515] or a double jury of twenty-four as at Colchester or Preston;[516] and the election of the jury itself was often far from being a simple matter, as we see at Lynn. Occasionally the necessity of recognizing various interests within the town and giving to them special influence in the municipal constitution seems to have added a local complication, as in Canterbury, where the aldermen were in early times hereditary owners and lords of the several wards of the town, and retained in consequence rights which were not finally extinguished till the reign of Henry the Eighth; here two "triours" were chosen, one by the two outgoing bailiffs together with the aldermen, the other by the commons or "council of the thirty-six"; these two triours then appointed twelve men from among the council, and the twelve finally chose the bailiffs for the next year.[517]

In appointing the other members of the corporation there was the same diversity of method, with a free use of the plan of nomination, so that a mixed system was sometimes evolved where half the corporation was elected by the people and the remainder nominated by the mayor or council. The town councillors might be chosen yearly by the burgesses, or by a jury nominated for the purpose; they might be turned into a new class of permanent officials by being elected for life; or made into an exclusive aristocratic body by being allowed to fill up all vacancies themselves; and in towns with a double council any two of these plans might be tried together; or both bodies might be chosen by some one system. An inevitable tendency to make themselves as independent as possible of the people over whom they ruled naturally guided the councillors to the belief that the manner of their election was best managed by themselves, and there were cases where not only the upper but the lower chamber became self-electing bodies in which the members held office for life.[518]

In short every conceivable experiment in government was tried in one town or another, or in the same town at different times, to the great confusion of systematic order. In one the original council of twelve or twenty-four might be maintained in its early representative character;[519] in another its constitution was gradually transformed. Sometimes besides the upper council the burghers set up a second chamber of sixteen or eighty or twenty-four or thirty-six or forty or forty-eight,[520] and the "worshipful and discreet members of the clothing," or the "high election," had to share their powers more or less with the "low election", "the sad and discreet" company arrayed in plain suits with no finery of fur and velvet. Hereditary owners of land might sit on the council of one borough, and non-burgesses join the council of another. Aldermen might be forced on the people, or they might be forbidden by the authorities.[521] As occasion served the townsfolk perhaps attempted to form a representative council out of a jury of electors or of arbitrators, or from a committee of the common assembly, or delegated members from the crafts.

Underneath this apparent confusion certain broad tendencies can be discerned; and it may be that with further study these tendencies will be found to have borne a different character in various districts of the country, and to have been influenced not only by political traditions, but by special conditions of trade and industry. As yet there are not collected materials to justify any general theory; but something may be learned by observing the constitutional changes which actually took place in a few boroughs; and by judging how far these constitutional changes can be adequately summed up in the theory of a continuous backsliding from popular freedom to the despotism of a privileged group of opulent traders. A few instances which have been chosen at hazard may serve to illustrate how various were the conditions under which civic life was carried on, and how these conditions influenced the political situation, and were reflected in the temper and form of government. They fall naturally into three groups.

I. Occasionally it seems to have happened, as at Southampton, that the original single council of twelve was retained till after the Reformation, in spite of sporadic attempts of the commons to vindicate their strength, whether through the general assembly or by some other means.

II. In the great majority of towns however a second council was formed—in most cases by creating a sort of committee of the general assembly. Whether the common people refused to come to assemblies as was stated at Norwich, or whether their absence was but a pretext of the governors, it is hard to say; but apparently a system commonly grew up of calling together on important occasions a group of selected citizens. Bailiffs and mayors who were anxious to get rid of unruly and, as they judged, superfluous elements in the town meetings; or who wished to compel a sufficient number of voters to come together to carry on business; might fall back on the expedient of sending out summonses to certain chosen householders whenever an assembly was to be held, and might thus in informal fashion create a sympathetic and obedient gathering to endorse the action of the ruling body. Presently perhaps fines were inflicted in case the summons was neglected; and when it was once clearly established that a definite number of members were thus bound to assemble at the mayor's bidding for the conduct of business, and when further this body was given the power of the whole assembly in deciding on all matters that concerned the common interest, it is clear that a council of the commons had been created—a permanent body endowed, whether with or without their consent, with the burghers' rights of legislation. In a number of towns, such as Coventry, Hereford, Leicester, and many more, the summons to the council was sent out by the mayor, and the system to some extent represented a victory of the oligarchy; we can perhaps trace in Nottingham the informal growth of this custom and its effects.

III. There were boroughs, however, in which the second council was the monument of a popular victory; and of these Norwich and Sandwich may serve as instances; in Lynn the system was developed under peculiar circumstances.

NOTE A.

I add here some very brief notes of constitutional changes in a few boroughs, which took place in the later middle ages. They all indicate a widespread struggle between the upper and lower sections of the community during the fifteenth century. A closer study shows that this movement must not be compared to the flicker of an expiring flame, but rather expresses the quick burning of a new fire. In some of the instances given below the oligarchy seems to have proved the more powerful, in others the middle class.

In 1373 the custom of Colchester was that the whole community chose four "sufficient men" (afterwards termed headmen), one from each ward, "of good conversation, and who had never been bailiffs;" and these, being sworn, elected five more from each ward, who likewise had never been bailiffs, making together with themselves twenty-four. Two at least of every five thus chosen were to be of the common council. The twenty-four elected the two bailiffs, eight aldermen, and other officers. Then bailiffs and aldermen together chose sixteen of the "wisest and most understanding people in the burgh;" which sixteen jointly with them carried on the government. "They were to meet in assembly at least four times a year; and if any burgess had a proposition to make to his governors he was to deliver it to the bailiffs in writing, and receive an answer at the next assembly." Edward the Fourth in his new charter directed bailiffs and aldermen and the sixteen to choose sixteen other persons, four from each ward, to be a common council with "power to make reasonable ordinances and constitutions for the good of the borough." The first sixteen were afterwards styled Primum Concilium, the latter Secundum Concilium.

Assemblies were held in the moot hall for electing officers and making bye-laws. No ordinances could be passed unless twenty-five members were present. Fines were raised from those who did not come or who came after the doors were shut. (Cromwell's Colchester, 264-5, 269.)

Canterbury was originally governed by a portreeve appointed by the king; but at least as early as the thirteenth century the portreeve was replaced by two bailiffs, who were assisted by a council of twelve aldermen, or "wisest men," and by thirty-six "probi homines" or "jurati." There is reason to believe that the bench or chamber of twelve exercised from the first the powers which belonged to them in the fifteenth century. They were sworn to keep the law days twice a year, to preserve the memory of the limits and bounds of their aldermanries, and to give good counsel to the mayor; they received all the accounts of the money in the cofferer's keeping; and with them rested the power to make all bye-laws. (See the cofferer's oath in muniments of city. A. 1.)

There were some peculiar features about this upper council. The six aldermanries of which the city consisted had been originally held by the Crown "in capite," but when Henry the Third granted the city to the citizens to hold in fee-ferm the offices were annexed to the fee-ferm, and the owners from that time held of the citizens. The wards, however, still remained the property of certain families in the county of Kent, estates which could be bequeathed by will, and which descended for generations from father to son. Their hereditary governors need not be either freemen or inhabitants of the city, and might moreover make their profit if they chose by leasing out the post. At one time S. Augustine's held an aldermanry at Canterbury (Madox, 252); and at the inquisition of 1285 it was proved that William de Godstede, who held the aldermanry of Westgate from the community of the city at a rent of 3*s*. 4*d.*, had leased it to the rector of Sturry, two miles away, for 100*s*. a year. At the same time their position in the city was most influential, for not only had they the usual police control of their wards as in other towns, but they were *ex-officio* members of the chamber of twelve, who formed the counsellors of the mayor in the government of the town. There they claimed superior place and privileges to their brethren, ranking in dignity next to the mayor and above the other six members of the chamber; the fine for reviling the mayor being 100*s*.; for the aldermen, 60*s*.; for the men of the chamber, 40*s*.; and for the thirty-six men of the council, 20*s*. The council of thirty-six may possibly have arisen out of the necessity of securing the attendance at the burghmote of a sufficient number of freemen. Their duties as defined by the oath customary in 1456 were very limited in character. "This hear ye, mayor, that I will be true to King Edward and his heirs, and true attendance make to the mayor of the city or his deputy at such times as I shall be desired or called, and keep the days of the burghmote, and truly keep the counsel of the said burghmote, and all other things do as one of the common council." They seem to have had no control over the town treasure, nor any power to propose laws, and at first had apparently no power even to reject them. It would appear that juries were chosen among their body at the burgh court, and they took part in the election of the bailiffs.

A violent dispute broke out in 1445 as to the right mode of electing the bailiffs, and when Cardinal Beaufort visited the city bribes were used to win his influence in settling the quarrel. The matter ended by the grant of a new charter to the city in 1448, by which the bailiffs were replaced by a mayor. By this charter, the king gave power to hear pleas and to collect such tallages as the mayor and aldermen may consider necessary for the maintenance of the city, but of the council of thirty-six there was no mention. As early as

1429, however, its share in the government seems to have been recognized. The name "common council" was recognized in the oath used in 1456; and that it represented the people at large is clear from the statement in 1489 that the thirty-six were "sworn to the council of this city by the assent of all the commonalty of the city." Finally in 1474 it was decreed that every act or ordinance made by the mayor and aldermen "with the assent of such of the thirty-six citizens for the commonalty of the said city chosen as it shall like the mayor and aldermen" was to be enrolled in the common chamber; and in this same year ordinances were made by the mayor, five aldermen, the sheriff of Canterbury, and two chamberlains; seven names are then given (who may possibly have formed the rest of the chamber of twelve with the five aldermen already mentioned), and thirty-six citizens (not mentioned by name) elected by the community for the public good of the city. In 1497 certain business in London was said to have been done by order of the mayor, aldermen, council, and commonalty. (Records of Burghmote Court. Hist. MSS. Com. ix. 140, 146, 167, 169-173. Hundred Rolls, i. 49-55.)

In Shrewsbury, before the plague, twelve men were chosen who apparently elected the bailiffs, and presented their accounts yearly to six men chosen by the commonalty. In 1380 the town was torn by dissensions, and apparently some change had been made in the municipal constitution, for the commonalty under the direction of the Earl of Arundel now agreed to return to the form of government practised at the time of the plague. This lasted till 1389. Discords and debates still, however, continued, and the commonalty met in 1389 in the presence of the abbot and various lords to find a remedy for the misgovernment of the town. It was agreed that the bailiffs should nominate a council of twenty-five, which council in its turn should elect for the coming year the bailiffs, the coroners, and six cessors. The cessors were to oversee the spending of town moneys and to make up their accounts for six auditors chosen by the commonalty. All burgesses were to be present at elections. The bailiffs only appointed the serjeants. The collectors of murage might be dismissed during their year of office for any fault. Any burgess who resisted these ordinances or gave his opinion in the common assembly was to be punished. Ordinances were to be read openly every year.

A new composition made in 1433 gave the council of twenty-five right to choose a serjeant in addition to the two appointed by the bailiffs; he was to collect the rents due from burgesses for the ferm of the town. Further, the commons' rights in electing the six auditors were affirmed and protected from encroachment "in deceit of the said commons." The members of Parliament were also to be elected by the whole of the commons. All the burgesses were ordered to attend at the guild hall when summoned, and the common seal was to be kept by four men chosen by the commons. Lastly, the bailiffs and commons were to elect twelve worthy men who were to serve as continual assistants to the bailiffs for the term of their lives. In case of death the bailiffs and commons were to elect another councillor. The burgesses entreat that this composition shall be confirmed by Parliament because in the case of previous accords the commonalty could not bring action against the bailiffs for contravention of them.

In 1444 the council of twelve were given the name of aldermen. The common council was to act for the whole body of burgesses, who in the assemblies at the guild hall were no longer to answer in their own persons, but to show their advice to the twenty-four who were then to consult among themselves and to elect a speaker who was to declare their will to the bailiffs and aldermen.

At the same time the nomination of the electing jury of twenty-five was taken out of the hands of the bailiff; henceforth they were to elect two of the common council, and these two were to appoint the twenty-five electors, as well as the six auditors and the coroners. The commons were also to choose a chamberlain or treasurer. (Owen's Shrewsbury, i. 168-174, 207-9, 212, 216.)

In Winchester "of the heads of the city should be four and twenty sworn instead of the most good men and of the wisest of the town for to truly help and counsel the mayor"; and the mayor was to be "chosen by the common granting of the four and twenty sworn, and of the commune, principal 'sosteynere' of the franchise." The mayor and the twenty-four then nominated four men to serve as bailiffs, and two of these were chosen by the commons. For levying taxes six men were chosen "by the common granting and sworn, three of the four-and-twenty and three of the commune." This was in and before the fourteenth century. At a later time the twenty-four named two men for mayor and the mayor chose one; while for the two bailiffs the twenty-four chose four men and the commonalty selected one of them, and in their turn chose four more, of whom the twenty-four selected one. The common seal was kept in a large coffer with two locks; one of the twenty-four was chosen to keep one key, and one of the commons to keep the other. (Eng. Guilds, 349-50, 356. Kitchin's Winchester, 164-5.)

In the early fifteenth century laws, etc., were made by the mayor and his peers and all the community of the city. (Gross, ii. 258-9.) The "full assembly" of 1477 mentions the mayor and fifty-seven of his peers then present (Ibid. 262). It is a matter for inquiry whether the thirty-three citizens added to the twenty-four were specially summoned householders, and whether Winchester followed in its common council the type of Leicester or of Norwich.

Leicester had originally a council of twenty-four; and the commons had a right at first to gather at elections or at a Common Hall and watch the proceedings of the council. They had, however, no right to interfere with business, and in 1467 a fine was imposed on any who cried out or named aloud one of the mayor's brethren to the office of the mayoralty. In the fifteenth century there were rumours and speech of ungodly rules and demeanings among the people, and in 1489 "whereas such persons as be of little substance or reason, and not contributors, or else full little, to the charges" still continued "their exclamations and headiness," they were excluded as a body from the Common Hall, and the mayor, bailiffs, and Twenty-four, were ordered only to summon forty-eight and no more of the most wise and sad of the commoners after their discretion. In the later part of the fifteenth century orders were made by the mayor and "his brethren called the Twenty-four and the whole company of the Forty-eight, then and there assembled, for and in the name of the whole body of the corporation of the town." (Hist. MSS. Com. viii. 423; Thomson, Mun. Hist. 55-6, 80-84.)

In 1553 "the mayor and burgesses" of Gloucester claimed to have had power time out of mind to ordain, constitute, and hold a court in their Council House, and to call many and divers men to their council at the same court and to compel and swear them in of their council. This summoning of additional councillors seems to have made up the "Common Council." In 1526 it was stated that "it has been the custom time out of mind to elect certain chief burgesses, sometimes more sometimes less in number," to form a common council; and the number was then fixed at forty, twelve of whom were to be aldermen.

CHAPTER XII

THE COUNCIL OF SOUTHAMPTON

THERE are two grounds on which Southampton may claim to stand first among examples of early municipal government. For centuries it was the great port of the south—the harbour where for England the trade of the whole world converged, where carracks of Flanders and galleys from Venice met to pour upon its wharves the treasures of the northern and the southern seas. And for centuries its government survived, as perhaps such a government survived nowhere else in England, in the order appointed by its first planters, with none of its hedges broken down by compromise, nor its pure springs stained by infiltration of popular and democratic fervours. It is possible that the two facts are intimately bound together, and that the destiny of a Channel port determined the somewhat unusual lot of the Southampton municipality.

The industrial experiences of Southampton had been very felicitous. Nearly forty trades are mentioned in the town records of the thirteenth century, and there were many more than these, carried on not only by the English inhabitants but by settlers come from Burgundy, Flanders, Denmark, and Lombardy, and the French colony established in Rochelle Lane and French Street. Wool of all kind was sold in the market, coarse, black, broken, and lambs' wool, much of which was sent to the Isle of Wight to be made up into web. Coloured "Paris candles" were manufactured as early as 1297. Cheese was made in great quantities, and cider. Bends of elms for ploughs were brought from Abingdon.[522] Hemp was grown for the making of cords, and the shipbuilding trade for which the town was so noted in the time of Henry the Fifth must have been already practised in far earlier days, to judge from the history of the Southampton shipping.[523]

Home industries, however, held a very modest position in Southampton compared with the fine figure made by its foreign commerce. Ships from the West bringing "cloth of Ireland," perhaps drugget from Drogheda or from Sligo, met vessels carrying wine from the French ports, herrings and wax and tapestry from Brittany, alum from Biscay and from Genoa, Eastern spices from the depôts of the Rhine, while harbour dues were paid for salt-fish, pitch, bitumen, charcoal, and wood from the ports of the Baltic.[524] The great glory of the town lay however in its direct trade with the Mediterranean. When in the reign of Edward the Second Venetian and Genoese ships first began to carry their wares to England they cast anchor in its harbour,[525] and for two hundred years Southampton became the centre of English traffic with the Italian republics.[526] An attempt to make it a free port in 1334 came to a speedy end, but the advantages the scheme offered must have been practically secured by the privileges which the kings granted both to the foreign merchants who came to trade and to the town itself as a commercial centre. In 1337 the merchants of the Society of the Alberti in Florence did the carrying trade of wool from Southampton to Gascony,[527] and three years later part of a tenement near the sea was let to the Society of the Bardi, the Florentine bankers. In 1378 the King allowed merchants of Spain and the Genoese and Venetians who carried all the Levant trade, to unlade and sell their goods at its wharfs instead of being forced to go to the staple at Calais;[528] and again in 1402 Henry the Fourth granted special permission to the Genoese to disembark at Southampton and carry their goods thence to London by land.[529] From 1353, when Winchester was made a staple for wool, Southampton as the port from which alone all its bales must be shipped to the Continent had a practical monopoly of the southern export trade.[530] It was the only harbour to which might be carried "Malmseys and other sweet wines of the growth of Candye and Rotymoes, and in any other place within the parts of Levant beyond the Straits of Morocco." Carracks from Genoa and Venice, ships from Spain, Portugal, Almayne, Flanders, and Zealand thronged its harbours, bringing their wines and spices, and carrying away wool for the weavers of the Netherlands, or cloth for the dyers of Italy and the traders of the Black Sea.[531] Attracted by its dazzling prospects of wealth, London vintners and cloth-workers rented great cellars for storage, and held houses and lands in the town; and so brilliant was the promise of its future that in 1379 a Genoese merchant got leave from the king, for the better security of his merchandise, to occupy the castle which had just been rebuilt, and promised in return to make Southampton the greatest port of Western Europe. But before he could carry out his plans the merchants in London, furious at so dangerous a rivalry, had him assassinated at his own door.[532]

Nor was commercial enterprise left to the foreigner, for even in the fourteenth century native traders were sending out English ships to do business in foreign ports.[533] In 1391 one merchant took a lease for the whole year of the customs of the town by land and water; while another wealthy burgess, William Soper, put the towers of the Water Gate in repair at his own cost, and rented them and the adjoining buildings for a hundred and twenty years, promising to repair and maintain them. At the end of the fourteenth century the large sums which passed from hand to hand, and the numerous bonds for payment of debts from £60 to £100 bore witness to the growth of trade.[534] The wool dues in the port were able to bear a charge of £100 a year granted by Henry the Fourth in 1400 for the repairing and fortifying of the town walls; and in 1417 Cardinal Beaufort, Lord of Southampton and the greatest wool-merchant in all England, lent £14,000 to Henry the Fifth on security of customs on wool and other merchandise in the various ports of

Southampton, and before a third of it was repaid he advanced another £14,000 on the same security.[535]

The prosperity of the citizens was shewn by their refusal any longer to interrupt business during the Winchester fair. In 1350 they had already quarrelled with the bishop on the subject; but he had carried the day, and the town had again submitted to the old rules that while the fair lasted there should be no weighing and measuring at the great beam in the market place, that if a merchant came carrying wares he should only be allowed to remain if he swore that they were not intended for sale, and that the bishop's bailiff should live in Southampton during the fair to see that the contract was carried out. If it was broken the inhabitants were bound, not only in their lands and houses but in all their goods and chattels, to pay a penalty of a thousand marks within three months.[536] From this intolerable state of things the citizens were strong enough to free themselves by negociations with the bishop in 1406,[537] and in 1433 they gained the right to have a fair of their own every year for three days at Trinity Chapel near the town.

Nor had the town yet exhausted its good fortune. A law of 1455 which forbade merchant strangers from Italy any longer to ride about the country buying up with ready money wools and wool cloth from the poor people, and only allowed them henceforth to buy in London, Southampton, or Sandwich,[538] drove foreign traders to settle in the town if they wanted to carry on their business at all; and many more were added to their number the next year when the whole body of Italian dealers living in London were driven out by a popular riot, and passing by Winchester, fixed their new homes in Southampton,[539] which must then have contained within its walls the great majority of all the Italian merchants in England. The monopoly of the whole export trade of Southern England was confirmed to the town by law in 1464; and finally Henry the Seventh created it a staple of metals, and gave the exclusive right of melting tin ore to its guild.[540]

Smugglers and illegal traders bore their testimony to the profits to be made in Southampton waters. Light boats[541] pushed by night into every creek and cove along the coast to land their casks of wine; and in the town strange tailors were hard at work cutting up stuff into garments for the foreign market so as to avoid the duty on exported cloth. It was decreed in 1407 that no alien tailor, coming in a ship or galley, should have any shop, house, or room in the town for the making of any "robes, jepone, ne autres garnements" until he had made agreement with the masters of the craft; so vessels of "Spayne, Portingall, Almayne, Flanders, Zelonde, and others in their vyages" came bringing with them "tailors of divers nations," who now however simply abode in their ships and cut up the cloth there at their leisure, and in 1468, four years after the monopoly of the wool trade had been again secured to Southampton, it had to pass a new law against these plunderers of the custom house.[542] Indeed, the magnitude of commerce at the end of the century may be measured by the scale on which corruption and false dealing could be carried on even by the town authorities themselves. In 1484 two London citizens, one a brewer, the other a "gentleman, and clerk of all the King's ships," owed to the mayor, sheriffs, and bailiffs of Southampton £1,200. These officers, however, had apparently got into some difficulty about the sale of 1,086 sacks of wool in which they were concerned, and drew up an agreement with their debtors that they would forgive this debt of £1,200 if they might have a promise that they should be held "harmless in their own names, and not as mayor, sheriffs, and bailiffs."[543]

There was, however, another aspect of Southampton trade. We have a glimpse of the hidden side of the town life during the thirteenth and fourteenth centuries in account books of the Hospital of St. Julian or God's House, which owned a hundred and eight tenements inhabited by working people, the prosperous ones living in houses of their own, the more luckless seeking shelter in selds or open warehouses. But from the one class as from the other, the Hospital pressed in vain for a rent which the tenant scarcely ever paid. One of the richer kind is pardoned 56*s.* arrears; the attorney is forgiven a sum of 50*s.*; the goldsmith who owes £4 8*s.* 6*d.*, manages to pay most of his debt in salt. Others pledge their carpets; some pay 1*d.* or 1/2*d.* or 3*d.* at a time for large accounts against them; in other cases there is the brief entry "died in poverty and so nothing;" or poor tenants "run away from the town in poverty," and the selds that sheltered them stand empty. Such is the tale of misery—a misery scarcely alleviated by the alms distributed by the Hospital to the poor—in 1299 three bushels of wheat given in Advent; in 1306 one-and-a-half quarters of beans and twenty-nine quarters of peas; in 1318 thirteen quarters of beans. After the burning of a great part of the town in 1337 by a fleet of French, Spaniards, and Genoese, matters grew yet worse, and in 1340 the arrears amounted to four times as much as the yearly rents. The Abbot of Beaulieu owed five years' rent for the "cheseseld." There was due from the five parishes of Holyrood, St. John, St. Michael, St. Lawrence, and All Saints within the Bar, £127 in 1340, £155 in 1342.[544] Large tenements were broken up into smaller ones where the people huddled together in their misery, and the terrible legacy of a very poor population clinging in extreme destitution to the slums and low suburbs of the town was apparently handed on to the next century, for so far as the published records tell, Southampton was the only town in the fifteenth century that gave regular out-door relief to paupers. In 1441 the Steward's book gives an account of £4 2*s.* 1*d.* given away in alms every week to poor men and women.[545]

In Southampton, in fact, riches did not gather in the people's coffers while men slept. Wealth which was hard to win, was harder still to keep in the great port of the southern coast, where life and goods were held by a precarious tenure whenever England had a quarrel across the water. At any moment the plea of military necessity might justify all kinds of irregular and intermittent interference of royal officers, and the government of Southampton became a matter of divided authority and shifting responsibility which was probably unparalleled elsewhere in England. A special guardian of the king's ships[546] interfered in the harbour; and a receiver and victualler to the king's troops[547] interfered in the shops and market of the town. The Constable of the Castle[548] long survived the constables of other towns, and was given powers determined by the court view of the necessities of the times; so that in 1369, we find a captain of the castle with authority to arrest all rebels against the king or the government of the town, and to watch against regrators, artizans, or workmen who should offend against the law.[549] At a time when the mayor of most boroughs was commissioner for array-at-arms, the mayor was here jointly responsible for military defences with the constable and apparently took quite the second place.[550]

Military discipline in fact pressed relentlessly at all points on a place continually vexed by war and alarms of war and calls to arms. On Sundays and holidays all children from seven years old were called out to practise shooting with bows on the common, while the town cowherd kept the cattle out of the way.[551] When war broke out every man had to go out and take his share of fighting, and no one save the mayor was even allowed to provide a deputy instead of bearing arms in person. If the inhabitants had no heart to fight, summary punishment was meted out as a warning for future times; and when in 1338 the mayor, bailiffs, and burgesses fled before an attack of the French, the custody of Southampton was seized into the king's hands, and its franchises forfeited for a whole year.[552] Besides the cost of three or four ships[553] to protect the harbour, with wages for masters and men, and money for their food and rent, Southampton was bound to have "ready for defence against the foreign enemy great plenty of armour, weapons, and other artillery and things needful." There was a town gunner who was paid sixpence a day to make gunpowder, gunstones and lathe-guns.[554] Generation after generation of unwilling tradesmen had to repair and maintain and defend walls over a mile long and from twenty-five to thirty feet high, with twenty-nine great towers; and to strengthen the sea-banks and ditches. The work was divided out among the people; lightermen and boatmen were bound to bring up every year boatloads of stones and heap them up against the walls on the sea side, while the townspeople put in piles and kept them in order.[555] The towers were manned by the various crafts, one by shoemakers, curriers, cobblers, and saddlers; another by mercers and grocers; a third by goldsmiths, blacksmiths, lockyers, pewterers, and tinkers; and so on.[556] But so heavy was the cost of repairs, that after the burning of the town by the French, when the king, in 1338 and 1340, ordered the fortifications to be strengthened and a stone wall fronting the sea built at the expense of the inhabitants,[557] the people simply fled away; and the Earl of Warwick and his successors, under the title of "guardians of the town," were posted in its castle with men-at-arms and archers, "to take order" about the wretched fugitives, and compel any inhabitants who attempted to leave the town to return and live there "according to their estate," and if they refused, to seize their houses, rents, and possessions for the king.[558] And in 1376 the poor commons and tenants prayed that the king would take the town into his hand and forgive them the rent, since for the last two years they had spent not only the whole ferm which he had granted them (nearly £300 a year) on the walls, but had been forced to give besides £1,000 of their own money, so that half the people had deserted their homes to escape the intolerable burdens thrown on them,[559] and the rest were going.

The long miseries of the Hundred Years War were soon followed by the harassing problems of the Wars of the Roses. For Southampton was reputed wealthy, with its unusually imposing ferm of £226 and the big roll of the king's customs, and there were always people waiting to dip their hands into so rich treasury. The royal generosities at its expense were an old story. A large part of the ferm was settled on successive queens from the thirteenth to the seventeenth centuries,[560] and however low funds might run the town always tried to keep well at court by paying at least the Queen's jointure. Great nobles and servants of the king's household were not forgotten, and took their grants as they could get them, partly in money, partly in wine or foreign fruits or spices. But when two warring parties each claimed the treasure of Southampton as its own, the municipal finances became a perilous matter for the council to deal with, and the crises of the Wars of the Roses are marked by calamity to the town budget.[561] In 1457 the ferm was only made up by contributions from seventeen burgesses amounting to over £42.[562] Matters were more serious in November, 1458, and the mayor had to go to London, from whence he writes to entreat the auditors "that ye will, as diligently as ye can or may, with one heart, one will, and one thought effectually to labour, that an end be had of the books of the bailiffs in all haste goodly, and to warn the steward that was to make his book ready against my coming home, for we must with all the diligence we can or may make provision of money to be had in short time or we be like to be sore hurt, and that God defend for we have had too much." One of the auditors accounts was over £30 too short, "the which is to me right strange, so much money as he received the last year and this year too, I cannot understand it…. I remit it to your wisdoms." Another account included nothing but the bare fees. These matters must be thought on "right specially" but "if ye will with good heart and will undivided and without any ambiguity every man heartily and diligently put his hand we shall once be brought out of thraldom." As to political news he is as cautious as he is anxious. "And so much to do will be amongst them, God spede the right." "I can no more, but I beseech God guide us in all our work."[563] A few months after the mayor was summoned to the Exchequer in London about his accounts, but before the day was fixed the Lancastrian Lord Exeter suddenly sent his secretary to the town with a receipt under his seal and sign manual for the last half-year's rent. "Milord prayed us so fair to be paid here (that is in Southampton and not in London) and said he had never so great 'myster' ne need that he is paid," and promised his help in case of any difficulty in London, "for we told him what hurt and loss it was unto us." So the town paid sadly, and the mayor anxiously wrote to their Recorder in London to try and get them out of the scrape. "And [we will] make aready all the money that we may in all haste possible whatsomever befall," he adds earnestly.[564]

It was indeed hard to gather money at the moment, for in 1460 the Earl of Wiltshire, Treasurer of Henry the Sixth, making an excuse to get to Southampton under pretence of intercepting Warwick, found five great carracks of Genoa lying in the port, seized them all with all their wealth, filled them with his soldiers, provided them with victuals from the town without payment, and fled to Flanders with his booty.[565] Then came the new rulers, and Edward the Fourth ordered Southampton to pay the treasurer of his household £133 6s. 8d., and to the Earl of Warwick as constable of Dover castle an annuity of £154 out of the same ferm.[566] What with one trouble and another Southampton fell into arrears with its rent, and a burgess (the very Richard Gryme who had been mayor a year before and had made the advance to Lord Exeter) was thrown into the Fleet in London till it should be paid; two of his fellow-townsmen were sent riding to Westminster "to labour for his welfare," and £20 was at last handed over before he was set free.[567] The same year the sheriff, also summoned before the Exchequer, rode to London at the town's cost; and he only got off by having his debt paid by the Recorder, who was afterwards repaid by the town.[568] There was further trouble in 1469-70 when the Kingmaker, as the restored Constable of Dover under Henry the Sixth, demanded his pension from the ferm, and the mayor travelled to London "to reckon with the Earl of Warwick," and spent twelve days there, "for the which twelve days the cost cometh to 50s. 6d."[569] Then a few months later came the other constable of the victorious Edward the Fourth, and the town had to pay him too and bear the double charge that year.[570]

All these financial difficulties were made yet more acute by the character of the municipal wealth. Of the £393 which made up the revenue of the town in 1428,[571] £302 3s. 4d. came from tolls; and the foreign commerce on which such sums were levied had to be maintained amid wars with France, quarrels with Brittany, attacks of Hanseatic and Breton and Genoese and Venetian traders always on the watch to seize ships on any plea of wrong done to their merchants, or in defiance of pirates that swarmed in the Channel, and of smugglers that haunted the coast. Again and again the people make complaint that the foreign merchants that used to bring their goods no longer came, and for lack of tolls to pay the ferm the burgesses had been forced to borrow £400 for their rent, and that many citizens had been driven from the town, and others were going unless something could be done to lighten their burdens.[572]

These were some of the special problems with which Southampton had to deal—perils of war, its consequences of military rule and divided authority within the town, a complicated and difficult finance, a trade at once wealthy and precarious, heavy expenses to be met in good times and in bad, a very poor class living side by side with a very rich one. The form of trouble might vary from year to year, but trouble was always with them. Bargainings, abject petitionings and arbitrary favours, concessions now on this side now on that, stern exactions and lavish gifts, left the town open to endless changes and chances of fortune.[573]

The general conditions, in fact, must have made the growth of popular government practically impossible; and from the beginning the town was probably ruled by a narrow oligarchy. Its first constitution was, perhaps, framed under the influence of a powerful Merchant Guild, such as would naturally be formed in a wealthy commercial centre—a fraternity not unlike the contemporary guild at Lynn or the latter one at Coventry.[574] It seems that in the twelfth century two king's bailiffs had the care of all the royal property, the collection of the ferm, the gathering in of the king's debts, and so forth.[575] Meanwhile the Merchant Guild elected its own aldermen, scavins, usher, and other officers, to protect the liberties and customs granted to it by Henry the First and confirmed by Henry the Second and his sons.[576] In 1199 John granted to "the burgesses" to have their town at ferm,[577] and it is probable that the alderman of the guild was charged with the collection and payment of the money, for in the course of the next generation he appears as mayor of the town.[578] Both offices, mayor and alderman, were carried on side by side in his person. He shared the government with the bailiffs, as chief of the town and the guild, bound to maintain the statutes of both, and having the first voice in all elections concerning both. If the bailiffs failed to do justice, he summoned the jurors and judged in their place. He had charge of the common coffer and the keys of the town gates, and kept the assize of bread and of ale.[579] By virtue of his old title and office the mayor was still called alderman in the fourteenth century,[580] and in 1368 he apparently acted at the head of the guild organization with its four scavins.[581]

The peculiar position of an alderman of the guild thus turned into a mayor, is no doubt marked by the fact that he was never, as in other boroughs, the elect of the whole community, nor even of a jury chosen by the people. In the fifteenth century it was admitted that from time immemorial the custom was for the outgoing mayor, in the presence of the bailiffs and burgesses, to nominate two burgesses, and the assembly was forced to elect one of these two, unless they chose to re-elect the mayor himself, which indeed was often done. The system was probably that which the guild had originally adopted for choosing its aldermen, and which went on unchanged under the new circumstances. His place as mayor, indeed, seems to have been an honour slowly and reluctantly conceded,[582] for in 1249, after "Benedict the son of Aaron" had held office (possibly for eleven years) the burgesses obtained a royal patent granting that neither they nor their heirs should ever again have a mayor in Southampton.[583] Twelve years later, however, the list begins again, though in a manner as informal as before, for long after his authority in Southampton was undisputed, the mayor was officially ignored in that capacity at Westminster, and charters from the time of Henry the Second to that of Richard the Second were addressed to "the burgesses."[584] It was only after a charter of Henry the Fourth, which among other things appointed the mayor and four aldermen as justices of the peace,[585] that the style seems to have changed, and the letters patent of Henry the Fifth are addressed to "the mayor and burgesses."[586] At last, in 1445, under Henry the Sixth, Southampton was made a perpetual corporation to be known by the name of "mayor, bailiffs, and burgesses,"[587] and this phrase henceforth replaced the old style.[588]

With the group of officials through whom the alderman ruled the guild we have no immediate concern. But when the mayor had taken his oath of office in S. Michael's Church (perhaps in the north chancel aisle which was called "Corporation Chapel"), he found himself at the head of an administrative body of twelve "discreets" and twelve aldermen of the wards. The aldermen set over the five wards (three of which were ruled by two aldermen, and the remaining two by three, making twelve in all) acted as a kind of police to keep the peace in their respective wards, to enroll the names of all the inhabitants and of their sureties, to take up malefactors, and to make the round every week or fortnight to see that all was in good order;[589] and it is possible that they took part in some work of the mayor's council in the fourteenth century.[590] The twelve "discreets" were elected every year by the whole community in an appointed place, and like the twelve portmen of Ipswich were sworn to keep the peace, to preserve the town liberties, to do justice to poor and rich, and to be present at every court.[591] They had joint charge with the mayor of the treasure and the common chest of charters and deeds, and no document could be sealed with the common seal unless at least six of them were present. They themselves elected the two bailiffs, the common clerk, and the serjeant of the town.[592] Finally in 1401, two years after the same privilege had been conceded to Nottingham, the charter of Henry IV. gave the discreets power to choose out of their own body four aldermen, who together with the mayor were to be justices of the peace, and were to be aided in their work by four discreet persons chosen by the mayor and community. From this time doubtless the mayor and his four brethren became the chief aldermen of the five wards;[593] and the town council, as in Nottingham, elected some of its members to sit as aldermen in scarlet robes, and some to be plain "discreets" or "burgesses."[594]

The two charters which finally determined the constitution of Southampton were granted within a year of the similar charters to Nottingham. The first, in 1445, which formed a deed of incorporation under the title of mayor, bailiffs, and burgesses, recognized elections by the official body, a custom which appears in the charter of 1401; while the second made the town into a county, in order to protect the merchants and mariners who were incommoded by the sheriff of the county serving writs on them.[595] In the actual government of the place it does not seem that these charters brought about much change. The mayor still presided over meetings of aldermen and burgesses at the Guildhall in Bargate Tower,[596] or in the Audit House which stood in the middle of the street in the very centre of the fish, poultry, and pig markets; and the whole community might be gathered together for the common business at the discretion of the rulers.[597] Nor did the charter of incorporation alter the old style used in local business. In affairs that concerned the commonalty, whether it was an agreement with some other borough about tolls, or ordinances for the town, or a concord with a neighbour as to the limits of the town's jurisdiction, or the leasing of the customs by land and sea for a year, or grants of land—in all such matters the ancient custom was to use the name of the "mayor and community"; and even after 1445 the old form "mayor and community" is still retained in all acts that related to public property and the town treasure, all leases, water supply, fines due to the Queen, license to hold a fair, and the like.[598] That the distinction between burgesses and commonalty was a real one in the eyes of the people is proved by the fact that on three great occasions when a solemn consent of the whole town was required, the signature of "the commonalty" or "the whole community" was formally placed alongside of that of the official class—once in the treaty with the Archduke Philip in 1496; once in the treaty with Maximilian as to the marriage of Prince Charles of Spain to Henry's daughter the Lady Mary; and once again in an important transaction concerning the common lands of the town.[599]

It thus seems probable that administration in Southampton underwent singularly little change from first to last, save the raising of councillors into self-elected aldermen and justices of the peace. Whether the system of close election by the council recognized in the charters of 1401 and 1445 was new, or whether, as is equally probable, the custom was already of old standing, it seems plain that no popular disturbance or protest was excited by these charters. It was not till fifteen years later, in 1460, that the commons rose in open revolt under the leadership of the sheriff and five burgesses, and then the battle raged round the election of the mayor.[600] A hundred or more rioters rushed to the Guildhall, broke in upon the meeting there with drawn daggers and loud cries, and proceeding at once to elect their leader the sheriff as mayor, carried him in triumph on their shoulders, and set him on the mayor's seat, while another of the ringleaders was appointed in his place as sheriff. But the riot had no great results. The defeated party procured a patent which declared that their old custom of election was to be observed, and a mayor was lawfully chosen by it; but as they were unable to displace the usurper, the quarrel finally ended in a compromise whose only effect was slightly to increase the part taken by the aldermen in elections. By this new system the mayor and aldermen met in the audit house a month before the day of election, and chose four burgesses for nomination; on the day of election they again met and struck two names off the list. The remaining two names were proposed to the burgesses and one of them elected by ballot; the outgoing mayor let it be known which was to be elected, and the ballot was a matter of form. The people put their necks once more under the yoke, and the mayor nominated his successor and handed on to him the traditions of office which he had himself received.[601]

Twenty years later there seems to have been another impotent effort to reform the system of election. At this time all such attempts were watched from the Court with suspicious fear; and Richard the Third wrote to the mayor, bailiffs, and burgesses, pointing out that by their letters patent they had truly the right both to elect municipal officers and to remove them for reasonable cause, and directing them, since "certain indisposed persons are about to trouble and vex you in due execution of the said grant, so to punish the said indisposed persons as shall be the good and fearful example of others, and if they be such persons whom ye may not accordingly punish in that behalf, to certify us thereof to the intent we may provide such a lawful remedy in the same as may accord with your said privileges."[602]

In these dissensions it does not seem that the popular anger was excited by alleged political usurpations, but simply by corrupt administration, especially perhaps in relation to public money and the common lands. There was certainly financial trouble. In 1459, as we have seen, the auditor's accounts had fallen short by large sums; and as from of old one of the auditors was appointed by the mayor, and the treasure chest was kept in the mayor's house and the keys by the mayor and discreets, there was probably ground for suspicion on the part of the people.[603] The remedy, however, was slowly and hardly won, and it was not till 1505 that a very moderate reform was carried out by passing a decree that the mayor's salary should be paid through the steward by the auditors; "to the intent following that no mayor from this day forward take upon him to receive or handle any of the town's money, that is, to wit, he shall make no fine except it be at the audit house, calling to him two or three of the aldermen or of the discreets at the least, and the money thereof coming to be put into the Common Box in the said audit house."[604] In course of time it was also ordered that the common chest should be kept in the guild hall[605] instead of the mayor's own house.

In the same year, 1459, there was probably some alarm also as to the common lands.[606] The 376 acres of Southampton Common, the various closes, the God's House Meadow, and the Saltmarsh, were, as we have seen, the special care of the "community";[607] and a quarrel had been going on for centuries with S. Julian's Hospital as to a tract of marsh which was claimed by the town as part of its common in spite of all the fences raised by the warden of S. Julian's to vindicate his claims.[608] In 1459 a new warden perhaps suggested the plan which he carried out a few years later, after the failure of the popular revolt, when he disseised the town in 1466 of a part of the great marsh or common, having bought over the mayor by a grant of some of the land in question to be held of the hospital. Under a later mayor in 1471 the burghers again broke down the fences put up by the hospital,[609] and appealed to the king and council to defend their ancient privileges. "Ancient men" (one aged 104 and more) gave their depositions as to boundaries,[610] and an award was finally made in 1504, followed by the necessary legal settlements, in 1505. A new quarrel arose when the corporation attempted to raise a tax for keeping up the sea-banks or cutting sluices to save the fields from floods; and proposed, if this failed, to enclose and hire out a part of the common land to pay these expenses.[611] The townsmen, on the alert for danger, sent in eager declarations that the poor commons "will be ever ready to withstand all manner of persons with their bodies and goods that would attempt to usurp upon any point or parcel of the liberties and franchises of the town." They would not hear of letting any part of the common; as to paying any money for sluice, bridge, or cut made by the corporation, "they pray your wisdoms in that matter to assess none of them, for they intend to pay none in no wise"; unless indeed some better and happier times might befall them, "remembering your poor commons are not as yet at a fordele in riches, trusting to God to increase under your masterships."[612] The period of wealth, however, tarried, and so did the taxes; so a few years later the corporation ordered part of the marsh to be enclosed. Upon this three hundred of the commons, men and women, marched out to the waste, broke down fences and banks, and triumphantly proceeded to the guild hall, making "presumptuously and unlawfully a great shout" to the annoyance of the court within. Flushed with success they next walked two and two in procession with their picks and shovels to the mayor's house near Holy Rood Church and Cross, and one cried out, "If master mayor have any more work for us we be ready"; after which they went home without doing further harm. Four days later one of the king's council came down with letters ordering the arrest of the chief offenders, and perpetual banishment was proclaimed against the ringleaders who had fled, while six other men were seized, taken to London, and put in the Marshalsea. The Southampton rioters were struck with terror and repentance. Petitions were got up in every parish for the prisoners; the town promised to restore the banks, and never sin again in like fashion; the corporation sent out a proclamation that all those who had taken part in breaking down the banks should go out to build them up again, and only when this was done was the petition for mercy forwarded to London. Finally, sentence was given by the cardinal and the council that the prisoners should be sent home, and at their coming to Hampton should sit in the open stocks under the pillory, till the mayor and his brethren and the king's lieutenant walked down the street, when the penitents were to plead for mercy and forgiveness and confess their guilt. All this was done; the mayor, in the name of his brethren, magnanimously, of his great mercy, accepted the apology and promised that no grudge should be borne against them. "And thereupponne [he] commaunded them owt of the stokkes, and hadd them to the audite hous, and bound them by obligacon to be good aberying ageynst the kinges grace and the mayor and his brethryn hereafter, and so delyveryd them."[613] The municipal dignity was vindicated, though the quarrel was still left to drag on for the next two hundred years.[614]

In spite of irritation over questions of financial fraud and the management of the common lands, however, there seems to have been little political activity in Southampton. The civic life stretches out before us like stagnant waters girt round by immutable barriers. Scarcely a movement disturbs its sluggish surface. The twelve perpetually gather round the mayor and rule the town with a despotic power which hardly suffers change during the centuries from John to Henry the Eighth. Even the modest claim of townsfolk for some closer connexion with their mayor only reveals with what a steady hand the venerable oligarchy maintained its ancient discipline. Against their consecrated order the commons from time to time made a riotous and disorderly protest;[615] but there is no attempt to bring about real constitutional reform. We scarcely hear of the general Assembly; there is no appeal to old traditions of freedom; no talk of a representative council of the commons; no organized resistance of the crafts—possibly because these, however numerous, were too poor and weak (if we may judge from their inability to maintain the walls and towers, even when grouped together) to make head against a very powerful corporation. Mere outbreaks of unorganized and intermittent revolt, which were occasionally kindled by some grave scandal, died away fruitlessly before the steady resistance of the authorities in power, and such paroxysms of transient activity on the part of the people remained without permanent result.

Southampton had, in fact, a peculiar history and a fixed tradition in government, which left its people in a singularly helpless position before authority. The conditions, political and commercial, of its municipal life necessarily gave the expert a supreme place in administration; and it is possible that a compact body of merchants had from the first imposed their methods of government and election on a population who had no voice in the matter. The state of affairs was exactly reflected in the attitude of the mayor, who held a place of singular pre-eminence and might. Far removed from popular criticism or control, as direct minister of the king[616] he conducted a vast mass of business in absolute independence, both of the community and of the guild, not only as being the king's escheator, the gauger and weigher of goods at the king's standard, and measurer over the assize of cloth, the mayor of the staple of wool, and mayor of the staple of metals under the king's orders, but also as the king's admiral within the town and its liberties, with supreme control of the port and coast from Christ Church Head to the Needles thence to Hill Head at the mouth of Southampton Water, over the port of Cowes and of Portsmouth;[617] and even as a sort of secretary for foreign affairs, for we must remember that nowhere, save in London, was the "foreign" question so big and important. Settlers from France or the Netherlands, such as those in Sandwich or Norwich, who took up their dwelling there and became absorbed in the general body of the townsfolk, formed a very different class from the merchant visitors who flocked to Southampton to look after business interests which extended all over the country, and to a great extent conducted the whole carrying trade of the south; and who, as strangers under the peculiar protection of the king, constituted a foreign colony, ruled by special laws and kept under special supervision.[618] In all these different departments of his government the mayor ruled by other laws than the municipal ordinances; he did not need the municipal seal for his decrees, nor the assent of the community for his acts; and the great departments in which his actions were removed from all possibility of local criticism, and local control must have made absolute rule the easier and less singular in all other relations of his office.

Nor ought we to forget wholly the outer influences which were acting on Southampton from the world beyond the water. With Flanders it seems to have had little direct communication. So long as the Mediterranean galleys carried its wool to the Netherland ports, and returned to pick up their freight for the homeward journey, the associations and commerce of Southampton were with the great cities of Italy, too far removed from it in every conceivable respect to serve as schools of political freedom; and with the communes of France whose liberties had long suffered decay, and in the fifteenth century were finally extinguished by the policy of Louis the Eleventh, the subtle enemy of popular liberties.[619] It is hard to tell how far Southampton may have been affected by such foreign associations, but at least they did not tend to weaken the influences at home which made for oligarchic rule. Undoubtedly if we compare this town with other English boroughs where civic life was more free and expansive in its growth, the municipal record, in spite of its brilliant commercial side, is one of singular monotony, and leaves us with the sense of a stunted developement in the body politic. Southampton, in fact, was by its position and dignity called to play so great a part in the national history, both in war and commerce, that all claim to private and local independence was superseded. At a far earlier date than other towns its destiny was merged in the fortunes of the whole commonwealth,[620] and the king suffered no deviation from the service required of it to the state. In a very remarkable way Southampton anticipated the history of boroughs which under the Tudors were drawn into the same duty and service; through successive centuries its burghers acquiesced in the expert administration of a small official class, scarcely fettered by popular control; and abandoned the pursuit of new ideals of communal life or new experiments in government.

CHAPTER XIII

THE COUNCIL OF NOTTINGHAM

PROBLEMS of government sat lightly on the people of Nottingham. Singularly favoured as it was by fortune compared with many other towns, there is something phenomenal in the record of a town so tranquil, so uniformly prosperous, so exempt from apprehension, with so complacent a record of successful trading and undisturbed ease. Administration was carried on in its simplest form, and few sacrifices were demanded of the inhabitants, whether of labour or of money, compared with the efforts which were required of less fortunate towns. The interest, in fact, of its history lies in the quiet picture that is given of a group of active and thriving traders, at peace with their neighbours, and for the most part at peace with themselves.

The position of Nottingham was one of great military importance; for lying almost at the centre of the kingdom, the town held the approach to the one bridge over the Trent by which the main road from the south struck northward: and further commanded the navigation of the river from the point where, broadened by the confluence of the Derwent and the Soar, it became a great highway of internal communication. Throughout its history, therefore, from the time of the Danes down to the time of the Civil War, Nottingham could not be left out of account when any fighting was going on. But England was in the main a land of peace, and the occasional and intermittent importance of an internal fortress was wholly different from the consequence that attached to a border castle like that of Bristol, or to outposts against foreign foes such as the walled seaport towns of the coast. Hence the military advantages of its site made but little mark on the character and history of the town, and the castle which crowned the sandstone cliff that rose precipitously from the waters of the river Lene played no great part in the life of the mediæval borough. Lying well out of reach of all foreign foes, it fell into no misfortunes such as Rye, which was destroyed by fire twice in half a century, nor was it impoverished by taxes for defence against the French such as threatened to leave Southampton desolate; and its merchants were only occasionally required to make contribution towards the protection of the coast and the safety of the sea-borne trade which added to their wealth and luxury. Thus, when the keeping of the sea was given in 1406 to the English merchants, their elected Admiral of the Fleet, Nicholas Blackburn, wrote a peremptory order to Nottingham for £200 as its share of the cost;[621] but the merchants' experiment failed, and they were relieved of their responsibility before they had levied any second toll.

But the same geographical position which, under other circumstances, would have made of Nottingham a strategic centre, did under the actual conditions of English life assure the fortunes of the borough in industry and commerce. By land and by water, trade was almost forced to its gates. The bridge which spanned the Trent, after it had fallen into ruins as the property of the kings, was granted by Edward the Third to the townspeople, who willingly undertook the heavy charges of its repair and maintenance; each division of the town territory was made responsible for one or two of its nineteen low arches,[622] and the wardens appointed to oversee the whole appeared from time to time before the municipal officers with laborious and portentous accounts. Over this bridge all traffic from south to north was bound to pass; while boats from Hull and the eastern ports travelled up the river to unload at the quays of Nottingham. Thus the burghers, more fortunate than those of Canterbury, Norwich, or Shrewsbury, had no cause to fear the troubles of a shifting commerce, of manufacturers driven away to seek for brighter prospects, or of merchants forsaking the old ways for some new trade route. A uniform prosperity seems to have reigned in the town. Traders of every kind were in 1395 winning more than the law allowed them,[623] and the market-place, which is said even now to be the largest in England, was covered with booths; there were twenty fish-boards, thirty-two stalls in the Butchers' House, thirty in the Mercers' House, twenty in the Drapers' House, and so on, the rents of which were rapidly rising in the second half of the fifteenth century;[624] and the stately Guild Hall, besides its council room, and its upper prison for felons and gaols for debtors with iron grating to the street, had its storage room for merchandise. Buyers and sellers crowded to the market, for new burgesses were still willingly admitted[625] on the payment of 6s. 8d., and it was only at the close of the next century that the ready hospitality of the town gave way to a jealous exclusiveness. Strangers without number paid for license to trade, besides rents for stalls or shops;[626] and the number of suits between burgesses and "foreigners" or non-burgesses, was so great that sometimes in a single year twenty rolls or more were closely written on both sides with the records of these suits alone—a fact which points to trade dealings with the outer world on a scale quite unknown to previous times.[627] Even the geological position of the town added to its sources of wealth, and the corporation as well as traders made profit from the neighbouring coal-mines.[628] All kinds of industries seem to have flourished. As early as 1155, when probably there were few places in England where cloth was dyed, bales were sent to Nottingham to be coloured red, blue, green, and tawny or murrey; and if their scarlet dye was liable to turn out not scarlet but red[629] even in 1434, we must remember that at this time for a fine scarlet dye English cloth had to be sent to Italy.[630] Nottingham manufacturers made linen as well as woollen goods.[631] Its famous workers in iron lived in Girdler Gate and Bridlesmith Gate. There was a foundry for bells well known in all the neighbouring counties, and the bell-founder, besides his bells, made brazen pots. Moreover, there were artists of repute.[632] Among English churches of the early Perpendicular period, there is none more beautiful than S. Mary's, lifted high above the market on the steep hill side.[633] The Nottingham goldsmith was sent for to repair the cross in Clifton Church.[634] The town had its own illuminator, Richard the Writer; and its image-maker, Nicolas Hill, who sent his wares as far as London (on one occasion as many as fifty-eight heads of John the Baptist, some of them in tabernacles or niches) and as he worked also in painting or gilding alabaster salt-cellars, was commonly known as the "Alablaster Man."[635]

The wealth of Nottingham was possibly not equal to that of towns like Bristol or Lynn, where at a time when capital was scanty the burghers had accumulated in their coffers good store of gold and silver. But a general air of substantial comfort and well-being seems to have pervaded the town. The subsidy roll of 1472 which gives a list of 154 owners of freehold property, from one whose tenth was 74s. 7-1/2d. down to one whose tenth was set down at 1/4d.,[636] the inventories of household goods, and the legacies which occur from time to time, show a considerable class of citizens living in wealth and luxury, and a yet larger class of comparatively well-to-do people after the measure of those times. While the richer merchants were building or adorning with handsome carved oak houses which a later age called "palaces of King John," humbler tradesmen contented themselves with homes such as are described in a builder's contract of 1479, where the little dwelling with a frontage of 18 feet on the street, was to have two bay windows and to cost altogether about £6.[637] Before the latter part of the sixteenth century[638] at least there is no indication of poverty such as we find in various other towns, in Southampton, or Romney, or Chester, or Canterbury—all places which had to suffer from special causes of distress—and even the wills do not contain the frequent bequests for the relief of the poor and of prisoners which occur in places where the calls of distress were more pressing and insistent. The financial problems of the corporation were perfectly simple and regular, and presented no more formidable difficulty than the keeping in repair of the great bridge. When the ferm of the town was reduced to £20 by Edward the Fourth it was done, so far as the municipal records tell the tale,[639] without any of the complainings of utter misery and desolation by which such favours were commonly won; and in the next half century there is no more serious hint of distress than is marked by the fact that in 1499 two of the butchers' stalls and a few other holdings were lying vacant, and that the Corporation had borrowed some small sums.[640]

Nottingham was unfretted too by trouble from without. Set on the outskirts of Sherwood Forest, but exempted since the time of John from the Forest laws and the jurisdiction of the Forest officers,[641] its very position tended to free it from the neighbourhood of any powerful lord who could threaten its citizens, diminish its rights, or tax its people with petty wars or law-suits, as

Liverpool and Bristol and Lynn were taxed and harassed. In its only trouble—an occasional dispute as to the control of the waters of the Trent—it was invariably supported by the Crown. Sometimes weirs and fishing nets obstructed the river; sometimes when the water was low boats coming from Hull had to be dragged along from the banks, and the river-side owners demanded fines for use of the towing path, so that the price of goods in Nottingham was increased to "a great dearness." Then the Nottingham men would hasten to move the king by "a clamorous relation"; and forthwith royal commissioners were sent down to inquire into the obstructions; royal proclamations were issued to forbid the exacting of river-side tolls; and royal orders forbade the neighbouring lord of Colwick to divert the waters of the Trent to his own uses to the injury of Nottingham.[642]

Nor were its burghers troubled by claims of any ecclesiastical power within the town walls, such as those which vexed Norwich and Exeter and Canterbury. Ecclesiastical interests indeed play no great part in Nottingham. Two churches already existed under Cnut, and before the fourteenth century one more was added.[643] But no abbey had been founded within its liberties, and the yearly journey of the mayor and his brethren to carry Whitsuntide offerings to the mother church at Southwell was but a picturesque ceremonial that recalled the time when Paulinus first founded there a centre of mission work among the pagans.[644]

As for Court factions and dynastic intrigues, distant traders with much work of their own on hands were generally prompted by a prudent self-interest to side with the dominant power in the State. The burghers easily transferred their sympathies from the Lady Anne of Bohemia to Henry the Fourth;[645] they stood by Henry the Sixth so long as the triumph of the rebels was doubtful, but no sooner were the fortunes of Edward the Fourth in the ascendant than by gifts out of their treasure and little detachments of their militia they testified to a new loyalty, and thus obtained the renewal of their charter and a reduction of their ferm for twenty years, "to have a reward to the town of Nottingham" "for the great cost and burdens, and loss of their goods that they have sustained by reason of those services."[646] In 1464 they ordered off a little troop in red jackets with white letters sewn on them[647] to join the king at York, and once more at Edward's restoration in 1471,[648] the town spent about £60 for "loans for soldiers" and liveries, besides many other costs. In October of 1482, the jury "presented" an offender charged with wearing the livery of the intriguing Richard of Gloucester;[649] but before the battle of Bosworth the town hospitably entertained Richard himself, and in its castle he received the Great Seal;[650] while no sooner was the day lost for York than a deputation was sent in hot haste to make peace with Henry the Seventh and obtain a safeguard and proclamation.[651] Stall-holders and burghers, in fact, intent on their own business, only asked that Court quarrels might be settled with the least possible trouble to themselves; and throughout the Wars of the Roses the Nottingham men did just what the men of every other town in England did—reluctantly sent their soldiers when they were ordered out to the aid of the reigning king, and whatever might be the side on which they fought, as soon as victory was declared hurried off their messengers with gifts and protestations of loyalty to the conqueror. Meanwhile they went steadily on with the main business of trade and watched the rents of their booths and the profits of their shops going up and their wealth constantly accumulating.[652]

Like all boroughs that held under the Crown, Nottingham won very early the rights of a free borough. Henry the Second from 1155 to 1165 granted its burgesses freedom from toll, a market, the monopoly of working dyed cloth within the borough, and free passage along the Trent; and further gave them power to tax inhabitants of all fees whatever for common expenses.[653] Originally governed by a reeve who collected its yearly ferm and managed its affairs on behalf of the king, Nottingham obtained by charter from John in 1189 a Merchant Guild, and leave to elect a reeve of the borough who should answer for the ferm to the Exchequer.[654] In 1230 the burgesses were allowed to appoint coroners, and (the ferm being fixed at £52) to levy a tax for weighing at the common scale all goods brought to the town.[655] A charter of 1255 granted them the freedom from arrest for debt which was being so commonly given at this time; the return of writs; and an order that no sheriff or bailiff should interfere in the exercise of justice in Nottingham unless "the burgesses" had not done their duty. And ten years later they were freed from the aid of 100*s.* formerly paid to the sheriff for his good will and that he should not enter their liberties.[656]

In the reverses of the Welsh war, when Edward the First summoned two great provincial councils of knights and burgesses to bestow a grant for completing the conquest of Wales, Nottingham used his necessities to secure its own profit; for three years the town had been in disgrace, with all its franchises forfeited, but in 1284 it not only regained them, but won permission to elect a mayor "by unanimous consent and will" of "both boroughs of the same town"—that is the French and the English boroughs which from the time of the Conquest had been established side by side, each governed by its own bailiff[657] according to the different laws and customs of the two peoples. During the Scotch war in 1314 their position as masters of the northern road possibly disposed Edward the Second to grant readily any favours they might demand; and immediately after Bannockburn they received power to hold all pleas before the mayor, and alien sheriffs or bailiffs were forbidden to enter the borough.[658] Yet later one of the first acts of Henry of Lancaster, after the deposition of Richard in 1399, was to make interest with the keepers of the stronghold of middle England. He gave lavishly all he had to give: the assize of tenure formerly held before the judges; all fines, forfeitures, and ransoms which had not yet been handed over; the election of four justices of the peace; the placing of the mayor upon all commissions of array of men-at-arms, so that neither sheriff of the county, nor officer of the court could henceforth tax the town for military aid without his assistance and consent.[659] In 1448 Henry the Sixth completed the emancipation of Nottingham by granting it a charter of incorporation under the title of "the mayor and burgesses of the town of Nottingham." By this charter the town, with the exception of the king's castle and gaol, was entirely separated from the county and made into a shire; its bailiffs became sheriffs, and were henceforth not to go out of the town to take their oath, but were to be sworn before the mayor; and the mayor himself was made the king's escheator.[660] If the king in these difficult times, with Normandy almost lost, and England on the eve of rebellion, offered bribes for loyalty, he required a due return; and in 1450 the Nottingham men had to pay their part of the bargain, by hiring men to go to the help of the sovereign at Blackheath against Jack Cade, which they accomplished by leasing some of their common lands for a sum of £20 to be paid in advance.[661]

Unfortunately, owing to the loss of the Old Red Book of Nottingham and other records, it is only by piecing together scattered hints and fragments that we can discern anything of the early constitution of the borough. In the first charters or official dealings with the court, we hear of "the Burgesses" only, with no mention of reeve or bailiff; until after the creation of the mayor in 1284, when the formal style is changed to "the Mayor and Burgesses." Whatever was the actual significance of the term "burgesses" we know that it already had a technical meaning, for a charter granted by Edward the First to "the Burgesses and Community of our town" in the days before the mayor had replaced the reeve,[662] shows that even then the two words were used in a special sense; and this original distinction remains throughout the records of the fourteenth and fifteenth centuries. In general, the business of the town was done in a somewhat elaborate manner by "the mayor, burgesses, and community," or "the mayor and his co-burgesses and the community"; but it seems that there were some affairs which were given over to the "mayor and burgesses"—an occasional treaty with another town,[663] or the letting of tenements or property acquired by the corporation and set apart for special public purposes such as the ferm, or of lands assigned for the expenses of the bridge; while on the other hand, where the common property of the people in house or land was in question transactions were carried out in the name of the "mayor and community."[664] There are perhaps no more than two cases before the middle of the sixteenth century in which common lands were leased by the "mayor and burgesses," and these happened as late as 1511 and 1514, and were probably acts of a specially corrupt administration.

By the Nottingham folk themselves, therefore, the word "burgesses" was from the thirteenth century onwards applied to a body which could be distinguished from the commonalty; and in the use of the words we seem again to catch the double meaning, first of the corporate body of citizens as opposed to the ancient "communitas"; and then of the governing council or assembly as opposed to the whole congregation of the freemen. When this secondary use of the words grew up in Nottingham we cannot say, as we know absolutely nothing of the early government of the town. It is only through one or two brief notices which have been saved from the general destruction of old records that we detect the presence in the council chamber of a recognized group of officials or councillors; and these notices belong to a late time. Meetings were held in the town hall in 1435 and 1443, in which a council of justices of the peace and "trustworthy men" did business with the consent of the commons;[665] and in 1443 we hear of a fine to be paid by "burgesses" who neglected to come to the hall when summoned, the fine being (as we learn from other towns) the customary sum levied from absent members of a regularly appointed council.[666] And from another entry copied from the records of three years later we know certainly that a council of twelve did exist in 1446. "Ordered that twelve and the mayor chosen to order, end, and dispose of as they think meet of all things belonging to the commonalty of the town without interruption or contradiction of any person within the town. All orders are with the consent of the commonalty."[667]

Whether the order of 1446 was the bringing in of a new method of administration, or an extension of the powers of an established council, or merely a declaration of the law that it should do its business "without interruption or contradiction" of any of the townsfolk, we cannot certainly tell, for the old Red Book is lost and the phrase is only preserved for us in a note made by a town clerk a hundred and fifty years later, whose comment on it, "And there shall you see the erection and election of the council," is of little value in deciding the matter.[668] In the absence of any direct evidence, the traces of an earlier council certainly suggest the idea that in the twelve we may have the successors of a body resembling the twelve portmen elected in royal boroughs for the general administration of the town, and that from 1399 the four justices of the peace formed part of this council. The commonalty had the right of entering the town hall during the meetings of the council, and of confirming the ordinances of the governing body by their "assent and consent"; and these powers might of course be more or less left in suspense or fully exercized as opportunity required. No doubt in a big and busy borough any frequent gathering of the townspeople was impossible, and it is very probable that (as at Sandwich), when the mayor did business in the borough court, any burghers who happened to be present[669] were taken to represent the general assembly of the commons, and bye-laws or necessary orders passed by them were understood to have received "the consent of the community." In the majority of instances the numbers who attended were probably few, but their presence is from time to time distinctly marked, as in the meeting of 1435; in the assembly of a hundred and thirty burgesses in 1463 to make laws; and in the calling of the commons together in their common hall in 1480.[670]

If the administration followed this well understood routine, it is probable that the conduct of public business underwent no great change when two new charters, in 1446 and 1448, settled the final order of government in Nottingham, and made it into a county. No mention was made in these charters of the existing council (unless indeed the term "burgesses" was commonly understood to mean the council),[671] but by the second in 1448 it was enacted that "the burgesses" should elect from time to time *from amongst themselves* seven aldermen (to answer to the seven wards of the town), one of whom was always to be mayor, while all the seven were to be justices of the peace. The aldermen were to hold office for life, and in their scarlet livery with suitable furs and linings, after the fashion of the aldermen of London,[672] were manifestly the leading members of the council; and the six burgesses who completed that body were within a few years known as "common councillors," to distinguish them from the heads of the wards.[673] The constitution of the Nottingham council seems in fact to have been exactly the same as that of Canterbury or of Southampton; and here no doubt, as in other places, the official governing body did at some time take to itself in a special sense the title of "the Burgesses," leaving that of "the Community" to the freemen at large.

The new charter, whether it introduced any change in older methods or no, at least seems to have awakened no resistance. A Council of Twelve which ruled before 1448 ruled in like manner afterwards, though now seven justices of the peace sat in it instead of four. As for what may seem to us the crucial fact that henceforward aldermen were elected for life, and elected by their own fellows and not by the people, it is possible that even this change, if indeed it was a change at all, seemed less revolutionary to the men of Nottingham in those days than it does now, for there is no trace of any conflict concerning the matter either at the time or for half a century afterwards. Indeed the same method of election was used for the councillors themselves, who also were appointed for life.[674] It appears that while the aldermen were always selected from among the six councillors, the councillors were chosen from "the clothing"—a very important body composed of sheriffs and chamberlains or treasurers who had passed out of office, but still wore their scarlet robes on great occasions.[675]

The oligarchy thus established was however no more in absolute possession of the field than an oligarchy of the thirteenth century. The people's right to hold a general assembly was admitted by the governing class as late as 1480, and claimed by the commonalty a century later. The jurors of the Court Leet long acted as representatives of the general body of burgesses for purposes of criticism and remonstrance. For certain kinds of business touching the community the custom of electing special juries was maintained; as in 1458 when "twenty-four upright and lawful men from the aforesaid town of Nottingham, as well as twenty-four upright and lawful men from each wapentake of the county aforesaid"[676] were summoned to report on the state of the bridge. It seems probable that at least six burghers took part in the election of municipal officers; and in 1511 the inhabitants claimed some share in the elections by virtue of "the statute of free elections in such cases ordained."[677] Above all the burghers exercized their ancient rights over the common property of the people. For in those days Nottingham boasted of great possessions[678] in land. From the low cliff of red sandstone which lifted it out of the floods that constantly swamped the lower grounds, the townsmen looked out over the common fields and closes and Lammas lands that stretched round it on every side, and formed until the Act of 1845 a broad belt of open country which cut off the borough from its surrounding dependent villages, and might in no way be used for building. These wide reaches of pasture were yearly distributed in due proportion among the burghers by common consent of the mayor and the whole community. In the division, and in questions of boundaries and fences and fields, the commonalty were all directly interested; and they never consented to hand over to the undisputed management of a council rights which touched them so nearly.[679] They asserted their claim to attend the meetings when the lands were divided or let out on lease, to take part in all decisions, and to keep a close watch on the councillors lest these should be tempted to pass over their own names when the poor lands were divided and to distribute among themselves all the best closes.[680] At the very end of the fifteenth century their verdict was still decisive. In 1480 the commons being called together to the Common Hall by the mayor on a question as to the common lands, "the said commons would in no wise agree" to his proposal.[681]

It is therefore probable that the charter of 1448 did not mark for Nottingham the moment of a serious constitutional revolution. Such little evidence as we have seems to show that the state of affairs was singularly like that which we have already seen in Southampton at the same date; that things went on pretty much as they had done for years past, and that the burgesses neither suffered, nor thought they suffered, any usurpation of their rights, or any grave loss of customary liberties. The system established in 1448 had been in full working for over half a century before any struggle, so far as we know, took place between the governing class and the people; and even then it was not suggested that the disturbance was caused by any change in the legal form of government.[682] For in 1500 Nottingham was in as sorry a plight as Norwich had been in 1300. It was practically handed over to the rule of publicans and licensed victuallers, who, with or without the law, held their own bravely against all opposition. When brewers and bakers and vintners rose to power they took care that the assize of bread and beer and wine should not be brought to mind; when butchers and cattle-dealers became aldermen and chamberlains they encouraged a confusion which was most profitable to themselves as to the limits of the common pastures, letting gates and bridges fall into ruin, and "although they have been often required by the whole community of the whole town of Nottingham to make common boundary marks, as their predecessors had done, have hitherto refused to do so;"[683] even as common trespassers they put their cattle and sheep in the meadow in the night time unto the great harm of their neighbours.[684] The officers appointed by the council dutifully served the interests of their masters: "We often complain of his demeanour, and have no remedy"[685] is the comment of the Mickletorn jury about the common serjeant. Year after year the protests of the commonalty were heard at the local courts. Jurors of the quarter sessions laid their grievances before the justices of the peace, themselves the main offenders; while the jury of the Mickletorn or Leet asserted their right to address the town council (when they could be persuaded to take their places at the court) and "in the name of the burgesses and commonalty of this town," to declare the wrongs of the people.[686]

It was in 1511 that the struggle between rulers and burghers culminated. In the August of that year the council seems to have violated the ancient custom, and leased common pastures by the authority of "the mayor and burgesses," the witnesses being six aldermen and six of the common council[687]—a style which had not been used before in dealing with these lands. This meddling with the rights of the community apparently heralded an outbreak of revolt. At the next Court Leet, in October, 1511, the Mickletorn jury presented the mayor who had been in power when the lease was granted, and charged him with encroaching on the common lands, and making his servants "riotously break off our common pasture hedges; it is thought contrary to right and to the common weal." Six months later, in April, 1512, the jury extended their attack, and the actual "Master Mayor" was presented for being the first beginner of a muck-hill, for misusing the time of the common serjeant, and for selling unfit herrings in the market and excluding other men who would have brought as good stuff and sold eight for a penny where he sold five, though as clerk of the market he should have increased and bettered it instead of impairing it, "and upon this runneth a great slander in the country and a great complaint." He was charged, along with "all his brethren," with failing to account for money in his charge "to the great hurt of the town and commons." Further the mayor and chamberlains together were presented for not repairing the two gates of the town; and the chamberlains for not looking after a public well; and the mayor's clerk, "the which takes our wages not as a beneficial servant unto us in no matter that any burgess of this town hath to do, but he repugnes and maligns against the burgesses and commons that they be not content with his demeanour."[688]

The commons went further than this, however, and raised the question of their ancient rights of assembling in the common hall and taking part in the election of officers.[689] At this point the authorities became genuinely alarmed. A month later, May 21, the Recorder or legal adviser of the corporation wrote a formal letter of advice to the governing body on these crucial matters of election and assembly. "I am informed," he says, "that divers of the commons of your town confederate themselves together and make sinister labour to do others to take their part and say as they do, and intend thereby to make aldermen and other officers at their pleasure; and if that should be suffered it should be contrary to all good politic order and rule, and in conclusion to the destruction of the town. Wherefore now at the beginning wisely withstand the same and call your brethren and the council together, and if ye by your wisdom think that by calling of these confederates every of them severally before you ye cannot order them without further help, then my advice is that ye send some wise person to Mr. Treasurer[690] that it would please him to see reformation, if he be in England, and else that he would write to my Lord Privy Seal, or to my Lord Steward, now in his absence to see this matter redressed, ascertaining you have spoke with my Lord Steward in this matter, and he gave me advice thus to write to you; for if ye shall suffer the commons to rule and follow their appetite and desire, farewell all good order. For if they be suffered now they will wait to do in like case hereafter." In a postscript he adds, "In any wise beware of calling of any common hall at the request of any one of them that make this confederacy. I doubt not but divers of you remember the saying of Mr. Treasurer of the inconveniences that had ensued upon the calling of the commons together in the city of London and in other cities and boroughs."[691] The sympathies of Mr. Treasurer were duly enlisted, according to the Recorder's advice, and on the very day when a new mayor took the place of the last, he wrote urging him to stand firm against those commons who would "combine themselves to subvert the good rule of the town and would make aldermen and put them out at their pleasure, contrary to the good order of your charter and privilege of your town." He begs them, if there be any of such "wilful disposition to subvert the good rule of the same your said town, that with all diligence certify me of their names, and I trust to see such remedy for them as shall not be to their contentment, but I shall see them shewn condign punishment as they have or shall deserve."[692]

The shibboleth of "good order" had its accustomed effect, and the governing body carried their point, though in leases of the common lands they presently returned to the old style.[693] The new mayor, John Rose, known to the people as the butcher chamberlain who in 1500 had let their landmarks be removed, and who since then had grown into innkeeper and victualler, ruled for eighteen months.[694] His successor, appointed in January, 1515,[695] was Master Thomas Mellers, an alderman who had a very bad reputation in the presentments of the Court Leet; after he had reigned two years, a mercer of Nottingham tried to kill him with a dagger while he was joyfully dining with an alderman; but he survived to rule again in 1522.[696] Again the jury returned to the charge. In 1524 the outgoing mayor was presented at the July sessions for not keeping the assize of bread,[697] and in October the matter was pressed on the attention of the newly-appointed mayor. Two years later, however, Nottingham was for the third time put under John Rose, who in the interests of firm government determined to suppress once for all the importunate presentments of the jury. During the whole time of his mayoralty, "in the default of the said Master Rose there was no verdict given of the jurors sworn for the body of this present town ... to inquire of things inquirable afore you justices of record," nor was the assize of victual ever put in execution; and by this the town had not only been greatly disordered but had been put in danger of forfeiting its liberties and franchises.[698] The next year (1527) the jury were again roused by the fact that three aldermen, one of them being Rose, the last year's mayor, had by their united efforts filled all vacancies with victuallers; and a formal petition was addressed to the mayor and his brethren in the name of the whole town. They called to remembrance the law that "No victualler should be chosen to no such rooms as judge of victual," and told again the long tale of their grievances. They declare that these elections were illegal, "the burgesses and commonalty of the said town not being made privy, nor thereunto consenting, contrary to the corporation of the said town, and also contrary to the statute of free elections in such case ordained," and that therefore the whole town might be made to suffer the loss of their liberties and franchises for non-using or misusing the same. In the lately elected aldermen "the want of discretion and debility of reason" was well known to the whole town, so that the common voice and fame of it ran through the shire; and the jurors thought "that the most wisest and discreetest men ought to have been chosen to such rooms by you and the burgesses *and commonalty.*"

Further the jury, "in their most humble manner," observed that the king had been deceived in the matter of the last subsidy; for in addition to their other crimes the three aldermen, when their substance was assessed for a subsidy at £50 or £55, had "embezzled" the record, and changed the figures to a nought.

Finally they pray "by the whole minds and agreements" that the present counsel of the town might use and continue in his place "like as he unto the same was elect and sworn, and that according to right and good conscience he may have his fees that is behind to him contented and paid."[699] All this the jury spoke in the name of the people, "whereunto we, the aforesaid jurors, in the name of the burgesses and commonalty of this town and borough are fully content and agreed."

In these troubles, it does not seem that the revolt of the people was excited by any definite constitutional change, nor was the charter of 1448 called in question or brought forward as the origin of later evils, nor was any protest made against the election of councillors for life. Complaints multiply against corrupt administration of the law, or the holding of office by unfit and illegal men. But the claim of the people to a share in elections is vague and indefinite, and neither in 1511 nor in 1527 do the commons appeal to precedent. Opinions as to their rights are tossed to and fro, balanced by contending winds of doctrine. In defence of the system of close election the council call to witness the charter and privileges of the town; while on the other hand the commons declare that elections are illegal if the commonalty as well as the burgesses are not "made privy nor thereunto consenting." Possibly the explanation lies in a common tendency of practice to drift away from the theory with which it had first kept company, and finally to disown its old accomplice. No doubt the commons inherited theoretically an inalienable right to take part in elections; but it had apparently become the practice that the people should only exercise that right in a certain definite way through the half-dozen representatives who attended the elections, and not through a common gathering; and thus the situation was one in which either side might indefinitely urge law and custom without ever bringing conviction to their opponents.

It is indeed conceivable that the true peril to popular liberty was of a far more subtle character than the words of any charter would suggest, and rather grew out of developements in the unwritten constitution of the borough, than in the written law. Not only in elections, but in the meeting of the general assembly, insidious changes may have been brought about by the mere growth of common custom. In the institution of "the Clothing" there were latent possibilities which time alone could bring to light. For over half a century sheriffs and chamberlains were quietly bowed out of office, and transferred with all their fur and finery to the brilliant company of the liveried ex-officials to await a happy re-election. But in due course, as its numbers multiplied, the Clothing was made manifest to all men in its stately ranks or "clene scarlet" as the very body-guard and sworn defenders of the central group of high officials, the traditional depositories of power. Surrounded and shielded by a band of forty or fifty friends who had already held office and might hold it again, men dedicated to their interests and disciplined to their methods, the mayor and his brethren were no longer left face to face with the whole community. Under the established custom by which any burgesses who were present at an assembly were taken to represent the whole body, it was evidently easy even while outwardly observing constitutional form, to summon to the meeting only members of the Clothing; and the decrees of the council having been submitted to this loyal gathering were assumed to have obtained the assent of the commonalty. Popular control might thus be absolutely extinguished, and that without revolution or going beyond the letter of the law, when a council chamber crowded with the official class[700] replaced the assembly of the commons, and exercized its powers simply by preserving its name.

The plan of forming a select committee of the General Assembly nominated by the mayor seems to have been a very favourite custom. In Coventry, for example, the mayor summoned certain citizens who were added to the twenty-four to form a common council. Their number was perhaps at first uncertain, for in 1444 we hear of a meeting of fifty-three, twenty-four of the council and twenty-nine other burgesses; but apparently from 1477 twenty-four citizens always assembled with the twenty-four jurats to form the common council of forty-eight. Generally, as in Leicester or Gloucester, a fixed number of representative citizens was summoned. A lower chamber of this pattern evidently assured the triumph of the oligarchy; and the idea of popular control was perhaps more completely banished by this narrow and formal interpretation of the common right of meeting than by mere idle neglect of the assembly. In Nottingham, so far as we can judge from the few council minutes preserved during the sixteenth century, the mayor and his brethren acted with perfect independence of the burgesses at large, and no longer mentioned the name of the community even in ordinances which touched the common lands.[701]

Still, however, the jury fought with indefatigable zeal for some control over administration.[702] They never let slip a chance of reprimanding their governors. Again and again the mayor was presented for refusing to enforce judgment on bakers, butchers, and brewers,[703] and with his brethren was charged with innumerable frauds on the people. Sometimes we find the jury busied about securing a capable schoolmaster;[704] sometimes they were demanding to have the accounts laid before them—the accounts of the bridge and the free school and the sums raised for the burgesses of Parliament, "and how the residue of the money is bestowed, for our money is therein as well as yours was, and therefore it is convenient that we know."[705] As Englishmen had once looked back to the times of the good King Edward, so the men of Nottingham turned wistfully to the golden past when the Red Book had been the charter of their liberties, and vainly prayed that the necessary parts of the book (doubtless the ancient town ordinances) should as of old be read yearly in the hearing of the burgesses.[706] Clinging to the ideal of a primitive liberty, these inveterate conservatives robbed reform of all the terrors that attached to what was new. What had been might safely be again. Nor was there any tendency to riot or disorder. All must be done in a constitutional way, and within the limits of tradition. Towards the end of the sixteenth century, therefore, there was a good deal of tinkering at the municipal constitution. On March 29 (1577) the number of councillors was increased from six to twelve, all as before to be chosen by the Clothing.[707] The democracy had probably very little to say to this change, for the order was made by forty-five burgesses "being then all of the degree of chamberlains" who seem here clearly to be acting as though their assent to an ordinance were equivalent to the consent of the whole community.[708] Six months later, however, it occurred to the people to make some use of the ancient custom of summoning a jury of forty-eight from town and suburbs for public business; and they proposed to have the common council elected by such a jury—to which suggestion the ruling class agreed. They further demanded that the councillors should attend at the Leet when the Mickletorn jury presented offences and gave their verdicts. All this was, as they claimed, a return to the authentic custom of former days, "according to the Red Book as we do think."[709] But in November the Leet jury were still praying that this agreement should be carried out, and there is no evidence that they ever succeeded. In any case, two years later, when the people once more urged their old claim to have the accounts made public and "to hear the end and reckoning of any subsidy when any is,"[710] they advanced a new demand for reform yet more radical; and suggested that all the common councillors should be utterly abolished, leaving only the aldermen and two coroners to form an upper chamber, "and that the forty-eight may be joined to you to confer in any matters for the town, as there is in other places where their corporations are better governed than this is,"[711] and that the same forty-eight as representing the commons should be given a definite share in the management of the bridge and school.[712]

But all these efforts proved vain, and the Council and Clothing continued their victorious career. As late as 1598 the commons endeavoured to revive the old constitution of the town and to call a general assembly through summons by the constables of the wards; and even collected money to institute a suit that they might inquire into a corrupt lease of common property by a member of the council. In the curious account preserved of the examination and depositions of the ringleaders in calling the assembly together the passionate determination of the people still finds voice, and there was at least one among them to maintain stoutly that he did not care if he died in a good cause.[713] The beginning of the next century found the contest slowly dragging along, the Mickletorn jury still protesting against the negligence of the councillors[714] and the people still discussing new constitutions with increasing nicety of detail, and debating the merits of two chambers of twenty-four and forty-eight,[715] or of twenty-eight each.[716] Meanwhile the twelve of the council are mentioned as existing unchanged in 1604.[717]

By this time the men of Nottingham had adopted in turn all the constitutional means of securing popular freedom that lay in their reach. They had consistently appealed to the old ordinances which in theory at least endowed them with sovereign power. The Mickletorn jury had been incessantly called on to right their wrongs by force of law. The cumbrous machinery of the general assembly had been dragged out in its noisy inefficiency. The custom of summoning forty-eight jurors for public purposes had been seized on as an institution out of which a chamber of the commons might be created and representative government established. But the mediæval history of Nottingham closes with the utter failure of schemes so industriously cherished. Doubtless reform had tarried too long in coming. Whether the general commercial prosperity had drawn all activity into trading enterprise and diverted it from politics, whether a common well-being had tended to an acquiescent conservatism, whether the variety of trades carried on in the town had, as in modern Birmingham, resulted in the absence of effective trade organization or of any strong and commanding craft guild to serve as a centre of union, or whether in this wealthy community buried in the Midlands there was some lack of ready interchange of thought and discussion with the outer world, the fact remains that resistance to the dominion of an oligarchy was of late and ineffectual growth, and when it did appear it seems to have mostly lost its energies in talk. In 1600 the men of Nottingham were still discussing the formation of a House of Commons to represent the will of the people—an experiment which Norwich had tried two hundred years before, and for which in municipal life it was now two hundred years too late.

Thus in the history of civic freedom Nottingham seems to stand midway between Southampton and Norwich. Not only did it in the fifteenth century closely follow Southampton in the critical dates of its municipal history, but it is certain that its local administration must have been a matter of no less importance to the Crown from a military point of view. In times of disturbance it was all-important to the king to keep a firm hold on the Midlands and on their central stronghold, and preserve as it were a "buffer state" between north and south, east and west; and we have seen how quick was the central government to take alarm at any "confederacy" to "subvert the good rule of the town," and how anxiously, as in Southampton, it interfered to protect the select oligarchy against the "sinister labour" of the commons. On the other hand the belief of its people in an ideal liberty, steeped as it is in strong emotion, is far removed from the apathy of the

Southampton burghers. In the aspirations of its commonalty Nottingham comes nearer to Norwich, but here there is a profound difference not only in the conduct of the controversy between rulers and subjects but in its final issue; and the council of the commons which the oligarchy was able to assemble by stealth in Nottingham has no likeness to the lower chamber created by the middle classes themselves in Norwich.

CHAPTER XIV

THE COMMON COUNCIL OF NORWICH

WHEN we turn from the southern to the eastern coast the first impression is that of being transported to a new atmosphere. It is not only that the outer forms of administration are different, for these differences, however interesting, are but the changes rung on a common system of local self-government. But in the political temper, the vitality of the popular institutions, the vigour of reform, we breathe a bracing air unknown in the Southampton docks and slums.

For the traders and artizans of the eastern coast lived in an exhilarating clime. Across the water the towns with which they traded were full of the movement of a free expansive life, very different from the political depression of the communes which the Southampton traders knew best. It was to the eastern coast that immigrants came flying from tyranny and clamorous for freedom; and traders from the eastern towns who watched in the streets of Ghent and Bruges and Ipres and Dinant, the violent and tumultuous life of cities where the people were still fighting for liberty, doubtless brought back from oversea tales of the passionate temper of independence which swept through the manufacturing boroughs of the Netherlands.

But however this may be, the towns of the east were distinguished by an intense vitality; and among the eastern boroughs where civic life was keenest and most fertile in experiment, Norwich was the pioneer in the way of freedom,—twenty or forty years ahead of Yarmouth in time[718]—beyond Colchester in the generosity with which the commonalty was called to share in the work of government[719]—happier and stronger than Lynn in having secured the union of its people into one undivided community for civil purposes. It is not impossible indeed that it stands in the forefront of all the English boroughs for the quality and value of its political experiments, and the elaborate finish of its constitution.

Originally, as we have seen, four bailiffs ruled the four great leets of the city, from 1223 to 1403. Their mode of administration has been very minutely described.[720] Each leet was for convenience' sake divided into sub-leets, the lesser divisions being at first probably twelve in number and afterwards ten. The sub-leet was itself composed of as many parishes as grouped together would contain at least twelve tithings, and could therefore produce sufficient capital pledges to hold a leet court. For all purposes of business every tithing was supposed to be represented by its own capital pledge, who was probably chosen by the tithing men, but who, once elected, seems to have held his post for years, perhaps for life. He lived in the parish, perhaps in the very street of his tithing, and was generally a man of substance, one of the respectable middle class of the city, and occasionally might even aspire to enter the official body. In the whole city the number of capital pledges was probably a hundred and sixty.[721]

The business of each sub-leet was taken in its turn before the four bailiffs all sitting together in the little thatched tolbooth that stood in the central market place. There the capital pledges appeared to answer for their tithings at the view of frankpledge; and when this business was over they served as a jury for "presenting" offences at the leet court.[722] Year after year there came up the same body of comfortable well-to-do burghers, who did their business quietly, without thought of entering into any controversy with the government, like the juries of Nottingham and Southampton.[723] Whether this was the result of summoning the pledges in small groups from one sub-leet at a time, or due to the fact that in Norwich the people already possessed other means of expression, there is not as yet enough evidence from other towns to show, but the fact is important.

In later records we learn what was doubtless true in 1223 as well as in 1365, that one of the bailiffs was chosen for each great leet; and we also have the first account of the manner of their choosing. A body of twenty-four men, six from each leet, was elected by the whole community, and the twenty-four then chose the bailiffs.[724] The first mention of a custom in fragmentary records by no means implies its first institution, and this mode of election may have dated from the earliest times. It also appears that before the close of the thirteenth century the bailiffs were assisted in judicial business by a select body of citizens, whose share in considering the case of offenders seems to show that they were "present in the court as informal assessors to the bailiffs, or, in other words, forming the court of which the bailiffs were the sole executive;"[725] and it is possible that for other business also some of the leading citizens were summoned to attend at assemblies, and their name affixed to deeds, separately or collectively.[726] A complaint of "the mean people of the commonalty"[727] shows that administration and taxation had even at that early time fallen into the hands of a small body—the bailiffs and "the rich"; and the "customs" of the city (which were perhaps drawn up about 1340, but which must in many respects contain traditional usages of an earlier date) give us some idea who were "the rich" here spoken of. A body of twenty-four men elected by the community, six from each of the four great leets, is there described as forming a court for the control of the whole trade of the city. It appointed supervisors over the various crafts, and received reports of fraud in trade—charges which, if it had not been for the intervention of the twenty-four, would have gone to the leet juries. And the same body of twenty-four had official supervision of the city finances and received all accounts of the treasurers and collectors of taxes or town money.[728] Once more, in 1344, we find them exercising yet another function—"the twenty-four in the same year elected and ordained by the whole communitas, in the presence of whom, or of the greater part of them, if all cannot be present, the business of the city touching the communitas might be enrolled."

Lastly it appears that the twenty-four gradually assumed the power of making laws for the community, and "used this custom that they might remedy new defaults and mischiefs arising by making new ordinances for the common profit of the town and the citizens and of others coming or conversant there."[729] Apparently the assembly itself was almost superseded, for on the plea that when assemblies were summoned for the common good of the city and the country, the citizens did not take the trouble to come, to the great hindrance of public business, it had been ordained some time before 1340 that for the calling together of the commonalty the bailiff's serjeant should summon certain of the most worthy and discreet men of each leet who were to be fined two shillings if they failed to obey the summons.[730]

A council of leading citizens, though it was already organized in this elaborate way early in the fourteenth century, scarcely appears in records of the later thirteenth century, and even then dimly in a vague inchoate form. It is, however, important to notice that from the very beginning two official styles were in use in the city documents, which seem at no time to have been interchangeable one with another. In the Pipe Roll of 1255 there seems to be a distinction between "the citizens" and "the men of Norwich";[731] and both in this year and later, whenever the borough has any dealings with Westminster it is "the citizens" who ask for favours, and it is to "our beloved citizens, they and their heirs," or to "the bailiffs and citizens their heirs and successors" that grants are made throughout the thirteenth and fourteenth centuries.[732] Exceptions to this form are rare. In 1347 when Edward the Third asked for soldiers to be furnished for the French war he addressed himself to "the mayor, bailiffs, and the whole community";[733] but as there was at that time no mayor in Norwich, the phrase was possibly that of a new clerk brought into the War Office in a hurried rush of business. In 1355 he sent a close letter to the "bailiffs and commonalty" of Norwich to provide him with a hundred and twenty armed men; and in 1371 a letter to the "bailiffs, good people, or commons" of Norwich to fit him out a ship. In all these cases it is obvious that the king's claim on the people was altogether independent of any obligations resting on them as citizens of a chartered borough. Very rarely did the community address the king. In 1304 and 1307[734] the "mean people of the commonalty of the city" asked his aid; and once "the commune of the town of Norwich" sent a special petition to Parliament. The city liberties had been forfeited into the King's hands in 1285, and the royal officer set over it had wrongfully distrained the people's goods to the value of £300;[735] but since "the citizens" in the technical sense of a corporate body possessing certain rights ceased to exist when the city lost its franchise, the Norwich people had to fall back on that which lay behind all chartered corporations—on that out of which all other rights had sprung; it was to "the commune of the town" that wrong had been done, and "the commune" appealed against it. On the other hand, whenever a question arose as to common lands or common property the business was always done in the name of "the commonalty" or "the bailiffs and commonalty," and in such cases the style of "the citizens" was never used.[736]

There seems, therefore, ground for thinking that from first to last the Norwich burghers officially described themselves by two distinct styles, which to the common understanding had different meanings, and were not used at hazard. I venture to suggest that here and elsewhere "cives" was the term used for the corporate body of citizens possessing chartered rights; while "communitas" stood for the citizens in another aspect, as the community which held property and enjoyed privileges by immemorial custom, before the charter of a free borough had been obtained. The holding of common property was probably the signal survival of customary rights, the others being gradually merged in the privileges enjoyed by charter; and hence it was in deeds relating to land that the traditional form of "cives et communitas" was chiefly preserved. In every town in England, however, whatever might be its special constitution, we find other rights universally claimed by the commons, which carried an authority that their opponents never dared in any single instance to gainsay, even when they sought to evade it. We may, perhaps, date back to a distant past the claim of the whole community to have all laws ratified by their "entire assent and consent," to be made privy and consenting to all elections, to know verily how the town moneys were raised and spent, to admit new burgesses by the common vote of the people. These were rights which the oligarchies constantly endeavoured to make void from the time of Henry the Third to the time of Henry the Eighth; yet no attempt was ever made to deny or to revoke them. It may be that their authentic force was derived from that obscure time of which no memory is, when the ancient "communitas" slowly built up the great tradition of its customary rights; and that when the remembrance of the primitive community had by lapse of time fallen into the background its power was still present, and to the last the name was one of dignity and carried with it a mandate from an older world. No doubt, however, in the vulgar tongue "commonalty" came to be used in a popular sense, and sometimes with an air of obloquy or contempt, to describe the general mass of citizens who had the right of meeting in common assembly, as distinguished from the official class. For by degrees old lines of division between the ruling and the subject classes were drawn sharper and deeper—when government by the select few took legal form; when a council of twenty-four sat as assessors in the courts, audited the town accounts, controlled its trade, and claimed to make its laws; when the assembly was reduced to a gathering of special men called by the bailiff's serjeant; and when even the attendance at the leet began to fall off as at the end of the fourteenth century[737] its business passed more and more into the hands of the twenty-four. Then the word "communitas" took a new shade of meaning. Before 1378 "the citizens" had come to mean in common talk the governing council, as opposed to the "commonalty" who were left outside.

It is true that the legal privileges of the community still remained. They had a claim on part at least of the public property. No new burgher could be admitted save by the act of the whole commonalty, or of twelve of them who might be taken to represent the entire body.[738] Taxes might only be assessed by will of the whole commonalty[739] or of the greater part of the same. Whatever might be the prevailing habit, the twenty-four had no legal right to act in the name of the whole people, and if the commons refused to obey their ordinances they could not appeal to any court of law to enforce their submission. In the Assembly Rolls the burghers are mentioned as sharing in the business of elections, grants of money, and taxation.[740] That they asserted their rights in a way which seemed to the governing class "contrarious" we gather from the fact that in 1378 "the citizens" (who in this case must certainly have meant a very limited body) presented a petition to Richard the Second in which they declared that of late "many of the commonalty of the said town have been very contrarious, and will be so still unless better remedies and ordinances be made for good government"; and they pray that the bailiffs and twenty-four citizens to be elected yearly by the commonalty may have power to make ordinances and to amend them from time to time when necessary.[741] A ship which they had just built at the king's orders possibly commended their request to his judgment, and the grant of the desired charter placed the council in a position of absolute authority, having power to issue ordinances without the consent of the people, and to enforce them by appeal to the royal courts.

What controversies and threats of revolution agitated the men of Norwich for the twenty-five years that followed this great change we do not know. The exact position of the twenty-four in the municipal assembly is not easy to trace from the paucity of existing documents.[742] The rolls which survive might be expected to shew some sign of the effect of the charter of 1378 by which the official authority of the twenty-four was established. Yet such is not the case. The description of the Assembly both before and after remains exactly the same. A select group of citizens attends at every meeting, and takes the whole charge of administration. Yet it is worthy of notice that neither before nor after 1378 is any order or resolution ever attributed to the twenty-four, though such orders are constantly referred to the action of the "tota communitas." Throughout these rolls the only authorities mentioned are the bailiffs and the commonalty.[743] If it is possible to believe, as I have suggested, that the right of the community to give or withhold consent in legislation was an immemorial custom which could not be abrogated by charter, the failure of the twenty-four to carry their point can be understood. No doubt party feeling on both sides ran high. It became necessary for a settlement to have a new charter; and in 1403, probably, at the instance of the ruling class, the city bought a fresh constitution at the heavy price of £1,000.[744] By this charter Norwich was made into a county; the four bailiffs were replaced by a mayor and two sheriffs, to be elected by the citizens and commonalty; and, in confirming previous grants, the customary phrase used in the charters of earlier centuries, "the citizens" was replaced by "the citizens and commonalty"—a term which is recognized in the charter as being already in use,[745] but which had not until now been invariably employed as the official style.

The charter of Henry the Fourth seems to have been in effect a confirmation of the charter given by Richard the Second, and to have set the victorious conclusion to the whole system of oligarchical government expressed by the council of twenty-four. The people were quick to appreciate the difficulty of making use of the powers which had been attributed to them and to perceive the tendency of the charter. A crisis was brought about by the very first elections held under the new constitution. The charter ordered that the sheriffs were to be elected, not as the old bailiffs had been by the electors of the four Leets, but by "the citizens and commonalty." In the ordinary assemblies, however, made up of the twenty-four and "others of the community," at which Parliament men, city treasurers, and officials, had been chosen, the twenty-four were practically supreme, and elections carried out in these gatherings were, as a matter of fact, in their hands. On March 1st, 1404, a mayor was chosen, and twelve days later two of the bailiffs were made sheriffs (the mayor's book says by the "cives").[746] The altered mode of appointing the sheriffs, as compared with the more popular custom of electing the old bailiffs, immediately roused the commons. An assembly was called to frame ordinances for the new state of things, and the people determined by their own authority to create a representative council of the burghers at large. It was ordered that eighty persons should be elected to attend all assemblies and act in the name of the people. To this council was given the right of nominating the sheriffs; the eighty were to go apart by themselves and name three persons, but if the commons did not approve of their choice they had again to retire and choose other names until their masters were content. Then the town clerk and some of the eighty carried the three names to the mayor and the twenty-four "probi homines"; the mayor chose one and the twenty-four the other.[747] The new council took part in the Michaelmas elections of that same year 1404, when the mayor was reappointed, and two new sheriffs were chosen.

This settlement evidently excited violent hostility, and in 1415 a Composition was framed to put an end to the discords by which the city was "divided and dissolved and in point to have been destroyed."[748] This document did not err on the side of any lax notions as to the seriousness of a written constitution. With pedantic nicety it touched almost lovingly on the minutest details of ceremony and dress, as well as on the greater problems that vexed the state—the position of the twenty-four; the rights of the commons; and the share which the two parties were to have in appointing the officers of the city.

The effect of this Composition of 1415 was to create a miniature copy of the English kingdom, a little community governed by its three estates, the mayor, the co-citizens of the mayor's council, and the commons. The twenty-four "probi homines" now became "the twenty-four co-citizens of the mayor's council," the mayor having the same authority over them "as the mayor of London hath,"[749] and the dignity of the municipal House of Lords was fitly marked by their dress, a livery "furred and lined as the estate and season of the year asketh."[750] Above all it was decreed that they should no longer be a body elected yearly but should "stand corporate perpetually," and even if this should accidentally not be embodied in the charter to be asked for later, "the citizens" declared that they could establish that law for themselves and not by point of charter, in virtue of the right given them in 1378, to make such ordinances as they chose in difficult or defective cases for which no remedy clearly existed in the city constitution.[751]

On the other hand the organization of the lower chamber was made more complete, and the relative position and authority of the two houses of the mimic parliament were defined with punctilious exactness. The common council was reduced from eighty to sixty members,[752] to be elected from the four wards by all citizens "inhabiting and having houses on their own account." It had its Speaker,[753] its own mode of procedure, its system of elaborate etiquette in all dealings with the upper house. Henceforth it was to take a part in legislation which entirely annulled any claim "the citizens" might have put forward by virtue of their charter of 1378; for though the mayor and the twenty-four preserved the right of proposing all new laws, "they shall nothing do nor make that may bind or charge the city without the assent of the commonalty." All ordinances made by the upper body must therefore be formally laid before the common council, and if it seemed to them that the matter "needeth longer advice and deliberation of answer, they shall ask it and all that seemeth expedient for the city by the common speaker of the mayor and of his council." If needful they could ask for "a bill of the same matters to be delivered to them," that they might give their answer in the next assembly; and "the mayor shall be beholden as ofttimes as they ask it to grant them for to go together in an house by themselves without any denying, and none other with them but the common speaker, and if they will have more to them as oft as they ask, the mayor shall be beholden to send for them without any withsaying. And in matters that seem to the aforesaid sixty persons for the common council that needeth not great nor long advice, be it lawful if they will, to go apart by themselves or in to the floor with their common speaker, and goodly and speedily, without great delay to come in with their answer as them seemeth speedful and needful to the purpose." Finally, in "all other points that be necessary to be had for the welfare of the city that come not now to mind, it is committed to the whole assembly thereupon to ordain and make remedy by ordinance and assent of the whole commonalty for profit of all the city."[754]

In the matter of elections, however, the general assembly reappeared in full force. When a new mayor was to be chosen the two councils were summoned to the hall; "and also all the citizens dwellers within the same city unto the aforesaid election shall freely come as they are beholden, and the doors of the hall to all citizens there willing to enter and come in shall be open and not kept, nor none from thence forbarred nor avoided but foreigners." After the mayor and the twenty-four had proclaimed the election from the bench they withdrew to the chamber, and the whole people in the hall then chose from among those who had already been mayors or sheriffs two names of "sufficient" persons, "and if that any variance happen among the commons in the hall that it may not clearly be known to the common speaker by no manner of form by him unto them, for to be put or showed, which two hath the most voices, then the common speaker and the common clerk shall go up to the mayor and to him shall declare the variance of the people in the hall. And then the mayor shall give to the common speaker in commandment for to call together the sixty persons for the common council of the city, or as many as there be there into an house by themselves. Which there shall try the aforesaid variance in the same form as it hath been and yet is used in the city of London." The names were carried to the chamber by the common clerk, the common speaker, and the recorder, with six of the common council; the six commons returned to the hall, leaving the three officers to take the votes of the mayor and council, and bring back to the commonalty the name of the elected mayor.

The election of all other municipal officers was carefully divided between the two parties in the state. The mayor and the twenty-four elected the common clerk, one sheriff, one chamberlain, one treasurer, one coroner, two keepers of the keys, two auditors, and eight constables. The common council chose the common speaker, a second sheriff, chamberlain, treasurer, and coroner, two keepers of the keys, two auditors, and eight constables. The whole assembly appointed the common serjeant, the recorder, the bell-man, and the ditch-keeper; they also chose the men who were to gather in the king's taxes, appointing four men in each ward to assess the tax and two to collect it. The new mayor named two sword-bearers, of whom the assembly chose one; in the same way the mayor nominated four persons for serjeants, and the assembly chose two of them.[755] Members of Parliament were chosen by the common assembly.

Thus the commons of Norwich made their decorous entry on the official stage, with a punctilious care to secure their dignity and make fast their liberties by countless ceremonial ligatures. The Composition which vindicated their right against the oligarchy proved, however, like the Ordinances of 1404, a hard saying to many; and disputes between the mayor's council and the commonalty were so violent[756] that the citizens appealed to Henry the Fifth in 1417 for a charter which should make the late agreement legally binding. The mayor's council no doubt brought influence to bear in high places, for their position was now somewhat bettered. By the charter, for which the city had to pay over £100,[757] the twenty-four, now first called aldermen, got rid of one serious difficulty in their way by securing the clause that they "shall stand perpetually as they do in London," and henceforth the old ceremony of annual election was simply recalled by the custom of reading out the names every year before the wards. In the composition it had been settled that in making "new ordinances for the welfare of the city that come not now to mind it is committed to the whole assembly thereon to ordain by ordinance and assent of the whole commonalty,"[758] but the new charter decreed that the mayor and aldermen should have full power to amend the laws and constitution with assent of the sixty of the common council.[759]

For the rest of the century the government of the city[760] remained of this pattern. The four great leets which had once elected the bailiffs now became the four wards, and were ultimately divided into twelve small wards. Each of these was represented in the upper council by two aldermen chosen for it by the electors of its own great ward. Each great ward also elected a fixed proportion of the members of the common council. The sheriffs held their "tourns" for the four wards, and appointed for each ward a jury drawn from the "men of good name and fame." Meanwhile the leet courts of the sub-divisions over which the bailiffs used to preside carried on an obscure and feeble existence, and the capital pledges which formed the leet juries sank into insignificance[761] under the combined usurpations of the sheriffs and the two councils. Once when the capital pledges attempted to secure to the small trader some advantage in landing their goods at a staith where apparently they escaped some city tolls, the governing body promptly repressed their insubordination.[762] Evidently the administration of the city was neither more lax nor more popular because its governing body was enlarged.

In the obscure years of conflict between 1378 and 1415 we are told nothing about the men or the organizations of men that made the revolution. But we know that a very important movement was going on in Norwich itself in the growth of the craft guilds. Long forbidden by the civic government because of the loss to the city chest when the craftsmen were withdrawn from the common courts, they apparently made matters easy for themselves by regular payment of fines, and continued to flourish.[763] Between 1350 and 1385[764] a number of guilds were either founded or reconstituted so as to obtain public recognition in the city,[765] and the one fact that we catch sight of in their ordinances amid the absolutely monotonous and formal recital of religious duties, is that they were in some cases allowed to choose their own aldermen and council, instead of being subjected as before to the twenty-four. The importance of this is at once evident in the ordinances of 1404, where the guilds take a very prominent place; and in the composition of 1415, when they were finally sanctioned and given a completed form.[766] Not only was the power of choosing their own officers granted to every trade, but it was decreed that "citizens of the city shall be enrolled of what craft he be of" on pain of forfeiture of his franchise; and that all "that shall be enfranchised from this time forth shall be enrolled under a craft and by assent of a craft." Such a rule practically made the craft-masters the judges of a new candidate for the city privileges, for if they refused to admit him to the guild he could never become a burgess.[767] On the other hand it was commanded that all the members of a craft must become freemen; foreigners were to hold shops under tribute and fine for two years and a day, and were then forced to buy the franchise of the city. "The master of the craft shall come honestly to him and give him warning to be a freeman or else spear in his shop-window." If he did not obey within fourteen days the master with an officer of the mayor again visited him with his spear, "and he so speared in, nor no other, shall not hold his craft within house nor without." Thus no trader or shopkeeper could remain exempt from the dues and charges of the city, and the whole commonalty was placed under the police supervision of the craft masters. The very dress of the crafts was made a matter of strict definition; all liveries and hoods of former days were to be given up, and the crafts were to wear liveries the same as those of London.[768]

If, however, during the years of conflict the craft associations may have done good service to the commonalty, they were met by a counter organization of the merchants and upper class. It seems to have become common after the Peasant revolt, when a new terror was stirred as to what the poor commons might do if left to follow their own will and appetite, for the richer sort to unite for self-protection and the preservation of their authority. In Norwich a Guild of S. George was founded in 1385 as a fraternity with the usual religious colour, and a - "going each Monday about in the city remembering and praying for the souls of the brethren and sisters of the said guild that be passed to God's mercy."[769] At first an informal body, consisting apparently of the wealthier and more powerful people, both lay and ecclesiastic, of Norwich and the surrounding country, its weakness lay in the fact that it was "desevered by constitutions and ordinances made within the city," and according to the old rule by which the formation of any guild was forbidden, it was, in fact, an illegal body. The governing class, however, probably enlisted considerable sympathy at court in the negociations for the charter of 1417; and the associates of S. George won from Henry the Fifth in 1418 permission to constitute themselves into a permanent society, and received a sword of wood with a carved dragon's head to be carried before their alderman on S. George's day.[770] The great people of the county and their wives entered the order, bishops, monks and rectors, counts, knights, and merchants—something like four hundred of them—all men of substance who rode on horseback to the guild assembly, where the uniform of S. George was varied by the mayors, sheriffs, aldermen, or masters of crafts, riding in the garments of their order. The government of the society was put in the hands of a very close corporation, and the alliance between Church and State in the guild is manifested by the association of the prior, mayor, and sheriffs of the city in its government.[771]

The real danger of such a fraternity lay in the peculiar position of Norwich, and the impossible task of local government which had been thrown on its burghers. Beyond the city territory lay a great manufacturing district—a whole county studded with villages where weaving and worsted making were carried on in every house—and over all this district Norwich had the supervision of the woollen trade. The difficulties of the arrangement by which, in 1409, at the request of the commons, the mayor, sheriffs, and commonalty were granted the right of measuring and sealing all worsteds made in Norwich or Norfolk,[772] must have been extreme. The great employers settled in the city who organized the country labour and supplied cloth for the export trade were thus given a certain judicial authority in the county; while the great wool sellers—land-owners whose vast flocks of sheep[773] pastured on the broad downs of undulating chalk, and who were turning into traders on their own account—were forced in their own interest to meddle with Norwich politics. Besides the general commercial questions which affected both city and county, there must have been many a vexed question as to the tenants who owed suit and service to the courts of their lords, but who as artizans were subject to Norwich rule and whose fines were swept into the Norwich treasury. On every hand the door was thrown open to trouble. If the Norwich corporation was to busy itself in county affairs, the county was bound to exert some control over the Norwich corporation, whether by guilds of St. George, by securing office in Norwich for sympathetic mayors, recorders, or sheriffs, by winning the help of the Earl of Suffolk or of bishop or prior, by choosing the Norwich members for Parliament, or if all other means failed, by bribery and violence and the stirring up of street factions.

From one point of view, therefore, the story of the long years of strife and calamity which followed the reformation of the Norwich constitution in 1415 is singularly interesting. In presence of a foreign foe internal dissension is suppressed, and the main story is no longer, as in Nottingham, that of a struggle between the two classes of the community itself. When a mayor of alien interests is imposed on Norwich by a foreign faction he stands alone, and aldermen and commons hold apart from him as betrayer of the common interests. The enemies whom Norwich had to fear came from without the community itself, and if the story of the city remained a singularly troubled one, the troublers of its peace were not those of its own household. Factions of the State and factions of the shire flung confusion into the city politics, and the old burning question of ecclesiastical rights embittered every local dispute.[774] Norwich was befriended by the Duke of Gloucester and had a persistent enemy in the Earl of Suffolk, and its fortunes swung backwards and forwards with the rise and fall of court parties. From the day when the recorder, John Heydon, betrayed the city into their hands, the county despots whom we know so well in the Paston Letters, meet us in its streets and assembly hall, ever followed by the curses of the people. Heydon of Baconsthorpe, Esq., sheriff in Norwich in 1431, and recorder from 1441-3,—the man whose putting away of his wife had created such a scandal that the very mention of it made him turn pale, the land-jobber, the smuggler of wool, the exactor of bribes, the parasite of the great lords whose support he could buy, the organizer of outrages and murder, the audacious schemer willing to spend two thousand pounds rather than lose the control of the Norwich sheriff, the patron of liveried followers, the "maintainer" in the courts of men who defied the law, the overbearing bully whose very presence was enough to cow the commons into refusing to present their complaints to the king's judges,[775]—can be pictured by every one who tracks his tortuous ways through the letters of the Pastons. In conjunction with Sir Thomas Tuddenham and others he overwhelmed the city with extortions, oppressions, and wrongs. These men "through their great covetousness and false might oppressed all such citizens as would not consent to make such mayors and sheriffs as they liked," "purposing for great lucre to have as well the rule of the city of Norwich as they had of the shire of Norfolk,"[776] and "trusting in their great might and power which they had and have in the country by the means of the stewardship of Lancaster and other great offices and for divers other causes that no man at that time durst make resistance against them, knowing their great malice and vengeance without dread of God or shame of the world." Even when the people sought to buy the favour of Sir Thomas, he took their money "by briberous extortion against all faith and conscience," and yet showed them no mercy.[777]

It is just possible that the danger to the city called into being a fraternity to confront the society of S. George, and that the burghers in their turn seized on the machinery of the religious guild. We catch one passing glimpse of a curious association known as "Le Bachery"; which was declared by the mayor and commons to be merely a company of citizens who out of pure devotion kept up a light in the chapel of the Blessed Virgin in the Fields (the ancient place for the assembly of the people) and from mere motives of decency had chosen a livery; but in whose pious and decent union the hostile fraternity saw an association fashioned to break the power of S. George, and made haste to use against it the old argument applied to its own youth—the charge of being an "illegal guild."[778]

The association was founded in stormy days. After Heydon was turned out of office by the people for betraying their interests to the prior,[779] his friend of S. George's guild, the mayor Wetherby, an ally of Tuddenham and a "hater of the commons," led the party of the county and the priory, and till his death fourteen years later the city knew no peace. Four times between 1433 and 1444 its franchises were forfeited for riot or stormy elections; twice the common seal was violently taken out of the treasury by aldermen and commons to prevent the sealing of proposals rejected of the people. Wetherby forced on the election, as his successor, of a mayor refused by aldermen and commons. John Qwerdling, falsely pretending to be common speaker, had carried to the chamber a name not set down by the commons for election; Hawk the town clerk had written down a wrong return; Nicholas Waleys had taken bribes enough to win him the name of "ambidexter"; the two city serjeants had packed juries, and the gaoler had threatened and struck the resisting commons on the head with his mace. The mayor's faction held the guild hall, while the aldermen's party retired to a private house, and having elected another candidate, put the offending officers out of their places, took the common seal out of the guild hall into their own keeping, and lest by any chance their election should be held invalid, refused to disperse till the mayor came down to confirm it, and called the bishop to join them in opposition to the prior. For the moment Wetherby yielded, but revenged himself by applying for a commission from the king to examine into the state of the city.[780] The enraged citizens kept up the broil till 1436, when another commission was appointed which forced the commons to submit, to restore the seal to its accustomed place in the treasury, and to put back the officers they had displaced in 1433.[781]

At the next election, in 1437, commissioners were sent by the privy council to see that all was done in order according to the charter, and in case of riot to seize the franchises of the city into the king's hand;[782] and thus quiet was secured. But Norwich was not to keep its restored franchise long. Riots and daily disturbances "concerning their liberties" broke out between the city and the prior;[783] in June the inhabitants of Norwich had to appear before the Privy Council, and in July the franchises of the city were seized and the place committed to the custody of John Welles, a London alderman who was made citizen and alderman of Norwich.[784] At the prayer of the bishops of Norwich and Lincoln the liberties were once more restored in 1439, to be as quickly lost again.[785] For Thomas Wetherby "who bare a great hatred to the commons" watched for an opportunity of making fresh trouble. By his counsel the abbot of S. Bennet's at Holm prosecuted the city in 1441 for certain mills it had built on the Wensum; and Thomas Tuddenham, John Fray, and William Paston (a friend of the abbot's), judged the case at Thetford and gave it against the the city, ordering the commons to pay £100 damages to the abbot and £50 to the prior. At this the assembly gathered in great numbers, crowded to the hall, in January, 1442, and took away the common seal that the award might not be sealed. By the influence of the Earl of Suffolk, the abbot, and Wetherby, the city was prosecuted for rebellion, and in spite of the protection of the Duke of Gloucester the mayor was ordered to appear in London, where he was fined £50 and imprisoned in the Fleet, and the liberties of the city were again seized into the king's hands. The mayor being thus fast in the Fleet, Wetherby got the common seal out of the chest, sealed the bond of £100 to the abbot of S. Bennet's at Holm, £50 to the bishop, and £50 to the prior, without the knowledge of the mayor, sheriffs, or commons; and then destroyed the new mills.[786]

This led to fresh troubles. On the Shrove Tuesday of 1443 the mayor and commonalty, at this time united in the mysterious guild of "Le Bachery," raised an insurrection, declaring they had power enough in the city and adjacent country to slay Thomas Brown the bishop,[787] the abbot of Holm, and the prior of Norwich. John Gladman, a merchant, rode with a paper crown as king at the head of a hundred and thirty people on horseback and on foot. At the ringing of the city bells three thousand citizens assembled, armed with swords, bows, arrows, and helmets, surrounded the priory, laid guns against it, and at last won a glorious victory, and forced the monks to deliver up the hateful deed falsely sealed with the common seal which bound the people to pay 4s. a year to the prior and to abandon claims to jurisdiction over certain priory lands.

Such a triumph was naturally followed by a fresh visit of royal commissioners in 1444.[788] Wetherby and the prior brought a long list of charges against the mayor;[789] while the city protested that Tuddenham and Heydon alone had made mischief out of their peaceful show; and that Gladman had only "made a disport with his neighbours, having his horse trapped with tynnsoyle and other nice disguisy things, crowned as king of Christmas," while "before him went each month disguised after the season required, and Lent clad in white and red herring skins and his horse trapped with oyster shells after him."[790]

Meanwhile the king had his own grievance against Norwich, for the city had unluckily brought a suit for £100 which it had formerly lent him, and now refused to advance any more money when he sent to solicit it.[791] Once more, therefore, in 1444, its liberties and franchises were confiscated. But now at last troubles began to lighten. Thomas Wetherby died, as well as the bishop who had supported him,[792] and the new bishop, of an old Norwich family, was for peace. In 1447 the liberties were restored, and in 1448 the king visited the city.[793] Two years later however, Heydon was again to the front, ready with Tuddenham to spend £2,000 in buying favour in high quarters in London, and £1,000 to secure a sheriff in Norwich committed to his interest.[794] It was suggested that the Norwich folk, the mayor with the aldermen and all the commons, should ride to meet the Duke of York when he visited the city, "and all the women of the same town be there also, and cry out on them also, and call them extortioners, and pray my Lord that he will do sharp executions upon them ... and let that be done in the most lamentable wise, for Sir, but if my Lord hear some foul tales of them, and some hideous noise and cry, by my faith they are else like to come to grace."[795] The commission of judges[796] finally sent to try Heydon for felony, his defiant ride through the town into the abbey, the rumours that he was to bear rule once more, his mode of meeting and outwitting or terrorising the commissioners by turns, all these are told from day to day almost in the Paston Letters. Finally, in 1452, Judge Yelverton arranged some kind of peace in Norwich,[797] helped possibly by the poverty and exhaustion of the city.[798] By giving a loan to the king and a present to the queen with a promise to befriend her in her anxieties, Norwich got a new charter in 1452.[799] In this the guild of S. George, which seems to have been united to the corporation about 1450, was apparently victorious.[800] It was agreed that the day after the mayor left office he should be chosen alderman of the guild, and the common council was taken into the council of the guild.

For the next seventy years the citizens were occupied by strife with the prior, which dated back to the day when the Norwich burghers were given the city into their hands.[801] The bickerings of three centuries ended in a compact drawn up in 1524, when questions of jurisdiction, tolls, pasturage, water, and rights of way were settled; and it was admitted that the mayor, sheriffs, citizens, and commonalty might go to the cathedral church on feast days and occasions of solemn processions, the mayor with sword and maces borne before him, on condition that he claimed no jurisdiction, while the prior and monks "of their amiable favour shall forbear as far as they lawfully can or may" to arrest any of the corporation or the citizens during these great processions.[802]

Such stories of local wranglings might well be left forgotten and obscure if there lay in them nothing more than vulgar quarrels. But the political experiment of Norwich was one of such serious purpose and such singular quality, that even in its failure it kindles our sympathy with men who for two hundred and fifty years had been laboriously working out the problem of administration. With an admirable political sagacity they had used in turn every form of local organization to perfect their experiment in self-government. They had taken the principle of an elected jury and adapted it for use in their courts, their council chamber, and their legislative assembly. They had turned to the problem of the general assembly, altogether useless in its primitive and unwieldy form, and developed out of it (taking a pattern from London) a representative council which should guide its deliberations and express its will. The craft-guilds were organized, and it is possible that in the struggle their discipline gave order and strength to the commonalty. When the battle grew hot the machinery of the religious guild was brought into play on either side, and S. George measured his force with the Virgin of the Fields. No doubt these various methods have no claim to originality, being frankly copied from customs known elsewhere; nor is it in the discovery of a new path that the merit of the Norwich burghers lies, but in the sound political instinct by which they steadily directed their way into the broad track whose ultimate goal is civil freedom, rather than the narrow road of privilege. As we watch the growth of the house of representatives which was established among them, an independent deliberative assembly elected by the commons; and compare it with the chamber of magnates at Nottingham that by a fine mockery was supposed to typify a gathering of the whole community; we have a just measure given us of the value of this more liberal experiment in municipal politics—an experiment so early in time, so serious in conception, so strong and orderly in execution, that it might have justified an enduring success.

But in spite of all the ingenuity and sagacity and resolution which the men of Norwich brought to their fine attempt at ordering public life, misfortune still waited on their steps, and from the outset the disaster of the fifteenth century darkens and throws long shadows. For Norwich was fighting with its doom already proclaimed—harassed by the harsh dry climate in which fine cloth needed for the foreign market could not be woven; by the hurry of the new export trade which drove masters to set up their mills by the streams of Yorkshire and Gloucestershire, where labour was free and cheap; by changes in methods of making worsted which shifted the manufacture over to the Netherlands; and by the false economy which to help a failing trade, made

English weavers refuse Norfolk yarn to foreign buyers—the Norwich burghers had still to endure the last calamity of pestilence, and the sweating sickness, which first burst on them in 1485, filled up the tale of disaster. Industrial difficulties alone might have been conquered. But a more insidious danger threatened all their liberties. By a fatal accident of position and circumstances the city, as we have seen, had been invaded and conquered by the county—by a society wholly separate from it in political developement. It had bitterly proved the truth of the extreme apprehension with which men of the towns at that time looked on the intrusion among them of "foreigners," bringing into their newly ordered civic life the feudal traditions of the county magnates, scattering liveries among their people, and pouring into their law courts a commanding army of retainers—"because," to use their own words, "by such maintainers and protectors a common contention might arise among us, and horrible manslaughter be committed among us, and the loss of the liberty or freedom of the city, to the disinheritance of us and of our children; which God forbid that in our days by the defeat of us should happen or fall out in such a manner."[803] The story of Norwich shows that in a provincial town, as in a greater state, a constitution framed for home uses and needs may be shattered by the violence of foreign affairs over which it has no power, against which it has no arms, and for the guidance of which it has no instructions.

NOTE A.

Mr. Hudson believes that in Norwich the word "citizen" at first meant merely an enfranchised equal, being frequently described as "par civitatis," and that from the thirteenth century onwards the most prominent idea which it imported was that of a privileged trader, in which sense it is used through the series of Leet Rolls. In one class of documents, however, at the close of the thirteenth century, he finds it apparently restricted to a limited body of substantial burghers, into whose hands the management of the public business had gradually passed. In enrolled deeds which have been examined for the years 1285-1298 a great number of persons are described merely as drapers, tanners, fishmongers and so on, while others are mentioned as "merchant citizen of Norwich," or "tanner, citizen of Norwich," and others again are put down simply as "citizen of Norwich." Out of the hundred and fifty persons to whom the words "citizen of Norwich" are applied there are fifty who are apparently of no trade; and of the remaining hundred, thirty-two are merchants, twenty-four drapers and linendrapers, and the rest, about fifty, belong to a variety of occupations, but generally to the skilled handicrafts. No smith is mentioned as citizen, and very few among the butchers and bakers. From these facts the general conclusion is drawn that the word "citizen" was being gradually restricted by the most important burghers to themselves, the lower classes of those who held the freedom of the city being massed together as the "communitas." (Arch. Journ. xlvi. No. 184, 318-319.)

The argument, however, rests on entries made in the last years of the thirteenth century, between 1285 and 1298, at a time when the state of things in Norwich was exceptional. The city rule was that every man who bought and sold in Norwich should have "made his ingress" into the town and become of the "franchise" or "liberty." How often the law was evaded we see from the presentments of the leet courts. (For the last ten years of the thirteenth century see Town Close Evidences, 12-15.) It would seem that as the prosperity of the city increased new inhabitants had begun to flock to it who were far more concerned in making their own bargains than in carrying out the laws and customs of the borough; and who, especially the poorer sort engaged in humble trades, were anxious to escape the payments and responsibilities of citizenship. Blomefield (iii. 73) states that about 1306, owing to difficulties in paying the ferm, it was ordered that every one who had traded for a year and a day in the city must take up his freedom, paying for it a fine of 40s. if he were not entitled to the franchise by birth or service. Since every citizen was bound to have a house, building went on fast, and can be measured by the increase of rents from houses. For "in 1329 Simon de Berford the King's escheator on this side Trent gave the city much trouble concerning a number of houses, shops and tenements lately erected by grant of the city on the waste grounds of the said city, on pretence that all the waste belonged to the King and not to the citizens, and that the rents of all such buildings should belong to the Crown (Custom Book fo. 2) by which means great part of the city rents, namely all the rents *de novo incremento* or new increased rents, would have been lost from the city to the value of £9 11s. 8d. a year, by which we may calculate the surprising increase of the inhabitants of this place from the beginning of Edward II. to this time. The small rents or old rents of houses erected upon the city waste from its original to Edward the Second's time amounted to but 9s. 2d., so that if we compare the new increased rents with the old ones we shall find in about thirty years' time nineteen times as many houses erected upon the waste as there were before, an argument sufficiently showing how populous it grew by its flourishing trade, and indeed its increase continued as surprisingly till that fatal pestilence in 1349.

"To remedy this imposition the citizens sent to Thomas Butt and John Ymme, their burgesses in Parliament, then held at Winchester, to complain of the usage to the King and Parliament; upon which the King afterwards directed his writ to the said Simon, certifying him, that by the grants of his progenitors, Kings of England, the citizens held the city and all the waste ground by fee-farm, in inheritance, and that therefore he had nothing to do to molest them in letting out such void grounds to be built upon for their profit and advantage towards paying their fee-farm. This writ bears date at Reading March 25, in the 4th of his reign." (Blomefield, iii. 80-1.)

These facts seem to indicate that citizenship was a less frequent thing among the inhabitants of Norwich at the end of the thirteenth century than in the first half of the fourteenth century—and was at that time possibly confined in practice to those who gained it by birth or service, and that purchase was rare.

For the very different law made by the Bishop of Norwich in 1307 for Lynn see p. 408. He may have desired to secure for Lynn the small traders who found themselves hard pressed by the Norwich decree of 1306.

CHAPTER XV

THE COMMON COUNCIL OF LYNN

It was not in Norwich alone that the people, refusing submission to a governing plutocracy, made the experiment of creating a lower house of commons to represent the burghers at large. The peculiar difficulties that beset popular government in that city were absent in other towns, but in no case was the experiment a simple matter. Everywhere unforeseen dangers were presently disclosed, dangers new and various, and capable of overwhelming the new movement in ultimate ruin and confusion. Even at the moment when Norwich was forming its second chamber, the town of Lynn, but a very few miles away, was developing a common council wholly different in its origin and its constitution, and threatened by occasions of failure and betrayal of which Norwich had no experience.

The case of Lynn is one of singular interest. Nowhere else in England was there a corporation more wealthy, or more formidable from its compact organization and great authority. On the other hand nowhere else perhaps was there a community of "mean people," burgesses and non-burgesses, so prosperous, active, and united; sustained as they were in every emergency by the effectual protection of their lord the Bishop, who, in his jealousy of the governing class, was forced to become the ally of the subject people, and to make their cause his own. Under these circumstances the conflict between the commons and the plutocrats who ruled over them had some original characteristics, and the problem of church and state in Lynn emerges in a new and subtle form.

The ruling class of the town was from the first the governing body of the Merchant Guild.[804] For here, as in other leading ports, it is evident that the rich traders quickly became dominant in civic affairs, even though their association in a Guild Merchant of itself gave them no right to govern. In Lynn a powerful merchant class must have been formed at a very early time. Through the town lay the one way by which Norfolk could be entered from the west; and its port was the only outlet for the trade of seven counties. Lynn was therefore the centre for the largest cattle market in the east of England, whence the export trade drew supplies of wool and fells and hides;[805] its middlemen and merchants held in their hands the commerce with Gascony, the Rhineland, Zealand, "the parts of North Berne," with Prussia, and Dacia, and the Hanse towns; and as early as 1271 the German merchants had some sort of local organization there under their alderman Symon, a citizen of Lynn, of whom we hear that he gave a pledge on behalf of some Lübeck merchants to the amount of £200.[806] No interest in the borough could compete with the great commercial company[807] by whom the whole volume of trade that was borne over the waters of the Wash "rowing and flowing," was ultimately controlled. Under the name of the Holy Trinity it had obtained a charter from John, and by the time of Edward the Second had nearly nine hundred names on its bede-roll. The sons of its old members were allowed to enter the guild on payment of 6*s.* 8*d.*; while others, men and women, were willing to give 60*s.* or 100*s.* to be counted among its brethren, the men looking to share in the political as well as commercial benefits it offered, while women were perhaps consoled with its spiritual gains; and men and women alike paid the same entrance fee to be enrolled after death in consideration of the eternal advantages of such membership.[808] In 1392 the guild employed thirteen chaplains yearly to say masses in the churches of S. Margaret, S. Nicholas, and S. James, used much wax for lights in churches and chapels, and from the profits of the common staith gave alms and fulfilled works of charity.[809]

The spiritual blessings of the guild, however, pale before the financial and political boons it had to offer. As a great trading company it heaped up wealth and increased power. The aldermen and his brethren made laws to regulate the commerce even of those burgesses who did not belong to their select company, but carried on business by virtue of the charter of free trade granted to the whole borough.[810] The guild owned along with other property the common staith and all its appurtenances, the quay where by its decree "no bad persons, nor any spiritual persons should work,"[811] and the right of passage for a boat beyond the port.[812] The monopoly of various profitable trades was secured to its members, as for instance the sale of mill-stones,[813] paving-stones, and grave-stones which were sold at from 20*s.* to 30*s.* apiece. The brethren of the guild were the bankers and capitalists of the town.[814] They lent money out on usury, and not only did the corporation come to borrow from their treasury, but in 1408 more than fifty townsmen were in their debt for sums varying from £1 to £119. The trading activity of the company may be measured by the fact that in 1392 the guild had in ready money £60 13*s.*, and in divers merchandise £200;[815] and in 1408 the loans came to £1,214. In 1422 its wealth was £1,403, of which the debts due to it made up £1,210. Its expenditure was generous and magnificent. Large sums were spent on the new guild hall, beginning in 1422 with £132 4*s.* The silver plate in its treasury weighed in the first half of the century 440 ounces. A silver wand was borne before its dean; and its members were carried to their graves under a covering of cloth of gold.[816]

Financial transactions on such a scale as this would in any case have given the guild control over a town government whose expenses were fast increasing, and which in every time of need turned to its coffers for money. But the company of the Holy Trinity exerted far more than an indirect authority over the corporation. It was in effect itself the real governing force in Lynn. By a charter of Henry the Third its alderman (who held office for life and was thus absolutely independent of popular control) was joined with the mayor in the rule and government of the borough: in case of the mayor's absence or death he was appointed in his stead,[817] and in the election of a new mayor he took the leading part.[818] Moreover, the twenty-four jurats of the council, who had the control of all town business, and from among whom alone the mayor might be chosen, were bound to be brethren of the guild. Under these conditions the "Potentiores"—the "great men of the town"—as they were commonly called in the time of Edward the First, ruled without restraint, and with a high hand assessed taxes, diverted money from the common treasury, profited by illegal trading, used customs contrary to common or merchant law, and bought the king's forgiveness if any complaint was made of their crimes. Against their despotism there was no protection for the burgesses of humbler station—the middle class which went by the name of Mediocres, and the yet lower layer of the people known as the Inferiores, traders and householders who were not burgesses, and whose prosperity, if fairly well established, was of a less brilliant character than that of the upper classes.

There was, however, a disturbing element in the history of the Lynn corporation which was absent in Southampton, Nottingham, or Norwich. The lord of the manor was close at hand, and the governing class had to reckon with his claims and expect his interference. Local disputes magnified his power. Thrown together as natural allies against the potentiores, the mediocres and inferiores were forced to rely mainly on the protection of the Bishop. He on his part, whether for the sake of developing the trade of his borough, or for the sake of increasing the population dependent on himself rather than on the rival power of the mayor, stipulated—and this at the very moment when Norwich was compelling all its traders and artizans to buy its freedom—that the mayor should not have power to force the franchise on any settlers old or new who might take up house in the town while preferring to remain free of the charges of citizenship. He won from the mayor, moreover, in 1309, a Composition for the protection of both mediocres and inferiores, which not only became the charter of all their future liberties, but was also the fullest recognition of his own authority.[819] From this time, in spite of efforts on the part of the municipality to evade the composition, the mean people, confident of their legal position and assured of the support of a powerful patron, formed a society differently compacted from that which we find in other boroughs, and played a part in the politics of Lynn which was perhaps unique in town history. The "community" of Lynn differed from the "community" of other boroughs in being made up, as is formally stated in 1412, not only of burgesses, both potentiores and mediocres, but also of inferiores[820] or non-burgesses.

The first detailed account of the constitution of Lynn is given in Letters Patent of Henry the Fifth in 1417, where the "ancient custom" which ruled the town was recapitulated.[821] When a mayor was to be elected the alderman of the guild appointed four "worthy and sufficient" burgesses, who added to themselves eight comburgesses, and this jury of twelve elected one of the twenty-four jurats as mayor, and appointed the other municipal officers for the coming year.[822] The council of twenty-four jurats, which was drawn wholly from the ranks of the merchant guild and elected for life, filled up its own vacancies, so that when any one of them died or resigned his office or was expelled, the townsfolk appeared as mere spectators in the hall, while the mayor and remaining jurats chose "one of the more worthy, honest, discreet, and sufficient" of the burgesses to fill the vacant place. If it became necessary to elect any other officers the mayor nominated four comburgesses, who named in their turn eight others to form a jury.

In later days it was supposed that so long as these ordinances were observed "mayor, jurats, burgesses, and community, rested happily under the sweetness of peace and quiet throughout the days of prosperous times."[823] Prosperous times there had certainly been[824] if we judge by the growth of the town's budget. In 1354 the corporation spent £176; in 1355 £94; in 1356 £266; in 1357 £92; in 1367 £165; in 1371 £163; in 1374 £249. The year 1377 was very costly to the burghers, whose expenses suddenly mounted to £874. It was the year of the quarrel with the Bishop of Norwich,[825] and Lynn had to give £318 15s. to the king, his mother, and others "labouring for the community" when the Bishop laid his complaint before the council "for a certain transgression done to him in the town"; and to pay £116 10s. for the expenses of the mayor, aldermen, and burgesses who went to London on the same business. They were required further this year to spend £113 on making an enclosure for the defence of the town; and £103 10s. on a town barge, doubtless fitted out at the king's demand to serve as a war vessel. All this naturally ended in a heavy debt; the corporation had only been able to raise £650 6s. 2d. and had to borrow £160 from the guild, and to leave the salaries of the mayor, clerk, serjeants, and chamberlains unpaid. The next year, however, it made an effort to clear off its debt and actually spent nearly £773, paying off £241 10s. to its creditors. From this time expenditure grew fast. In 1380 it was £351, and in 1382 £204; in 1385 £304; in 1389 £394; in 1399 £461.[826] In 1403 the borough had to lend to the king over £333 which was not repaid till 1425.[827]

The municipal debt of course grew as fast as the municipal expenditure, and in 1408 the corporation owed the guild between £400 and £500.[828] The council of jurats borrowed generously from the fraternity in their capacity of town councillors, and lent as generously to the corporation in their capacity of members of the guild. The inevitable abuses which belong to financial administration conducted on this system presently made themselves felt. Perhaps there was an attempt at reform when in 1402 changes were made in the manner of keeping and auditing accounts, and each of the four chamberlains had to return a separate statement of receipts and outgoings.[829] But if so the remedy was ineffectual, and for the state of Lynn, as for far bigger states, the question of finance ended in a question of revolution, or was at last the pretext of revolution. The angry discontent of the community finally broke out in 1411, when the people demanded the repayment into the town treasury of a sum of £458, which the last five mayors had spent without the consent of the community in litigation with the Bishop, to the serious prejudice and extreme depoverishment of the town. The five mayors on their side, at the head of the potentiores, retorted by claiming from the town £280 to repay losses which they had incurred in its service during their terms of office.

Thus the traditional "sweetness of peace" was at an end, and Lynn was presently plunged into the excitement of a revolution. Fortunately for the people the ruling body found itself face to face with all its enemies at once; for the mediocres and inferiores, alike excluded from places of honour and power, were as of old drawn into close relations and were together thrown on the protection of their lord the Bishop for the defence of their rights; while the Bishop himself, with whom the municipality had been dragging on a long quarrel for the last thirteen years, was probably in no conciliatory mood. Everything, however, was conducted on strictly constitutional lines. By common consent a committee of eighteen men of the town was appointed to deal with the grievances of the state, and every section of the town society was required to give pledges of obedience to its decision. The mayor and twenty-two potentiores bound themselves in sums of £100 each to submit to the decrees of the eighteen; eighty-four of the mediocres pledged themselves in sums of £50 each; and sixty-six of the inferiores in sums of £5 11s. 2d. On the committee itself each of the three classes that made up the community was represented. There were twelve burgesses, of whom seven were potentiores and five mediocres, and six non-burgesses or inferiores.

At first all seemed to go well for the popular party. The decisions of the committee were eminently satisfactory. The compensation money which the late mayors had claimed was altogether refused; and they were ordered to repay to the town treasury the £458 illegally spent without consent of the community. A decree was made that henceforth the mayor should only have, according to ancient custom, £10 for his year's fee and whatever the community might put by for his reward having regard to his merit or demerit; and that he should answer to the town for all arrears of contributions during his mayoralty. It was declared that the non-burgesses had been deprived of the privileges secured to them by the composition of 1309, and an order was made that from this time they "shall have and use all rights to the said inferiores granted." This was a declaration of ancient law and custom; but the committee went further and began the process of "mending the constitution" by issuing a decree that for the future each mayor should choose and take to himself a council consisting of three potentiores, three mediocres, and three inferiores, which nine persons together with the mayor should have full power to deal with the rents, etc., of the community.[830] By these ordinances which mark the triumph of the alliance between the mediocres and inferiores with the lord of the manor behind them, just as the composition of 1309 had marked their triumph a century before, the non-burgesses were formally given a share in the actual control of administration—a circumstance which so far as published records go has no parallel in the history of any other borough. The decrees were agreed to (how reluctantly was to be proved later) by the corporation on April 8, 1411, and signed by persons chosen from the three orders of inhabitants;[831] in November, 1412, they were confirmed by Henry the Fourth; and once more on April 10, 1413, by Henry the Fifth.[832]

At the same time, in 1411, the important question of elections was raised; and for the sake of securing to the commonalty a due share of power along with the alderman and his brethren, it was suggested that "certain new ordinances and constitutions concerning and about the elections of the mayor and the rest of the jurats, and officers, and ministers," might be drawn up. The commons were to meet together a week before the day of election, and choose from among themselves a common speaker—a prolocutor he was called in Lynn. All burgesses who desired it might freely come to the guild hall for the election, and the congregation having been made, after public proclamation that none but a burgess or minister might give his vote,[833] they should choose two names from among the jurats, and from these two names the mayor and jurats were to select one as mayor. Throughout this proceeding the prolocutor and clerk were practically set to act as spies[834] on one another in the interests of their several parties, the prolocutor guarding the people's interest, and keeping watch at the elbow of the common clerk (the nominee of the mayor and jurats) as he went from burgess to burgess in the hall to inquire for whom they wished to vote, or as he carried the nominations to the mayor, and wrote down the decisive votes of the upper chamber "severally and secretly." In like manner the election of the other officers was also regulated;[835] and above all, the burgesses were, for the first time, given a share in the election of the council of twenty-four, being allowed at every vacancy to nominate two candidates; if these were rejected they were again to choose two other names, and so on until the jurats were satisfied. In its new constitution Lynn, like Norwich, decided to shape its system after "the manner and form in which it was used in the city of London;" but in Lynn there were special difficulties, and the new scheme could only be brought "at least to the greatest possible conformity with them of London, forsomuch that in the aforesaid town there are not had aldermen, wards, recorder, nor divers other things as in the city of London."[836]

Unhappily for "the sweetness of peace" parties were so evenly matched in the committee of eighteen that the reforms were only passed by a majority of one vote.[837] Moreover, the agreement—drawn up by the committee on April 8, 1411, set forth and assented to by the mayor and community in May, signed by their orders in July, and sealed with the common seal in December—was not confirmed by charter till the following November, 1412.[838] Thus, when the burgesses met on August 27, 1411, to choose a new mayor, their ordinances were still but a common agreement and without any sanction of law if they were disputed. Burgesses and non-burgesses gathered in force, some three hundred or so strong, to see what was going to happen. The question was raised as to what form of election should be used, and a proposal was made to delay the business. But the mayor having put it to the meeting that all who wished to proceed with the election were to sit down and the others to rise up, all save six "suddenly as in a moment fell on the forms, benches, and ground"; and a hundred and forty-eight burgesses insisted on going on with the business. The next point was how the electing jury was to be named, and the hundred non-burgesses present begged to have "a little voice" in the matter, which was refused. The alderman of the guild and the inferiores having been thus set aside, the burgesses were left in possession of the field, and they proceeded, with a compromise between the old and new systems, to nominate, as the alderman had formerly done, the first four members of the jury, two jurats and two mediocres, who then added to themselves eight burgesses. In the following year the people again assembled, burgesses and non-burgesses together to the number of three hundred, in spite of a notice on the rolls of process for "quieting these dissensions," and again carried out the elections after the new mode.[839]

The balance of forces, however, was too even to give the victors any security of tenure, and government worked with great friction. It seems that the mayor of the popular party strengthened the radical vote by admitting to the franchise "foreign" inhabitants (probably some of the inferiores) against the will of the council; while the reformers insulted the guild brethren in their own guild hall; and in 1415 "without consent of the mayor and burgesses" quit-claimed the debts of the town—debts owed, as we have seen, to the guild.[840] By their enemies the new ordinances were declared to have "furnished the fuel of grief and hatred," and according to the malcontents the late agreement had only caused "immense expenses, charges, losses, and intolerable damage by reason of discords, strifes, and other ills," and must inevitably "redound to the final destruction and pauperization, but also the desolation and probable overthrowing of all that town." In 1416 an appeal was made to Henry the Fifth, whose sympathy here, as in Norwich at the same time, was with the oligarchy; and he summoning the parties before him[841] ordered a final concord between them. To "pluck up by the roots and extirpate strifes" the new ordinances were utterly annulled, the former customs of the town recapitulated, and the old constitution restored. The alderman received again his ancient position,[842] the jurats became once more a self-electing body, and the town was subjected to the system dear to the potentiores, and against which the people had risen in vain. From this time the old method of election was resumed and carried on throughout the century.[843] Murmurs of discontent still seem to have been heard occasionally. In 1419 one of the townsmen challenged the alderman of the guild at the election assembly. "We would know," he said, "by what authority or right you call up four persons to make our mayor"; but he was put down by a speech about "our charter," and after this meeting it would seem that the public were no longer admitted to the meetings of the corporation.[844]

Defeated on the great issue of the election of the mayor and jurats, the commons fell back on the idea of a chamber of representatives. An attempt had already been made, in 1411, to form a council of nine, which though appointed by the mayor was to be drawn from the three orders of the community, and to act for them; but this scheme came to an end with the annulling of the ordinances. No sooner, however, was the old power of the potentiores restored by Henry the Fifth than the idea of a common council immediately revived among the people, possibly inspired by the example of Norwich which had only a year before secured the charter that gave its common council a permanent status. It was decided that each of the nine constabularies or wards in Lynn should choose three burgesses "having sufficient tenure in the town" who should take part in all business concerning taxes, tenths, fifteenths, allowances, repairs of houses, walls, bridges, watercourses, ditches, all payments, rendering of accounts, and other charges of the borough. This new body of twenty-seven became at once generally known as the common council, and was formally confirmed by the Bishop in 1420. The community bound itself to obey any decree which was issued in the name of the two councils,[845] and from December, 1418, when the noble jurats and the discreet burgesses met for the first time in the guild hall, the whole conduct of town business passed into their hands.[846] Henceforth decrees and ordinances were made with the assent of "the whole congregation";[847] but it is obvious that the institution of the common council in this form marked the final separation between the interests of the two lower classes of the community, and the irrevocable close of their alliance. As in 1411 the inferiores had been declared incapable of any share in electing officers, so now they remained without any part in legislation, while the mediocres entered happily into their inheritance.

So the revolution of Lynn flickered out. For the new common council cannot be said to have represented after all a very formidable concession to democratic demands. Unlike the council of 1411 it apparently took no account at all of the inferiores. The electorates of the constabularies seldom numbered more than twenty people and sometimes as few as twelve, and the whole body which elected the new council did not consist of more than a hundred and fifty persons.[848] To prevent any trouble, moreover, there was a provision that if any man proved unfit, the mayor and aldermen and the councils of twenty-four and twenty-seven might choose another in his place.[849] With such safeguards the new representatives might be trusted to work in complete harmony with the older body; the potentiores had taken the mediocres into their counsels and formed an alliance with them, and the inferiores, left outside the door of the common hall, deserted by their old confederates, and dependent on a lord whose influence was steadily on the decline, sank into obscurity and silence. In course of time the jurats rose to the full dignity of an upper house, and effectually secured in their own hands the whole administration of the nine constabularies by an order (in 1480) that a jurat must be chosen as alderman in each constabulary, that the alderman and constable together shall keep the peace and settle debates, and that if they could not reduce rebellious persons to quiet, no burgess in that constabulary might be suitor in any court, spiritual or temporal, without the leave of the mayor.[850] Finally, in 1524, the two ruling classes obtained a charter which formed their corporation into a close self-elective body; the mayor was to be elected by the twelve aldermen, and the twelve aldermen by the common council, and the common council by the mayor and aldermen.

In the last state of the council we see the strength given to the upper classes by a common alliance, by the humiliation of the non-burgesses, and by the increasing weakness of the lord of the manor. It would, however, be impossible to maintain that in Lynn a primitive democratic government had been gradually submerged by a usurping oligarchy. If we compare the demands put forward in 1309 by the inhabitants at large—demands for freedom of trade and some assurance that they should not be unjustly taxed—with their claims a century later to be formally represented in the administration of the town, we see what strides had been made in that hundred years in the notion of popular government; and so far as it was not violently thwarted by alien influences the movement of the early fifteenth century was in the direction of widening liberty. In the new governing body more than twice as many members sat as in the old council of the potentiores, and two orders of the community were represented instead of one; while the commonalty lost none of the ancient customary rights which had originally belonged to it. The non-burgesses still made their appearance with the rest when taxes were to be levied or the common property allotted. In 1435, when the mayor was sent to Bruges as one of the king's ambassadors on commercial matters, his journey and its expenses are ordered "by the full advice and assent of the twenty-four and the common council and of all the burgesses and merchants of Lynn."[851] During the first years of Henry the Sixth loans of money to the king and the receiving of re-payments was done in the name of and with the consent of the whole community;[852] in 1448 arbitrators to decide on a disputed question about a tenement were in like manner elected by the whole community;[853] and in the levying of taxes the whole three orders acted together as of old, so that in 1463, when a sum of £36 had to be raised, of the eighteen men chosen to assess the tax, six belonged to the jurats, six to the common council, and six to the "communitas."[854]

Still, however, from the point of view of any real extension of liberty, the revolution had failed, and as in Norwich it had failed from purely external causes. The temporal sovereignty of the Church had destroyed the political freedom of the State. From the time when the Bishop had broken their society into two sections, which could never again unite for civil purposes, an ecclesiastical tradition stood between the people and freedom. The crucial moment for liberty in Lynn had occurred a century before, on that day in 1309 when the Bishop had won from the corporation the right to create as a bulwark of his power a class of inhabitants protected in every material interest of their lives, but cut off from the body of free citizens, and carefully debarred from political independence. For a time the system by which a privileged class was allowed to buy the protection of the borough without paying the fair price, and to maintain a position within its walls by the authority of a power without, seemed to work well for both parties to the cunning bargain—indeed, to offer certain advantages. Dependent on the Bishop for all their rights of trade and privileges, the inferiores were content to let him fight their battles, which he did so effectually that the mediocres themselves were attracted to their party, and made common cause with them to the apparent profit of all concerned. But the only strength of a corrupt alliance utterly false in principle lay in the support given by the Bishop, and no sooner did this begin to fail than the whole scheme utterly collapsed. The question of elections raised at the August meeting of 1411 gave the potentiores their opportunity to break up the confederation from within by detaching the hundred or hundred and fifty mediocres from the rest of the party of resistance, leaving the non-burgesses to shift for themselves; and when these, suddenly alive to their hapless situation, tried to recover ground and begged to be taken into the family of citizen-voters, even by "a little voice," there was no place found for their repentance. The common council which the community had striven to create finally represented only a handful of privileged people instead of the general body of inhabitants, and any hope of the political developement of Lynn as a free community was once for all arrested. The betrayal of the common cause of civic equality brought its exact recompense on the day when every weapon of the unenfranchised inhabitants was seen to be broken and useless. In the common assembly they had no votes. In the common council they had no representatives. The machinery of all their seventy-five guilds[855] could not in any way be so handled as to further the power of the people; for so long as the great body of craft-holders and artizans lay outside the borough franchise it was impossible for them to employ their organizations in the service of the common cause. Deprived of the close connection between the borough and the craft which existed in other towns, they could neither aspire to send delegates from the trades into the council chamber, nor could they make the crafts the only way of entrance into the freedom of the city.

The main result of this breaking up of the "communitas" of Lynn into three fractions which could never again be united, was the final affirmation of power in the hands of a small ruling class. In Lynn it was always the merchants who conquered. One by one they vanquished their opponents, the Church, the mediocres, the inferiores. A singular and pathetic unity pervades the history of the town from first to last. Lynn had won from land and sea a little space of ground, a little tenure of life, and there, lighted by a passing gleam of beneficent fortune, it made its brief experiment—a single experience consistent from first to last, and scarcely subjected to accident or change. The old borough still retains some subtle charm of a lingering distinction. Even now as we look at the homes of its last traders—the heavy double doors which shut off the great court from the street, the houses built round three sides of the open square, and lifted at the back straight out of the waters of canals cut to give passage to the ships and barges which drifted up on every rising tide, almost brushing as they passed the windows that opened on rich chambers dark with carved work in wood—we seem to breath the strange air of a remote place and time in which this old city of dead merchants lies ever steeped. The very fashion of the place still affirms perpetually that when the end came the ancient rulers of Lynn made a proud exit, bequeathing their heritage to none, and leaving their silent dwellings to suffer indeed the presence of strangers, but with no pretence of acquiescing welcome.

CHAPTER XVI

THE COMMON COUNCIL OF SANDWICH

THE attempt in various boroughs to create a municipal house of commons for the protection of popular liberties is so striking a fact in the town history of the fifteenth century that, for the sake of again observing the experiment under a new set of conditions, we may take one last example of the building up of a representative council. The case of Sandwich differs considerably from that either of Norwich or of Lynn, though one significant fact is common to all three boroughs. In each of these towns the effort to work out the new constitution was frustrated; and, singularly enough, it was frustrated in every case, not by any evidence of inherent weakness in the scheme itself, but by the operation of external and accidental causes. In Norwich the system was possibly wrecked by difficulties in the working of what we may call foreign affairs—that is by the ill-defined and impossible relations of the town to the country, when the town claimed to interfere with interests over which its authority was limited, while these interests had no regular representation in its councils, so that intrigue came in to replace recognized and orderly influence, and the natural distinctions of parties within the town were submerged in factions more or less external and artificial, and in the corrupt political ambitions to which these gave opportunity. In Lynn an equally artificial state of parties was created and maintained by the miniature strife between the Church as a temporal power and the civil government. The existence of a large body of commons delivered by the Bishop from taking up the just burdens of citizenship, as dependents on his protection, withdrawn from a full share in the responsibilities of their fellow-townsmen and used as a sort of occupying army for the maintenance of his rights over the borough, was fatal to the healthy developement of municipal self-government. But in Sandwich an altogether new problem is suggested—the problem of local self-government in the members of a confederated state, in which the several communities might tend towards democracy while the central administration remained the stronghold of aristocratic tradition.

For Sandwich must not be considered as if it stood alone like Norwich, independent and self-contained. Under the constitution of the Cinque Ports, as we have seen, certain weighty matters, such as military defence, finance, foreign trade and foreign traders, the higher matters of justice, and so on, were under a central government represented either at Dover or at the Brodhull, and the several towns were mainly concerned with local affairs. It is possible that in the conduct of daily business of a comparatively simple kind there was less necessity than in the greater boroughs for the supremacy of experts, and apparently administration did not so soon harden into the despotism of an oligarchy. There was much, moreover, which was favourable to popular movements in the general conditions of Kent and Sussex, which, even as early as the twelfth century, were centres of important mining and manufacturing industries, and in whose midst there arose more than once movements of liberal and radical thought like those which in our days have come from the coal-fields and iron mines of the north. The trading vessels which put out from the ports across the German Ocean kept the people in constant touch with the commercial towns of the north European coast where municipal life was most vigorous and enduring. And of the strangers to whom Sandwich gave shelter, till at last almost a third of its streets were occupied by foreigners, the main body were traders or artizans from the Netherlands who, wherever they sought refuge after their desperate battle against oligarchy in their own country, must have carried with them their sturdy creed of independence and freedom of political discussion, and would have inevitably ranged themselves on the popular side of town politics, whether as enfranchised voters or as unenfranchised talkers.

Thus the men of the Cinque Ports long preserved a fine tradition of vigorous independence; and in Sandwich, as in the other ports, the burghers actually maintained in practice something of the early democratic theory of government. The mayor, jurats, and other officers, elected by the whole commonalty,[856] carried on the administrative and judicial work, but when a question arose as to the making of new laws or the granting of cesses the whole people were called together to a hornblowing,[857] and "the mayor and commonalty at a common assembly may make such decrees as they think proper." Any gathering of freemen, no matter how small, who assembled with the mayor, was "deemed a meeting of the whole body," and its ordinances were consequently binding; but the mayor might send the common wardman, or whom he pleased, to shut up all the windows of cellars and shops and so forcibly persuade dealers and artizans to join the congregation.[858]

This mode of government by a single council of twelve checked by the *referendum* lasted unchanged till the middle of the fifteenth century; and it was certainly less difficult for the system that in larger boroughs so quickly developed into the rule of a plutocracy, to keep its democratic character in a small community which had only increased from the three hundred and eighty-three inhabited houses of the Conqueror's time to four hundred and twenty households in 1565,[859] and in which the forces that made for freedom and popular government were strong. It would seem indeed that the mayor's difficulty was not so much to force the freemen to fulfil their civic duties, as to check the too active zeal of inhabitants not enfranchised, and Sandwich had to reiterate its laws that only free "barons," indwellers, and householders, should attend at elections, and at last had to inflict on any offender a fine of 21$d.$ and the loss of his upper garment.[860]

In the middle of the fifteenth century, however, there was a movement to amend the primitive constitution of the town. The first change was probably intended to bring Sandwich into harmony with the prevailing fashion. In 1437 its eight wards were made into twelve, and a jurat sat over each, with power to appoint every year his own constable and deputy constable.[861] Other reforms followed under the auspices of Richard Cok, who was mayor five times in thirteen years, and who was again chosen for the sixth time in 1470 to make peace with Edward the Fourth after his triumph over Henry the Sixth.[862] During his first mayoralty (in 1441) an order was issued that no one might sit on the bench at court but the mayor, the jurats, and the king's bailiff; in other words the dignity of the upper chamber was asserted, and all intrusion and interference with its consultations made impossible. The increasing authority of the council was immediately met by an organization of the commons to protect their own interests, such as we have seen at Norwich and Lynn half a century earlier. During Cok's fifth term of office, in 1454, a representative council of seventy commons was formed, who, with the consent of the mayor and jurats, were to make all manner of elections and all scots and lots. In this way about one citizen householder out of every six was given a share in the government—a scheme so different from that of either Norwich or Lynn that it suggests how far Sandwich must have outstripped those towns in the habit of popular government.

From this time we can trace a steady conflict between the two parties in the town, the official or governing class and the commonalty. The common council was remodelled ten years later, in 1464, and its members reduced to thirty-six. It is very probable that this change was brought about by the policy of the governing class; for at the same time the mayor and jurats set up a claim to be the authoritative judges of the fitness of men sent by the commonalty to serve as councillors, and it was ordained that the people should henceforth nominate forty-eight persons, sixteen out of each parish, and that the mayor and jurats should then choose thirty-six of these to be of the common council. Their triumph, however, was short, for in 1471, immediately after Cok's last mayoralty, the controlling choice of mayor and jurats was set aside, and it was decided that the commonalty should elect for themselves, without any interference or dictation, twelve men from each of the three parishes to be of the common council, to consult with the mayor and jurats "whenever the mayor pleases" for the benefit and utility of the town, and to make and establish decrees for its profit.[863]

For over half a century the democratic party had their way. Popular representation was recognized as part of the Sandwich constitution, and so far as the town itself was concerned, it would seem that liberal ideas of government and civic freedom prevailed in a far greater degree than in either Norwich or Lynn. All went well till the time of Henry the Eighth. Then a singular danger declared itself, and the story of the sixteenth century is that of the ruin of popular liberties in Sandwich. The governing class had in each of the Cinque Ports a source of peculiar strength. Out-numbered and out-voted as they might be in each separate port, they reigned supreme in the Brodhull court, where their majority was certain, and where they could carry matters with a high hand; and it was there that the governing bodies of the various ports, all alike threatened with public criticism of their acts and limitation of their powers, formed a combination for the protection of their common interests. All devices to establish freely elected common councils, or any representative bodies to express popular opinion, received their quietus at the Brodhull court in 1526. The respectable assembly of mayors, jurats, and delegates there gathered passed a resolution that the duties of electing the mayor and jurats, receiving the king's bailiff, and appointing the bailiffs to Yarmouth, should be given over in each port to a committee of thirty-seven persons; and in each corporate town to a body of twenty-four, who were to be nominated by the mayor and jurats.[864] In 1528 a new mayor of Sandwich was elected after the new fashion, the whole commonalty nominating three jurats, one of whom was then chosen by the appointed committee of thirty-seven.[865] That the freemen did not give up their rights without a fight we may judge from the fact that in 1535 they again elected their mayor after the ancient custom of the town; but it was a losing battle, and as a matter of fact no popular liberties survived this century. The common council was reduced to twenty-four members, and both the upper and lower councils alike were appointed by the mayor and jurats. The election of the mayor was taken from the people, and the jurats succeeded in turn to the post by order of seniority.[866] Finally even the right of the commons to vote at assemblies was taken from them in 1595, to be restored in 1599, and again taken away "for their insolence and disorder" in 1603.

In Sandwich, therefore, it is obvious that the reform movement failed, not through inherent vice or defect of its own, but by the overpowering pressure of an external force—on this occasion by the federal council of the united states that made up the confederation of the Cinque Ports. No doubt the easy victory of the whole confederation was made possible by the decaying fortunes of the town; for at the time of its defeat the vigour and the glory of Sandwich had departed. Works for the preservation of the port had been constantly going on since the thirteenth century when the artificial canal known as the Delf was dug, and put under the charge of overseers; though after a brave struggle of two hundred years diggers and sluice-makers could no longer hold their own against winds and sands that silted up their harbour. In 1483 the town, under the threat of breaking up the whole wall they had built, ordered the gentlemen and yeomen of the country who had pastures by the stream to scour their dykes and make sluices; though neither the forced efforts of the county squires, nor the royal grant to the town in 1548 of all the plate and treasures of the parish churches to carry on the works of the harbour;[867] nor a later Act of Parliament for deepening the Stour, could rescue Sandwich from its doom. In its decrepitude liberty slipped from its grasp. But the disaster of a later time must not wholly obscure with its shadow the records of days when Sandwich was rejoicing in brighter fortunes. If in the decay of its prosperity and hope the oligarchy fixed their yoke on the neck of the people, and inaugurated the rule of the plutocrats, their victory was not quickly won; for throughout the fifteenth century, as we have seen, when by the necessity of the times the question of stricter organization of public life was here as elsewhere forced into prominence, the commons of Sandwich neither renounced their rights to self-government, nor failed to take an adequate part in moulding the new constitution. It is indeed not impossible that the oligarchic congregation of the Brodhull mainly drew its force for the suppression of popular independence from the support or even the instigation of the Court; for we can easily understand that at a time when under the policy of the Tudors England figured as a great power in Europe, laden with obligations and with hatreds, her ministers were driven to look anxiously to her first line of defence against foreign foes. The policy of securing the main ports in the hands of a little group of loyal officials, easily controlled from headquarters, and no friends to common riots or rebellions, must inevitably have followed the revival of the ancient tradition which saw in the safety of the realm the whole purpose of the Cinque Port confederation.

CHAPTER XVII

CONCLUSION

WITH the reign of Henry the Eighth a wholly new chapter opens in the history of the towns. In the preceding centuries we have traced their gradual rise out of obscure poverty into an illustrious opulence and dignity. Already in the time of Langland the poet's imagination was arrested by the exalted position of the mayor, the "days-man" who could lay his hand upon the highest and the lowest—on the royal majesty and the mean people of the commune. When, a hundred and fifty years later, another poet pictures the court of Fame, where she sits

"Under a glorious cloth of estate ...
Encrowned as empress of all this world of fate."[868]

he sees in the crowd of applicants who press round the throne to solicit her favours the men of Dartmouth and Portsmouth and Plymouth, the burgesses and bailiffs of the Cinque Ports, mingling with messengers from Thrace and Rounceval. Nor were their claims to stand in such a court but a fantastic fiction of poetry. We have seen how the commune and the borough—originally in spite of their collective character mere feudal lordships like the rest, introduced under the sanction and protection of ordinary feudal custom and according to the fictions of feudal law—became in course of time a potent force for the rending asunder of the mediæval framework of society. Patronized and encouraged by the king, nourished in great measure at the expense of the baronage, lay and ecclesiastical, these insidious communities of the people had gradually revealed a character of their own alien to the whole feudal tradition. Under the shelter of their walls the forces of the middle class were mustered for battle against the ancient supremacy of the nobility and the Church. Charters "for the accommodation of the burgesses in doing their business quietly" became the cover for their irresistible attack; and the common bell which rang out to assemble the congregation of enfranchised burghers perpetually announced in every borough of the kingdom the ultimate triumph of "the common people of the realm."

We have also noted the manner in which during these centuries the boroughs remained strongholds of a robust faith in political freedom.[869] Theories of liberty taught by statesmen and philosophers, and debated by barons and knights in their own manner at Runnymede, on the battle-field, or in the council chamber, assumed in the towns homelier forms, and became the vulgar property of the people. The burgher too had his notion of an ideal freedom—a freedom which had never entered within the range of his experience, but in which he still believed with a transcendent faith. In what manner the faith had come to him it is hard to say, through what legal fiction, from what mysterious tradition, by what dominant instinct of race. To quell the enemy and the accuser he might call to witness Domesday or Magna Charta, or liberties registered in the Old Red Book of the town "as we do think," or in the customs of the elders; or for lack of better authority, the fable of a lost charter of the Saxon House, or a shadowy local legend, or tale of freedom "long before the Conquest,"[870] served as evidence of repute. But for the believer testimony was superfluous; the very vagueness of his faith was not without advantages, since the fancied world of the past might be adequately furnished with types of all that was desired in the present. Imagination was stimulated by the rivalry of factions, and political discussion never ceased. No doubt the vulgarization of the notion of freedom, thus thrown into the market-place for burghers to cut and trim to their own needs, has had a permanent effect on English thought.[871] In communities where strictly personal ambition in government was reduced to its lowest expression, where the only possible tyranny was that of a class or of a group, and where the whole society of burghers was nourished on a tradition of equal and indestructible rights, the privilege coveted by ordinary folk was not the pleasure of exercizing authority, but the right to suffer no coercion. Among the townsfolk the "gentleman" was not the man who ruled his neighbour, but the enfranchised equal among his fellows. It may not be altogether fanciful to detect, in the noble translation of a church collect, not only the fine intuition of the scholar, but an echo of the spirit of free and equal liberty that was quickening among the people at large. If the phrase "Cui servire est regnare" carried to English ears a foreign thought, the English words introduced a new and characteristic meaning—"Whose service is perfect freedom."

Lastly we have seen how chequered was the fate of liberty—how often it was obstructed and impaired in its passage through the market-place and the bye-lanes of the city, driven from shelter to shelter, banished from the Guildhall, mocked by a false homage. Between the twelfth century, when the trading communities had represented a new democracy and led the attack on the then established magnates of society; and the sixteenth century, when a ruling oligarchy had been formed out of their ranks, a vast change had taken place in the political relations of the prosperous middle class. In their conduct of the great struggle for emancipation from the county potentates, feudal or official, and in their development of a general freedom of trade, the more prosperous burghers who had first come to the front in affairs had proved the champions of a new liberty. The strong government which they had established through the administration of a select body of experts had abundantly justified itself in setting the independence of the towns beyond attack; and long before the fifteenth century had opened the boroughs, represented by their magistrates and councillors, held an impregnable position. Meanwhile, however, the wave of industrial progress began slowly to lift up out of their dumb helplessness the masses who had till now learned obedience of poverty and despair, for "While hunger was their master would none strive." Imperceptibly the whole scene was changed, and a new conflict was seen to be preparing. By the slow changes of time what had been the democracy of 1200 had become the oligarchy of 1500. On the one hand the plutocrats of the boroughs had made their way into the circle of the privileged classes; in a thousand points their interests now coincided with those of the officials and the gentry in the counties; and their conservative instincts had won the confidence and sympathy of the court. On the other hand the humbler sort of traders and artizans, congregated more and more thickly at the busy centres of industry, made familiar with the uses and methods of association, and impatient both of tyranny and of want, were beginning to form a new democracy, and to constitute to the comfortable classes an alarming social danger. In every borough the problems which confront the modern world were formulated. On all side agitators proclaimed the right of the workers to have a voice in the organization of trade, and the right of the common burghers to share in the control of municipal affairs. The demand of the people that government should really be carried on by their consent, so easily stifled in the thirteenth century, became in the fifteenth loud and persistent; and riotous confederacies of labourers and artizans added excitement to the political demonstrations in the streets. A new terror invaded the council-chamber of the Guildhall—the terror of the mob. While the craft-masters hastened to fortify the guild against the forces of misrule, town councillors made strong the borough administration in the interests of good order. The history of the municipalities in the fifteenth century is far from indicating an era of political apathy, or of mere civic indolence and corruption. In the records of the trade fraternities we see the opening of an industrial war. In the constitutions and ordinances of the towns we see the foreshadowing of a political revolution. The original struggle with feudal forces had closed in triumph for the boroughs, and a new conflict now takes its beginning. Faction fights, crafty intrigues, intricate constitutional changes, these signalise the opening of a new controversy—the controversy between the middle and the lower classes.

At the very moment however when this division of social forces had declared itself, and when it seemed as though the attention of England was to be concentrated on the new social problem, the whole movement was suddenly arrested. All speculation as to what might have happened in the course of a natural evolution is utterly vain. It is probable indeed that the poorer classes, unfed, untaught, and undisciplined, were at that time wholly unprepared to enter on any struggle for industrial and political emancipation, and if the battle had been really fought out, must have suffered a crushing defeat. Centuries of discipline have been needed to consolidate their forces, and very possibly the course of freedom was best served by delay. As a matter of fact however the social question was cast aside by external and arbitrary forces. It was engulfed in the political revolution inaugurated by the early Tudors. So violent was the change that it is only in our own age that the controversies which were opening in the fifteenth century have again taken the foremost place.

For from the moment when the history of national politics begins under the Tudor kings, the whole character and significance of the local centres of government undergo a profound change. Henry the Seventh, as we have seen, had laid the foundation of a vast commercial policy; but until the reign of Henry the Eighth, England, unconscious of its capacity and of its destiny, stood aloof from European affairs; and with her small population, her inadequate navy, her somewhat old-fashioned army, her feeble political influence, was little more than an upstart in the august society of continental nations. From this position she was raised by the genius of Wolsey into a State of which it might be said that its Crown "is this day more esteemed than the Emperor's Crown and all his Empire;" and of whose minister a Venetian ambassador reports that "he is seven times more powerful than the Pope."[872] In a very few years England, courted by French and Spanish kings, and able to treat on equal terms with Pope and Emperor, boasted of being mediator and arbiter of European politics. The pride of a great mission exalted the imagination of her people, and a poet of the Renascence in his vision of "all manner of nations" who dwelt on the field of fame, marked the gate of chalcedony which gave entrance to "Anglia."

"The building thereof was passing commendable;
Whereon stood a leopard, crowned with gold and stones,
Terrible of countenance and passing formidable, ...
As fiercely frowning as he had been fighting."[873]

By the royal courage and appetite of Henry the Eighth, bent on making the whole people his accomplices for the carrying out of his personal will, the work of Wolsey was continued, though in a very different temper, and the national pride and confidence pushed to the highest point. If the policy of Cromwell had been fully carried out, the history of the Reformation and the fortunes of Europe might have been reversed by the intervention of England. We can well understand that amid these tremendous schemes local aspirations were forgotten and local quarrellings silenced. To perfect the policy of the new Monarchy the destinies of the several towns were submerged in the destinies of the whole Commonwealth. Sovereigns no longer viewed with interested regard or with indifferent tolerance, as of old,[874] the growth of borough franchises and the developement of local governments. Street riots were no longer matters of the parish, but of the State. The king's hand was stretched out over the wealthy corporations whose liberties had grown into such vast proportions, and like the baronage and the Church, the boroughs were laid prostrate before the throne.

For under the Tudor system of government the king was the necessary centre of every interest in the country.[875] He alone could impose a common policy and give expression to a national will. To him all classes looked to defend their cause and ensure their prosperity, in the implicit faith that he lived for them alone and to perform their will. In the royal power lay the one force by which England could be held together. At an earlier time, indeed, the common folk had repudiated the doctrine of the king's absolute supremacy as it was now understood. "They say that the king should live upon his commons, and that their bodies and goods are his: the contrary is true, for then needed him never to set Parliament and to ask good of them."[876] But now new maxims were scattered abroad—"that the king can do no wrong, however much he may wish to do it; that not only the property but the persons of his subjects are his own; and that a man has a right to no more than the king's goodness thinks fit not to take from him." Parliament almost ceased to exist, until in course of time, packed with members carefully nominated, and by the craft of the king elaborately duped, it was turned into a mere instrument by which the most ruthless acts of royal aggression could be given the stamp and semblance of law.[877]

The new centralized government was carried on by means of a vast official system which extended from the highest to the lowest departments, and reached out to the farthest limits of the country. In its efficient form it was practically the creation of the first Tudor king. With Warwick the baronial leaders of an earlier time had passed away; and the weakened remnant of the baronage which emerged from the civil wars had been carefully depressed by Henry the Seventh. At the council-board their places were taken by officials who received their orders directly from the king; and when the barons returned to office and council they returned as fellow servants with the new officials, and holding the same functions. Henry the Eighth carried out the same policy. The great nobles might complain of "low-born knaves" who surrounded the king; but when the minister "clapped his rod upon the board" silence fell on an obsequious council—and barons and commons alike trembled before the son of an Ipswich merchant or a Putney blacksmith.

For the tremendous power of Wolsey or of Cromwell lay in the fact that the whole hierarchy of officials, from the most exalted to the most base, was directly responsible to him. Every figure of any importance in the country was perfectly well known to the minister at the head of affairs, and on every subordinate through the length and breadth of the land the court kept vigilant watch. If an official at any point disagreed with the opinions held at head quarters he was forthwith turned out of office, and the ease with which

Henry and his successors made national revolutions is the measure of the absolute perfection to which the machinery of their administration had been brought. In the boroughs it is impossible to exaggerate the effect of this political revolution. The consequence to which the towns had risen made of them all-important centres of administration for the maintenance of general order. Two-thirds of the members of Parliament were sent from the boroughs, and the control of these members, therefore, meant the control of the House of Commons. For a two-fold reason, therefore, the tendency long shewn by the Court to sympathize with the governing oligarchy in the municipalities inevitably took from this time a new force. Under the oligarchic system of administration the towns could be held for the king by a mere handful of loyal officials; and the influence of the Crown was naturally flung on the side of the representatives of good order, as it was understood by the government. In the interests of the whole State a new policy was developed. Municipal independence was struck down at the very roots, and the free growth of earlier days arrested by an iron discipline invented at Westminster, and enforced by a selected company of Townhall officials, whose authority was felt to be ultimately supported by the majesty of the king himself. The number of the town councillors was constantly diminished, and the liberties of the commons curtailed. Under the new conditions the individual life of the borough ceased to have the same significance as of old, and an era opened in which its highest destiny was to be employed as an instrument of the royal will for national ends, and its only glory lay in forming one of the members of a mighty commonwealth. To follow out the internal record of municipal politics on the old lines, as though the story of the sixteenth century were the natural consequence of their earlier course of developement would be radically false; and I therefore pause on the threshold of the new state of things. The history of the boroughs as schools in which the new middle class received its training for service in the field of national politics, and as the laboratories in which they made their most fruitful experiments in administration, ends before the close of the fifteenth century. It may be that as the working class in its turn rises to take its place alongside of its predecessors on the stage of public affairs, the towns will again become centres of interest in the national story, as the workshops of an enlarged political science.

FOOTNOTES:

[1] Journ. Arch. Ass. xxvii. 461, 488.

[2] Freeman's Exeter, 146-7.

[3] Book of Precedence, E. E. Text Society, part ii. 8-18, 79, etc. 143, etc. Manners and Meals (E. E. Text Soc.), 175.

[4] Paston Letters, ii. 319.

[5] Lamond's Walter of Henley 123-145. Monum. Franciscana (Rolls Series), i. app. ix.

[6] Manners and Meals, pp. 250, 251, 252.

[7] Ibid. 258-260.

[8] Ibid. 274.

[9] "Take not every rope's end with every man that hauls," ran the warning to the young. "Believe not all men that speak thee fair, Whether that it be common, burgess or mayor." Manners and Meals, 183. See Songs and Carols (Percy Society, vol. xxiii.) viii. ix. xviii.

[10] Manners and Meals, 182.

[11] Percy Society, vol. xxiii. Songs and Carols, see songs xxxii. and xxxv.

[12] Commonplace book of the fifteenth century edited by Miss Toulmin Smith. Catechism of Adrian and Epotys, p. 40, lines 421-8.

[13]

"Men's works have often interchange
That now is nurture sometime had been strange.
Things whilom used be now laid aside
And new fetis [fashions] daily be contrived."

—Caxton's Book of Courtesy (E. E. Text Society), 45.

[14] Manners and Meals, 271.

[15] Ibid. p. 265.

[16] The popularity of the "Ship of Fools," with its trite, long-winded, and vague moralities, is an excellent indication of the intellectual position of the new middle class.

[17] Songs and Carols (Percy Society, xxiii.), song xxx.

[18] Songs and Carols (Percy Society, xxiii.) lxxvi.

[19] Hist. MSS. Com. ix. 174.

[20] Book of Precedence, 106. "Money maketh merchants, I tell you, over all." Skelton's Poems (ed. Dyce) i. 277.

[21]

"'Though some be clannere than some, ye see well,' quoth Grace,
That all craft and connyng came of my gift."

—Passus xxii. 252-3.

[22]

"Son, if thou wist what thing it were,
Connynge to learn and with thee to bear,
Thou would not mis-spend one hour,
For of all treasure connynge is the flower;
If thou wilt live in peace and rest
Hear and see and say the best."

Book of Precedence, 69. Another rhyme gives the lesson in ruder form.

"Learn as fast as thou may and can
For our Bishop is an old man
And therefore thou must learn fast
If thou wilt be Bishop when he is past."

—Manners and Meals, 383.

[23] See Manners and Meals, lii to lxii.

[24] At Lynn there was in 1383 a Guild "of young scholars"; at Worcester the Guild of S. Nicholas kept "time out of mind a free school within the said city in a great hall belonging to the said Guild called the Trinity Hall." The Guild of Palmers supported a school at Ludlow; and so did Guilds at Stratford and at Deritend. The Guild of Kalenders in Bristol had in the twelfth century kept a school of Jews, and when that business came to an end were still charged with education, public lectures, and the management of a free library. (English Guilds, 51, 205, 196, 221, 288. See Hunt's Bristol, 112, 249, 260.) The Drapers had a school at Shrewsbury (Hibbert's Inf. of English Guilds, 33); and the Merchant Tailors in London (Clode, 35). I learn from Mr. A. F. Leach that at Ashburton the Grammar School founded 1314 by Bishop Stapledon of Exeter (who also founded Exeter College) was entrusted to the Guild of St. Lawrence, whose chantry-priest was the schoolmaster. The school is still kept on the site of the Guild Chapel, the original tower of which forms part of the School.

[25] Hunter's Deanery of Doncaster, vol ii. 5-6.

[26] Bentham's History of Ely Cathedral, 2nd Edition, 182. Hull Grammar School Gazette, 1891, No. 8, p. 88. See Riley's Liber Albus, xix. There was a grammar master at Ewelme Almshouse 1461 (ibid. 627), where teaching was to be free (ibid. ix. 217-8). Four new grammar schools were opened in London in 1447, and during the reign of Henry the Sixth nine were set up in London alone (Pauli's Pictures, 452). In 1472 Prior Selling, of Christchurch, reports to the Archbishop of Canterbury that he has provided a "schoolmaster for your grammar schools in Canterbury, the which hath lately taught grammar at Winchester and at S. Antony's in London" (Hist. MSS. Com. ix. 105). John Syre, the grammar school master in 1436, lived in Gayhow's tenement, S. Alphege parish (ibid. 139). The Almshouse of the poor sisters in Reading was in 1486 turned into a grammar school (Coates' Reading, 15); there was a school in Appleby taught by a chantry priest before the middle of the fifteenth century (Transactions of Cumberland and Westmoreland Arch. Soc. part ii. vol. viii.); and one in Preston whose master was made a burgess in 1415 (Memorials of Preston Guilds, 14). In Liverpool there was an endowed free school before the reformation (Picton's Memorials, ii. 55-6). Miss Dormer Harris has learned from the town records that the expenses of the grammar school at Coventry in the fifteenth century, were paid by the Trinity Guild—in other words, by the Corporation. It is evident that when William Bingham, who founded a grammar school attached to Clare Hall, Cambridge, says that in 1439 he passed seventy deserted schools in travelling from Hampton to Ripon by way of Coventry (Boase's Oxford, 108), we cannot infer from this any decay in education. It may have indicated a shifting of population, or more probably perhaps the results of the effort made in 1391 to prevent villeins from being put to the clerical schools in preparation for taking minor orders and so gaining emancipation from their lords. Rot. Parl. iii. 294.

[27] In the royal accounts the principal artizans in each craft audit such parts of the accounts as deal with labour and sign every page (Rogers' Agric. and Prices, iv. 502).

[28] Richard the Redeless, pass. ii. 41.

[29] The Will of Sir John Percivale, published by the Governors of the Macclesfield School. I am indebted to the kindness of Mr. A. F. Leach for this reference—as well as for that about Stockport, and the reference to the School Gazette and the Town Records of Hull. He informs me that the first school founded by a lay person of which we have as yet any record was at Wotton-under-Edge, and was founded by a woman, Lady Berkeley, in 1385.

[30] Baines' Hist. of the County of Lancaster, i. 296-7.

[31] The author of Piers Ploughman criticizes the education given by the clerics of his day. "Grammar that ground is of all" was neglected so that no one could now either "versify fair" or construe what the poets wrote.

"Doctors of degree and of divinity masters
That should the seven arts conne and assoil *ad quodlibet*,
But they fail in philosophy, an philosophers lived
And would well examine them, wonder me thinketh!"

—Passus xviii. 107-118.

[32] The "alphabet and the humanities" did not imply culture in anything like our sense of the word, nor yet Latin from the literary point of view, but the old ecclesiastical discipline, which included above all things *logic*, and which ultimately led, if the pupil advanced far enough, to the scholastic philosophy. Thus for example in the *Epistolæ obscurorum virorum* one of the (priestly) correspondents is made to protest against the introduction of the study of Vergil and other new-fangled writers.

[33] Hist. MSS. Com. viii. 281-2.

[34] Hist. MSS. Com. x. part 4, 425-6.

[35] Nottingham Records, i. 246, 263.

[36] Ordinances for Dame Agnes Meller's School, Nott. Rec. iii. 453-6. The Mayor of Chester had the payment of the master at Farneworth, Lancashire. (Hist. MSS. Com. viii. 370.) In Coventry the corporation (*i.e.*, the Trinity Guild) paid the master.

[37] Ibid. iv. 191.

[38] Nott. Rec., iv. 214.

[39] Collectanea (Oxf. Hist. Soc.), ii. 334-6.

[40] Paston Letters, i. 431. Hunt's Bristol, 112.

[41] Introduction by Miss Toulmin Smith to Ricart's Calendar. Lives of the Berkeleys, i. 5, 7. Skelton was possibly a native of Norfolk, perhaps of Norwich. Skelton's Poems, ed. Dyce, I. v. vi.

[42] Caxton's Book of Courtesy, 33-41. See Manners and Meals, lix. Skelton's Poems (ed. Dyce), I. 75, 377-9.

[43] Directions not to spare the rod were constant. Manners and Meals, 384. See the poor boy's complaint, p. 385-6. Tusser's lines show that the system was not confined to the lower schools.

"From Paul's I went to Eton, sent
To learn straightways the Latin phrase;
Where fifty-three stripes given to me

At once I had,

For fault but small, or none at all,
It came to pass thus beat I was.
See, Udall, see the mercy of thee

To me, poor lad!"

Erasmus, in his Praise of Folly, singles the schoolmasters out as "a race of men the most miserable, who grow old in penury and filth in their schools— *schools* did I say? *prisons! dungeons!* I should have said—among their boys, deafened with din, poisoned by a fetid atmosphere; but thanks to their folly perfectly self-satisfied so long as they can bawl and shout to their terrified boys, and box and beat and flog them, and so indulge in all kinds of ways their cruel disposition." One such master he tells of who to crush boys' unruly spirits, and to subdue the wantonness of their age, never took a meal with his flock without making the comedy end in a tragedy. "So at the end of the meal one or another boy was dragged out to be flogged." Boase's Oxford, 76-77.

[44] The Commonweal (ed. E. Lamond), 21-23, 30.

[45] Manners and Meals, xxiv. Cf. ibid. xxvi. xlv.

[46] See Crossthwaite. Rep. Royal Com. on Markets, 25.

[47] "Feria" or Saint's day. The place originally held by the fair is illustrated by the ancient custom in Leicester, that when merchants went to the great fairs, when the "fairs were up no plea was holden no more of them that were at home, than of them that were at the fairs;" this was altered by Crouchback's charter of 1277, so that those who stayed at home might be tried in case of complaint. Hist. MSS. Com. viii. 423-4.

[48] The Fair of Wycombe was held on the Day of S. Thomas the Martyr from time out of mind. It had begun to decline by 1527, and the Mayor and Bailiffs bitterly complained that now scarcely any one came to keep up the fair and that the shopkeepers kept their shops and stalls at home in the town as usual. A strict order was made by the Council in 1527 that "no manner of man nor woman" should keep open shop in the town on that day or show their goods in the street, but should "resort unto the Fair there as it is wont to be kept." Parker's Hist. of Wycombe, 29.

[49] Rep. Royal Com. on Markets, 1, 7, 9.

[50] Ibid. 19, 25.

[51] The grants of fairs and markets in the thirteenth century were about 3,300; in the fourteenth century about 1,560; in the fifteenth century to 1482 about 100; Report on Markets, 108-131.

[52] Rep. on Markets, 9. On the other hand in Scotland the right of market was one of the ordinary privileges of a trading town. Ibid. 26.

[53] Ibid. 19. Sometimes not till the fifteenth century, as in Norwich.

[54] Ibid. 9. For the setting up of the beam and directions about weighing, Ibid. 57, 25. Paston Letters, ii. 106. Kingdon's Grocers' Company, I. xiii-xv., xviii., xix., xxiv.-xxxiii. Schanz, i. 579-82. Towns were compelled to keep standard measures by Stat. 8 Henry VI. cap. 5; 11 Henry VI. cap. 8; 7 Henry VII. cap. 3. The Commons asked Henry VII. to have measures made at his own cost; he agreed, but refused to take the cost. When they were made in 1495 members of Parliament had to carry them back to their several towns from London. 11 Henry VII. cap. 4.

[55] Boys' Sandwich, 431, 496, 498, 509.

[56] Report on Markets, 25. Cutts' Colchester, 154-7. Nott. Rec. i. 314-16.

[57] Hist. MSS. Com. ix. 152. For the uncertainty as to the stone of wool, Rogers, Agric. and Prices, i. 367.

[58] Plumpton Correspondence, 21.

[59] Rogers' Agric. and Prices, i. 660. The introduction of carriers and posts was later in England than in France. Denton's Lectures, 190-5.

[60] Hist. MSS. Com. v. 489. In very many towns the churchyard was without any enclosure even in the fifteenth century. For the overseer of the streets and his hog-man see Boys' Sandwich, 674.

[61] Nottingham Records, iv. 190.

[62] Blomefield, iii. 183.

[63] Parker's Manor of Aylesbury, 14-15.

[64] In 1388 town officers were ordered to clean their towns of all that could corrupt and infect the air and bring disease. 12 Richard II. cap. 13. The shambles were commonly at the very corner of the Tol-booth or Moot Hall. Hewitson's Hist. of Preston, 36. See Shillingford's Letters, 89. But in 1487 the Londoners after sixteen years continual remonstrance obtained a statute that no butcher was to kill any beast within the walls of the town, and that the same law was to be observed in all walled towns of England except Berwick and Carlisle. 4 Henry VII. cap. 3.

[65] A grant for paving was given to Liverpool in 1329. Picton's Mun. Rec. of Liverpool, i. 10. Southampton appointed in 1482 a "pavyour" who should dwell in a house of the town at a price of 13s. 4d. rent free "and to have yearly a gown." Davies, 119, 120. Nottingham decided in 1501 to have a town paviour at a salary of 33s. 4d. and a gown; and gave order that the chamberlains were to find stones and sand. Nottingham Records, iii. 309. See vol. i. p. 18, note.

[66] Hist. MSS. Com. v. 493. In Canterbury, where the inns were very numerous, there was a law that no hosteler should "disturb no manner of strange man coming to the city for to take his inn, but it shall be lawful to take his inn at his own lust without disturbance of any hosteler." Hist. MSS. Com. ix. 172.

[67] Married women might become merchants on their own account and carry on trade, hold property and answer in all matters of business before the law as independent traders. (Eng. Gilds, 382. Mun. Records, Carlisle, ed. Ferguson and Nansen, 79. Hist. MSS. Com. ix. 174.) Women might become members of the Merchant Gild at Totnes by inheritance, by purchase, or by gift. (Hist. MSS. Com. iii. 342-3.) Their property was carefully guarded, and no tenement held by the wife's right could be alienated or burdened with a rent unless the wife had given her free consent openly in the Mayor's Court. (Nott. Records, i. 83, 265.)

[68] Hist. MSS. Com. v. 540. Boys' Sandwich, 498.

[69] The brokers were paid by a fixed tax on the merchants' goods which passed through their hands. Boys' Sandwich, 497, 506-7.

[70] Hist. Preston Guild, 16.

[71] Blomefield, iii. 168. Gross, ii. 43, 175, 220. Nott. Records, i. 445-6, 159, 201; ii. 47, 241. See also the serjeant-at-mace in Sandwich (Boys, 504-5), at Nottingham (Rec. iii. 73).

[72] For typical market rules see Reading, Gross, ii. 204-7. Southampton, Ibid. 220.

[73] See Schanz, i. 621-2

[74] The loaf was changed in weight not in price with the price of corn; the lowest rate conceived by ancient writers was 12d. a quarter of corn; the unit of bread was 1/4d. loaf. (Hist. MSS. Com. ix. 175.) Twelve kinds are mentioned in the fifteenth century, but in the Assize only three sorts were recognized—Wastel or white or well-baked bread; Coket (seconds); Simnel, twice baked bread, used only in Lent. (English Guilds, 102. Boys' Sandwich, 543.)

[75] Manorial Pleas, Selden Soc. xxxviii. For control of bread and beer at the time of Domesday see Rep. on Markets, 18. In Norwich supervisors of bread were appointed before 1340. The system seems to have worked well, for no troubles as to the assize of bread are recorded, as in other towns. Leet. Jur. of Norwich, Selden Soc. xxxvi.

[76] Rep. on Markets, 25.

[77] Hist. MSS. Com. ix. 288. In certain departments, as in the fixing of the prices of bread and ale, in measures, in various rules about buying and selling, the towns simply carried out laws made by the central government; while in other things such as the regulation of the price of meat, poultry, fish, and wine, they were from time to time given authority to fix their own standard.

[78] Andover, Gross, ii. 310. Cutts' Colchester, 154-7.

[79] In 1383 the price of unsweetened wine was practically left to the towns for about a hundred years. Schanz, i. 647. For common consumption wine was sweetened with honey and flavoured with blackberries. Archæol. Cantiana, vi. 328.

[80] Liber Albus, 289, 373-86, 686-91, Liber Custumarum, 117-120, 385-6. Statutes 22 Edward IV. cap. 2. Hist. MSS. Com. ix. 172.

[81] Ricart's Kalendar, 81-84.

[82] Piers Ploughman. Pass. xxii. 398-404.

[83] Nott. Rec. iii. 357.

[84] Select Pleas of the Crown, Selden Soc. 88-9. Hist. MSS. Com. ix. 172. Gross, i. 45. English Guilds, 353, 381-4.

[85] English Guilds, 353.

[86] Journ. Arch. Ass. xxvii. 476. English Guilds, 392.

[87] Gross, ii. 1 175. Rep. on Markets, 16.

[88] English Guilds, 390, 392, 406.

[89] The town liberties did not always extend over the whole town territory. The liberties of Carlisle were confined to a small district in the centre of the modern town, and did not extend beyond the limits of this "ancient city." Hereford up till 1830 was divided into two parts, the In-Borough where the inhabitant householders had the elective franchise and the Out-Borough comprising all beyond the In-Borough that was under the corporate jurisdiction. Papers relating to Parl. Representation, 1829-32.

[90] Collectanea, ii. (Oxford. Hist. Soc.), 13.

[91] Freeman's Exeter, 143.

[92] Gross, ii. 262. Rot. Hund. i. 356, 3 Ed. i. When an unusual press of people was drawn to the town by some festival or public occasion orders were issued to allow country dealers to bring food within the walls and sell it without paying toll or any other manner of charge. Davies' York, 167.

[93] Hist. MSS. Com. v. 606-7. Gross, i. 48-9. See Vol. I. p. 182, n. 4. Sometimes the monopoly was given to the townspeople (Gross, i. 46; ii. 28, 46, 205, 255); in other cases to the Merchant Guild which had power to enroll non-residents among its numbers. (Gross, i. 47, 52, 122, 139, 153, 191, 218.) In cases of abuse there was an appeal to the king. (Rep. on Markets, 25, 60.)

[94] Picton's Municipal Records of Liverpool, i. 17, 18, 28. It is evident that the system of protection was not universally popular, for when in 1515 a commission was sent to examine why Liverpool had so decayed that its contributions to the Exchequer had fallen off, a complaint was made that the mayor had caused the decline in the customs revenue by the enfranchisement of strangers living in the borough, who were thus freed from the payment of dues that had once gone to the Crown. (Picton's Memorials, i. 38.) Leland writing in 1533 says: "Irish merchants come much thither as to a good haven," and in the margin he adds, "at Liverpool is a small custom paid that causeth merchants to resort." The trade of later days had even then begun: "Good merchants at Liverpool, much Irish yarn that Manchester men do buy there." (Ibid. i. 46.)

[95] Fosbrooke's Gloucestershire, i. 204-8. For the trade with Wales, ibid. 156-7. See also the rovers of the Forest of Dean and the troubles of Tewkesbury and Gloucester, in Stat. 8 Henry the Sixth, cap. 27. There were similar disputes between Shrewsbury and Worcester as to the limits of their jurisdiction over the Severn. (Owen's Shrewsbury, i. 300.)

[96] To encourage the carriage of corn in some places, probably in many, while the toll on every horse laden with a pack of marketable goods was 1*d[.]*, a corn-laden beast was charged only one farthing. (Materials for Hist. Henry VII. vol. ii. 332.) For a case of toll illegally levied on victuals see Rep. on Markets 57.

[97] Collectanea (Oxford Hist. Soc.), ii. 120; 50-51. In the sixteenth century when the victuallers' laws were no longer enforced to any extent, other measures were found necessary to keep a constant supply of corn in the bigger towns.

[98] See Collectanea (Oxford Hist. Soc.), ii. 49.

[99] Riley's Mem. 180.

[100] Ibid. 181.

[101] Nottingham Records, iii. 354. Hist. MSS. Com. ix. 172-5. Ibid. v. 531.

[102] Preamble of Canterbury regulations for brewers and bakers drawn up in 1487. (Hist. MSS. Com. ix. 173.)

[103] Ibid. For suburban trades see girdlers and embroiderers in London. (Schanz i. 608. Rolls Parl. iv. 73.)

[104] For the attempt at free trade in Winchester in 1430, following the example of Coventry and New Sarum, see Gross, ii. 261. Another rule of the assembly in the same direction was passed in 1471, apparently in the attempt to find a new source of income for payment of the ferm. Ibid. 262.

[105] Muniments of Canterbury. In Southampton there was a class of Outburgesses who did not live in the town; they were allowed to vote for a mayor and members of Parliament, but might not be present at a common council. (Davies' Southampton, 197.)

[106] Preston Guild Rolls, xvi. xx.

[107] For breach of this custom see Rep. on Markets, 57 (Wallingford), 60-61. (Bosworth, Lafford.)

[108] Preston Guild Rolls, xii.

[109] Ibid. xii. xxiv. xxix. xxx.

[110] Rep. on Markets, 61.

[111] In 1209 there were fifty-six foreigners in the Shrewsbury Guild; forty years later they had increased to 234. (Hibbert's Influence and Development of English Gilds, 18.)

[112] Many merchants of Lynn were made freemen of Canterbury and also admitted to the Brotherhood of the Monastery, by letters of fraternity which gave them a share in certain spiritual benefits. Is it possible that any trading privileges were connected with this?

[113] As far away as Nottingham oxen and sheep were forestalled and sold to butchers of London. Nott. Rec. iii. 48.

[114] Leet Jurisdiction of Norwich (Selden Soc.), lxxiv.

[115] Select Pleas of the Crown (Selden Soc.), 88-9.

[116] Case of the Abbot of Westminster against Southampton. Rot. Parl. i. 20-21. Trial before the King's Bench at Westminster in 1201 where the Burgesses of Northampton claim that unjust toll is taken from them by the Abbot of Thorney, which he defends by virtue of custom and an older charter than Northampton. Select Civil Pleas (Selden Soc.), i. 11. See a case at Plymouth, 1495; Hist. MSS. Com. ix. 273. Leicester and Nottingham; Ibid.

viii. 416-417. Southampton and Bristol; Report on Markets, 56. Winchester; Ibid. 55. See also Ibid. 62; Gross, ii. 257-8; 177-182; 147; 379. A merchant from the Cinque Ports who insisted on the privilege of burgesses to pay no toll with regard to some wool in Blackwell Hall, in the time of Henry the Eighth, had to defend his rights and won his case.

[117] Retaliation in taking of toll is expressly mentioned in the charter of London. Stubbs' Select Charters, 104.

[118] 1238. Gross, ii. 173-174.

[119] Gross, ii. 256.

[120] Hist. MSS. Com. xi. 3, p. 16. For agreement between Southampton and Portsmouth 1239, Marlborough 1239, Bristol 1260, Netley Abbey 1288, Bishop of Winchester 1312, Lymington 1324, New Sarum 1329, Coventry 1456, see Davies' Southampton, 225-228; Abbot of Westminster Rot. Parl. i. 20-21. Other instances Rep. on Markets, 40-41. Select Civil Pleas (Selden Soc.), i. 11. Nottingham Rec. i. 55, ii. 349, 362. Gross, ii. 389-90, Hist. MSS. Com. ix. 212.

[121] Journ. Arch. Ass. xxvii. 416-7. When a gun was made for Lydd, metal for it was bought at Winchelsea and Hastings. (Hist. MSS. Com. v. 516-517, 521.) The Nottingham founder sent to Lincolnshire for his bell metal. (Nott. Rec. ii. 143, 145).

[122] Ibid. ii. 179; iii. 19, 21, 29.

[123] Hist. MSS. Com. viii. 414.

[124] Select Pleas of the Crown (Selden Soc.), i. 89. Rep. on Markets, 50-52.

[125] See Calendar of Letters from Corporation of London. 1350-1370, ed. by Dr. Sharpe.

[126] Piers Ploughman. Pass vii. 250.

[127] These can be traced from 1285 to the time of James I.; they were probably Jews who had come with the Conqueror and were allowed to get land. Survey of Birmingham, 50.

[128] For example William Hollingbroke of Romney, whose wife Joanna sold blankets in 1373, was one of the members sent to Parliament and headed the list of taxpayers in a ward named after him Hollingbroke Ward from 1384 till 1401. Then his widow took his place till she retired from business in 1404, and the once opulent family, for a time represented by a single trader Stephen, seems finally to have become extinct in 1441. The chief position in local trade then passed to the Stuppeneys who settled in the town in 1436 and whose local fame is still recalled by the fact that even now the yearly

election of the Mayor of Romney takes place in the church of S. Nicholas at the tomb of one of them who was Jurat of the town.

[129] Hist. MSS. Com. v. 523-531.

[130] Between 1353 and 1380. Ibid. vi. 545. Ibid. iv. 1, 424-8. Ibid. v. 533. The mayor of Liverpool, who in 1380 had property to the value of £28 6s. 4d., made up of domestic utensils, grain in store, wheat sown, nine oxen and cows, six horses, and eighteen pigs, was no doubt a very rich man in his own borough. Picton's Mem. Liverpool, i. 30.

[131] Hist. MSS. Com. v. 534, 535, 536, 539, 541-3.

[132] Piers Ploughman. Pass. iv. 83. A prosperous cook at Oxford in 1400 married his daughter to one Lelham "Dominus de Grove." By the marriage contract the cook was to give to Lelham twenty marks to be paid at intervals; to the bride and bridegroom he was to give three tenements in Oxford; he was to make provision for them in his own house for eight years, and when after that they were to be set up in a house of their own he was to provide them with a bed, blankets, sheets, and all other furniture needful for the same bed, a vessel for water, a wine vase, two tablecloths, two towels, twelve silver spoons, two cups, two brass pots, one chawfre, four plates, one dozen vessels for garnishing the supper, two salts, two candle-sticks. Hist. MSS. Com. xi. 3, 75-6.

[133] See Nott. Rec. iii. 74-76, 342, 353, 358-60, 461, 463. The holding offices of all kinds by victuallers and brewers was forbidden (Stat. 12, Ed. II. cap. 6. 6 Ri. II. st. 1, cap. 9, H.M.C. ix. 174, xi. 3, 19), as a protection to the people from fraudulent administration of the laws concerning food; but these statutes were everywhere broken.

[134] (See pp. 352-3.)

[135] H.M.C. ix. 173-4.

[136] According to Thorold Rogers (Agric. and Prices, iv. 502-5) about 20 per cent. in excess. Skilled workmen, such as architects, artists, trained clerks, &c., were paid at very modest rates, though sometimes they were given honour by being boarded as gentlemen.

[137] Statutes, 12 Richard II. cap. 3.

[138] Riley's Liber Albus, 261-2.

[139] For particulars of truck wages see Stat. 4 Edward IV. cap. 1. This payment on the truck system was spoken of as a new thing in the middle of the fifteenth century (Wright's Political Songs, ii. 285), and is referred to in Libel of English Policy. It was forbidden by town ordinance in Winchester and Worcester. (English Guilds, 352, 383.)

[140] Piers Ploughman. Pass. vii. 213-14.

[141] Piers Ploughman. Passes vii. 215-249.

[142] For a description of the various deceits practised in cloth-making see 3 Richard II. stat. cap. 2. Stat. of Westminster 7 Richard II. cap. 9; 15 Richard II. cap. 10. In 1221 the jurors of Worcester were already complaining that the assize of the breadth of cloth was not observed. Select Pleas of the Crown, Selden Soc. 97.

[143] Piers Ploughman. Pass. i. 33-4.

[144] Hist. MSS. Com. ix. 259; xi. 3, 70-73, 111. Davies' Southampton, 82. Hunt's Bristol, 74, 97-8.

[145] Survey of Birmingham, 50, 51, 52. See above, p. 63.

[146] Journ. Archæol. Ass. xxvii. 110-148. This as one among many proofs tends to show how wealth was passing not so much to the mere land-owners as to the new tenants who were combining the cloth trade with big sheep farms—the enterprising speculators who were on the watch for the cheap lands of ruined lords to increase their own business.

[147] Members of the Pepperers Company began to replace the Jews at the King's exchange in the thirteenth century (Kingdon's Grocers' Company, i. x-xii.)

[148] Von Ochenkowski, 112, 125. The upgrowth of the true class of merchants is shewn in the Hull Guild whose ordinances date from 1499 (Lambert's Guild Life, 157-160) and the York Mistery of Mercers of 1430, (Ibid. 167).

[149] For the forbidding of exportation of gold and silver and the consequent regulations about travellers by sea, see 5 Richard II. St. i. cap. 2.

[150] The Chancellor of England was given power to enquire and judge on dealings of "dry exchange," and also Justices of the Peace of the neighbouring counties. Stat. 3 Henry VII. cap. 6. Compare Luchaire, Communes Françaises, 242-4.

[151] When in the parable of Piers Ploughman the wicked Lady Mede defends corrupt gain by the argument that merchandise cannot exist without meed or reward the answer of Conscience is that trade is nothing but pure barter.

"In merchandise is no meed I may it well avow
It is a permutation apertelich [evidently] one penny-worth for another.

"—Piers Ploughman. Pass. iv. 282, 315, 316.

See also the limits set even on barter—

"For it is simony to sell what sent is of grace
That is wit and water, wind, and fire the forth:
These four should be free to all folk that it needeth."

Ibid. Pass. x. 55-7. Here, however, he has doubtless in his mind the lord's mill on the hill or by the stream, the rights of turbary and of gathering wood in the forest, and the great need of the people—protection in the law-courts.

[152] Von Ochenkowski, 165, 167, 245-9.

[153] Piers Ploughman. Passus x. 26.

[154]

"And though they wend by the way the two together,
Though the messenger make his way amid the wheat
Will no wise man wroth be, nor his wed take;
Is not hayward yhote [ordered] his wed for to take;
But if the merchant make his way over men's corn,
And the hayward happen with him for to meet,
Either his hat or his hood, or else his gloves
The merchant must forego, or the money of his purse."

—Piers Ploughman. Pass. xiv. 42-50.

[155] Hist. MSS. Com. v. 443. For merchants' marks in S. George's Church, Doncaster, see Hunter's Deanery of Doncaster, i. 14.

[156] Plummer's Fortescue, 235.

[157] Piers Ploughman. Pass. vii. 278-285.

[158] Ibid. Pass. xiv. 50-51.

[159] See Ship of Fools, Barclay, 43, st. 4.

[160] Lib. Eng. Pol. Wright's Political Poems, ii. 178.

[161] Hist. MSS. Com. v. 601-4.

[162] Hunt's Bristol, 75, 93-5; 126-8.

[163] Hunt's Bristol, 94-5, 108. A Bristol grocer left 350 ounces of silver plate to be divided among his children. Ibid. 108. The first fork we hear of in England in 1443 belonged to a citizen family in York. "Unum par cultellorum vocat' 'karving knyves' et unum par forpicum argenteorum." (Plumpton Correspondence, xxxiv.)

[164] Piers Ploughman. Passus, xv. 90. For Wood's account of Oxford houses, see Boase's Oxford, 48-9.

[165] Boys' Sandwich, 149, 185, 186.

[166] The plate of S. Mary's, Sandwich, amounted to about 724 ounces of silver, and there was a good deal of silver gilt; it had splendid brocade of gold of Venice and of Lucca, and a mass of vestments of white damask powdered with gold of Venice, and blue velvet powdered with fleurs de lis, or with moons and stars, and so on. (Boys' Sandwich, 375.) A burgess of Wycombe, Redehode, fitted up the church with beautiful screens of carved wood, and added other gifts to its store of jewels and gilt crowns for Our Lady, and other ornaments of amber, silver, jet, turquoises, with rich garments and ermine fur, damasks, velvets, silks, a baldachino bearing green branches with birds of gold, magnificent robes of cloth of gold, &c., and splendid plate. (Hist. MSS. Com. v. 554-5.)

[167] An ironmonger, Richard Fallande, set up a tablet in Hospital Hall to remind the townsfolk of the dangers and terrors of the old ford, of passengers drowned, of poor people pitilessly turned back, or wayfarers robbed of hood or girdle to satisfy the ferry-men's greed. People were constantly drowned and

"Few folke there were coude that way wende
But they waged a wed or payed of her purse
And if it were a begger had breed in her bagge
He schulde be ryght soone i bid for to goo aboute
And of the poor penyles the hireward wold habbe
A hood or a girdel and let him goo withoute."

(English Illustrated Magazine, May 1889, p. 951.) For Rochester Bridge, see Hist. MSS. Com. ix. 285.

[168] Davies' Southampton, 115.

[169] Hist. MSS. Com. ix. 247. For similar bequests, Ibid. x. 4, p. 529-30. Ibid. ix. 208-10. The Common Weal (ed. E. Lamond), 18, 19.

[170] Ibid. xi. 7, 169, 174, 175, 180-1. Ibid. ix. 57, 275, 137, 145. Davies' Walks through York, 30-1.

[171] Piers Ploughman. Pass. i. 22.

[172] See the surprising lists of these stores in the Paston Letters, iii. 312, 270-4, 297 8, 282 9, 136, 313. Compare vol. i. p. 259.

[173] Hist. MSS. Com. x. 4, 297. Paston Letters, iii. 23, 35, 46, 49, 219, 258. See vol. i. 260-2.

[174] Paston Letters, iii. 114-15.

[175] Paston Letters, iii. 194. Hist. MSS. Com. vii. 599.

[176] Richard the Redeless, Passus iii. 145, &c.

[177] Plumpton Correspondence, xxxix. xl.

[178] Sometimes their servants also reached posts of importance. John Russel, one of Fastolf's servants, paid a sum down to be appointed Searcher at Yarmouth. And Thomas Fry, a steward of the Berkeleys under Henry the Seventh and Henry the Eighth, was "raised by them to be of principal authority and in commission of the peace of the city of Coventry, and a steward of great power in that Corporation." (Berkeleys, ii. 215.)

[179] The Poles of Hull were rising into importance. (Paston Letters, ii. 210.) Sir John Fastolf possibly sprang from this class, for his relation Richard Fastolf was a London tailor. (Hist. MSS. Com. viii. 265.) Two London drapers, a mercer and a grocer were among the forty-seven Knights of the Bath created at the coronation of Elizabeth, queen of Edward the Fourth. (Three XV. century Chronicles, 80.) See the marriage of Whittingham, Mayor of London, whose son entered the Royal Household (Verney Papers, 15-17); of Verney, mayor in 1465 and knighted in 1471 (Ibid. 13, 22); of Sir William Plumpton (Plumpton Correspondence, xxvii.); of Sir Maurice Berkeley (Hunt's Bristol, 101).

[180] Paston Letters, iii. 383.

[181] For the whole story see Paston Letters, ii. 341, 347, 350, 363-5.

[182] Paston Letters, iii. 109, 219, 278.

[183] Nottingham Records, i. 169.

[184] Plumpton Correspondence, 12. The lady was sister to Godfrey Green, who seems to have been of good family, possibly a connexion of Sir William Plumpton (17 note). Green did a good deal of business for Plumpton (22-3), and was one of the trustees of a settlement, lxxii. note.

[185] See Clément, Jacques Cœur.

[186] Ibid. 134.

[187] Clément, Jacques Cœur.

[188] (See p. 327).

[189] See Hist. of Eng. People, ii. 142-3, 151, 164-6, 170-2, 188. Brinklow's writings afford a very good illustration of the radical temper in politics which at this time was developed in the towns.

[190] Stat. 3 Henry VII. cap. 11. The Common Weal, 88-90.

[191] It was often forbidden to employ any woman save the wife or daughter of the master (Hunt's Bristol, 82; Riley's Mem. 217).

[192] Lambert's Guild Life, 238-9; Hist. MSS. Com. xi. 3, p. 11, 87.

[193] Kent had sunk from the fifth to the tenth place in wealth among counties during the Hundred Years' War. In 1454 the wool of Lincolnshire, Shropshire, and the Cotswolds, represented the best, and that of Kent almost the worst quality; this may account for the decline of Canterbury. The difference in quality would of course tell much more on the prosperity of a district when the home manufacture of cloth was developed.

[194] Schanz, i. 610-11 (1455); 33 Henry VI. cap. 4; Rot. Parl. v. 324.

[195] Schanz, i. 600; Stat. 11 Henry VII. cap. 27.

[196] Lib. Cus. 127. I suspect that the question of these fulling-mills in London was much complicated by the supply of water becoming inadequate to the needs of the growing city, and the great resentment felt by the fullers of cloth against the intrusion of the cap-makers on their domain over the running streams. There is some evidence that this was the case, and it is probable that the want of water-power was one of the causes which drove the woollen manufacture from certain towns.

[197] 22 Edward IV. cap. 5. There had been trouble about fulling machinery in London as early as 1298. (Lib. Cust. Rolls, Series, 127-9.)

[198] In 1416 £22 6s. 8d. was received as a fine for offences from foreigners in Romney. (Hist. MSS. Com. v. 539.) In Sandwich the tax on foreigners was assessed by the mayor and jurats. Every indweller having aliens in his service was to keep back as much of their wages as would pay his tax. (Boys' Sandwich, 787.)

[199] See Schanz, i. 414-6.

[200] Hunt's Bristol, 82, 93, 111. The complaint seems to have been against master-weavers who employed their own servants and not the Bristol journeymen. See Rymer's Fœdera, v. 137.

[201] See Hibbert's Influence of Eng. Gilds, 64.

[202] See the Commons' Petition in Parliament, 50 Edward the Third (1376), Rolls of Parliament, vol. ii., p. 332. "Et come les bones gentz des touz Citees & Borghs parmy ceste terre si pleignent durement, q̃ ... toute manere de gentz Aliens, & autres qi ne sont pas Fraunces en les dites Citees & Borghs, poent venir illeòqs demourrer auxi longement come lour plest, & tenir overtz Hostiels, & recepter̃ q coñqs persones qe lour plerra: Et s'ils eiount ascunes Marchandises ils les vendent as autres Estraungers, pur revendre sĩ bn par retail come autre˜ qcoñq manere˜q lour mieltz semble pur lours Profitz demeisne. Par qi les Marchauntz Denizeins sont trop anientiz, la Terre voide de Moneie, les closures des Citees & Borghs desapparaillez, la Navye de la

terrẽ bn pres destruite, le Conseil de la terre par tout descovert, toute manere d'estraunge Marchaundise grandement encherie; & qe pys est, par tieles privees receites les Enemys auxint priveez oũ q les loialx Liges: De qi n'ad mestier de autres tesmoignes fors̃ q sentir & vewẽ q molte app'tement en touz degreez la provent."

[203] Stat. 1 Richard III. cap. 9.

[204] Stat. 1 Richard III. cap. 9. About 1528 the London shoemakers complain that whereas the King had granted leave that a fraternity of forty-four foreigners might exercise the craft of shoemakers in the city, by colour of this grant 220 foreign householders employing over 400 apprentices and servants, had set up in the business. An amusing account is given of the attitude of this foreign company to the English searchers of the craft. There had once been 140 Englishmen of the cordwainers' livery but now there were only twenty, and the wives and children of those who had been ruined were turned into water-carriers and labourers. These foreigners did not come to settle, but having made their fortunes went off home, while others took their places. (Schanz, ii. 598-600.)

[205] Schanz, ii. 596-8. They pray that the former laws may be put in force, ordering strangers only to dwell in the houses of Englishmen, to sell only in gross and not by retail, and to remain only a month in any town after their first coming.

[206] In the same way Bristol in 1461 forbade its weavers to employ their wives, daughters, and maidens at the loom, lest the King's people likely to do the King service in his wars should lack employment. (Hunt's Bristol, 82.)

[207] The customs of Coventry in this respect are exceedingly interesting.

[208] Stat. 25 Henry VIII. cap. 18.

[209] Stat. 21 Henry VIII. cap. 12. In the reign of Henry the Eighth there were complaints that Worcester, Evesham, Droitwich, Kidderminster, and Bromsgrove, had fallen into decay from the growth of the free-traders. (Stat. 25 Henry VIII. cap. 18.) See also the coverlet makers of York. (34 and 35 Henry VIII. cap. 10.)

[210] Piers Ploughman. Passus ix. 187.

"'It is nothing for love they labour thus fast,
But for fear of famine, in faith,' said Piers."

Passus ix. 214, 215.

[211]

"Fridays and fasting days a farthingworth of mussels
Were a feast for such folk, or so many cockles."

Pass. x. 94, 95; see 72-87. Pollard's Miracle Plays, 31-2.

[212] Children who had served in husbandry till the age of twelve "shall abide at the same labour without being put to any mystery or handicraft" (Stat. 12 Rich. II. cap. 5).

[213] It is important in the town ordinances to observe the effect of local circumstances. For instance, in Coventry the weavers were allowed in 1424 to take as many apprentices as they liked, "sine contradictione alicujus," while the number in other trades was limited. This was just such an order as might be expected of a town council of rich merchant clothiers and drapers.

[214] See Chap. V.

[215] The customs of Norwich, 1340, forced some responsibility for these servants on the masters. (Leet Jurisdiction (Selden Soc.), lxvi.)

[216] No general laws for the whole kingdom which seriously limited the employment of apprentices were passed before the sixteenth century, but the various towns made such local laws as seemed necessary. In most cases masters were bound to enrol their apprentices in the town court; and at the end of the fifteenth century the Town Councils and the Guilds were making serious efforts to enforce the law. Miss Dormer Harris tells me that the capper's apprentices in Coventry were bound by surety for £5 to fulfil their covenant. If an apprentice left his master before the seven years were over, the master might not take another till the time had expired unless he delivered the £5 to the keepers for the use of the craft. The masters of crafts there appear to have been very reluctant to take apprentices, especially after 1494.

[217] In Norwich in spite of the statutes of 1436 and 1503 (15 Henry VI. cap. 6; 19 Henry VII. cap. 7) the crafts persisted in making rules by which apprentices were compelled to pay 20*s.* or 30*s.* for entry into the common hall (compare the composition of 1415 in the Norwich documents)—a fine which meant that the craftsmen were practically denied the freedom of the city, and therefore the position of master, and were thus forced to swell the body of journeymen. An Act passed in 1531 ordered that no apprentice should pay more than 2*s.* 6*d.* for entry into the common hall; or 3*s.* 4*d.* at the end of the term for the freedom of the company; but the companies evaded this law by asking only the statute sum for the freedom of the company, but making the candidates swear they would not trade without license, for which they had to pay at the company's pleasure. This was again forbidden by Henry in 1537 (Blomefield, iii. 181-2). Among the weavers of Newcastle in 1527 all who had finished their apprenticeship were admitted to membership on payment of 13*s.* 4*d.*, but any man of the craft desirous to be of the

fellowship a brother thereof, with power to set up shop, had to pay £20 (Newcastle Guilds). The London grocers in 1345 paid 20*s.* for each apprentice; the apprentice who wished to belong to the fraternity paid 40*s.* on leaving his master (Kingdon's Grocers' Company, i. 11, 12).

[218] Compare Riley's Mem. Lond. 244, 181, 278, 354. Black's Leathersellers, 39.

[219] In London no apprentice after his term was to use his trade till he had been sworn to the franchise. (Liber Albus, 272.)

[220] Journeymen among the cutlers and founders who had not served their time as apprentices could only get such wages as the overseers of the trade allowed to them after examination. (Riley's Mem. Lond. 439, 514.) The system was probably widespread to judge from the many ordinances concerning wages. Unskilled journeymen must be spoken of in the ordinances of the bladesmiths. (Riley's Mem. 570.) For serving-men who worked by the day for the glovers see ibid. 246. In 1449 at Coventry a reasonable wage seems to have been 4*d.* a day; but a capper's journeyman in 1496 got 12*d.* a week working twelve hours a day (reference to Coventry records given me by Miss Dormer Harris).

[221] 7 Henry IV. cap. 17.

[222] The law was done away with when it turned to the hurt of the employers. In a later state of the cloth industry some of the old centres of industry such as London and Norwich and Bristol found their wealth decayed; and decided that their trade was starved for want of workmen while the young people were growing up to idleness and vice. Then the masters, actually threatened with the loss of their manufacturing industries, insisted on new laws allowing them to take apprentices without regard to the Act of Henry the Fourth (11 Henry VII. cap. 11; 12 Henry VII. cap. 1).

[223] Hudson's Notes about Norwich; in Norfolk and Norwich Arch. Soc. vol. xii.

[224] English Guilds, 284-6, 337, 350. See in Exeter the relations of the Tailors' Guild to the suburbs. (Ibid. 310.) Possibly the system may even then have been like the ordinary system which generally prevailed till the end of the last century. In Dereham in Norfolk the site of a line of hovels is still marked in which a group of shoemakers lived and worked for the Norwich masters, whose collector came round every week to collect the finished work. A rich farmer seems to have served as a sort of contractor in the tailoring trade; the upper floor of his house immediately below the roof formed a long room without any partitions in which ten or twelve tailors worked by day and slept by night, and the contractor dispatched their work to the Norwich dealer.

[225] Chap. XII. p. 385. See also the monopoly of the York weavers in the twelfth century, with the control of trade in the whole county which it must have implied. (Gross, i. 108, note.)

[226] English Guilds, 383.

[227] Von Ochenkowski (Wirthschaftliche Entwickelung, 128-133) scarcely seems to distinguish sufficiently between the objections to the competition of the dealers or masters from the suburbs, and to the employment by town manufacturers of labour outside the town. The resistance would necessarily have come from different quarters and for different reasons.

[228] Cf. The Common Weal (ed. E. Lamond), 49.

[229] The well-known rioter is described by Skelton. Poems (ed. Dyce), ii. 43-4.

[230] This was sometimes done by royal charter. (Hibbert's Influence of Eng. Guilds, 96.) All the facts are against the theory of Marx that the merchant was by some hostile force prevented from buying labour, though allowed to buy other commodities. The limitations were of the merchants' and dealers' own making for their own purposes. It is equally improbable that the guild organization excluded division of labour in the workshop. (Marx, Capital, &c. i. 352.)

[231] This uniformity is well illustrated in the later ordinances of the Hull Guilds. (Lambert, Two Thousand Years of Guild Life; Gross, ii. 272.)

[232] Clode, Merchant Tailors, p. 2.

[233] In 1311 the "hatters" and the "dealers who bought and sold hats" in London were two quite distinct callings. (Riley's Mem. 90.) The distinction was well known in 1327 between the saddlers and the various orders of workmen employed in manufacturing for them. (Ibid. 157-8.)

[234] A separation of the guilds into these groups is sufficient of itself to shew of how little value the generalizations of Marx are as to the relations of the crafts to capital; and how misleading it is to represent the guilds as providing the main opposition to merchants or capitalists, especially in the matter of refusing the supply of labour. (See Marx 1. 352.)

[235] Seligman (Two Chapters on Mediæval Guilds, 69) states that the crafts were not charitable associations giving relief to poor members till the fifteenth century. Out of twelve crafts mentioned in English Guilds, nine gave relief to poor, and three do not mention it. For the Braelers in London, 1355, see Riley's Mem. 277; the White tawyers, 1346, ibid. 232; the Lorimers, 1261, Liber Cust. 78-80. Most of the ordinances in Riley's Mem. make no mention of relief, but the ordinances are so manifestly incomplete—merely

additions or alterations made for some special purpose—that no argument can be drawn from them. The vast majority of religious or social guilds had some charitable provisions, and in many cases these were certainly trade guilds. The probability seems to lie on the side of help given to poor members from the first.

[236] The way in which the guilds fought in defence of their voluntary courts of arbitration, and the objection of the towns to these, is in itself proof enough of the importance to their members of a tribunal, however voluntary and arbitrary, which might relieve them from the interference on every occasion of the local magistrates, and the party politics of the town. The advantages of association in case of being called before the greater courts is evident from the account of mediæval procedure given in Sir J. Stephen's History of the Criminal Law. The illustrations afforded by the Paston Letters are without number. See Manorial Pleas (Selden Soc.), 136. For the heavy cost involved by the corrupt practices of lawyers, judges, pleaders, and attorneys, see the action brought in 1275 by an advocate against an employer who had withdrawn from the case; the advocate sues for his fees and also for having been prevented by the stopping of the case from getting a very large sum of money out of the other side. (Ibid. 155-6.)

[237] It was a disgrace to the lord if any of his "livery" appeared in the law courts. The protection extended to the members of a craft was really efficient. See the punishment of a grocer who in 1404 had turned another of the company out of his house. (Kingdon's Grocers' Company, i. 93.)

[238] The grocers in London claimed control over every one who kept a shop of spicery even if he did not wear their livery (Kingdon's Grocers' Company, i. 66); but those who refused the livery were fined. The liveried members paid 2*s.* 6*d.* for the dinner, and "every man out of the clothing as us seemed they might bear." (Ibid. ii. 239, 258.) A list was kept of those who wore the livery, those who wore gowns, and householders and bachelors not in livery. (Ibid. 175-177.)

[239] These divisions must be taken in a general sense. Five orders are mentioned among the Merchant Taylors (Clode, 8-9); but these really fall into three main groups. For our present purpose the "Bachelors," an intermediate rank formed in some of the richer crafts, may be omitted.

[240] See Du Cange.

[241] Riley's Mem. Lond. 258. See the case of the London bakers where a special ordinance was needed to make the servants liable to punishment for the grossest frauds in the absence of the masters. (Ibid. 181-2.)

[242] If a craftsman not admitted to the freedom of the guild took work, the customer in case of fraud had only the protection of the common law, and could not appeal to the town or guild ordinances. (English Guilds, 322.)

[243] From time to time there were protests on the part of the members of the craft against the power of the oligarchy. There was such a case in the London Grocers' Company, when an attempt was made in 1444 to limit the power of the wardens in appointing new members. (Kingdon's Grocers' Company, i. 123.)

[244] English Guilds, 30, 35, 289. Twelve of the discreetest of the smiths at Coventry elected the keepers, and formed the court to try offenders.

[245] Lambert's Guild Life, 113, 129; English Guilds, 156, 159, 162, 217, 160, 169, 31, 164, 167, 318, 445. The weavers' guild was governed by a council of twenty-four as early as the thirteenth century. (Lib. Cus. 424.) In religious or social guilds there were cases where the election of officers was made by the assent of all the brethren (English Guilds, 47, 49, 148, 213, 232), or "with the assent of the *elder part* of the brethren and sistern of the guild" (ibid. 150); but the prevailing custom was the appointment of picked men to choose the officers. (English Guilds, 62, 64, 71, 75, 83, 89, 91, 97, 119, 266.) In one case "all the brethren whom the alderman should send for" were to elect officers. (Ibid. 35.) In another the alderman chose two men, the company chose two others, these four chose two more, and the six elected officers. In a later form copied for another craft instead of the "company" the "masters of the guild" chose two men. (Ibid. 276.) In one case a new provost was chosen by the four provosts of the past year. (Ibid. 186.) In the Grocers' Company the wardens appointed their successors. (Kingdon's Grocers' Company, i. 10, 14, 18.) A similar custom prevailed in the Southampton Guild Merchant.

[246] Riley's Mem. 348. In the Cordwainers' Guild of Exeter (1481) two of the wardens were chosen from the shop-holders, and two from the journeymen. (English Guilds, 332.) It would seem that among the coruesers of Bristol the journeymen had a certain recognized position, the visible sign of which was their having the right to provide lights carried in the municipal processions at certain feasts; and when in 1454 "divers debates and murmurs had arisen between the masters and crafts of the coruesers and the journeymen," and the masters and craft-holders sought to deprive the journeymen of this right, the attempt was vigorously and successfully resisted.

[247] In Ipswich when a youth in 1448 was apprenticed to a barber for seven years it was stipulated that he should get suitable clothing, shoes, bedding, board, and chastisement. (Hist. MSS. Com. ix. 259.) At Romney in 1451 it was decreed that at the end of his service the apprentice should receive from his master 10*s.* or a bed of that value. (Ibid. v. 543). A decree against using

daggers or knives or making any affray was limited by the phrase, "provided always that it shall be lawful to any inhabitant to correct his servant or apprentice according to the law." (English Guilds, 390.) But on the other hand when a master among the tailors at Exeter chastised his servant so far as to bruise his arm and break his head, he had not only to give a fine to the craft but to give the servant 15*s*. and a month's board and to pay his doctor. (Ibid. 322.)

[248] A master retiring from trade might sell and devise the services of his apprentice to a new master, but if there was any suspicion that a sale had been so managed that the apprentice lost credit for one or two years of the service which he had actually fulfilled both the masters were deprived of the freedom of the city and craft. (Paston Letters, i. 378.)

[249] See note A at end of chapter.

[250] Statutes 6 Henry VI. cap. 3.

[251] Statutes 12 Richard II. cap. 3.

[252] English Guilds, 395, 285-6; Hist. MSS. Com. v. 530; Riley's Mem. Lond. 246.

[253] Riley's Mem. Lond. 307; English Guilds, 285-6. Piece-work was common in many trades. In Newcastle the guild of fullers and dyers in their ordinances of 1477 regulated the price of fulling and shearing the various kinds of cloth by piece-work at so much a yard. The weavers also worked by the piece. The Newcastle slaters had been formed into a guild and had ordinances in 1451 with similar regulations; the bricklayers and plasterers were in a guild in 1454 (Newcastle Guilds). There was piece-work among the tawyers. (Riley's Mem. Lond. 330-1.) In Winchester the weavers probably worked at from 3*d.* to 4*d.* a day, as they were ordered to take from Hallow Eve to the Annunciation for their work but 1*s.* 6*d.*, and from the Annunciation to Hallow Eve but 2*s.*

[254] In 1265 Leicester weavers were allowed by the guild to weave by night as well as by day. (Gross, ii. 144.)

[255] Riley's Mem. Lond. 232-3. This was true of a great number of trades. (Ibid. 244, 245-7, 258, &c. For Lincoln tailors, English Guilds, 183. Kingdon's Grocers' Company, i. 20-21.) In this last company public notice was given of a servant who had left his master to prevent his being engaged by another.

[256] Hibbert's Influence of English Guilds, 64.

[257] Riley's Mem. 247-8, 250-1, 256.

[258] Lib. Cus. 84.

[259] Riley's Mem. 495.

[260] Mem. Lond. 495-6. The friars from time to time appear as supporters of the poorer people. In Coventry the White Friars was the meeting place for the fellowship of the crafts and for the tilers' company in the fifteenth century; and Friar John Bredon played the part of a local agitator. The policy of the Friars was often, as in Canterbury, part of a general antagonism to other religious establishments. (Hist. MSS. Com. ix. 98.)

[261] Mem. Lond. 543-4. The suppression of the May-day festival of the journeymen shearmen in Shrewsbury was very possibly a similar putting down of confederations and conspiracies. (Hibbert's Inf. and Dev. of Eng. Gilds, 120-2.) See also the Bristol Coruesers, p. 119, n. 1.

[262] Riley's Mem. Lond. 609-12, 653. Clode, 4, 22-29.

[263] The town records of Shrewsbury note in 1516 a reward to the king's messenger bearing letters concerning the insurrection of the apprentices of the City of London. (Owen's Shrewsbury, i. 284.)

[264] See p. 102, note 2.

[265] See Note A, p. 160.

[266] English Guilds, cxxi. For an exception at Hull see Lambert's Guild Life, 188. For Canterbury see H.M.C. ix. 173-4.

[267] "The people must cheerfully maintain the government, within whose functions however it does not lie to support the people." Cleveland's Presidential Address. Mar. 6, 1893.

[268] Stat. 11 Henry VI. cap. 12.

[269] Nott. Rec. i. 268-272, 316-318. See also Hist. MSS. Com. vi. 582.

[270] Piers Ploughman. Pass. iv. 80-118. There is an instance of a guild in which no parson, baker, or wife, was admitted. (Eng. Gilds, 271).

[271] Piers Ploughman. Pass. iii. 222.

[272] Riley's Mem. 182. A summary of the conflict on the price of wine is given in Schanz, i. 642-50. By 5 Richard II. Stat. i. cap. 4 if a vintner refused to sell at the right price the mayor might deliver the wine to any buyer at statute cost.

[273] Kingdon's Grocers' Company, i., xvii., xviii.; Schanz, i. 651.

[274] Norwich Town Close Evidences (Brit. Museum.), 16.

[275] Riley's Memorials, 174-5. Many other examples might be given. A later instance occurs when the London Corporation brought a complaint against

the society of hoastmen in 1603 about the raising of the price of coals in London and the scanty supply, so that "without great difficulty the city cannot be provided sufficiently of sea-coals for the poor." The fraternity of hoastmen make a statement of their reasons concerning the prices of sea-coals to the Privy Council in answer to the complaint of the Mayor and Aldermen. (Newcastle Guilds, 44.)

[276] The chief objection of the public to the "unreasonable ordinances" by which the crafts closed their corporations was the "common damage to the people," probably as tending to raise prices. (P. 102, n. 2.) The Coventry Leet opposed the crafts in this matter.

[277] These grants were all of early date, in the twelfth century. Ashley, Woollen Industry, 15-17; Madox, 26, 191, etc., 212, etc., 283-4. The Nottingham weavers paid a rent of 40s. for their guild to the King from the time of Henry the Second. For this they raised a contribution from each loom, and obtained a grant that those who paid might work in the outskirts of the town. (Nott. Rec. iii. 27, 58, ii. 36.)

[278] Riley's Lib. Cus. 130 etc.

[279] Ibid. 121, 123. The survival of the weavers' court may be seen in 1321. In certain cases where the bureller was fined by the Mayor, the weaver was punished by the bailiffs of his own guild. (Ibid. 422-3.)

[280] Riley's Lib. Cus. 423.

[281] In 1327 Edward the Third granted a charter to the girdlers of London, which took in all the girdlers of the kingdom, ordered them under the same rules, and set them under the Mayors of whatever city they might be in. (Riley's Mem. 154-5).

[282] Some charters were given by Edward the Fourth and later Kings to companies of Tailors, Merchants, and so on, which gave them an existence independent of the town, and power to make their own ordinances. (See p. 173.) No list has been made out of these companies, and the subject needs investigation. From the cases which I have met with I think it may probably turn out that such charters were generally given to companies with a foreign trade, and given for reasons referring to that trade. The second charter of the Merchant Tailors in 1390 allowed them to make ordinances among themselves and of their own authority. (Clode, 3.) This charter seems to have freed them from the Mayor, but if so they were again put under his control in 1436. (Ibid. 5, see pp. 189-191, 193.) This was followed by a violent attempt in 1442 to have a Mayor of their own company, which failed and caused much anger. It is evident from the charter of Henry the Seventh, in 1502, which confirmed their independence, that they dealt in "all and every kinds of merchandises" "in all quarters and kingdoms of the world." (Ibid.

7, 195.) By this they were again given full power to make ordinances for themselves without interference, so long as these were not contrary to the laws of the kingdom nor to the prejudice of the Mayor; and the Mayor was wholly deprived of the power of search among their subjects—a most important measure, since the master and wardens "had a great number of householders with their servants to rule and govern." (Ibid. 197-200.)

[283] Though guilds were forbidden in Norwich they existed, doubtless by the payment of annual fines. In the case of the tanners the complaint in 1287 against them was clearly that in case of disputes they "made plaint" to their own aldermen and not to the bailiffs. (Hudson's Leet Jurisdiction in Norwich (Selden Soc.) p. 13.) The cobblers had apparently an important guild from the money paid; the saddlers, tanners, and fullers had also guilds in 1292. (Ibid. 39, 42, 43.) The King reserved the power of creating guilds, and it was possibly to prevent his exercising it that towns like Norwich and Coventry obtained by charter the right to have no guilds. Such a privilege freed them from the fear of fraternities independent of the municipality, while it left them free to recognise informally associations whose recurring fines were really the tribute paid for existence.

[284] Some of those so-called religious, but really trading guilds, have been identified. It is clear that the guild of S. Benedict at Lincoln was a society of traders or merchants, who traded on loans from the common fund, paying back half of the increase they made on it. (English Guilds, 174.) Among other instances see the Guild of S. John Baptist at Hull (Lambert's Guild Life, 112, etc. 118, 232, 233); Corpus Christi (ibid. 124); Holy Trinity (ibid. 126.) A very curious and interesting account of the formal founding of the Pepperers' Company as the Fraternity of S. Anthony in the Monastery of Bury, 1345, is given in Kingdon's Grocers' Company, i., xvii. Compare the records given on 8-15. It had become the Grocers' Company by 1373. The Drapers' Guild in Shrewsbury was originally the Guild of the Trinity. (Hibbert's Inf. and Dev. of Eng. Guilds, 32.) For other instances see Chapter V. The custom was so common in the fourteenth and fifteenth centuries that it is highly probable that under any stress of difficulty it would have been resorted to in earlier days. The artizans must have been fully aware of the fact disclosed to us by the two forms of summonses for guild returns issued in 1388, one for the religious and one for the trading guilds—the fact that the two forms of association were regarded in a different way by the government. Some guilds are avowedly of a double character. (English Guilds, 126-128, 179-185.)

[285] See note A at end of chapter.

[286] Riley's Mem. 627; see also 118, 120-1, 153-4.

[287] Riley's Mem. 341.

[288] In the second half of the fourteenth century the London guild ordinances are in the main simply rules against bad or deceitful wares. See the chandlers, curriers and pelterers, cappers, potters, &c. Riley's Mem. 118, 358; Lib. Cus. 94, 101; goldsmiths, Schanz, i. 613-4.

[289] Mem. Lond. 293.

[290] Lib. Cus. 100.

[291] Mem. Lond. 280-2.

[292] Riley's Liber Custumarum, 101. See the case of the weavers infra p. 160, where the craft tried to shorten hours and the town forbade it.

[293] Ordinances of Pewterers. Riley's Mem. 243. See also glovers and hatters, &c., 239, 246.

[294] Ibid. 226.

[295] Riley's Mem. 226-7.

[296] Ibid. 218.

[297] Annual congregations made by the masons were forbidden by statute of Richard II., continued by later Kings (3 Henry VI., cap. i.). The anxiety of the government was quickened by the number of tilers who took part in the Peasants' Revolt. (Stubbs, ii. 496.) Cf. The Common Weal (ed. Miss Lamond), 88-9.

[298] Statutes of the Realm, 3 Edward IV. cap. 4; ibid. 4 Edward IV. cap. 1. A law of 1410 withdrew from the worsted-weavers and merchants of Norwich the supervision of the cloth trade that had been granted to them in 1348 (Ashley, Woollen Industry, 54-5); and handed over to the mayor, sheriffs, and commonalty of Norwich, the right of measuring and sealing all worsteds made in Norwich or Norfolk. (Blomefield, iii. 125.) A later law enacted that "the worsted shearers in Norwich shall make no ordinance but such as the Mayor and Alderman shall think necessary." (Stat. 1494, cap. xi.) In the fifteenth century the Privy Council took away from the Bakers' and Tailors' Crafts in London the right of search in their trades which had been granted to their Wardens, and restored it to the Mayor, and ordered the crafts to obey the Mayor after the old usages, customs, and laws of London. 1442. Proceedings Privy Council, v. 196; Seligman, Med. Guilds, 82; Schanz, i. 617.

[299] The mayor and aldermen of London had full jurisdiction over all the various trades quite early in the fourteenth century. Two master-masons were reconciled before the mayor of London in 1298. (Mem. Lond. 38.) For early part of the fourteenth century see ibid. 90, 118, 120, 153-4, 216, 156, 178, 245-6.

[300] In "the ordinances of the Hull Guilds from 1490 to 1723 there is no authorization by any but the mayor of the town." (Lambert's Guild Life, 188.) For municipal authority over the Shrewsbury Guilds see Hibbert, 40, 85-6. For Norwich, Blomefield, iii. 130.

[301] A law of 1413 ordered the registration of charters and approval of ordinances and bye-laws—a law which was repeated by the Statute of Henry VI. to prevent the masters of guilds and fraternities making ordinances to the damage of the King or the people, when it was again decreed that all their rules should be certified and registered by Justices of the Peace or by the chief magistrates of cities or towns. 15 Henry VI., cap. 6. See also 19 Henry VII., cap. 7.

[302] English Guilds, 283-286.

[303] Ricart, 78. The examples are too numerous to give. But see the ordinances drawn up in 1448 for the Tailors' Guild of Lynn by the Mayor and the Council. It was ordered that no new tailor should set up in business unless he was considered "sufficient in conning" not only by the two head men of his craft, but also by the mayor. Every tailor admitted to the guild had to pay a fine as entrance fee to the Mayor and another to the community, as well as his payment to the Guild; and paid a yearly fee to the town for any sewers and apprentices whom he employed. Quarrels between shapers and sewers were to be settled by the Mayor and the head men of the craft. If a tailor sent home an ill-fitting garment the buyer might bring his complaint to the Mayor's Court, and claim amends before the Mayor and the head men of the craft on condition of paying a fine of 3*s.* 4*d.* if he did not prove his case. (Hist. MSS. Com. xi. 3, 165-6.)

[304] Miss Dormer Harris has kindly given me the rules at Coventry as to how a craft was to proceed to the punishment of a member in 1518. The master of the craft was first to ask a "reasonable penalty;" if the offender refused to pay, the master was to apply again after three or four days and have the refusal recorded; and in case the refusal was repeated a second time he and three or four of the "honest men" of the craft were to come to the mayor; and the mayor and one of the justices were to command the offender to pay a double penalty; and if he refused yet again, to commit him to prison until it was paid to the craft. At the same time the offender was to desire the master to be "good master to him and his good lover." If the penalty were more than would suffice for a pound of wax, the remainder was to go to common box, *i.e.*, the city funds.

[305] The tilers were strictly ruled by statute as to how the various tiles should be made, thatch tile, roof tile, gutter tile, and so on; how the earth should be prepared and how big the tiles should be. Justices of the Peace, that is in

towns the Mayor and the Aldermen, were to hear the cases against offenders and appoint searchers. (17 Edward IV. cap. 4.)

[306] Mem. Lond. 308.

[307] English Guilds, 386, 398-9.

[308] Hist. MSS. Com. ix. 174.

[309] Nott. Rec. i. 197. In Winchester every bureller had to give one cloth yearly to the King's ferm. (English Guilds, 351.)

[310] Enforced contribution of crafts was common; and the cost considerable. (Gross, ii. 51; Hist. MSS. Com. xi. 3, p. 166, 225; ibid. ix. 173-5.) See Kingdon, ii. 260, 318, &c. In Coventry there were complaints in 1494 that the dyers, skinners, fishmongers, &c., were so "self-willed" that they could not be made to contribute to pageants. See Hibbert's Inf. and Dev. of Eng. Gilds, 63. For the whole question of plays and pageants see Davidson's Studies in Eng. Mystery Plays, printed by Yale University, 1892. The Corpus Christi processions became after the order of the Council of Vienne, 1318, exceedingly popular; the guilds of Corpus Christi, having charge of the procession, not of the plays (91-2), were probably generally composed of the upper class of people. A list of Miracle Plays and Mysteries has been made for students by F. Stoddard, California University, 1887.

[311] Von Ochenkowski thinks the relation of municipalities and crafts depended on the relative force of the three principles then contending for the mastery—feudal rights, the king's will, and the common law; in the conflicts between guilds and towns he sees the alternating forces of the king's law and of the common law. (Wirthschaftliche Entwickelung, 59-60.) Many homelier causes than this were probably at work.

[312] The surprising number of guilds formed under Richard the Second and during the next hundred years must strike any one who looks at the town records. As a single example see the list given for Shrewsbury in Hibbert's Inf. and Dev. of Eng. Gilds, 58-9. In many cases it can be proved that the new fraternity was really an old one, but its re-constitution is as important as a new creation.

[313] Boys' Sandwich, 678, 680.

[314] Hist. MSS. Com. ix. 173-4. "Provided always that any such masters so elected shall be none of the same crafts or mysteries whereof they shall be elected."

[315] Boys, 685, &c.

[316] Hist. MSS. Com. ix. 173-5, 148. Sometimes wealthy guilds united to gain a monopoly of power in the borough. There was a tendency to combine

even in the poorer social or religious fraternities. (Eng. Gilds, 219.) A decline took place in the number of miracle plays for the crafts. Pollard's Miracle Plays, xxx.

[317] See the curious provision made by the mayor of London at the request of the farriers to get their bills paid. (Riley's Mem. Lond. 294.)

[318] English Guilds, 285.

[319] Hist. MSS. Com. ix. 174.

[320] Shillingford's Letters (Camden Soc.) 4.

[321] Though this body of Twelve appears first in the records in 1344, it is impossible to doubt that it was of earlier origin, in view of the custom of other boroughs. In the same way the notices in 1288, 1301, and later, of the electing jury do not by any means imply that these were its first appearances, and all analogy would point to an opposite conclusion.

[322] Freeman's Exeter, 147, 149.

[323] Mr. Freeman seems to suggest that the Council of Exeter was formed by the habitual summoning of certain members of the Assembly to advise the mayor, and speaks of it as "a committee of the whole body." (Ibid. p. 152.) It is, however, not yet certainly ascertained whether the evidence bears out this view as regards Exeter.

[324] The regular list of recorders or law officers begins in 1354. Freeman's Exeter, 154.

[325] Freeman's Exeter, 146-7. English Guilds, 303, 307, 308.

[326] Both these classes admitted "out-brothers," probably "foreigners," who paid half fees.

[327] English Guilds, 313-316.

[328] Ibid. 318, 324, 327.

[329] Ibid. 321-2.

[330] His first charter to the Tailors was in 1461 (Gross i. 124 n 2); the second in 1466. A different instance occurs in Shrewsbury, when Edward the Fourth gave in 1461 a charter to the Fraternity of the Blessed Trinity making it into the company of the Drapers. (Hibbert's Influence and Development of English Guilds, 59.)

[331] English Guilds, 301, 307, 310. Gross i. 124.

[332] English Guilds, 309-311.

[333] English Guilds, 302-304.

[334] Ibid. 303.

[335] English Guilds, 304-8.

[336] English Guilds, 324.

[337] Ibid. 326.

[338] English Guilds, 323.

[339] Ibid. 331-4.

[340] Ibid. 334-7.

[341] This forms the earliest account we possess of the costs of a private bill. Ibid. 308-311.

[342] Freeman's Exeter, 146-154.

[343] English Guilds, 328.

[344] See Chapter XIII. p. 352-4.

[345] In 1376 the judges held that no guild could be established save by royal charter. (Seligman in his Med. Guilds p. 66, quotes Year Book 49, Edward III. fol. 36.) On the other hand in 1376 the commons presented a petition complaining that many of the mayors were prevented from exercising their office thoroughly by the special charters which had been granted to certain misteries and praying that these special charters might be withdrawn so as to strengthen the hands of the local authorities. (Rot. Parl. ii. 331 No. 54.) See Gross i. 113 note 2. For instances of royal charters to guilds see the Mercers of Shrewsbury (Hibbert, 64), the Tailors of London (Clode's Merchant Tailors), and various companies in Hull (Lambert's Two Thousand Years of Guild Life).

[346] A curious instance is given in Hull in which one of the county magnates made use of the guild as an instrument for getting hold of the borough representation in Parliament. (Lambert's Two Thousand Years of Guild Life, 182.)

[347] The story of the Hull Merchants' Company is very instructive. Ibid. 180, etc.

[348] See Chapter VIII. The union of crafts in a guild at Walsall (Gross ii. 248) before 1440 seems to have been very like the union of crafts at Coventry a century earlier to get control of the town government, "in eschewing of such great misorder and inconvenience as here of late hath fortuned and happened."

[349] Carlisle Mun. Rec. ed. Ferguson and Nansen 89-99.

[350] The town customs and bye-laws were drawn up in 1561 by "the Mayor and Council with four of every occupation in the aforesaid city, for and in the name of the whole citizens (Carlisle Mun. Rec. 28, 29, 59). In Beverley the alderman of merchants and twenty-one aldermen of various crafts gave assent in the fifteenth century to ordinances of the governors." (Gross, ii. 23.)

[351] Gross, ii. 380-3.

[352] See Chapter XIII. 374-5.

[353] Gross, i. 111, note 3. The cases of Durham and Morpeth here mentioned are very late.

[354] Ibid. 112, note 4.

[355] Ibid. i. 124 note 2. Von Ochenkowski (Wirthschaftliche Entwickelung, 67) argues that this regulation was made in consequence of the mediæval view of trade as a public trust not a mere individual act; and that skill in craft was taken as a test of uprightness of character and a pledge of fitness for citizenship. From this conclusion follows the belief, which in its turn supports the conclusion, that the rule was one imposed by the town authorities and not by the will of the crafts.

[356] Stubbs, iii. 607.

[357] This history has been treated by Dr. Gross in his "Gild Merchant." In the thirteenth century Merchant Guilds existed in at least one-third and probably in a much greater proportion of the English boroughs. (Gross, i. 2, 22, 158.)

[358] Ibid. i. 107.

[359] Gross, i. 74, 107, 108, note 3, 109. There were clergy and women in the Andover Guild (Ibid. ii. 299, 321); and in Coventry (English Guilds, 228).

[360] Gross, i. 66-71, ii. 236.

[361] Ibid. i. 43, 61, 158-9.

[362] Ibid. i. 282-3.

[363] Gross, i. 61-63, 85. Sometimes the grant of a guild was given before the grant of other rights. In other cases it followed. Thus in Gloucester the first charter was given by Henry the Second "to my burgesses of Gloucester" in 1155. The Guild did not appear in the charter till 1200, when John granted certain municipal rights to "our burgesses of Gloucester," and others mainly of a trading sort to "our burgesses of Gloucester of the Merchant Guild"; and in 1227 a charter of Henry the Third seems for the first time to enact

that burgesses must not only dwell in the borough, hold land, and pay lot and scot, but must also "be in the Merchant Guild and Hanse."

[364] Ibid. i. 43-52, 158-9.

[365] Ibid. i. 63, 85, 114. "In some places their powers appear to have been gradually enlarged during the thirteenth century so as to embrace jurisdiction in pleas relating to trade." (Ibid. 65.)

[366] Ibid. i. 114-115.

[367] Gross, i. 117, 159-60.

[368] Ibid. i. 116.

[369] Dr. Gross holds that all guilds of merchants formed after the decline of the Gilda Mercatoria in the thirteenth century must be considered as being merely craft-unions of the ordinary kind—in most cases superseding the Guild Merchant (i. 129).

[370] By Dr. Gross's definition, "What had once been a distinct integral part of the civic body politic became vaguely blended with the whole of it." (Gross, i. 159-60, 163.)

[371] This is stated to have been very rare. (Ibid. p. 114.)

[372] Ibid. 118, 163. The appellation of the Guild Merchant "was more frequently applied to the aggregate of the crafts" than to the governing body of the borough. (Ibid. i. 114.) In Carlisle had the term "been used at all, *it would probably have been applied* to the eight guilds aggregately, rather than to the Corporation." (Ibid. ii. 40.) In proving that the later Guild Merchant was "an aggregate of the crafts," Dr. Gross carries us at a single step into a much later period (pp. 118-123), where the name tells us little apart from the history of the borough. The case of Coventry seems a doubtful instance.

[373] Gross, i. 161, 163. Lynn is given as an illustration of this change, but the evidence is not adduced.

[374] Ibid. i. 118. No instance is given of this.

[375] Dr. Gross argues that any struggle which did take place was not between the Guild Merchant and the crafts, but between "the governing council (the "magnates," "potentiores," etc.) on the one side and the burgesses at large ("communitas," "populus," "minores") on the other." (Gross i. 110, 285.) The "magnates" of Norwich (Hudson's Mun. Org. p. 24-5), or "les riches" of the city records, ruled in a city where there was no Guild Merchant. The "potentiores" of Lynn seem from the printed records to have been the Guild Merchant. In the town records "communitas" cannot be understood as synonymous with "populus," still less with "minores."

[376] Gross, i. 109. "Not a single unmistakable example of such a conflict has ever been deduced." On this point Seligman (Mediæval Guilds, 57-8) speaks very dogmatically on most inconclusive evidence, so far as this is given in his notes. The analogy on p. 58 of craft guilds including smaller unions is not shewn, nor their common occurrence proved.

[377] In London, Norwich, and the Cinque Ports, there was no Guild Merchant at any time. In Lynn, Andover, Southampton, and Bristol it was all-powerful. In Nottingham no influence of its action can be traced; the guild mentioned in John's charter (Nott. Rec. i. 9) is only once mentioned afterwards, in 1365. (Ibid. i. 189.)

[378] Gross, i. 107.

[379] See Lynn, Gross, ii. 157. Southampton, ibid. 216-226. Andover, ibid. 4, 8, 294, 344. Derby, ibid. 51-3. Newcastle, ibid. 184-5; other instances, i. 69. For Reading see vol. i. 302. For the variety in relations of the Guild to the town see Gross, i. 73.

[380] As at Oxford and Lincoln, Lib. Cus. 671. Gross, ii. 146. It is very probable, however, that these were confirmations of older institutions.

[381] Gross, i. 109.

[382] Ibid. i. 33.

[383] Ibid. i. 31. See also Bury St. Edmunds, ii. 30-3.

[384] See p. 219, note at end of Chapter.

[385] Barnstaple, Gross, ii. 12.

[386] Bury St. Edmunds, Gross, ii. 33-4.

[387] Gross, i. 117. Is there any reason to think that if the enjoyment of monopoly was split up and divided among the crafts, the exercize of authority was split up and transferred in the same proportions?

[388] When wealthy individuals of a craft, men perhaps almost in the position of merchants, were admitted to the Guild, no argument can be drawn from this as to the relation of the craft itself to the Guild.

[389] Gross, i. 114-5. In the instances here given (p. 116, note 1) of regulations made for craftsmen by the Guild Merchant it is necessary to define the exact relation between the Guild and the governing body of the town. (See Andover in 1314. Gross, ii. 308. Compare Leicester, ibid. 144.)

[390] Gross, i. 125-6, 159-60.

[391] Ibid. i. 75, 76.

[392] All the materials which I have used in speaking of Coventry have been given me very kindly by Miss Dormer Harris, who has made a careful study of the town records on the spot, and will soon, it is hoped, publish the result of her researches.

[393] Compare Chesterfield, where a Guild was established in 1218 to guard the "liberties of the town"; in case of need its aldermen were to choose twelve men to go before the justices or elsewhere to help these "liberties" of the town; and any one suffering loss for them was to be repaid by the Guild. (English Guilds, 165-167.)

[394] Compare the very small numbers of the Reading Guild, which was a survival of olden times (Vol. I. p. 302, note 1). S. Alban's was larger, but apparently of a more doubtful character, even in the eyes of the prudent burghers. (Ibid. 296-7.)

[395] They got land from Isabella, and built their church at Bablake—the first church built by the burghers.

[396] The taking of a common name may have been connected with the license to mortmain. S. John's Guild had got a license in 1342 and land to build its church, but some extended license must have been needed for a larger society which desired to possess new property.

[397] Mercers' obits were celebrated in S. Catherine's Chapel; drapers' obits usually in the Lady Chapel belonging to S. Mary's or the Merchant Guild.

[398] The early guildhall of York belonged to the guilds of S. George and S. Christopher; and when the new hall was built in the middle of the fifteenth century these two guilds retained considerable power in it. (Davies' Walks Through York, 49-51.) Sir William Plumpton and his wife joined the fraternity of S. Christopher at York, 1439. (Plumpton Corr. lxii.)

[399] Cf. Norwich (p. 395). This arrangement was probably made for the sake of financial security (see p. 215-6).

[400] English Gilds, 232.

[401] Accounts of the Guild of Corpus Christi are preserved from 1488. The brethren and sisters of the Guild seem to have been spread all over England, and are mentioned at London, Lynn, and Birmingham. They were of all ranks and of all trades and callings. (Hist. MSS. Com. i. 101.) The Prior of the cathedral, the Prior's bailiff, the vicar of Trinity, various craftsmen of the town and vicars of the neighbourhood, merchants of Queenborough, Dublin, Drogheda, Bristol, Kingston-on-Hull, London, and many other places, a "merchant of the Staple," and great men of the neighbourhood, such as Thomas Grey, the Marquis of Dorset, Lord Hastings, and others belonged to its association.

[402] S. Mary's Hall was begun in 1340, and finished in 1413.

[403] The Twenty-four were self-elected; the mayor was elected by the Twenty-four; the common council were appointed and summoned by the mayor.

[404] Compare the case of Southampton where a guild merchant had imposed its methods on a town government.

[405] The list compiled in 1449 of living craftsmen who had held office gives fifteen drapers and eleven mercers, and seven dyers; as against two wire-drawers, two whit-tawyers, and two weavers. The dyers in Coventry were often cloth merchants of great consequence.

[406] In the time of Richard the Second the fullers and tailors first attempted to form a guild, and even obtained a patent which licensed their society to hold property worth a yearly rental of eight marks.

[407] The complaint against the dyers is shown in a petition to Parliament in 1415 (Rot. Parl. iv. 75), in which the community of Coventry say that by reason of a confederacy among the dyers they cannot get their cloth dyed under 6*s.* or 7*s.* a dozen, whereas last year's price was 5*s.*; and forty pounds of wool was now 30*s.* which was last year 20*s.*, &c. The dyers are also great and common makers of cloth and take all the flower of the wool for their own cloth, the remnant serving the common people. The petitioners request that on the day of the mayor's election, those that elect him (that is twenty-four members of the ruling guilds) shall also appoint four persons, two drapers, one dyer, and one woder, sworn to keep watch over the dyers, and present them for any "fault or confederacy" to the mayor, bailiffs, and justices of the peace—in other words to the officers of the Trinity Guild. For the first fault he was to pay a fine to the king, for the second a fine and half a year's imprisonment. They also prayed that no one who was a dyer should make vendible cloth. These conditions being refused they claimed the suppression of the guild.

[408] The mayor and his brethren carried their complaint to the king in 1424, and by royal writ the assemblies were forbidden. In 1422 the governing guilds issued an order that all wardens should bring the ordinances of the crafts before the mayor, recorder, and bailiffs, and eight of the general council by whom honest, lawful, and good rules should be allowed; and no ordinances might be made against the law in oppression of people, upon pain of imprisonment or fine at the king's will. In 1424 arbitrators were appointed by the mayor's order to decide the disputes between the master weavers and their men; and rules were drawn up for the whole craft. It is obvious that this is very different from regulation by a guild which still retained the crafts within its own association.

[409] They gave forty marks for a fresh license for their guild with mortmain up to ten marks, and leave to elect four masters at the Nativity to rule the craft and to plead in courts for the whole body. As of old they seem to have failed in carrying out their scheme in spite of the license, and in 1448 a petition was presented by them (whether it was voluntary may well be doubted) that the union between the fullers' and tailors' crafts should be severed. At the suppression of the guilds the shearmen and tailors held a mill and tenements in mortmain for the support of their chauntry.

[410] Cf. Exeter, Chapter VII.

[411] How little freedom was left to far the most powerful craft of all—the dyers—we see from the law of 1530, that if any masters and journeymen of the dyers can be proved before the mayor and justices to have hindered any one from becoming a dyer, they are to be fined. If the journeymen refuse to work for the new dyers, then, without hindrance from the craft or the journeymen, they may hire others not inhabitants. In 1530 it was ordered that a certain Robert Perkins was to become a dyer without "let or hindrance" from craft and journeymen. In general the corporation resisted the tendency of the lesser crafts to prevent the setting up of new masters—a policy which is easy to understand in the rule of merchants, as opposed to that of the manufacturers.

[412] Posted up on the door of S. Michael's in 1494:—

"Be it knowen and understood
This cite should be free and now is bond
Dame Goode-Eve made hit free
And now the' be customes for woll and the drap'ie.
Also hit is made that no prentice shall be
But XIII. penies pay shall he,
This act did Robert Grene
Therefore he had many a curse I wene."

(Sharp's Antiquities, 235.)

[413]

"This city is bond that shuld be free,
The right is holden from the C̄ialte.
Our cōins that at Lamas open shuld be cast
They be closed in and hegged full fast....
If ever ye have nede to the cōialte
Such favour as ye show us such shall ye see.
We may speke fair and bid ye good morwe
But luff from our herts ye shall have nevr....
Cherish the cōialte and so they have their right

For drede of a worse chance by day or by night.
The best of all littel worth shuld be
And ye had not had help of the cōialte."

(Sharp, 235.) Perhaps it was from the talk of the streets in some such local disturbance that Langland quoted when he wrote the lines quoted in Vol. I. p. 26.

[414] The Coventry craft-masters' apprentices paid their fines to the mayor "for the use of the city," not of the guild; the "searchers" for the trades were appointed and the regulations made at the Leet Court, not at meetings of a guild; the same officials attended, but they had to act as representing the municipality.

[415] As in Lynn, Bristol, and, later, Norwich.

[416] It is a subject for inquiry whether any Guild Merchant gave its name to a municipality unless it had been made responsible for the payment of the ferm, and held openly and to the knowledge of the exchequer some property or rents or tolls for the purpose.

[417] The Coventry Guild held town property for public purposes before this, apparently as a private arrangement.

[418] It is possible that in the earlier part of Richard's reign the fear inspired by the Peasant Revolt may have quickened the spirit of organization among the wealthier classes. In the Guild of Lichfield, established by charter in 1387, the master of the Guild and the Forty-eight were "steadfastly to abide together and see that good rule be kept in the city." (Gross, ii. 145.) Similar combinations of the richer classes seem to have been very general.

[419] English Gilds, 244-6, 249, 250.

[420] Gross, ii. 353.

[421] Hist. MSS. Com. iii. 316. This states that all the burgesses and the commonalty of the borough of Bridgewater have ordained that they will choose yearly two seneschals of their guild, and one bailiff to attend on them; such seneschals to have power to punish those offending against these ordinances. If any one among them shall maliciously impute to another a charge of theft, forgery, neifty ("nativitatis," the being a born bondman), murder, adultery, or excommunication, and be convicted thereof before the seneschals, he shall be amerced and bound to the commonalty to make satisfaction to the other at the award of his peers. No one shall implead another without the borough under pain of amercement. Any one neglecting to appear before the seneschals when summoned is to be amerced. Those opposing execution or distress made by order of the seneschals to be amerced and bound to the commonalty in forty pence. No one is to buy flesh

or fish before 9 A.M. for regrating under pain of becoming bound to the commonalty in the price of the flesh or fish so bought or sold. If any one is elected to the office of seneschal of S. Mary's or of the Holy Cross in the church of the said borough he shall render account for the moneys arising therefrom to the said seneschals whenever summoned so to do. Any person refusing any one of those offices, if elected thereto, is to be bound to the commonalty in the sum of 6s. 8d. The seneschals are to render account for all moneys received by them each year upon the morrow of the circumcision of our Lord. This deed has a large fragment of the castle seal or seal of the lord of the fee still attached. (Hist. MSS. Com. iii. 316.)

[422] Their meetings for business were held in a small chamber attached to the church of S. Helen, which is still the exchequer chamber of their successors, the governors of Christ's Hospital. (Hist. MSS. Com. i. 98.) Dr. Gross (i. 83-4, note 11) gives the names of some towns where the government was guided by a "simple social-religious gild." The instances suggest different problems, and need separate examination of the special circumstances.

[423] Madox, 217. How many later declarations of the poverty of *corporations* was due to this convenient system of dealing with their funds?

[424] This system was devised before the doctrine of Trusts was adopted, in the reign of Henry the Fourth; but even after that doctrine was accepted the holding of property by a friendly corporation would have put considerable difficulty in the way of recovering money owed by the municipality.

[425] English Gilds, 231-5.

[426] See Note A at end of Chapter.

[427] See Chapter XIV.

[428] Dr. Gross is one of the latest writers who insists especially on the passage from democracy to oligarchy. (i. 108-110, 125-6, 160, 171, 285.)

[429] Gross, i. 23-6; ii. 115 et sq. Compare Hist. MSS. Com. ix. 239, for the forms used in 1291. For elections in 1310 see Ibid. 242.

[430] In Romney an instance is given in 1442 of a man being arrested who had come, not being free, to hear the common council. Hist. MSS. Com. v. 540. For Wycombe, Ibid. 557.

[431] Journal Archæological Association, xxvii. 464.

[432] Ibid.

[433] Hist. MSS. Com. v. 493.

[434] Boys' Sandwich, 429. See also Berwick, English Guilds, 344.

[435] Journ. Arch. Ass. xxvii. 462. If a townsman struck the mayor and was too harshly punished the friends of the prisoner might call a jury "of the discreetest and stoutest men of the city," who should ordain a just penalty. In Rye as in Hereford the old custom was that the man who struck the mayor was to lose his right hand (Lyon's Dover, ii. 352); in Preston there was some punishment for a mayor who struck a burgess in or out of court (Custumal, Hist. Preston Guild). In Canterbury if a bailiff did wrong to any "that may be found by two lawful men of syght and of hyerth" complaint was made to the twelve aldermen; and if they charged the bailiff in vain to amend the wrong, the case was carried to a court of the thirty-six, the aldermen, and the most wisest men, "and by them right shall be ordained" (Hist. MSS. Com. ix. 171).

[436] Hist. MSS. Com. v. 559.

[437] Hunt's Bristol, 103-5.

[438] For the variety of modes in which juries were elected then and later see Rep. Mun. Corporations, 27.

[439] We find also special juries—for example a jury of masons and carpenters to judge "because of a waterfall which fell from the house and gutter of Richard Maidstone upon the house and ground of William Bennett" (Hist. MSS. Com. ix. 169); and groups of umpires appointed to settle differences (Boys' Sandwich, 786).

[440] This was the custom in Exeter. At Bayonne every new citizen was sworn upon a book containing the charter and statutes of the commune (Luchaire, 47).

[441] Ricart, 2.

[442] At Wycombe and Dartmouth two Italian copies of the Pandects of Justinian and commentaries were used in the fifteenth century to bind up the corporation books.

[443] See pp. 310-11, 334-6, 366-70. A decree of 1328 in Preston was made by "the mayor, bailiffs, and burgesses, with all the commonalty, by a whole assent and consent." (Thomson, Mun. Hist. 105.)

[444] Mr. Maitland describes the communal organization of the villein tenants on the manor of Bright Waltham in 1293 (Manorial Pleas, Selden Soc. 161-4, 168). They formed a "communitas" which held property, could receive a grant of land, could contract and make exchanges with the lord (172). These rights were recognized in the manorial courts, though at Westminster they would have been held very irregular (163). They elected or recommended the reeve, shepherd, ploughman, swineherd (170), the whole ville "undertaking" for him (168). The steward kept watch that no land of

servile tenure should be treated as free, and the villeins themselves were very unwilling that a villein should set up as a freeman on the ground of holding a freehold acre (164).

[445] In Barnstaple a deed concerning a tenement in the High Street in 1416 was sealed with the seal of the commonalty, not that of the mayor. (Hist. MSS. Com. ix. 213.) In Rye there was a seal of the community different from the mayor's seal, which last was first used in 1377. (Ibid. v. 489, 511.) Also in Lydd (ibid. 530-2).

[446] See note A at end of chapter.

[447] Worcester, Eng. Guilds, 378.

[448] Frequent cases indicate that where the common lands played an important part in the wealth or industry of a borough the burgesses long preserved an interest in municipal affairs. Thus, in Haverford West, where the townsfolk up to 1832 took a very real part in the election of their officers and the control of business, the common meadow still contained over a thousand acres. (Report on Mun. Corporation, 233, etc.) And at Berwick-on-Tweed, where also affairs were administered by the whole body of burgesses, the annual value of the lands whose profits went to the freemen was near £6,000. (Ibid. 31.)

[449] Piers Ploughman, pass. xi. 239.

[450] Merewether and Stephens, ii. 590-2.

[451] Norwich Town Close Evidences, p. 16. A copy of this volume (a private publication printed in connection with the Town Close case in 1885) may be found in the British Museum.

[452] Norwich Town Close Evidences, 18-19.

[453] Ibid. 17.

[454] It was at this time that the mayor was given power to distrain for sums levied on the commonalty. (Hist. MSS. Com. xi. part 3, 186-7.)

[455] Hist. MSS. Com. xi. 3, pp. 187, 240. Gross, ii. 155-6.

[456] Report on Markets, 62.

[457] Rot. Parl. i. 433.

[458] Madox, 94.

[459] In the list of taxpayers to the poll-tax of 1380 in Oxford, we find four aldermen mentioned—a vintner, a draper, and two others whose trade is not mentioned, but who had eight and ten servants, a number very greatly above the average. The vintner and draper each paid, like the mayor, 13s. 4d.; but

the man with ten servants gave only 12*d*.; and the man with eight is not registered as having paid at all. (Oxford City Documents, Oxford Hist. Soc. 8-45.)

[460] See Note A at end of chapter.

[461] In 1327 a violent dispute broke out between the great people of Andover and the rest of the community. The story of the election of a sort of council of fifteen of the richer people in 1303, and of incidents leading to the riot of 1327 can be traced in the entries quoted in Gross, ii. 297-321.

[462] Inaugural Address at Oxford by Mr. Froude, Oct. 26th, 1892.

[463] Cases occur in the towns under the game laws. The Jurats of Hythe present Henry Colle as "a common destroyer in killing hares with snares and pypys to the great destruction of the sport of the gentry and against the statute"; and another man "for keeping one ferret for hunting against the statute." (Hist. MSS. Com. iv. 1, 431, 2.)

[464] See Piers Ploughman. Pass. ix. 20-31; ii. 96; x. 223, *et sq.*

[465]

"Then louh (laughed) there a lord and 'by this light' said,
'I hold it right and reason to take of my reeve
All that mine auditor or else my steward
Counselleth me by their account and my clerk's writing.
With *spiritus intellectus* they took the reeve-rolls,
And with *spiritus fortitudinis* fetch it, will he, nil he.'"

—Piers Ploughman. Passus xxii. 461-466.

[466] "If any judgment be given," say the Hereford Customs, "or any execution of writs of our Lord the King, be to be impleaded or done, or if any doubt or ambiguity shall be upon any of our laws or customs, or anything else touching the whole commonalty, then the bailiff or steward, by all kind of rigour, may compel *the discreeter especially, or any other citizen whom they have need of*, to come unto them." (Journ. Arch. Ass. xxvii. 464.)

[467] Hudson, Mun. Org., 24-5.

[468] Royal Commission on Markets, 15, 16. The justices had a right to dismiss poor recognitors, and order the sheriff to cause lawful knights and other proved discreet men to be elected in their stead (Select Civil Pleas, Selden Society, 100). The records of the Manchester Court Leet Jury have only been preserved from 1552. The number varied from about fourteen to eighteen, who were yearly chosen at the court leets from the chief burgesses of the town. When the father died his eldest son or younger brother seems to have been made a juror in his stead. The jurors, in fact, were chosen

generation after generation from the same small number of families. The reeve and one or both constables were generally nominated from among the jury then in the box. (Manchester Court Leet Records, 177-8.) Cf. Ship of Fools. Barclay, 99.

[469] Ibid. 62. See Vol. I. 186, 165, note A. In Canterbury there was a law that if by the bailiff's fault the king should send a writ "in hindering of the liberty" of the town the bailiff should make restitution.

[470] In Colchester for example the number of people assessed for all moveables in 1301 was 390 and the sum raised £24 12s. 6d. In 1377, when it stood twelfth on the list of English towns, it is said to have had about 4,500 inhabitants.

[471] Thus in 1342 Nicholas Langton was elected mayor of York for the seventeenth time (Hargrove's York, i. 308) and two men bore rule in Liverpool for eighteen years between 1374 and 1406—one for twelve years and the other for six (Picton's Liverpool, i. 30).

[472] There was a great variety in the names of mayors during the fifteenth century. John Samon held the office several times, but generally speaking the mayors were not re-elected, and in no case did they hold office two years in succession. (See Nottingham Records.)

[473] Gross, ii. 117.

[474] Lincoln and London (Madox, 14; Gross, i. 80). Canterbury (Hist. MSS. Com. ix. 167).

[475] See Lynn and Southampton.

[476] Ricart's Kalendar, 72, etc. The Mayor in Nottingham was bound "to give his brethren knowledge for to see the game of the fishing" ... and "in likewise to give them knowledge of every bear-baiting and bull-baiting within the town, to see the sport of the game after the old custom and usage." (Rec. iii. 449.)

[477] Hythe, Hist. MSS. Com. iv. i. 432, 434.

[478] Hist. MSS. Com. v. 542. Ibid. vi. 572-580. Any man thrice convicted of "cursing the mayor and slandering him with good and grave people," was to be deprived of his freedom by sound of the bell of the Guild Hall.

[479] See ch. viii. Freeman's Exeter, 90.

[480] In Bristol the town clerk, the steward, and the attorney, had forty-two rays, and their under clerks thirty-two rays. (Ricart, xii. 81.)

[481] In 1476 Lydd paid 13s. 4d. for the writing out of its "Customall." The custumal of Sandwich written in 1301 was copied about 1465 by the Town

Clerk, John Serles. The Black Book of Hythe was copied in the same way. For Southampton see Hist. MSS. Com. xi. 3, p. 8. Instances are too numerous to give.

[482] See the Translation of Crouchback's Charter at Leicester (Hist. MSS. Com. viii. 404); a translation from the French in 1491 of the old book of laws and customs of Yarmouth (Ibid. ix. 305); a translation in 1473 of the ancient rules of the Guild of Southampton known as the Pax Bread. (Davies' Southampton, 133.)

[483] Hist. MSS. Com. v. 606-7. The clerk was also responsible for deeds which were constantly given into the keeping of the Mayor and Council.

[484] The Domesday Book of Dorchester compiled in the XV. century (Journ. Arch. Ass. xxviii. 29); the Liber Albus of Norwich in 1426 (Blomefield, iii. 141; Arch. Journ. xlvi. 302). Ordinances were drawn up at Rye in 1397 (Hist. MSS. Com. v. 489); the Fordwich Kalendar in the fifteenth century (Ibid. v. 606-607). The oldest Year Book of Sandwich is the Old Black Book in which entries are made in 1432 and end in 1487. Entries in its White Book begin in 1488 and end in 1526. The fact that the laws of the Scotch Marches were codified at this time shews the prevailing tendency.

[485] As in Romney (Hist. MSS. Com. v. 539).

[486] In 1386 the Cinque Ports paid for the copying of Magna Charta (Ibid. 533).

[487] Nottingham Records, ii. 340.

[488] Hist. MSS. Com. vi. 489.

[489] Ibid. ix. 223-4.

[490] First paper roll in Reading accounts 1463. (Hist. MSS. Com. xi. part 7, 175.) Accounts at Bridport, Southampton, and Hythe on paper under Richard the Second. (Ibid. vi. 492; xi. 3-8; iv. 1, 438-9.) Some of the guild returns were on paper in 1389. (English Guilds, 132-3.) In 1467 there was a rule in Worcester that the town clerk must be a citizen, and do his own work with daily attendance and not by simple and inefficient deputy, and must engross on parchment. (Guilds, 399.)

[491] Hist. MSS. Com. vi. 477.

[492] Ibid. ix. 108.

[493] Ibid. vi. 603.

[494] The difference is seen by comparing with their accounts such documents as presentments at sessions, bills for goods and the like.

(Nottingham Records, iii. xiv.) See also entries in the records made by Roger Bramston, mayor of Wycombe, in 1490.

[495] The possible difficulty of getting rid of a clerk is illustrated by what happened when the mayor, sheriffs, alderman, and commons of York, in 1475, by their whole and common assent, dismissed the common clerk "for divers and many offences—excessive takings of money, misguiding of their books, accounts, and evidences, with other great trespasses." They then wrote to D. of Gloucester to entreat his good lordship and that he would move the king to allow them to name another common clerk; and the Duke having sent letters to Lord Hastings and Lord Stanley, finally received an answer from the king that he had commissioned two serjeants of the law to examine the case, that they had reported in favour of the corporation, and that a new clerk might be elected. The grateful town agreed at a meeting of the council that the D. of Gloucester "for his great labour now late made unto the king's great grace" should "be presented at his coming to the city with 6 swans and 6 pikes." (Davies' York, 53-55.)

[496] Hist. MSS. Com. vi. 603. In Hereford the steward might be a "foreigner who is known of the citizens." (Journ. Arch. Ass. xxvii. 463-4.)

[497] In Sandwich the "town clerk's" salary was 40$s.$ a year, out of which he had to find parchment, except when he wrote out the cesses, when the commonalty might give him a shilling or two for the parchment and his trouble. Other small payments fell to him when a freeman was made or a corporation letter was signed or suchlike business done. (Boys' Sandwich, 476.) In 1390 Romney paid as much as 56$s.$ 8$d.$; then the salary fell to 40$s.$ in 1428; then to 32$s.$ 11$d.$; and then to 26$s.$ 8$d.$, with 3$s.$ 4$d.$ for parchment. (Ibid. 803.) This corresponded with the decline in the fortunes of Romney.

[498] The common clerk at Hythe, John Smallwood, secured for himself a following of thirty-six men sworn to help him in all his undertakings, and in 1397 he had even gathered sixty men pledged to bring about the death of four of his enemies. For four years the town refused to have any clerk at all, until at last Smallwood made his peace in 1414 by the gift of certain tenements and lands. (Hist. MSS. Com. iv. part 1, 437-8.)

[499] Davies' York, 207. Thomas Atwood, who was town clerk of Canterbury in 1497, seems to have been mayor in 1500. His brother William was one of the counsel of the city in 1497.

[500] Nottingham Records, iii. 59, 84.

[501] For his writing and one or two of his mottoes see Nottingham Records, III. ix.-xiii. ii. xvi. For Robert de Ricarto of Bristol, see p. 20. For Daniel Rowe of Romney, p. 61.

[502] Thompson, Mun. Hist. 82.

[503] See Paston Letters. Cf. The Common Weal (ed. Miss Lamond), 83-4.

[504] See the case of Norwich. The main effect of the new charters was simply to make the rate of progress apparent, and to some extent to help it forward by the mere process of reducing everything to formal legal arrangement, thus incidentally destroying vague liberties, or hardening the exercise of them into a fixed form which had lost all elasticity.

[505] Piers Ploughman. Passus ix. 174.

[506]

"But while Hunger was their master would none chide, Ne strive against the Statute, he looked so stern."

Ibid. Passus ix. 342, 343.

[507] Occasionally we find odd instances of growing independence. In Worcester "at some seasons of wilfulness" the people had shewn their revolutionary temper by choosing for serjeants and constables "persons of worship, to the dishonour of them and of the said city;" and an ordinance was made in 1467 that none of the twenty-four or the forty-eight might be appointed to these offices. (English Guilds, 409.) In like manner the great court of Bridgenorth decreed in 1503 that no burgess should be made serjeant. (Hist. MSS. Com. x. 4, 426.) In 1350 a guild was formed in Lincoln of "common and middling folks" who strongly objected to any one joining them "of the rank of mayor or bailiffs," or claiming dignity for his personal rank, and made a rule that if any such persons insisted on entering their society they should not meddle with its business and should never be appointed officers. (English Guilds, 178-9.)

[508] Piers Ploughman. Pass. xviii. 88.

[509] The differences of early charters should all be studied. See, for example, the charters of Nottingham and Northampton given in the same year (Stubbs's Charters, 300-302).

[510] The complexity and apparently inexhaustible confusion of their methods is well illustrated by the lists drawn up in 1833 by the commissioners appointed to inquire into municipal corporations. See appendix to the Rep. on Mun. Corpor. 94, 95; and especially the tables on pp. 102-132. Evidently the burghers have scarcely deserved the reproach of those who consider direct election by the people as the natural rude expedient of unlearned men grouped in political societies and ignorant of the wiser system of nomination which commends itself to trained legislators.

[511] Kitchin's Winchester, 164.

[512] P. 306.

[513] Municipal Corporations Report, 21.

[514] The modes of election of sheriffs and bailiffs were as various and complicated as those of mayor and council. For illustrations of this see Rep. on Mun. Corp. 24, 25.

[515] There was also a "Great Court" of twenty-four. Hist. MSS. Com. x. part 4, pp. 425-7. At Melcombe Regis (Hist. MSS. Com. v. 578) there was an electing jury of twelve. In Preston the mayor chose in open court two ancient discreet and honest burgesses, who took an oath that they would at once select twenty-four burgesses who should not bear any office in the town during the next year. The twenty-four having been chosen and sworn, elected a mayor, a bailiff, and a sub-bailiff; these three at once took their respective oaths, and the mayor before he left the hall appointed a mayor's bailiff and a serjeant. Laws were made by the "mayor, bailiffs, and burgesses, with all the commonalty, by a whole assent and consent." Government seems to have been carried on by the mayor and "twelve of those who with him are ordained," and who were known as aldermen or capital burgesses. By a guild law earlier than 1328 former mayors and bailiffs, though they might sit on the bench as aldermen, were not allowed to meddle with the twenty-four during the election, under penalty of a fine of twenty shillings or loss of citizenship. (Preston, Guild Record, xxiv. Guild ordinances in history of Preston Guild, by Dobson and Harland, 12, 17, 19-23.)

[516] To illustrate the variety of town constitutions I have given three or four, taken at random, in an Appendix at the end of the chapter. Other instances will be found in Chapters. XII.-XVI.

[517] See note A, p. 283, Hist. MSS. Com. ix. 171-2. This plan was perhaps modelled on a system common in ecclesiastical elections and possibly peculiar in Canterbury so far as municipalities were concerned. There was a dispute in 1435 about the mode of presentation to S. Peter's, Cornhill, to avoid the "great strife and controversy" between the mayor, aldermen, and common council. It was decided that the mayor and aldermen should choose four priests living within the city or a mile of it; that these four should name to the common council four clerks "most meet in manners and conyng"; and that out of these four the mayor, aldermen, and council should choose one. Three Fifteenth century Chron. (Camden Soc., 91-92).

[518] Report on Mun. Corporations, 20.

[519] In Bridport there were twelve jurors. (Hist. MSS. Com. vi. 489-90, 492-3.) In Southampton twelve "discreets," p. 308. The jurats in Romney and others of the Cinque Ports formed a similar body. So also in Carlisle, and in Pontefract. (Hist. MSS. Com. viii. 270-1.) A writ from the privy council was

addressed to "the mayor, bailiffs, and twenty-four notablest burgesses of our town of Northampton" in 1442. (Proceed. Privy Council v. 191.) Wells had a council of twenty-four. (Hist. MSS. Com. i. 106-7.)

[520] Oxford, by a charter of Richard the First, had a mayor and two aldermen. In 1255 Henry the Third made the aldermen four, corresponding to the four wards of the city, and joined with them eight leading burgesses mainly to keep peace in the city and to have charge of the assize of bread, beer, and wine. The twenty-four common councilmen were elected from the citizens at large. (Boase's Oxford, 42-44.) In Ipswich besides the twelve "honest and loyal" portmen elected yearly in the cemetery of S. Mary Tower there was a council of twenty-four; and seven of the portmen and thirteen of the twenty-four could together make rules for the town. (Hist. MSS. Com. ix. 242, 244.) In Yarmouth (Hist. MSS. Com. ix. 305; Blomefield, xi. 301-2, 342), twenty-four jurats (afterwards called aldermen) were chosen by the burgesses, and appointed all the officers of the town. Between 1400 and 1407 changes were made in the constitution. Two bailiffs were elected instead of four, and besides the council of twenty-four aldermen a common council was formed of forty-eight members. So also in Colchester and Norwich. Worcester had two councils, "the twenty-four above and the forty-eight beneath." (English Guilds, 379, 396. Also Leicester, Hist. MSS. Com. viii. 425.) Canterbury had an upper council of twelve and another of thirty-six. (Hist. MSS. Com. ix. 171-2.) For councils of seventy and eighty see pp. 374, 432. In Chester a charter of 1506 gave twenty-four aldermen and forty of the common council. (Hist. MSS. Com. viii. 359-60.) In Bristol (Hunt's Bristol, 85-86) and Liverpool (Picton ii. 26) the council was composed of forty "honest and discreet" men. Colchester had two councils of sixteen each. (Cromwell's Colchester, 265.)

[521] The manner in which the aldermen took their place in the system of municipal government has not yet been worked out. In London, Canterbury, and Lincoln they were hereditary owners of the various wards. The people of Coventry petitioned for aldermen over the wards in 1450, but the mayor and his brethren refused. In Lynn there were only constables of the wards.

[522] Hist. MSS. Com. vi. 551-569.

[523] Davies' Southampton, 263.

[524] Hist. MSS. Com. xi. 3. p. 42, 77-82.

[525] Davies' Southampton, 250.

[526] Gross, ii. 232.

[527] Davies, 253.

[528] 2 Rich. II. St. 1, cap. 3.

[529] Davies, 254.

[530] Ibid. 250.

[531] Hist. MSS. Com. xi. 3, 50, 87.

[532] Ibid. xi. 3, 81, 83, 86. Davies, 253-4.

[533] For example, Thomas Payne, whose barge, the "John of Southampton," traded with Zealand; or the goldsmith, William Nycoll, who was also a merchant, and sent his ship the "Marye of Hampton" to the Bay of Biscay under the charge of a cousin, his factor and purser. (Hist. MSS. Com. xi. 3. p. 78, 84, 88.)

[534] Hist. MSS. Com. xi. 3, pp. 70-73. Davies, 97-8. In 1399 Richard the Second granted to the Emperor for the war against the Turks a sum of £2,000, which was sent through a Genoese merchant and charged on the customs at Southampton. Hist. MSS. Com. xi. 3, 16. Bekynton, i. lx. note. In 1401 a second £2,000 was paid.

[535] Davies, 61, 256.

[536] Hist. MSS. Com. xi. 3, p. 66-69.

[537] Ibid. 77.

[538] Davies, 255.

[539] Ibid. 471.

[540] Ibid. 255-6.

[541] In 1411 the burgesses made a great wharf with a crane on it at the water-gate to increase merchandise and prevent the evading of customs. Davies, 112. For strangers brought their wines "very contemptuously" and landed them "within this realm where they think good themselves." (H.M.C. xi. 3, 50-52.)

[542] Hist. MSS. Com. xi. 3, 11, 87.

[543] Hist. MSS. Com. xi. 3, 90.

[544] Hist. MSS. Com. vi, 551-569.

[545] Davies, 294. This may have supported nearly 140 people.

[546] Davies, 82. For supplies for the King's ship see Hist. MSS. Com. xi. 3, 113.

[547] Davies, 79. Archers sent to the castle for the defence of the townsmen were charged to their account, and they had to submit patiently to their exactions; a letter from Edward the Fourth ordered the town to release one

of the Bowers who had been committed to prison "for his inordinate demeaning," and to go on paying him his wages like other Bowers. (Hist. MSS. Com. xi. 3, 99.)

[548] The castle wall was not pulled down before the end of the fifteenth century. Finally the castle hill itself, after its mound had been lowered and planed, was crowned in 1818 with a Zion chapel on the site of the Norman keep. (Davies, 76, 84.)

[549] Ibid. 81. For the inconvenience which a constable might cause to the town if he wished, see p. 83.

[550] See for one example among many, Davies, 81.

[551] Davies, 216.

[552] Ibid. 79.

[553] In the last year of Henry the Sixth the master of one of the King's ships received from the Mayor £31 10s. 10d. In the first year of Edward the Fourth he again paid for the victualling and custody of the ship £68 5s. 10d. (Davies, 110, 113. Hist. MSS. Com. xi. 3, pp. 85, 98.)

[554] Davies' Southampton, 214. For sum in 1468 ibid. 72, 100.

[555] Davies, 62-3.

[556] Ibid. 105.

[557] With help from the king if necessary. (Davies, 80.) The town had power to raise a tax on all goods carried in or out of the gates till the wall was finished. (Davies, 60.)

[558] Davies, 80. Hist. MSS. Com. xi. 3, p. 61. So a hundred and fifty years later Henry the Eighth forbade any citizen to leave Chester, because "the city standeth open in the danger of enemies," and requireth all "for its safety and defence." (Hist. MSS. Com. viii. 370.)

[559] Davies, 60, 61. Similar complaints were perpetually renewed in the next century.

[560] Davies, 35. Southampton was constantly in arrears of its ferm. Ibid. 34.

[561] Margaret of Anjou was allowed in 1445 a grant of £1,000 a year from the great and little customs of the town, and the annuity of £100 which was confirmed to her in 1454 was not resumed by Parliament till 1464.

[562] Davies, 37.

[563] Hist. MSS. Com. xi. 3, 111, 112.

[564] Hist. MSS. Com. xi. 3, 112-13.

[565] English Chronicle, 1377-1461 (Camden Soc.), 90. Davies, 471-2.

[566] Davies, 111. Hist. MSS. Com. xi. 3, 16. See also 98-99.

[567] Davies, 111, 37. In 1462 arrears of the ferm were remitted, and again in 1484 (Ib. 34). In 1463 a mayor of Southampton was deposed by the King's mandamus (Ibid. 168).

[568] Davies speaks of this John Ingoldsby who paid the debt as afterwards apparently one of the Barons of the Exchequer (p. 38.) A John Ingoldsby had been Recorder of Southampton from at least 1444 (p. 185) to at least 1459 (Hist. MSS. Com. xi. 3, 113) and very probably later.

[569] Davies, 36. Hist. MSS. Com. xi. 3. 100.

[570] In 1486 the pension of £154 was paid to the Earl of Arundel as constable of Dover Castle, part of it being given in kind. For other trouble, see Hist. MSS. Com. xi. 3. 98.

[571] The outlay of the town in this year was £383 9s. 7d. (Hist. MSS. Com. xi. 3. 141-2.)

[572] In this last case they were comforted by a promise of release for ten years from payment of 140 marks from the rent of £200 which had been assigned to Queen Joan, and by a grant to the corporation of the right to hold land to the value of £100. (Hist. MSS. Com. xi. 3, 42-3.)

[573] The Southampton trade did in fact utterly fail before a century was over. In 1530 its rent was reduced by £26 13s. d., and in 1552 the King ordered that when the customs at the port did not amount to £200, and no ships called carracks of Genoa and galleys of Venice should enter the port to load or unload, the town should not pay the accustomed rent of £200, but only £50. To this day certificates are still prepared every year on November 9th that no carracks of Genoa nor galleys of Venice have arrived at the port. (Davies, 38-9. Hist. MSS. Com. xi. 3, 49.)

[574] Unfortunately in the brief extracts from the Southampton records which have been as yet published, references to municipal government are so scanty that any sketch of it can only be drawn in faint and uncertain outline. In the opinion of Dr. Gross the Merchant Guild was originally a strictly private fraternity, and only became the dominant burghal authority in the fourteenth century. (Gross, ii. 231.) I have suggested here the idea of an earlier connexion; but the question needs full examination.

[575] Davies' Southampton, 163.

[576] Hist. MSS. Com. Report xi. Appendix 3. p. 43.

[577] Ibid. 44.

[578] Possibly in 1217, certainly in 1237. Davies, 170.

[579] Gross, ii. 220-5.

[580] Hist. MSS. Com. xi. 3, p. 57. See guild ordinances.

[581] Indenture in 1368 by mayor, four scavins, two bailiffs, the steward, sixteen burgesses named, and the whole community. Ibid. p. 66.

[582] In 1240 the style used is simply "the burgesses." Ibid. p. 7.

[583] Gross, ii. 214. Davies, 163.

[584] Hist. MSS. Com. xi. 3, pp. 40-2, 43, 46. Compare Nottingham.

[585] Davies, 154, 238.

[586] Hist. MSS. Com. xi. 3, p. 42.

[587] Hist. MSS. Com. xi. 3, p. 45.

[588] Ibid. pp. 46, 81, 84, 87, 106.

[589] Gross, ii. 222-5.

[590] In 1302 a lease of the ferm of the town to certain persons is granted by consent of twenty-two men named, but without any mention of their position, "and all the community of the town." (Hist. MSS. Com. xi. 3, 56.) Ordinances were made in 1349 by the mayor, aldermen, and community. (Ibid. 9.)

[591] Gross, ii. 220, 223, 225.

[592] Gross, ii. 220-3.

[593] See the office assigned to the aldermen in 1504, Davies, 76. For their dress, ibid. 235.

[594] Davies, 237-9. An ordinance was made in 1409 by the mayor, aldermen, and burgesses, and a similar one in 1486 by the mayor, aldermen, and burgesses in common assembly; and an ordinance in common assembly in 1504. (Hist. MSS. Com. xi. 3, p. 11.)

[595] Davies, 155. It is possible that at this time the chief aldermen were fashioned into a close body elected for life after the pattern of London; at any rate soon after this we find them and their wives in the orthodox scarlet robes with fur and velvet, in all points the same as those of the mayor. 235.

[596] Davies, 63, 71-2, 125.

[597] Gross, ii. 225. Davies (p. 136) says that whenever the guild became settled as the supreme authority, there entered at that period an element of restriction alien from the more ancient government of the towns; and traces

to the guild the narrowing of common privileges and subjection of the community to an exclusive system of local administration. It is possible that wherever a guild merchant did lay hold on a town government, as here, at Lynn, or at Coventry, the tendency may always have been to intensify the existing tendencies to the despotic rule of the richer citizens.

[598] Hist. MSS. Com. xi. 3, p. 7, 60, 61. Ordinances in 1368 and 1393, 9, 8; a concord in 1397, 74; lease of customs in 1390, 72; land in 1373, 1379, 69-70. For other instances see 1403, p. 76; 1410, 77; 1413, 79; 1421, 80; 1422, 80-1; 1433, 82; 1433, 44; 1439, 84; 1462, 85; 1466, 86; 1477, 87; 1482, 90; 1491, 90; 1494, 90-1; 1496, 91; 1507, 91.

[599] Hist. MSS. Com. xi. 3, p. 12, 91, 113.

[600] Hist. MSS. Com. xi. 3, 91, 107; Davies, 164. In Nottingham, as in Southampton, we have an occasional indication that the burgesses or common councillors, possibly under some fit of impatience at the pretensions of the aldermen, had intermittent tendencies to side with the people. In Southampton there was possibly at this time a certain bond of sympathy, for seven years earlier, in 1452, the burgesses complained that the aldermen had assumed the right of retaining, as justices of the peace, fines which had always gone to them towards the payment of the ferm; and their contention having been maintained in Parliament, royal orders were sent to the aldermen to molest the burgesses no more. Davies, 156.

[601] Davies, 164, 165.

[602] Hist. MSS. Com. xi. 3, p. 104. In 1617 two burgesses tried to oppose the "private nomination," but were called before the common council and forced to submit. (Davies, 164, 165.)

[603] Hist. MSS. Com. xi. 3, 11.

[604] Ibid.

[605] Davies, 71-2.

[606] As early as 1254 an inquisition of boundaries had been held by twenty-four lawful men. (Hist. MSS. Com. xi. 3, p. 7.)

[607] The same sense of insufficiency of the common to the increasing number of burgesses seems to have been felt as at Nottingham. In the next century a man was fined, because "being a bachelor and not keeping house, he ought not to keep any cattle at all" on it.

[608] The hospital had made encroachments and put up fences in 1438, which the then mayor had broken down (Davies, 52).

[609] Davies, 53.

[610] Ibid. 53. Hist. MSS. Com. xi. 3. p. 14, 91.

[611] Davies, 52.

[612] Davies, 57-8.

[613] Davies, 58-59.

[614] See, for 1549, Hist. MSS. Com. xi. 3, p. 14; for 1681, Davies, 52. The latest grant of the public land of Southampton was made on Sept. 16th, 1892, by the Mayor and corporation for a graving dock—part of the harbour improvements by which Southampton is to be restored to its old supremacy on the southern coast and once more to give room in its port to the largest steamers afloat. There was a far-away echo of old world controversies in the assurance of the mayor to the people that by this act of the corporation in giving the land at a nominal consideration there was scarcely anybody in Southampton who would not be benefited, and "not a soul in Southampton would be injured."

[615] In the following century we find them making presentments at the Court Leet about the mayor's misdoings (Davies, 123).

[616] As the King's servant orders were sent direct to him without mention of the community. (Hist. MSS. Com. xi. 3, pp. 16, 103.)

[617] By admiralty law the sea was supposed to reach up to the first bridge, and he therefore controlled the Itchen as far as Woodhill and the Test as far as Red Bridge, and as admiral held his courts of admiralty in the accustomed places on the sea-shore at Keyhaven, Lepe, and Hamble. Davies, 237-40. Compare the mayor of Rochester (H. M. C. ix. 287).

[618] See for example of one difficulty of this supervision, Davies, 475. For an illustration of his anxieties in the seizing of a carrack, see Hist. MSS. Com. iii. 111.

[619] See *Louis XI. et les Villes*. Henri Sée.

[620] See pp. 447-8.

[621] Nottingham Records, ii. 34-6.

[622] Nottingham Records, ii. 222-238.

[623] Ibid. i. 269.

[624] Nottingham Records, iii. 412, 62, etc. 39.

[625] For lists of new burgesses admitted in the latter half of the fifteenth and in the sixteenth century each paying 6*s.* 8*d.* and in the great majority of cases giving the names of two burgesses as pledges, see Ibid. ii. 303-305. In the fourteenth century only one pledge was needed. Ibid. i. 286. At the end

of the sixteenth century strangers who were made freemen paid £10. Ibid. iv. 170-1.

[626] Ibid. ii. 102, 242; iii. 349-52.

[627] Ibid. ii. xi. xii.

[628] There is notice of the transfer of a coal mine in Cossal in 1348. Ibid. i. 145

[629] Nottingham Records, ii. 147.

[630] Bekynton, i. 230.

[631] Nottingham Records, iii. 113.

[632] Ibid. ii. 142, 158, 166, 160; iii. 403, 445.

[633] Among the cases brought before the leet jury was that of a wager as to whether the painter of the rood-loft had been paid or not. (Records, iii. 143.)

[634] Ibid. ii. 178.

[635] Ibid. iii. 18, 20, 28, 83, 180, 499.

[636] Nottingham Records, ii. 284 *et sq*.

[637] Ibid. ii. 389.

[638] See Ibid. iv. 259. Similar entries become very frequent.

[639] Nottingham Records, ii. 246, 248, 254, *et sq*.; iii. 414, 416.

[640] Ibid. iii. 65, 68.

[641] Ibid. i. 120.

[642] In 1378 a commission was appointed to inquire into the obstructions of the Trent. Nottingham Records, i. 198. Again in 1382 the King was moved by the "clamorous relation" of the men of Nottingham and a royal proclamation was issued to forbid the raising of such tolls; while a new commission was appointed in the following year, 1383, to prevent Richard Byron, lord of Colwick, from directing the waters of the Trent to his own uses to the injury of Nottingham. (Ibid. i. 225, 227, 413.) Sir John Babington, who owned considerable land in Nottingham, seems to have quarrelled with the corporation about 1500. They appealed to Sir Thomas Lovel for help, who answered that he had written to him to demean himself as he ought to do until Lovel had examined the case and decided on it. (Ibid. iii. 402.)

[643] In the fourteenth century there were nearly 70 churches in Norwich.

[644] Ibid. iii. 362.

[645] Richard the Second seems to have handed it over to Anne of Bohemia. (Nottingham Records, i. 226.) And under Edward the Fourth it was granted to Elizabeth Woodville.

[646] Ibid. iii. 414, 416.

[647] One man was paid for cutting out the letters and another for stitching them on the jackets. (Ibid. ii. 377.)

[648] Ibid. iii. 421.

[649] Ibid. ii. 331.

[650] Ibid. iii. 237.

[651] Nottingham Records, iii. 239, 245.

[652] In 1461 the chamberlains' expenditure for the whole year came to £124. Ibid. iii. 418. In 1486 they render account for £440 11*s*. 4*d*. Ibid. 266.

[653] Ibid. i. 1.

[654] Nottingham Records, i. 8.

[655] Ibid. i. 22, 24.

[656] Ibid. i. 40-46.

[657] Ibid. i. 56, 58, 124, 168. The wife's dower differed in each. Inheritance went by borough English in the English town; in the French town it went to the eldest son. (Ibid. i. 186.) The jurors from the eastern and western sides always remained distinct. (Ibid. ii. 322, etc.; iii. 344.) By 1330 one of the boroughs had fallen into such poverty that it could no longer find a bailiff, and leave was given by charter to elect the bailiff from the inhabitants of any part of the town that seemed best. (Ibid. i. 109.)

[658] Nottingham Records, i. 78-80.

[659] Ibid. ii. 2-10.

[660] Nottingham Records, ii. 186.

[661] The land was let for thirty years at the yearly rent of a rose, and the corporation was to make enclosures of ditches and hedges. The agreement was made by the mayor, sheriff, and aldermen, "with the assent and consent of the entire community of the town." Ibid. iii. 408-410.

[662] Ibid. i. 56.

[663] Nottingham Records, i. 363; ii. 362; iv. 43. It will be seen that in this case the word community was sometimes used; the term varied no doubt according to the exact body in which the right was vested that formed the

subject of the treaty, and this again might depend partly on the date at which the right was acquired. Cf. the various styles used in Calender of Letters of London Corporation, ed. by Dr. Sharpe.

[664] Some instances of this style follow. There is a mortgage of rent of certain tolls by the "mayor and community," 1315. Ibid. i. 84. Settlement as to common pasture by "mayor, burgesses, and community," i. 150. Lease in 1390 by "mayor, chamberlains, and all the burgesses with the assent and will of the entire community," iii. 425. For similar phrases in 1401 and 1416 iii. 425-6; ii. 106-8. In 1435, ii. 362. In 1443, ii. 408. In 1444, ii. 424. In 1451, iii. 408. In 1467, ii. 269. In 1479 land bequeathed to "mayor, sheriffs, burgesses, and men of Nottingham," ii. 304-6, 307. For 1480, ii. 420. In 1482 an agreement about the Retford tolls is settled by "the mayor and his brethren and the commonalty of Nottingham," iii. 427. There is an extreme particularity in the phrase used in 1485, ii. 353. For a lease of land in 1494, iii. 431. For 1504, iii. 325-6.

[665] We may compare this with the Council of Southampton; see pp. 308-11.

[666] In 1435 we read of the mayor, and nine, or possibly eleven, burgesses named "and many other commons in the said hall," (Nott. Rec. ii. 362.) In 1443 there is something very like the council—the mayor, four justices of the peace named, John Orgram and other "trustworthy men" of the town, and the two chamberlains, who acted "with the assent of the whole community of the town." (Ibid. ii. 408.) For the fine see ii. 424.

[667] Ibid. ii. 424.

[668] The editor of the Records, Mr. Stevenson, accepts this statement of Gregory, and says that "The council had no existence prior to 1446, and it was at first merely a committee appointed by the burgesses for the management of the affairs of the town." According to him the townspeople were accustomed to assemble for the discussion of any important business, and "this was the system of government in use prior to the establishment of this committee in 1446." (Nott. Rec. iv. ix.) He believes further that "it was, no doubt, the abuses arising from this system and the inconvenience of having to call a meeting of the whole community for the consideration of every question connected with the ruling of the town that caused the burgesses to choose the committee of 1446." (Ibid. xi.)

[669] Ibid. iv. xi.

[670] Nott. Rec. ii. 362, 425, 420. The right of the burgesses to ask for the calling of a common hall is admitted in iii. 342.

[671] Ibid. ii. 186 *et sq.* There are passages in the charter which seem to convey this impression. In 1465 Elizabeth Woodville confirms a charter to "the mayor, sheriffs, burgesses, and men of the town," by whatsoever name they might be incorporated and known (ii. 255-7).

[672] Ibid. ii. 202-4. For boundaries of wards see iv. 174.

[673] Ibid. ii. 425; iv. xii. 2. The aldermen were still merged for general business in the council, and appear only three times, possibly acting as a kind of separate estate—once in 1450 when some land was let by the mayor, sheriffs, chamberlains, aldermen, and the whole community; once twenty years later, when in 1471 a complaint was addressed to the King by the mayor, aldermen, and commonalty; and once in 1504 when an ordinance was made by the mayor and aldermen to reduce certain fines to be paid by them for neglect of financial duties, to which they obtained the consent of councillors and commons. (Nott. Rec. iii. 325; iii. 408; ii. 334.) In the first two cases the word may have been used to denote the whole council.

[674] Ibid. iv. xii. xv.

[675] Nott. Rec. iv. xi. xii. xiv. xv. We have only records of the completed changes in the middle of the sixteenth century, probably because of the loss of documents. But in the time of Henry VII. the distinction was already established between the mayor and his brethren and the clothing (those who had served the office of chamberlain or sheriff). iii. 449.

[676] Ibid. ii. 227.

[677] See p. 350. In an agreement made in 1500 between the mayor, council and clothing the names of six inhabitants are included, apparently unofficial, and possibly representatives of the commons. (Nott. Rec. iii. 301.) The names set down for the election of the mayor and officers for the next year are the mayor, recorder, six aldermen, six common councillors, two sheriffs, the six (apparently) plain burgesses mentioned in the last list, and twenty-four others of the clothing. (Compare the lists ibid. iii. 301, 302.)

[678] For a list of the common property and common lands in 1435 see Ibid. ii. 355-361; see also iii. 62-66; in 1351 iii. 366 *et sq.*

[679] The importance to the burgesses of the common lands may be illustrated by their argument in 1577 against admitting new burgesses "for there is too many of them already; by making of them the poor burgesses commons is eaten up, to the great hindrance of all." At the same time they insisted that if a burgess let out his part of the land it should be to a burgess and not to a foreigner. (Nott. Rec. iv. 171, 172.)

[680] Ibid. iv. 282. "We present the new council for not setting the town's grounds to the true meaning of their new election, but hath taken the best

ground to the richest men, and let the poor men have nothing that are ancienter burgesses. Also we find that the whole house or the most of them overhipt (passed over) themselves as it came to them by order of their names in the book while they were disposing of Hartliff ground and the coppices, but now that the East Steaner and other good closes come to be disposed of, they share them themselves, and leaves poor men unserved that are both ancient and needful." This happened in 1606 when the council had got control of the land.

[681] Ibid. ii. 420. No doubt one of the grievances of the people under a despotic administration was the being deprived of any adequate control over the admission of new burgesses to share their lands. Compare Ibid. iii. 459 etc. with the constant remonstrance of the Mickletorn jury.

[682] The conflict of the sixteenth century lies really beyond our period in point of time, but the complaints of the people and the incidents of the fight throw much light on the working of municipal government, even in earlier days.

[683] 1500, Nott. Rec. iii. 74, 76. The chamberlain concerned in this business was John Rose.

[684] 1516, Nott. Rec. iii. 353. A very frequent charge against the aldermen.

[685] Ibid. iii. 344.

[686] Ibid. iii. 300. The Mickletorn mentioned in 1308 was held in the presence of the coroners and bailiffs, and presentments were made by decennaries of the daily market, (i. 66, 68.) Seventeen jurors are mentioned at the Mickletorn of 1395. (i. 268.) It is interesting to compare the procedure at Coventry, as taken by Miss Dormer Harris from the records. All petitions to be laid before the court were given in to the mayor four days before the meeting of the Leet; and these were inspected by twenty-four men summoned by the mayor. On the day of the Leet these petitions, if satisfactory, received the assent of the twenty-four jurats of the Leet.

[687] Nott. Rec. iii. 438.

[688] Ibid. iii. 338-40.

[689] As late as 1480 their right of assembly had been admitted, and at least six of the commons had taken formal part in elections and other business in 1500 and 1504.

[690] This Mr. Treasurer was Sir Thomas Lovel, Treasurer of the Household, Constable of Nottingham Castle, Steward of Lenton monastery.

[691] Nott. Rec. iii. 341-2.

[692] Ibid. iii. 342-3.

[693] In September, 1514, John Rose, mayor, and the burgesses of the town gave a licence to John Sye to enclose part of the common ground for his use at a rent of 2*s.* a year. (Nott. Rec. iii. 125.) But in February, 1515, when leave was given to the guardians of the free school to enclose land express mention is made of the mayor, burgesses, and community. (iii. 457.) The agreement in 1516 about the Lenton fair was made between the convent and the mayor, sheriffs, burgesses, and commonalty. (iii. 345.) See also 439-40.

[694] June 1513 to Dec. 1514. Again in 1520.

[695] Nottingham Records, iii. 342, 463.

[696] Ibid. iii. 423, 463-4.

[697] Ibid. iii. 357. He apparently neglected their entreaties. 358.

[698] Nott. Rec. iii. 359.

[699] Nott. Rec. iii. 358-60.

[700] Nottingham Records, iv. xiii. For a case in which this certainly happened see p. 356. The same thing seems to have happened in 1504. A law of 1442 had ordered that if the mayor and bailiffs did not render up their accounts before leaving office they should be fined, £20 for the mayor, £10 for the bailiffs; in 1504 the mayor and aldermen together issued a new ordinance reducing the fine to one half, an ordinance which was assented to by three common councillors, while for the commonalty appear the names of seventeen burgesses, of whom one was certainly one of the sheriffs. (Ibid. ii. 424; iii. 325.)

[701] Nottingham Records, iv. pp. xiii. xxvii. xxviii. 100, 101, 1552.

[702] Ibid. iv. 106-8, 215 *et sq.*

[703] Ibid. iii. 365; iv. 10.

[704] Ibid. iv. 106, 191, 223. The free school was left to the guardianship of the mayor, aldermen, and common council, and if they were negligent to the Lenton convent, now of course suppressed. (Ibid. iii. 453 *et sq.*)

[705] Nottingham Records, iv. 108.

[706] Ibid. iv. 238.

[707] Ibid. iv. 408-9. The burgesses seem to have twice at least acted with the people against or apart from the aldermen—once in the settlement about the town accounts in 1504 (iii. 325-6); and once in the complaint drawn up by the Mickletorn jury in 1527 against the mayor and aldermen (iii. 358-60.) The people may have hoped to strengthen this element of resistance.

[708] Mr. Stevenson thinks that the Clothing about this date became a portion of the council. Nottingham Records, iv. xiii. The other explanation seems to me to meet difficulties which this leaves unsolved.

[709] Ibid. iv. 171, 172.

[710] Ibid. iv. 191.

[711] Nottingham Records, iv. 191.

[712] Ibid. iv. 214, 237-8.

[713] Ibid. iv. 245-8.

[714] Ibid. iv. 253.

[715] Ibid. iv. 262-3, 265. See 268, xvi.

[716] Ibid. iv. 269, 282.

[717] Ibid. 270. For the final settlement see iv. xvii.

[718] Hist. MSS. Com. ix. 300-305. Blomefield, xi. 300-342.

[719] Cromwell's Colchester, 264-5.

[720] See Mr. Hudson's admirable work on Leet Jurisdiction in Norwich. (Selden Soc. vol. v.) For the four "vice-comites" of London see Round's Geoffrey de Mandeville, 363.

[721] Leet Jur. (Selden Soc.) v. p. xviii. lxii, xliii-li.; Hudson, Mun. Org. in Norwich: Arch. Journ. xlvi. no. 184, 312, 316.

[722] According to Mr. Hudson the Norwich Leet Juries were solely a "police" organization. They existed to make "presentments" which involved a certain amount of previous keeping of the peace in their own little neighbourhood. In their *individual* capacity the capital pledges were the precursors of the "petty constable" [see Selden Soc. v. lxii. no. 1, and cf. pages there cited]; in their *collective* capacity as juries they preceded the local "Justice of the Peace," a function usurped to a small extent between (say) 1360 and 1420 by the "twenty-four citizens," and afterwards wholly usurped by the "Court of Aldermen," who were the borough magistrates.

[723] Hudson, Leet Jur. in Norwich, lxxi., note.

[724] Ibid. xv. 1365. Arch. Journ. xlvi. no. 184, 322. In reference to the election of bailiffs or the "twenty-four" the word "leet" means a division of the city, not a court.

[725] Leet Jurisdiction in Norwich, xli.

[726] Besides the deed of 1290 (p. 367 n. 2) Mr. Hudson has kindly sent me the following extracts. Saturday, Vigil of Palms, 27 Edward I. 1298—John the carpenter and Alice his wife grant a messuage next the gates of Nedham to "Ballivi, Cives, et Communitas Norwici" "ad asiamentum muri civitatis erigendi." (City Domesday, fol. lxxiii.) On folio lxviii. of the same book there is a grant of a messuage near the cathedral to the commonalty, 31 Edward, 1302, in the following form: "to the four Bailiffs (named), Henry Clark, Robert de Holveston, ... Adam de Blicling, citizens of the said city (15 persons), and all the Commonalty thereof."

[727] Norwich Town Close Evidences, printed privately, 1885. (British Museum), 18.

[728] Arch. Journ. xlvi. no. 184, 322.

[729] They state in 1378 that this had already been the custom. (Town Close Evidences, 30.)

[730] Arch. Journ. xlvi. No 183, 315.

[731] Town Close Evidences, 7. The phrase used in 1218 (p. 5), "men of the city," is not the same.

[732] Ibid. 7, 13, 17, 18, 25, 26, 30. Arch. Journ. xlvi. no. 184, 325. See Note A at end of chapter.

[733] Town Close Evidences, 27.

[734] Ibid. 16, 18.

[735] Town Close Evidences, 10, 11, 17.

[736] Norwich Town Close Evidences, 14, 24, 27, 31, 32. The same form was used even after the charter of 1403, in 1420 and 1435. (Ibid. 46.) We find "the citizens" joined with "the commonalty" in the thirteenth century. An enrolled deed of 1290, in which license to build a stall in the market is granted by the "Communitas Norwici et cives ejusdam civitatis," is quoted by Mr. Hudson. (See Mun. Org., Arch. Journ. xlvi. no. 184.) The double style used is, I think, explained by a contention which occurred a century later, in 1379. "There was a discussion whether the stalls in the meat-market ought to belong to the commonalty or to the bailiffs. They are agreed that the said stalls shall in future remain to the commonalty for ever, without challenge or contradiction to the present bailiffs or the bailiffs in future." (Town Close Evidences, 31.) At that time a great reorganization of the market was in progress (see Kirkpatrick's "Streets and Lanes of Norwich," App. i. pp. 95, 96) with a view to getting as many stalls as possible into the hands of the authorities. As the bailiffs had certain sources of income allotted to them (they being personally responsible for the fee ferm rent) they need not be

blamed for trying to help themselves. On the other hand the attempt shows how significant was the use of the word "communitas" in the older deed (see p. 364 no. 1). I think it very possible that property set apart for a definite public purpose was held in the joint names of citizens and commonalty; but I am convinced this last word was never used in a formal way, but always expressed a tenure and control with which the "cives" or the twenty-four could not interfere.

[737] Hudson, Leet Jur. in Norwich, xxxvi. lxxiii. 63. Selden Soc.

[738] Arch. Journ. xlvi. 316-17.

[739] Town Close Evidences, 16-17.

[740] Ibid. 29. Evidently this was a time of very active municipal life. About 1372 the corporation seems to have begun copying out carefully older legal documents, and this copying and re-writing went on through the next century. The account-books which still exist began to be kept in 1393. In 1378 the income of the city was £374 17 s. 4d. Blomefield, iii. 103.

[741] Town Close Evidences, 30.

[742] Mr. Hudson informs me that there are rolls (more or less perfect) for about half the years between 1365 and 1385. Then they fail till 1413, when the constitution of the assembly had been entirely altered.

[743] I have to thank Mr. Hudson for his kindness in giving me this information. He tells me that an assembly on October 7th, 1372, is thus described: "Prima congregatio ibidem tenta die Jovis, &c. ... quatuor Ballivis (eleven persons specially named) et aliis de com'tate presentibus." This is the constant form in use, whenever the attendance is recorded, down to the last of these rolls in 1385. The number of persons specially named varies from eleven to seventeen. Their similarity in the course of each year suggests that they were specially bound to attend. In two years 1377-8 and 1379-80 the attendances are recorded several times, and, as in the first case the total number of persons named is twenty-five and in the other twenty-four, it seems reasonably certain that they were the actual twenty-four. This is confirmed by the fact that almost all the "committee," as they would now be called, are appointed from their number and almost the whole burden of administration is undertaken by one or other of them in conjunction with the bailiffs.

[744] Citizens left legacies to help in these expenses. Not only was £1,000 lent to the King, but heavy bribes had to be paid all round. Blomefield, iii. 120.

[745] Town Close Evidences, 36. In considering the new style two views present themselves. We may lay the whole stress on the association of mayor

and sheriffs instead of bailiffs with "the citizens and commonalty"; or, as I incline to think, we may also attach importance to the formal association in a charter of "citizens" and "commonalty," as marking an epoch in the civic history.

[746] Mr. Hudson has been good enough to give me these dates and facts, in which he has been able to correct Blomefield's statements, from evidence in the Norwich Conveyance Rolls, etc.

[747] Blomefield, iii. 123-124. Hudson, Mun. Org., Arch. Journ. xlvi. no. 184, 299.

[748] Town Close Evidences, 37-43.

[749] In 1354 it was ordered that London aldermen should not be elected yearly but hold office for life. (Stow's London, 189.) A common council appears as early as 1273; and again in 1347. It was then chosen by the mayor, aldermen, and representatives from the wards. At the end of Edward's reign the election was transferred to the trading companies, but restored to the wards in 1384; to be given back to the companies by Edward the Fourth in 1467; and restored to the wards in 1650. (Merewether and Stephens, 734-5, 1988-1992.)

[750] All that had been mayors were to ride in their cloaks whenever the mayor rode on pain of £20, each of the twenty-four on pain of 100s. The hat of the mayor cost in 1418 2s. 10d., in 1437 10s. 2d. (Rogers' Agric. and Prices, iv. 579.)

[751] Town Close Evidences, 40-1.

[752] Conesford elected twelve councillors, Mancroft sixteen, Wymer twenty, and the Ward over the Water twelve.

[753] The Speaker of the House of Commons is first mentioned in 1378.

[754] Town Close Evidences, 39, 40, 41.

[755] Town Close Evidences, 41, 42.

[756] Ibid. 45.

[757] Blomefield, iii. 134.

[758] Town Close Evidences, 41.

[759] Ibid. 45.

[760] In 1423 when the mayor and other judges sat in the city there appeared before them two coroners, 16 constables for the four wards, the constables for the liberties of Holmestrete and Spitelond, with the bailiff of the prior's liberties in those places, and four men out of each ward possibly for jurymen.

In 1424 a tripartite indenture was made by the mayor, aldermen, and commons, with constitutions for the better government of the city, and was ratified at a common assembly in the guild hall. (Blomefield, iii. 136-139.)

[761] Leet Jur. in Norwich, xx. lxxvi. lxxx.

[762] Leet Jurisdiction, lxxx.

[763] Arch. Journ. xlvi. no. 184, p. 326-7. Leet Jur. lxxxix. Before the end of the thirteenth century there were guilds of cobblers, fullers, saddlers, tanners. (Ibid. 13, 39, 42, 43.)

[764] In the list given in English Guilds there is one guild founded in 1307 and ten (or eleven, if we count the masons' guild on p. 39) founded between 1350 and 1385, some of them craft guilds, others nominally social or religious associations, though it is very probable that in many cases this was but a thin disguise for a craft guild. English Guilds, 14, etc.

[765] See saddlers' guild, which had existed a century before.

[766] The composition of 1415 decided that each craft in the city was yearly to choose two masters, whose names were to be presented for the mayor's consent, and who were to take their oaths before him. The Monday after the mayor's "riding" these masters were to make good and true search in their crafts and to present all offenders before the mayor for judgement; and half the fines were given to the sheriffs, half to the masters of the crafts. The mayor had to accept the presentment of the "masters"; he could not make search either himself or by any of the town officers; only if a craft refused to be searched or to elect masters the mayor might himself appoint two masters and order the search. If the masters concealed any notable default they were to be punished by the advice of the mayor and more sufficient men of the same craft. (Town Close Evidences, 41, 42.)

[767] On being enrolled each man must pay to the craft 40 pence, and to the chamber at least 20*s.* and "more after the quantity of his good." (Town Close Evidences, 42.) The profits of admission to the freedom of the city had in old times gone half to the bailiffs and half to the community, but now the craft claimed a definite share of the entrance money. (Arch. Journ. xlvi. no. 184, p. 328.) By the composition six men were to be chosen "to be of counsel with the chamberlains in receiving of burgesses."

[768] Town Close Evidences, 42-3.

[769] Hist. MSS. Com. i. 104.

[770] English Guilds, 443-4.

[771] Lambert's Guild Life, 108. English Guilds, 443-60.

[772] 1/2d. was paid for each piece sealed. The right was leased to two citizens at 20 marks rent. Blomefield, iii. 125. By the law of 1442 the weavers were to choose every year four wardens from the craftsmen of the town, who should in their turn choose two inspectors or overseers for the stuff out of Norfolk. The wardens tested the faulty goods and received half of any forfeited stuffs. The law of 1445 ordered them to choose four wardens for Norwich and four for Norfolk, and directed the wardens to make such laws as were needful for the improvement of the trade. (20 Henry VI. cap. 10; 23 Henry VI. cap. 3; 7 Edward IV. cap. 1.)

[773] See Paston Letters.

[774] Not only were there disputes with the prior of Norwich, but with the Hospital of S. Paul (Town Close Evidences, 7-8); the prioress of Carrow (Blomefield, iii. 64, 147); the abbot of Holme (ibid. 153-4); the abbot of Wendling (ibid. 147).

[775] "For the people here is loth to complain till they hear tidings of a good sheriff." (Paston Letters, i. 166.)

[776] The mayor and citizens were able if necessary to have in harness from two to five hundred men of the town. (Ibid. ii. 414.)

[777] Blomefield, iii. 144-155.

[778] In 1444. Blomefield, iii. 151, 152. The courts were held in the tolbooth, but the assemblies of the commons still gathered in the chapel of the Virgin Mary in the Fields. (Ibid. 92.) Most of the city business was done there as late as 1455. (Ibid. 160.) It appears that the citizens frequently availed themselves of other people's accommodation (the Priory, Black Friars, Grey Friars) rather than spend money in providing it for themselves.

[779] Ibid. iii. 153.

[780] William Paston was one of the commissioners. (Blomefield, iii. 148.)

[781] Ibid. iii. 144-6.

[782] Proceedings of Privy Council, v. 17-19.

[783] Blomefield, iii. 146-7, 153.

[784] Proceedings of Privy Council, v. 34, 45.

[785] Blomefield, iii. 147. New arrangements were made about the payments of the sheriffs by raising regular taxes; the sword-bearer and the three serjeants for the maces were given their offices for life.

[786] Blomefield, iii. 147-149.

[787] The bishop was on the side of the anti-popular party. At his death he left to John Heydon the cup he daily used of silver gilt with the cover. (Ibid. iii. 538.)

[788] Hist. MSS. Com. i. 103.

[789] Charges that the mayor had sealed with the common seal measures bigger than the standard measures for certain favoured citizens, and that the people were forced to sell to them by these measures; that he had made an evil use of the Pye-powder Court, using its summary and autocratic procedure to imprison many men wrongly and tyrannically (one John Wetherby had been imprisoned); and that he sustained an illegal guild in the city called Le Bachery. In 1477 a statute was made that the Pye-powder Court could only deal with contracts or bargains made during the fair. (Blomefield, iii. 169.)

[790] Ibid. iii. 149-50, 154-5.

[791] Ibid. 147, 152.

[792] He left £40 to Norwich towards payment of the city tax. (Blomefield, iii. 534.) The city, however, asked in vain for the money in 1454 and again in 1460. (159.) Walter Lyhert, made bishop in 1446, was of an old Norwich family. An ancestor of his had been citizen in 1261. (Ibid. iii. 535-6.)

[793] Ibid. iii. 156.

[794] Paston Letters, i. 151, 156, 158.

[795] Ibid. i. 151.

[796] Ibid. i. 123, 183-4, 199-200, 206, 211-2, 225.

[797] In 1460 Heydon left Norfolk for Berkshire. (Paston Letters, i. cxlii.)

[798] In 1456 the common stock was so much wasted that several of the aldermen remitted debts to the city. (Blomefield, iii. 160.) And even the guild of S. George was scarcely able to pay its way. (Hist. MSS. Com. i. 104.)

[799] All ex-mayors were allowed to be justices of the peace. Four of the justices of the peace were to have the powers of King's justices, and the aldermen were allowed to elect the under sheriffs, town clerks, and sheriffs' bailiffs. (Blomefield, iii. 158.)

[800] Hist. MSS. Com. i. 104. In 1452 it was ordered that no brother should wear a red gown save the alderman of the guild or any of the twenty-four aldermen of the city.

[801] The first attempt at a settlement was in 1205 about the rights of common of the townspeople. (Town Close Evidences, 4-5.)

[802] Town Close Evidences, 52-64.

[803] Vol. I. p. 221.

[804] Dr. Gross, taking the Trinity guild of Lynn as "a continuation of the old guild merchant," speaks of its "line of developement" into a "simple, social-religious fraternity" (i. 161); and notes that "though the ancient function of the guild had disappeared, its social-religious successor was a quasi-official part of the civic polity" (p. 162). He does not, however, enable us to trace any such "developement," or to distinguish "ancient functions" from later ones. From our first glimpse of the guild in the charters of John and Henry the Third to the patent of Henry the Fifth it seems to be singularly free from change, nor is any evidence produced during these centuries for its "transformation into a simple social-religious guild." In the case of Southampton Dr. Gross sees a developement of an exactly opposite kind (ii. 231).

[805] For a most interesting account of the Lynn cattle and sheep trade, and the Kipton Ash market, set up in 1306, for drafting off the sheep flocks, see Dr. Jessopp's paper in the Nineteenth Century, June, 1892, on "A Fourteenth Century Parson."

[806] Cunningham, Growth of English Industry and Commerce, 183.

[807] The guild did not include all the town traders (Gross, ii. 166-7), and probably tended to become an exclusive body since it could keep out all save the sons of its members by charging whatever entrance fees it liked (p. 164).

[808] Hist. MSS. Com. xi. 3, p. 210-11.

[809] Blomefield, viii. 515. Gross, ii. 159-170. The guild of Corpus Christi paid in 1400 103*s*. 2*d*. for meat and drinks and spices for its feast, and 169*s*. for making wax torches; and the beginning of the century was marked by the foundation of at least three other guilds, with right to hold land and buildings.

[810] Gross, ii. 166-7.

[811] Gross, ii. 166.

[812] A charter of 1305 secured its possession of certain property. The charter of 1393 was probably connected with the extension of the statute of mortmain to towns. (Hist. MSS. Com. xi. 3, 186, 191.)

[813] Hist. MSS. Com. xi. 3, p. 211. Gross, ii. 153. The best mill-stones in those days came from Paris, or from Andernach on the Rhine. A good mill-stone might cost from £3 to £4. (Rogers' Work and Wages, i. 113.)

[814] Even from the thirteenth century. (Gross, ii. 153.)

[815] Gross, ii. 159.

[816] Hist. MSS. Com. xi. 3, pp. 225-231.

[817] Gross, ii. 158, etc. 168.

[818] Compare this with Southampton, where the alderman was himself mayor.

[819] Gross, ii. 155-156.

[820] Hist. MSS. Com. xi. 3, p. 194.

[821] Hist. MSS. Com. xi. 3, 195-6. Beloe, Our Borough, p. 19.

[822] Beloe, Our Borough, 15.

[823] Hist. MSS. Com. xi. 3, 196.

[824] In 1345 the king called out a hundred men of the most vigorous to go to Gascony. (Ibid. 189.)

[825] See Vol. I. 291-2.

[826] Hist. MSS. Com. xi. 3, 218-223.

[827] Ibid. 158-9.

[828] Ibid. p. 229.

[829] Ibid. xi. 3, p. 224.

[830] Cf. for comparison and contrast the custom of Dinant after 1348. (Ville de Dinant. Pirenne, 45-6, 49-50.)

[831] Hist. MSS. Com. xi. 3, 191-4.

[832] Mr. Beloe says that the ruling class resisted, and instituted a costly suit to get a decree under the great seal setting aside the award, but he gives no particulars. (Our Borough, 17.)

[833] Hist. MSS. Com. xi. 3, 197, 200.

[834] Either officer convicted of false dealing was to lose his office and franchise for ever.

[835] The four chamberlains or treasurers were then to be chosen from the body of burgesses, two by the mayor and jurats, two by the burgesses. But, unlike Norwich, where the council and commons divided the remaining elections between them, in Lynn the only appointment left to the community besides the two chamberlains was the prolocutor. Coroners and constables were nominated by the people, and elected by the jurats, and the other officers, the common clerk, serjeant, janitors, bell-man and wait, taken from the general community both of burgesses and non-burgesses, were directly appointed by the mayor and jurats.

[836] Hist. MSS. Com. xi. 3, 196-202. There were "constabularies" which corresponded to wards, over which a captain was appointed in time of war or danger. (Hist. MSS. Com. xi. 3, 167.)

[837] Beloe, Our Borough, 16.

[838] Hist. MSS. Com. xi. 3, 191-4.

[839] Beloe, 17, 18. Gross, ii. 170.

[840] Ibid.

[841] Hist. MSS. Com. xi. 3, 195, 203.

[842] Instances of the important place held by the alderman in matters of town government in 1420. (Ibid. 246, and in 1431-42, p. 162-4.)

[843] In 1426 the alderman of the guild chose four fit persons who took the accustomed oath and entered the chamber; they chose four others, who, after being sworn, were brought into the chamber, and the eight then added to their number four more. The whole body of twelve, after sitting from the tenth to the third hour, were finally divided as to the election of the serjeant who had in some way offended the community, and at whose name a "great murmur now arose amongst the people" waiting outside. He was, however, chosen after asking pardon of the mayor and community for his offence. (Ibid. 160.) In 1477 another election is described, which was carried on in exactly the same way. (Ibid. 169.) And in 1470, when a constable had to be elected there was the same procedure.

[844] Beloe, 21.

[845] Hist. MSS. Com. xi. 3, 245, 246.

[846] The gradual change in the mode of electing burgesses for parliament illustrates the action of the councils in absorbing influence. In 1314 the jury to elect the burgesses had been chosen by a committee of twenty-six townsmen. But at least from 1425 the mayor assumed the right of choosing the first four of the jury, who then named the remaining eight. In 1433, if not earlier, the mayor was bound to select two of the twenty-four and two of the twenty-seven, and the added eight members were all taken from the same bodies; and in 1442 this custom was made into a permanent law. (Hist. MSS. Com. xi. 3. 240, 157-8, 163-4, 166-9.) About 1523 the burgesses were chosen by the twenty-four and twenty-seven voting personally in assembly; this assembly, called the "House," carried on all dealings with members, instructed them, paid them, and received their reports. The first effort of the burgesses at large to take any part in election was at the Long Parliament. (Ibid. pp. 148-9.)

[847] 1427, Ibid. 160; 1428, p. 161; 1441, p. 163-4; 1442, p. 164; 1466, p. 168. Cf. also p. 148.

[848] Hist. MSS. Com. xi. 3, 162.

[849] Ibid. 246.

[850] Ibid. 170.

[851] Hist. MSS. Com. xi. 3, 163.

[852] Ibid. 158-9, 161.

[853] Ibid. 167.

[854] Ibid. 168. The use of the word communitas in 1463 is here explained as showing how the term had "already lost its original meaning and was used to designate the humblest and least influential class of the burgesses." But community was used in exactly this sense in 1305. (Ibid. 187.)

[855] For some details of the seventy-five guilds of Lynn see the Norfolk Antiquarian Miscellany, edited by Walter Rye, Part I., pp. 153-183.

[856] Lyon's Dover, I. xi.; ii. 267-8, 287, 312, 370.

[857] In Dover the common assembly summoned in the same way was called a Hornblowing. (Boy's Sandwich, 797.)

[858] Ibid. 538.

[859] Ibid. 783-4. In 1565 291 households were English and 129 Walloons. But there were many foreigners in Sandwich at a far earlier time.

[860] In 1466 and 1492. Boys' Sandwich, 675, 679.

[861] Ibid. 787.

[862] Ibid. 673-6. In 1469 the commons of Sandwich at a Shepway court desire that the mayor may be kept in safe custody for such charges as they will allege against him. (Ibid. 676.)

[863] Boys' Sandwich, 677.

[864] Lyon's Dover, i. 206-7.

[865] Boys' Sandwich, 683.

[866] At the same time the jurats, who as late as 1492 need only have lived a year in the town, "he and his wife together," must now have been there at least three years. (Ibid. 679-701.) Jurats were ultimately chosen or nominated by the mayor in Dover and in Winchelsea. (Lyon, ii. 268, 371.)

[867] Boys, 686.

[868] Skelton's Poems. Ed. Dyce, 381-2.

[869] Green's History of the English People, i. 211-225.

[870] See p. 238. Mr. Maitland's Archaic Communities (Law Quarterly), 47.

[871] Brinklow's Papers (Early Eng. Text Soc.) illustrate the uncompromising ideas of radical reform fostered in towns.

[872] Bishop Creighton's Wolsey, 51, 59.

[873] Skelton's Poems. Ed. Dyce, i. 386.

[874] See Vol. I. Ch. VII.

[875]

"He rules his commonalty
With all benignity,
His noble baronage
He putteth them in courage
To exploit deeds of arms....
Wherever he rides or goes
His subjects he doth support,
Maintain them with comfort
Of his most princely port."

Skelton, ii. 81-2.

[876] Vol. I. p. 26, n. 5.

[877] "And then they (princes) daub over their oppression with a submissive, flattering carriage, that they may so far insinuate into the affections of the vulgar, as they may not tumult nor rebel, but patiently crouch to burdens and exactions." (Erasmus, Praise of Folly, tr.), 151.

Milton Keynes UK
Ingram Content Group UK Ltd.
UKHW012243180624
444315UK00005B/563